SAVAGE CONTINENT

'Ho... ... story and Lowe tells it very well' *Spectator*

... *press*

'An incisive portrait of Europe after the Second World War'
Melissa Katsoulis, *Sunday Telegraph*

'Vivid . . . Lowe has a good eye for revealing details' *Daily Telegraph*

'Meticulous' *Financial Times*

'Grimly absorbing, conveys the pity of war and its sorry aftermath
with integrity and proper sympathy' Ian Thomson,
Sunday Telegraph, Book of the Week

'A powerful and disturbing book, painstakingly researched and written
with both authority and an impressive historical sweep' James Holland

'Extraordinary, exceptional. Reveals a continent where moral values
were often missing and basically lawlessness prevailed for
several years' Trevor James, *Historian*

'An excellent account . . . Lowe's vivid descriptions of Europeans
scrambling for scraps of food, rampant theft and "destruction of morals"
are a timely reminder that a certain humility is in order when we look
at less fortunate continents today' *Independent*

ABOUT THE AUTHOR

After spending more than a decade as a history publisher, Keith Lowe is now a full-time author and historian. He is widely recognized as an authority on the Second World War, and has often spoken on TV and radio, both in Britain and in the United States. He is the author of the critically acclaimed *Inferno: The Devastation of Hamburg, 1943*. He lives in north London with his wife and two children.

www.keithlowehistory.com

KEITH LOWE

Savage Continent

Europe in the Aftermath of World War II

PENGUIN BOOKS

PENGUIN BOOKS

Published by the Penguin Group
Penguin Books Ltd, 80 Strand, London WC2R ORL, England
Penguin Group (USA) Inc., 375 Hudson Street, New York, New York 10014, USA
Penguin Group (Canada), 90 Eglinton Avenue East, Suite 700, Toronto, Ontario, Canada M4P 2Y3
(a division of Pearson Penguin Canada Inc.)
Penguin Ireland, 25 St Stephen's Green, Dublin 2, Ireland (a division of Penguin Books Ltd)
Penguin Group (Australia), 707 Collins Street, Melbourne, Victoria 3008, Australia
(a division of Pearson Australia Group Pty Ltd)
Penguin Books India Pvt Ltd, 11 Community Centre, Panchsheel Park, New Delhi – 110 017, India
Penguin Group (NZ), 67 Apollo Drive, Rosedale, Auckland 0632, New Zealand
(a division of Pearson New Zealand Ltd)
Penguin Books (South Africa) (Pty) Ltd, Block D, Rosebank Office Park,
181 Jan Smuts Avenue, Parktown North, Gauteng 2193, South Africa

Penguin Books Ltd, Registered Offices: 80 Strand, London WC2R ORL, England

www.penguin.com

First published by Viking 2012
Published in Penguin Books 2013

005

Copyright © Keith Lowe, 2012

Typeset by Palimpsest Book Production, Falkirk, Stirlingshire
Printed in Great Britain by Clays Ltd, St Ives plc

ISBN: 978-0-141-03451-5

www.greenpenguin.co.uk

 MIX
Paper from
responsible sources
FSC   FSC™ C018179
www.fsc.org

Penguin Books is committed to a sustainable
future for our business, our readers and our planet.
This book is made from Forest Stewardship
Council™ certified paper.

To Vera

Contents

PART I
The Legacy of War

PART II
Vengeance

PART III
Ethnic Cleansing

PART IV
Civil War

Illustrations

Section One

Section Two

Photograph acknowledgements

United Nations, 1, 2, 3, 4, 5, 6, 7, 10, 20, 22; Aldo de Jaco, *I cinque anni che cambiarono l'Italia* (Rome: Newton Compton, 1985), 8; Ullstein, 9, 19; US National Archives, 11, 16, 17; Alena Králová collection, 12; U.S. Army Signal Corps, 13; Bob Landry/Time & Life Pictures/Getty Images, 14; Christian Schiefer/Archivio di stato del cantone Ticino, 15; Pix Inc./ Time & Life Pictures/Getty Images, 18; Muzeum Regionalne Tomaszów Lubelski, 21; Leonard McCombe/*Life* Magazine/Time & Life Pictures/ Getty Images, 23; Dmitri Kessel/Time & Life Pictures/Getty Images, 24; Bert Hardy/*Picture Post*/Getty Images, 25; Associated Press, 26, 27; Museum of Genocide Victims, Vilnius, 28; Ria Novosti, 29.

Every effort has been made to locate and contact the copyright holder of picture 8. Readers with information about this photograph are invited to contact the publisher.

Maps

1. Territorial changes in Europe, 1945–7

Soviet acquisitions

Polish acquisitions from Germany

Other changes

Introduction

Imagine a world without institutions. It is a world where borders between countries seem to have dissolved, leaving a single, endless landscape over which people travel in search of communities that no longer exist. There are no governments any more, on either a national scale or even a local one. There are no schools or universities, no libraries or archives, no access to any information whatsoever. There is no cinema or theatre, and certainly no television. The radio occasionally works, but the signal is distant, and almost always in a foreign language. No one has seen a newspaper for weeks. There are no railways or motor vehicles, no telephones or telegrams, no post office, no communication at all except what is passed through word of mouth.

There are no banks, but that is no great hardship because money no longer has any worth. There are no shops, because no one has anything to sell. Nothing is made here: the great factories and businesses that used to exist have all been destroyed or dismantled, as have most of the other buildings. There are no tools, save what can be dug out of the rubble. There is no food.

Law and order are virtually non-existent, because there is no police force and no judiciary. In some areas there no longer seems to be any clear sense of what is right and what is wrong. People help themselves to whatever they want without regard to ownership – indeed, the sense of ownership itself has largely disappeared. Goods belong only to those who are strong enough to hold on to them, and those who are willing to guard them with their lives. Men with weapons roam the streets, taking what they want and threatening anyone who gets in their way. Women of all classes and ages prostitute themselves for food and protection. There is no shame. There is no morality. There is only survival.

For modern generations it is difficult to picture such a world existing outside the imaginations of Hollywood script-writers. However, there are still hundreds of thousands of people alive today who experienced exactly these conditions – not in far-flung corners of the globe, but at the heart of what has for decades been considered one of the most stable and developed regions on earth. In 1944 and 1945 large parts of Europe were left in chaos for months at a time. The Second World War – easily the most destructive war in history – had devastated not only the physical infrastructure, but also the institutions that held countries together. The political system had broken down to such a degree that American observers were warning of the possibility of Europe-wide civil war.[1] The deliberate fragmentation of communities had sown an irreversible mistrust between neighbours; and universal famine had made personal morality an irrelevance. 'Europe', claimed the *New York Times* in March 1945, 'is in a condition which no American can hope to understand.' It was 'The New Dark Continent'.[2]

That Europe managed to pull itself out of this mire, and then go on to become a prosperous, tolerant continent seems nothing short of a miracle. Looking back on the feats of reconstruction that took place – the rebuilding of roads, railways, factories, even whole cities – it is tempting to see nothing but progress. The political rebirth that occurred in the west is likewise impressive, especially the rehabilitation of Germany, which transformed itself from a pariah nation to a responsible member of the European family in just a few short years. A new desire for international cooperation was also born during the postwar years, which would bring not only prosperity but peace. The decades since 1945 have been hailed as the single longest period of international peace in Europe since the time of the Roman Empire.

It is little wonder that those who write about the postwar era – historians, statesmen and economists alike – often portray it as a time when Europe rose like a phoenix from the ashes of destruction. According to this point of view, the conclusion of the war marked not only the end of repression and violence, but also the spiritual, moral and economic rebirth of the whole continent. The Germans call the months after the war *Stunde Null* ('Zero Hour') – the implication being that it was a time when the slate was wiped clean, and history allowed to start again.

But it does not take much imagination to see that this is a decidedly rosy view of postwar history. To begin with, the war did not simply stop with Hitler's defeat. A conflict on the scale of the Second World War, with all the smaller civil disputes that it encompassed, took months, if not years, to come to a halt, and the end came at different times in different parts of Europe. In Sicily and the south of Italy, for example, it was as good as over in the autumn of 1943. In France, for most civilians, it ended a year later, in the autumn of 1944. In parts of eastern Europe, by contrast, the violence continued long after VE Day. Tito's troops were still fighting German units in Yugoslavia until at least 15 May 1945. Civil wars, which were first ignited by Nazi involvement, continued to rage in Greece, Yugoslavia and Poland for several years after the main war was over; and in Ukraine and the Baltic States nationalist partisans continued fighting Soviet troops until well into the 1950s.

Some Poles contend that the Second World War did not really end until even more recently: since the conflict officially began with the invasion of their country by both the Nazis and the Soviets, it was not over until the last Soviet tank left the country in 1989. Many in the Baltic countries feel the same way: in 2005 the presidents of Estonia and Lithuania refused to visit Moscow to celebrate the 60th anniversary of VE Day, on the grounds that, for their countries at least, liberation had not arrived until the early 1990s. When one factors in the Cold War, which was effectively a state of perpetual conflict between eastern and western Europe, and several national uprisings against Soviet dominance, then the claim that the postwar years were an era of unbroken peace seems hopelessly overstated.

Equally dubious is the idea of *Stunde Null*. There was certainly no wiping of the slate, no matter how hard German statesmen might have wished for one. In the aftermath of the war waves of vengeance and retribution washed over every sphere of European life. Nations were stripped of territory and assets, governments and institutions underwent purges, and whole communities were terrorized because of what they were perceived to have done during the war. Some of the worst vengeance was meted out on individuals. German civilians all over Europe were beaten, arrested, used as slave labour or simply murdered. Soldiers and policemen who had collaborated with the Nazis were arrested and tortured. Women who had slept with German soldiers were stripped, shaved and paraded through the streets covered in tar. German, Hungarian and Austrian women were raped in their millions. Far from wiping the slate clean, the aftermath of the war merely propagated grievances between communities and between nations, many of which are still alive today.

Neither did the end of the war signify the birth of a new era of ethnic harmony in Europe. Indeed, in some parts of Europe, ethnic tensions actually became worse. Jews continued to be victimized, just as they had been during the war itself. Minorities everywhere became political targets once again, and in some areas this led to atrocities that were just as repugnant as those committed by the Nazis. The aftermath of the war also saw the logical conclusion of all the Nazis' efforts to categorize and segregate different races. Between 1945 and 1947 tens of millions of men, women and children were expelled from their countries in some of the biggest acts of ethnic cleansing the world has ever seen. This is a subject that is rarely discussed by admirers of the 'European miracle', and even more rarely understood: even those who are aware of the expulsions of Germans know little about the similar expulsions of other minorities across eastern Europe. The cultural diversity that was once such an integral part of the European landscape before, and even during, the war was not dealt its final death-blow until after the war was over.

That the reconstruction of Europe was begun in the midst of all these issues makes it all the more remarkable. But in the same way that the war took a long time to end, so the reconstruction took a long time to get going. The people who lived amidst the rubble of Europe's devastated cities were more concerned with the minutiae of everyday survival than with restoring the building blocks of society. They were hungry, bereaved and bitter about the years of suffering they had been made to endure – before they could be motivated to start rebuilding they needed time to vent their anger, to reflect and to mourn.

The new authorities that were taking up office across Europe also needed time to establish themselves. Their first priority was not to clear the rubble, or repair the railway lines, or reopen the factories, but merely to appoint representatives and councils in each area of their countries. These councils then had to win the trust of the people, the majority of whom had learned through six years of organized atrocity to treat all institutions with extreme caution. In such circumstances the establishment of some kind of law and order, let alone any physical reconstruction, was little more than a pipe dream. It was only outside agencies – the Allied armies, the United Nations, the Red Cross – that had the authority or the manpower to attempt such feats. In the absence of such agencies, chaos reigned.

The story of Europe in the immediate postwar period is therefore not primarily one of reconstruction and rehabilitation – it is firstly a story of the descent into anarchy. This is a history that has never properly been written. Dozens of excellent books describe events in individual countries – especially in Germany – but they do so at the expense of the larger picture: the same themes occur again and again throughout the continent. There are one or two histories, like Tony Judt's *Postwar*, that take in a broader view of the continent as a whole – however, they do so over a much larger timescale, and so are obliged to summarize the events of the immediate postwar years in just a few chapters. To my knowledge there is no book in any language that describes the whole continent – east and west – in detail during this crucial and turbulent time.

This book is a partial attempt to rectify this situation. It shall not, as so many other books have done, seek to explain how the continent eventually rose from the ashes and attempted to rebuild itself physically, economically and morally. It will not concentrate on the Nuremberg trials, or the Marshall Plan, or any of the other attempts to heal the wounds that had been created by the war. Instead it is concerned with the period before such attempts at rehabilitation were even a possibility, when most of Europe was still extremely volatile, and violence could flare up once again at the slightest provocation. In a sense it is attempting the impossible – to describe chaos. It will do so by picking out different elements in that chaos, and by suggesting ways in which these were linked by common themes.

I shall begin by showing precisely what had been destroyed during the war, both physically and morally. It is only by fully appreciating what had been lost that we can understand the events that followed. Part II describes the wave of vengeance that swept across the continent, and suggests ways in which this phenomenon was manipulated for political gain. Vengeance is a constant theme of this book, and an understanding of its logic, and the purposes to which it was put, is essential if we are to understand the atmosphere of postwar Europe. Parts III and IV show what happened when this vengeance, and other forms of violence, were allowed to get out of hand. The ethnic cleansing, political violence and civil war that resulted were some of the most momentous events in European history. I shall argue that these were, in effect, the last spasms of the Second World War – and in many cases an almost seamless link to the beginning of the Cold War. The book will therefore cover, roughly, the years 1944 to 1949.

One of my main aims in writing this book was to break away from the narrow Western view that tends to dominate most writing on the period. For decades books about the aftermath of the war have focused on events in western Europe, largely because information about the east was not readily available, even in eastern Europe itself. Since the break-up of the Soviet Union and its satellite states this information has become more available, but it still tends to be obscure, and generally appears only in academic books and journals, often only in the language of the originator. So while much pioneering work has been done by Polish, Czech or Hungarian writers it has remained accessible only in Polish, Czech or Hungarian. It has also remained, largely, in the hands of academics – which brings me to another purpose of this book: to bring the period to life for the general reader.

My final, and perhaps most important, purpose is to clear a path through the labyrinth of myths that have been propagated about the aftermath of the war. Many of the 'massacres' I have investigated turn out, on closer inspection, to be far less dramatic than they are usually portrayed. Equally, some quite astonishing atrocities have been hushed up, or simply lost in the sweep of other historical events. While it might be impossible to unearth the exact truth behind some of these incidents, it is at least possible to remove some of the untruths.

A particular bugbear of mine is the plethora of vague and unsubstantiated statistics that are regularly bandied about in discussions concerning this period. Statistics really do matter, because they are often employed for political purposes. Some nations routinely exaggerate the crimes of their neighbours, either to distract attention from their own crimes or to further their own national causes. Political parties of all colours like to exaggerate the misdeeds of their rivals, and play down those of their allies. Historians also sometimes exaggerate, or merely pick the most sensational number from the range of figures available, to make their stories seem more dramatic. But the stories from this period are fantastic enough – they do not need exaggeration. For this reason I have tried where possible to base all my statistics on official sources, or on responsible academic studies if official sources are missing or suspect. Whenever statistics are in dispute I shall put what I consider to be the most reliable number in the main text, and alternative numbers in the notes.

That said, it would be foolish to imagine that my attempts at accuracy cannot be improved upon. Neither can this book pretend to be a 'definitive' or 'comprehensive' history of the immediate postwar period in Europe: the subject matter is far too broad for that. Instead it is an attempt to shine a light on a whole world of surprising and occasionally terrifying events for those who might never otherwise have discovered them.

My hope is that it will open up a debate about how these events affected the continent during the most painful stages of its rebirth and – since there is enormous scope for further research – perhaps stimulate others to investigate more deeply. If the past is a foreign country, this period in Europe's history still has vast regions marked only by the phrase 'Here be dragons'.

Note on Place Names

The map of Europe changed considerably in the aftermath of the Second World War, and the names of towns and cities changed with it. Thus, for example, the German city of Stettin became the Polish city of Szczecin, Polish Wilno became Lithuanian Vilnius and Italian Fiume became Yugoslavian Rijeka.

Except where there is an established English name for a city, I have tried always to use place names as they would generally have been accepted at the time. Thus, I have used Stettin when recounting events there during the war, but Szczecin when describing later events. Similarly I have given Russian names for Ukrainian cities like Kharkov or Dnepropetrovsk because, as part of the Soviet Union, this is how they were always referred to in contemporary documents.

There were, and still are, strong nationalist intentions behind the names given to towns, particularly in sensitive border areas. I would like to reassure the reader that these are not necessarily sentiments that I share.

PART I

The Legacy of War

I thought you'd be there waiting for me . . . What greeted me instead was the lingering stench of ashes and the empty sockets of our ruined home.

Samuel Puterman on his return to Warsaw, 1945[1]

We could see the physical destruction but the effect of vast economic disruption and political, social, and psychological destruction . . . completely escaped us.

Dean Acheson, US Under-Secretary of State, 1947

I

Physical Destruction

In 1943 the travel book publisher Karl Baedeker produced a guide to the Generalgouvernement – that part of central and southern Poland that remained nominally separate from the Reich. As with all publications in Germany at the time, it was just as concerned with disseminating propaganda as with giving its readers information. The section on Warsaw was a case in point. The book waxed lyrical about the city's German origins, its German character and the way that it had become one of the world's great capitals 'predominantly through the effort of Germans'. It urged tourists to visit the medieval Royal Castle, the fourteenth-century cathedral and the beautiful late-Renaissance Jesuit Church – all the products of German culture and influence. Of special interest was the complex of late baroque palaces around Piłsudski Square – 'the most beautiful square in Warsaw' – now renamed Adolf Hitler Platz. The centrepiece was the 'Saxon' Palace, built of course by a German, and its beautiful Saxon Gardens, which were again designed by German architects. The travel guide conceded that one or two buildings had unfortunately been damaged by the battle for Warsaw in 1939, but since then, it reassured its readers, Warsaw 'is being rebuilt once more under German leadership'.[1]

No mention was made of the western suburbs of the city, which had been converted into a ghetto for Jews. This was probably just as well because even as the book was being published an uprising broke out here, obliging SS-Brigadeführer Jürgen Stroop to set fire to virtually every house in the district.[2] Almost four square kilometres of the city were entirely destroyed in this way.

The following year a second uprising broke out throughout the rest of the city. This time it was a more general insurgency inspired by the

Polish Home Army. In August 1944, groups of Polish men, women and teenagers began ambushing German soldiers and stealing their weapons and ammunition. For the next two months they barricaded themselves in and around the Old City, and held down more than 17,000 German anti-insurgent troops.[3] The uprising only came to an end in October after some of the most brutal fighting of the war. Afterwards, tired of Polish disobedience, and aware that the Russians were about to enter the city anyway, Hitler ordered the city to be completely razed.[4]

Accordingly, German troops blew up the medieval Royal Castle that had so impressed Baedeker. They undermined the fourteenth-century cathedral and blew that up too. Then they destroyed the Jesuit Church. The Saxon Palace was systematically blown up over the course of three days just after Christmas 1944, as was the entire complex of baroque and rococo palaces. The European Hotel, recommended by Baedeker, was first burned down in October and then, just to make sure, blown up in January 1945. German troops went from house to house, street to street, systematically destroying the entire city: 93 per cent of Warsaw's dwellings were destroyed or damaged beyond repair. To complete the destruction they burned down the National Archive, the Archives of Ancient Documents, the Financial Archives, the Municipal Archives, the Archives of New Documents and the Public Library.[5]

After the war, when the Poles were turning their thoughts to rebuilding their capital, the National Museum held an exhibition showing fragments of buildings and artworks that had been damaged or destroyed during the German occupation. They produced an accompanying guide book, which, unlike Baedeker's guide book, was written entirely in the past tense. The intention was to remind the people of Warsaw, and the wider world, of exactly what had been lost. There is a realization implicit in both the guide book and the exhibition itself that those who lived through the destruction of Warsaw were no longer able to appreciate the immensity of what had happened to their city. For them it had happened gradually, beginning with the bombardment in 1939, continuing with German looting during the occupation and ending with the destruction of the Ghetto in 1943 and the final devastation in late 1944. Now, just a few months after their liberation, they had become used to living in shells of houses, surrounded on all sides by mountains of rubble.[6]

In some ways the true scale of the destruction could be appreciated only by those who saw its results without actually witnessing it taking place. John Vachon was a young photographer who came to Warsaw as part of the United Nations relief effort after the war. The letters he wrote to his wife Penny in January 1946 display his complete incomprehension at the scale of the destruction.

> This is really an incredible city and I want to give you an idea of it, and don't know how I can do it. It's a big city, see. Over one million pre war. Big as Detroit. Now it is 90 per cent *all* destroyed . . . Wherever you walk here it is hunks of buildings standing up without roofs or much sides, and people living in them. Except the Ghetto, where it is just a great plain of bricks, with twisted beds and bath tubs and sofas, pictures in frames, trunks, millions of things sticking out among the bricks. I can't understand how it could have been done . . . It's something that's so vicious I can't believe it.[7]

The beautiful baroque city described by Karl Baedeker just two years earlier had completely disappeared.

It is difficult to convey in meaningful terms the scale of the wreckage caused by the Second World War. Warsaw was just one example of a city destroyed – there were dozens more within Poland alone. In Europe as a whole *hundreds* of cities had been entirely or partially devastated. Photographs taken after the war can give some idea of the scale of the destruction of individual cities, but when one tries to multiply this devastation across the entire continent it necessarily defies comprehension. In some countries – especially Germany, Poland, Yugoslavia and Ukraine – a millennium of culture and architecture had been crushed in the space of just a few short years. The violence that brought about such total devastation has been likened by more than one historian to Armageddon.[8]

Those people who witnessed the wreckage of Europe's cities struggled to come to terms even with the local devastation they saw, and it is only in their tortured, inadequate descriptions that some of the destruction becomes imaginable. However, before we come to such human reactions to the crushed and shattered scenery, it is necessary to set down some statistics – because statistics matter, regardless of how elusive they can be.

As the only nation to have successfully defied Hitler for the entire duration of the war, Britain had suffered badly. The Luftwaffe had dropped almost 50,000 tons of bombs on Britain during the Blitz, destroying 202,000 houses and damaging 4.5 million more.[9] The pounding received by Britain's major cities is well known, but it is what happened to some of the smaller towns that shows the true extent of the bombing. The ferocity of the attacks on Coventry gave birth to a new German verb, *coventrieren* – to 'Coventrate', or destroy utterly. Clydebank is a relatively small industrial town on the outskirts of Glasgow: out of 12,000 homes only 8 escaped damage.[10]

Across the English Channel the damage was not quite so universal, but much more concentrated. Caen, for example, was virtually wiped off the map when the Allies landed in Normandy in 1944: 75 per cent of the city was obliterated by Allied bombs.[11] Saint-Lô and Le Havre suffered even worse, with 77 per cent and 82 per cent of the buildings destroyed.[12] When the Allies landed in the south of France more than 14,000 buildings in Marseilles were partly or completely destroyed.[13] According to government records for compensation claims and loans for war losses, 460,000 buildings in France were destroyed in the war, and a further 1.9 million damaged.[14]

The further east one travelled after the war, the worse the devastation became. In Budapest 84 per cent of the buildings were damaged, and 30 per cent of them so badly that they were entirely uninhabitable.[15] About 80 per cent of the city of Minsk in Belarus was destroyed: only 19 of 332 major factories in the city survived, and only then because mines set by the retreating Germans were defused by Red Army sappers just in time.[16] Most of the public buildings in Kiev were mined when the Soviets retreated in 1941 – the rest were destroyed when they returned in 1944. Kharkov in eastern Ukraine was fought over so many times that eventually there was little left to dispute. In Rostov and Voronezh, according to one British journalist, 'the destruction was very nearly 100 per cent'.[17] And the list goes on. Approximately 1,700 towns and cities were devastated in the USSR, 714 of them in Ukraine alone.[18]

Those who travelled across this ruined landscape in the aftermath of the war saw city after city after city destroyed. Very few of these people ever attempted to describe the totality of what they had seen – instead they struggled to come to terms with the more localized damage in each single city as they came across it. Stalingrad, for example, was nothing but 'lumps of walls, boxes of half-ruined buildings, piles of rubble, isolated chimneys'.[19] Sebastopol 'was now melancholy beyond words' where 'even in the suburbs . . . there was hardly a house standing'.[20] In September 1945 the American diplomat George F. Kennan found himself in the formerly Finnish but now Russian city of Vyborg, admiring the way that 'Rays of early morning sunshine . . . caught the gutted shells of apartment buildings, and flooded them momentarily with a chill, pale gleam.' Apart from a goat that he startled in one of the ruined doorways, Kennan seemed to be the only living being in the entire city.[21]

At the centre of all this destruction lay Germany, whose cities undoubtedly suffered the most comprehensive damage of the war. Around 3.6 million German apartments were destroyed by the British and American air forces – that is, about a fifth of all living spaces in the country.[22] In absolute terms the damage to living spaces in Germany was nearly eighteen times as bad as it was in Britain.[23] Individual cities suffered far worse than the average. According to figures from the Reich's Statistical Office, Berlin lost up to 50 per cent of its habitable premises, Hanover 51.6 per cent, Hamburg 53.3 per cent, Duisburg 64 per cent, Dortmund 66 per cent, and Cologne 70 per cent.[24]

When Allied observers came to Germany after the war, most of them expected to find destruction on the same scale as they had witnessed in Britain during the Blitz. Even after British and American newspapers and magazines began to print pictures and descriptions of the devastation it was impossible to prepare for the sight of the real thing. Austin Robinson, for example, was sent to western Germany directly after the war on behalf of the British Ministry of Production. His description of Mainz while he was there displays his sense of shock:

> That skeleton, with whole blocks level, huge areas with nothing but walls standing, factories almost completely gutted, was a picture that I know will live with me for life. One had known it intellectually without feeling it emotionally or humanly.[25]

British Lieutenant Philip Dark was equally appalled by the apocalyptic vision he saw in Hamburg at the end of the war:

> [W]e swung in towards the centre and started to enter a city devastated beyond all comprehension. It was more than appalling. As far as the eye could see, square mile after square mile of empty shells of buildings with

twisted girders scarecrowed in the air, radiators of a flat jutting out from
a shaft of a still-standing wall, like a crucified pterodactyl skeleton. Hor-
rible, hideous shapes of chimneys sprouting from the frame of a wall. The
whole pervaded by an atmosphere of ageless quiet . . . Such impressions
are incomprehensible unless seen.[26]

There is a sense of utter despair in many of the descriptions of German
cities in 1945. Dresden, for example, no longer resembled 'Florence on
the Elbe' but was more like 'the face of the moon', and planning directors believed that it would take 'at least seventy years' to rebuild.[27]
Munich was so badly devastated that 'It truly did almost make one
think that a Last Judgement was imminent.'[28] Berlin was 'completely
shattered – just piles of rubble and skeleton houses'.[29] Cologne was a
city 'recumbent, without beauty, shapeless in the rubble and loneliness
of complete physical defeat'.[30]

Between 18 and 20 million German people were rendered homeless by the destruction of their cities – that is the same as the combined
prewar populations of Holland, Belgium and Luxembourg.[31] Another
10 million people in Ukraine were also homeless, or more than the
total prewar population of Hungary.[32] These people lived in cellars,
ruins, holes in the ground – anywhere they could find a modicum of
shelter. They were entirely deprived of essential services, such as
water, gas, electricity – as were millions of others across Europe. Warsaw, for example, had just two working street lights.[33] In Odessa
water was only available from artesian wells, so that even visiting
dignitaries were given just a single bottle per day for washing.[34] Without these essential utilities the populations of Europe's cities were
reduced to living, as one American columnist described it, 'in medieval fashion surrounded by the broken-down machinery of the
twentieth century'.[35]

While the devastation was at its most dramatic in Europe's cities, rural
communities often suffered just as badly. Across the continent farms
were plundered, burned, flooded or simply neglected because of the war.
The marshes in southern Italy, so assiduously drained by Mussolini,
were deliberately flooded again by the retreating Germans, causing a
resurgence of malaria.[36] More than half a million acres of Holland
(219,000 hectares) were ruined when German troops deliberately

opened the dykes that kept the sea at bay.[37] Remoteness from the main theatres of war was no protection from such treatment. More than a third of the dwelling places in Lapland were destroyed by the retreating Germans.[38] The idea was to deny the turncoat Finnish forces any shelter during the winter, but it also had the effect of creating over 80,000 refugees. Across northern Norway and Finland roads were mined, telephone lines pulled down and bridges blown up, creating problems that would be felt for years after the war was over.

Once again, the further east, the worse the destruction. Greece lost a third of its forests during the German occupation, and over a thousand villages were burned and left uninhabited.[39] In Yugoslavia, according to the postwar Reparations Commission, 24 per cent of the orchards were destroyed, as were 38 per cent of the vineyards and about 60 per cent of all livestock. The plundering of millions of tons of grain, milk and wool completed the ruination of the Yugoslav rural economy.[40] In the USSR it was even worse: here as many as 70,000 villages were destroyed, along with their communities and the entire rural infrastructure.[41] Such damage was not merely the result of fighting and casual plundering – it was caused by the systematic and deliberate destruction of land and property. Farms and villages were burned down for the merest hint of resistance. Vast swathes of forest along the sides of roads were cut down to minimize the risk of ambush.

Much has been written about how ruthless Germany and Russia were when they attacked each other, but they were equally ruthless in defence. When the German army streamed into Soviet territory in the summer of 1941, Stalin made a radio broadcast to his people telling them to remove everything they could before fleeing: 'All valuable property, including non-ferrous metals, grain and fuel that cannot be withdrawn must be destroyed without fail. In areas occupied by the enemy, guerrilla units . . . must set fire to forests, stores and transports.'[42]

When the tables began to turn, Hitler likewise ordered that nothing should be left behind for the returning Soviets. 'Regardless of its inhabitants, every locality must be burned down and destroyed to deprive the enemy of accommodation facilities,' read one of Hitler's orders to his army commanders in Ukraine in December 1941; 'the localities left intact have to be subsequently ruined by the air force.'[43] Later, when things began to get more desperate, Himmler ordered his SS leaders to destroy everything: 'Not one person, no cattle, no quintal of grain, no railway track must remain behind . . . The enemy must find a country totally burned and destroyed.'[44]

As a consequence of orders like these, vast areas of agricultural land in Ukraine and Belarus were torched not once, but twice, and with them countless villages and farmhouses that might offer shelter to the enemy. Industry, naturally, was one of the first things to be destroyed. In Hungary, for instance, 500 major factories were dismantled and transported to Germany – over 90 per cent of the rest were deliberately damaged or destroyed – and almost every coal mine was flooded or collapsed.[45] In the USSR approximately 32,000 factories were destroyed.[46] In Yugoslavia the Reparations Commission estimated that their country had lost more than $9.14 billion worth of industry, or a third of the country's entire industrial wealth.[47]

Perhaps the worst damage was that which befell the continent's transport infrastructure. Holland, for example, lost 60 per cent of its road, rail and canal transport. In Italy up to a third of the country's road network had been made unusable, and 13,000 bridges were damaged or destroyed. Both France and Yugoslavia lost 77 per cent of their rail locomotives and a similar percentage of all rolling stock. Poland lost a fifth of its roads, a third of its rail track (about 10,000 miles in all), 85 per cent of all rolling stock, and 100 per cent of its civil aviation. Norway had lost half of its prewar shipping tonnage, and Greece lost between two-thirds and three-quarters of all shipping. By the end of the war, the *only* universally reliable method of travel was on foot.[48]

The physical devastation of Europe was more than merely the loss of its buildings and its infrastructure. It was more, even, than the destruction of centuries of culture and architecture. The truly disturbing thing about the ruins was what they symbolized. The mountains of rubble were, as one British serviceman put it, 'a monument to man's power of self-destruction'.[49] For hundreds of millions of people they were a daily reminder of the viciousness that the continent had witnessed, and which might at any time resurface.

Primo Levi, who had survived Auschwitz, claimed that there was something almost supernatural about the way the Germans had destroyed everything in their wake. To him, the broken remains of an army base at Slutsk, near Minsk, demonstrated 'the genius of destruction, of anti-creation, here as at Auschwitz; it was the mystique of barrenness, beyond all demands of war or impulse for booty'.[50] The destruction wreaked by the Allies was almost as bad: when Levi saw the ruins of Vienna he was overcome by a 'heavy, threatening sensation of an irreparable and definitive evil which was present everywhere, nestling in the guts of Europe and the world, the seed of future harm'.[51]

It is this undercurrent of 'anti-creation' and 'definitive evil' that makes the destruction of Europe's towns and cities so disturbing to contemplate. What is implied in all the descriptions of this time, but never overtly stated, is that behind the physical devastation is something far worse. The 'skeletons' of houses and framed pictures sticking out of the rubble of Warsaw are highly symbolic: hidden beneath the ruins, both literally and metaphorically, there was a separate human and moral disaster.

2

Absence

Death Toll

If the physical devastation of Europe defies easy comprehension, then the human cost of the war does so to an even greater degree. Any description of such things is necessarily inadequate. I am reminded of the novelist Hans Erich Nossack's attempt to describe the aftermath of the Hamburg firestorm in 1943: 'Oh, as I ride back in memory down that road into Hamburg I feel the urge to stop and give up. Why go on? I mean, why write it all down? Wouldn't it be better to surrender it to oblivion for all time?'[1] And yet, as Nossack himself realized, it is the duty of eyewitnesses and historians to record such events, even if their attempts to give them meaning are necessarily doomed to failure.

When describing catastrophes on such a vast scale, the historian is always presented with conflicting impulses. On the one hand he can present the raw statistics, and leave it to the reader to imagine what such numbers mean. In the aftermath of the war governments and aid agencies produced figures for just about every aspect of the conflict, from the numbers of soldiers and civilians killed to the economic effect of bombing on specific industries. Across Europe there was an official urge to measure, to estimate, to quantify – perhaps in what Nossack called 'an attempt to banish the dead by means of numbers'.[2]

On the other hand there is a temptation to ignore the figures altogether, and merely record the experiences of the ordinary people who witnessed these events. In the aftermath of the Hamburg firestorm, for example, it was not the fact of 40,000 deaths that upset the German population – it was the manner of these deaths. Stories of a raging inferno, of hurricane force winds and blizzards of sparks which set fire to people's hair and clothes – these things capture the imagination far more effectively than raw numbers. In any case, as people instinctively understood even at the time, the statistics were not reliable. In a city where bodies were concealed beneath mountains of rubble, where some had been fused together by the intense heat while others were reduced to mere ashes, it was impossible to measure the number of dead with any kind of precision. Whatever approach one takes, it is impossible to convey more than the merest glimpse of what such a catastrophe actually means. Conventional history is simply not equipped to describe what Nossack called 'something else . . . strangeness itself . . . the essentially not possible'.[3]

In some respects the Hamburg firestorm can be considered a microcosm of what happened to Europe in the war. As with the rest of Europe, the bombing had transformed the city into a landscape of ruins – and yet there were still parts of it that lay serenely, miraculously, untouched. As happened in many other parts of the continent, whole suburbs were evacuated in the wake of the firestorm, and remained virtually deserted for years to come. The victims, again as elsewhere, came from many nationalities, and all walks of life.

However, there are also some stark contrasts between the fate of this city and that of the rest of the continent. Horrific as the bombing of Hamburg was, it actually killed less than 3 per cent of the population. The death rate in Europe as a whole was more than twice that. The number of people who died as a direct result of the Second World War in Europe is truly mind-boggling: between 35 and 40 million people in total.[4] That is the equivalent of somewhere between the entire prewar population of Poland (35 million) and that of France (42 million).[5] Or, to put it another way, it was the same number of deaths as would have occurred had the Hamburg firestorm been repeated every night for a thousand nights.

The total figure masks some huge disparities between countries. For example Britain's losses, though horrific, were comparatively light. Approximately 300,000 Britons were killed in the Second World War – about a third as many as were killed in the First.[6] Likewise, over half a million French people were killed, around 210,000 Dutch, 86,000 Belgians and almost 310,000 Italians.[7] Germany, by contrast, lost almost 4.5 million soldiers and a further 1.5 million civilians. About as many German civilians died beneath Allied bombs alone as did Britons, Belgians and Dutchmen from all causes during the whole of the war.[8]

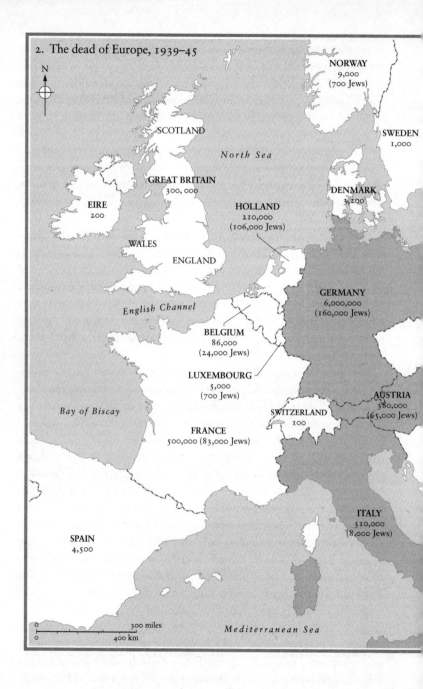

2. The dead of Europe, 1939–45

N

NORWAY
9,000
(700 Jews)

SWEDEN
1,000

SCOTLAND

North Sea

GREAT BRITAIN
300,000

DENMARK
3,200

HOLLAND
210,000
(106,000 Jews)

EIRE
200

GERMANY
6,000,000
(160,000 Jews)

WALES

ENGLAND

English Channel

BELGIUM
86,000
(24,000 Jews)

LUXEMBOURG
5,000
(700 Jews)

AUSTRIA
380,000
(65,000 Jews)

SWITZERLAND
100

Bay of Biscay

FRANCE
500,000 (83,000 Jews)

ITALY
310,000
(8,000 Jews)

SPAIN
4,500

0   300 miles
0   400 km

Mediterranean Sea

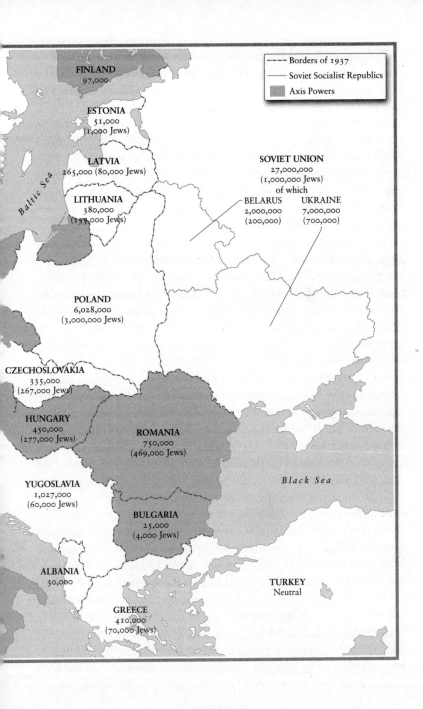

Borders of 1937
Soviet Socialist Republics
Axis Powers

FINLAND
97,000

ESTONIA
51,000
(1,000 Jews)

LATVIA
265,000 (80,000 Jews)

LITHUANIA
380,000
(133,000 Jews)

Baltic Sea

SOVIET UNION
27,000,000
(1,000,000 Jews)
of which
BELARUS   UKRAINE
2,000,000   7,000,000
(200,000)   (700,000)

POLAND
6,028,000
(3,000,000 Jews)

CZECHOSLOVAKIA
335,000
(267,000 Jews)

HUNGARY
450,000
(277,000 Jews)

ROMANIA
750,000
(469,000 Jews)

YUGOSLAVIA
1,027,000
(60,000 Jews)

Black Sea

BULGARIA
25,000
(4,000 Jews)

ALBANIA
30,000

TURKEY
Neutral

GREECE
410,000
(70,000 Jews)

Once again, the further east, the worse the casualties. Greece suffered about 410,000 war dead – a total that does not appear markedly worse than some of the other countries already listed until one realizes that Greece had a prewar population of only about 7 million. The war therefore killed about 6 per cent of all Greeks.[9] Likewise Hungary's 450,000 war deaths represented almost 5 per cent of the population.[10] In Yugoslavia just over a million people were killed, or 6.3 per cent of the population.[11] Deaths in Estonia, Latvia and Lithuania probably amounted to between 8 and 9 per cent of all prewar Balts.[12] As a nation, Poland suffered the most proportionally: more than one Pole in every six was killed – a total of over 6 million people in all.[13]

The highest absolute number of war deaths came in the Soviet Union: approximately 27 million people.[14] This incomprehensible figure once again necessarily hides huge regional variations. There are no reliable figures for the individual regions of Belarus or Ukraine, for example, which were not internationally regarded as separate countries at the time – but most estimates of Ukrainian war dead put the figure at between 7 and 8 million. If that figure is correct, one in every five Ukrainians was killed by the war.[15] The Belarusian death toll is reputed to have been the highest of all, with a quarter of the population killed.[16]

Today, as in 1945, it is almost impossible to grasp what such statistics mean in practice, and any attempt to bring the figures to life is doomed to fail. One could say that the total death toll represents an average of one killing every five seconds, for almost six long years – but such things are impossible to imagine. Even those who experienced the war, who witnessed massacres, who saw fields full of dead bodies and mass graves brimming with corpses are unable to comprehend the true scale of the killing that took place across Europe during the war.

Perhaps the only way to come close to understanding what happened is to stop trying to imagine Europe as a place populated by the dead, and to think of it instead as a place characterized by absence. Almost everyone alive when the war ended had lost friends or relatives to it. Whole villages, whole towns and even whole cities had been effectively erased, and with them their populations. Large areas of Europe that had once been home to thriving, bustling communities were now almost entirely empty of people. It was not the presence of death that defined the atmosphere of postwar Europe, but rather the absence of those who had once occupied Europe's sitting rooms, its shops, its streets, its markets.

From the distance of the twenty-first century, we tend to look back on the end of the war as a time of celebration. We have seen images of sailors kissing girls in New York's Times Square, and smiling troops of all nationalities linking arms along Paris's Champs Elysées. However, for all the celebration that took place at the end of the war, Europe was actually a place in mourning. The sense of loss was both personal and communal. Just as the continent's towns and cities had been replaced by a landscape of crumbling ruins, so too had families and communities been replaced by a series of gaping holes.

The Vanishing of the Jews

Some absences were of course greater than others. The most obvious absence, particularly in eastern Europe, was that of the Jews. In an interview for the oral history project at London's Imperial War Museum, Edith Baneth, a Jewish survivor from Czechoslovakia, summed up how this absence is still felt on a personal level today:

> When it comes to the point of thinking of the families which we all lost, it can never be put right. They can't be replaced – the second and third generations still feel it. When we have weddings and barmitzvahs, from other sides there are maybe fifty or sixty people from their family. When my son had his barmitzvah, and his wedding, there was no family what-soever – that's the way the second and third generation feel the Holocaust, they miss their family. My son hasn't *experienced* a family life – having uncles, aunts, grandmothers, grandfathers. There is just that *hole*.[17]

In 1945, while most people counted the family and friends that they had *lost* to the war, Jewish survivors tended to count those they still *had left*. Sometimes there were none. In the memorial book for the Jews of Berlin, the deaths of entire extended families are listed alongside each other – from tiny children to their great-grandparents. There are six pages of Abrahams, eleven pages of Hirsches, twelve pages of Levys and thirteen pages of Wolffs.[18] Similar books could be made for any of the Jewish communities that used to exist throughout Europe. Victor Breitburg, for example, lost his entire family in Poland in 1944. 'I was the only survi-vor out of fifty-four people in my family. I went back to Łódź to see if I could find some of my family members, but there was no one.'[19]

When all the losses are added up, the 'hole' Edith Baneth speaks of came to engulf not only entire families but entire communities. In Poland and Ukraine there were dozens of large cities where Jews made up a sizeable proportion of the population before the war. Wilno, for example, which is today known as Vilnius, the capital city of Lithuania, was home to between 60,000 and 70,000 Jews before the war. By the middle of 1945 perhaps only 10 per cent of them had survived.[20] Jews also made up around a third of the population in Warsaw – some 393,950 people in total – and yet when the Red Army finally crossed the Vistula at Warsaw in January 1945 they found only 200 Jewish survivors in the city. Even by the end of 1945, when handfuls of survivors had trickled back to the city, there were never more than 5,000.[21]

Jewish communities in rural areas fared just as badly. In the vast tracts of countryside around Minsk in Belarus the Jewish presence was reduced from about 13 per cent of the population to just 0.6 per cent.[22] In Volhynia, a mostly rural backwater of prewar Poland, 98.5 per cent of the Jewish community were killed by the Germans and their local militias.[23] In all, at least 5,750,000 Jews were killed during the Second World War, making it the worst and most systematic genocide in history.[24]

Once again, such statistics are difficult to understand until one begins to imagine what they might mean on a more human scale. Alicia Adams, a survivor of Drohobycz in Poland, puts the events she witnessed in stark terms:

Not only my parents, my uncles, aunts and my brother, but also all my childhood friends and all the people I knew in my childhood – the *whole population* of Drohobycz was wiped out, about thirty thousand people, they were all shot. So it wasn't only my closest family being killed, I watched everybody. I watched somebody being killed *every* day – that was part of my childhood.[25]

For those Jews who escaped or survived, returning to the empty and abandoned neighbourhoods of eastern Europe was a uniquely depressing experience. The famed Soviet writer Vasily Grossman had grown up in Ukraine, but was living in Moscow at the time of the German invasion. When he returned as a war reporter at the end of 1943 he found that all his friends and family had been exterminated. He was one of the first to write about what would soon become known as the Holocaust:

There are no Jews in the Ukraine. Nowhere – Potava, Kharkov, Kremen-chug, Borispol, Yagotin – in none of the cities, hundreds of towns, or thousands of villages will you see the black, tear-filled eyes of little girls; you will not hear the pained voice of an old woman; you will not see the dark face of a hungry baby. All is silence. Everything is still. A whole people has been brutally murdered.[26]

With the effective removal of an entire race from most of the continent a unique culture, built up over centuries, was also lost.

This was the murder of a great and ancient professional experience, passed from one generation to another in thousands of families of craftsmen and of members of the intelligentsia. This was the murder of everyday traditions that grandfathers had passed to their grandchildren, this was the murder of memories, of a mournful song, folk poetry, of life, happy and bitter, this was the destruction of hearths and cemeteries, this was the death of the nation which had been living side by side with Ukrainians over hundreds of years . . .[27]

The Jews were one of the few groups who came close to understanding the enormity of what had happened to Europe during the Second World War. The fact that they had been singled out and herded together gave them a unique perspective: they could see that the mass killings were not merely a local matter, but were taking place all over the continent. Even children understood this. The eleven-year-old Celina Lieberman, for example, tried to keep her Jewish identity alive despite being hastily fostered out to a Christian couple in Ukraine in 1942. She used to apologize to God each night for accompanying her new parents to church, because she solemnly believed herself to be the last Jew alive.[28]

And yet, even in the midst of this despair, there were still some small seeds of hope. Celina Lieberman was *not* the last Jew alive. After the war had passed on, Jews began to emerge from hiding even in the most unlikely places. Thousands had survived in the forests and swamps of Lithuania, Poland and Belarus. Thousands more had spent the war hidden in the basements and attics of sympathetic Gentiles. Even in destroyed Warsaw handfuls of Jews emerged from the ruins, like the biblical Noah stepping onto the shores of a changed world. They had weathered the flood of the Holocaust by hiding in sewers, tunnels and purpose-built bunkers – their own personal arks. Perhaps the greatest miracle, although it might not have felt it, was the survival of Jews in the concentration camps of Europe. Despite the best efforts of the Nazis to starve and work them to death, some 300,000 Jews lived to be liberated by the Allies in 1945. In all, some 1.6 million European Jews managed to escape death.[29]

The war also provided some rare examples of states acting honourably towards Jews in the face of serious pressure from the Nazis. For example, Denmark passed no anti-Jewish laws, expropriated no Jewish property, and ousted no Jews from government posts. When they discovered that the SS were planning to round up the country's 7,200 Jews, the Danish people conspired to evacuate almost the entire community in secret to Sweden.[30] The Italian people also resisted all attempts to deport Jews, not only in Italy itself but in the territories it had conquered.[31] When the SS demanded the deportation of Bulgaria's 49,000 Jews, the king, the parliament, the church, the intellectuals and the farmers vehemently opposed the measures. Indeed, the Bulgarian farmers were said to be ready to lie down on the railway tracks to prevent the Jews being taken. As a consequence, Bulgaria was the only country in Europe to see its population of Jews actually *increase* during the war.[32]

Finally, there are some astonishing examples of individuals who were willing to risk their lives in order to save Jews. Some of these people, like the German industrialist Oskar Schindler, are well known; but since 1953 more than 21,700 others have been recognized by the state of Israel for saving Jews.[33] Some of these people sheltered Jews despite their own intense prejudices against them. One Dutch clergyman, for example, admitted to feeling an intense aversion towards Jews, whom he thought 'unbearable . . . very different to us, another kind, typically of another race'. And yet he was still willing to be arrested and imprisoned in a concentration camp for helping them to escape the Nazis. It is from such unlikely sources that hope sprang during and after the war, not only for Jews but for the European people as a whole.[34]

Other Holocausts

While the extermination of the Jews was the most visible, continent-wide genocide, there were other equally devastating absences on a local scale. In Croatia 592,000 Serbs, Muslims and Jews were killed by the

Ustashe regime in an attempt to ethnically cleanse the entire country.[35] In Volhynia, after the Jews had been exterminated, tens of thousands of Poles were killed by Ukrainian nationalists. Bulgarians massacred Greek communities in the areas they invaded along the northern edge of the Aegean, and Hungarians did the same to Serbians in the Vojvodina region of Yugoslavia.

In many areas of Europe, unwanted ethnic groups were simply driven out of their towns and villages. This occurred all over central and eastern Europe at the beginning of the war, as the old empires clawed back the territory they had lost in the aftermath of the First World War. But the most dramatic exodus of an ethnic group occurred in 1945, when several million Germans were driven out of East Prussia, Silesia and Pomerania by the advancing Red Army, leaving a landscape of ghost towns behind them. When these parts of eastern Germany were handed over to Poland in the aftermath of the war, the arriving Poles described an eerie absence of life in what appeared to be otherwise perfectly normal streets. Some of the houses had dishes of food still on the tables, as if they had been abandoned in a hurry. 'Everything was empty,' remembers Zbigniew Ogrodzinski, one of the first Polish officials to be appointed in the German city of Stettin in the spring of 1945. 'You went into houses, and everything was there – books on the shelves, furniture, everything. There weren't any Germans at all.'[36]

In some rural parts of eastern Germany the absence of life seemed total. In the summer of 1945, a British major described his journey through the German province of Mecklenburg as he went to negotiate an exchange of goods with his Russian counterpart.

> Our road lay for the first kilos through the Forest of Rabensteinfeld, and then through good agricultural land, until we arrived at Crivitz. This journey was the most eerie I have ever made. The only humans we saw were old Red Army soldiers and sentries. The farms were deserted, barns emptied, fields devoid of cattle and horses, no fowls, in short a dead land. I can't remember seeing anything living (other than a few Red soldiers) on that 18 kilo journey to Crivitz. I never heard a bird sing or saw any wild creatures.[37]

During the course of just six years, the demographics of Europe had changed irredeemably. The density of Poland's population fell by 27 per cent, and some areas in the east of the country were now barely populated at all.[38] Countries that had once been ethnically mixed had been 'cleansed' so extensively that, to all intents and purposes, they now included only a single ethnic group.[39] As well as an absence of people, therefore, there was an absence of community, and an absence of diversity: large areas of Europe had become homogeneous. This process would only accelerate in the months after the war.

If the wholesale massacre of entire communities made the landscape seem eerie to outsiders, it was far more disorienting for the few who still lived amongst the emptiness. The survivors of the massacre at Oradour-sur-Glane in the Limousin region of France, for example, have never since fully come to terms with what happened to them. In the summer of 1944, in reprisal for local Resistance activity, all the town's men were rounded up and shot. The women and children were driven into the church, which was then set on fire. After the war the authorities decided not to rebuild the village, but to construct a new town nearby – Oradour itself was to be preserved for ever exactly as it was on the day of the massacre. It is still a ghost town today.[40]

Similar massacres, equally brutal, occurred in countless local communities across Europe. Perhaps the most infamous massacre of them all was that at Lidice, in Czechoslovakia, where the entire male population was shot in reprisal for the assassination of Reinhard Heydrich, the German deputy Reichsprotektor of Bohemia and Moravia. The children of the village were then taken to the Chełmno concentration camp, where they were gassed, and the women were incarcerated at Ravensbrück as slave labour. The village itself was then burned, and bulldozed, and the rubble carted away to allow the grass to grow over where the buildings had once stood. The purpose of this massacre was not merely to punish the local community for resisting the occupation, but to entirely delete that community, as if it had never existed. The Nazis then used the systematic destruction of the village as an advertisement of what would happen to any other village found to be even remotely involved in Resistance activities.[41]

The psychological impact of such total erasure of a community should not be underestimated. In 1945, after the liberation of the concentration camps, the surviving women of Lidice headed back to their village. They were unaware of what had happened to their community until they encountered Czech soldiers at the border. One of these women, Miloslava Kalibová, later described her reaction:

The soldiers lowered their heads and many of them had tears in their eyes. We said 'Oh no! Don't say there is even worse to come . . .' One of the soldiers spoke to me and I learnt from him that three years earlier all the men had been shot . . . Killing little boys. Killing all the men just like that . . . And worst of all, gassing the children. It was an enormous shock.[42]

When she arrived at the village she found 'only barren plains'. Nothing of the original village existed except in her own memory, and the memories of her fellow survivors.[43]

Such experiences were, at a local level, every bit as devastating as the Holocaust. The destruction of towns and villages was a loss not only to the surviving inhabitants of those places, but also to the whole surrounding area, and by extension to the continent as a whole, which, in the words of Antoine de Saint-Exupéry, was deprived of a 'cargo of memories . . . a cluster of traditions'.[44] Lidice, along with thousands of other villages, was switched off like a light.

Widows and Orphans

If the killing created some gaping 'holes' in the fabric of European society, there were also other, more subtle demographic absences, as if a single thread had been entirely removed from the tapestry. The most striking of these, and the one that was felt almost universally, was the absence of men. Photographs of provincial Britain on VE Day show street parties full of women and children celebrating the end of the war – apart from the old, or the occasional soldier on leave, men are mostly missing from the pictures. The people in these photographs are smiling, because they know that the absence of their menfolk is only temporary. In other parts of Europe there were no such certainties. Most German soldiers, and those from other Axis countries, were interned at the end of the war – many of these men would not be returning for years to come. And of course millions of men of all nationalities would never return. 'In our thousands of miles that we travelled in Germany,' wrote one British major after the war, 'the most outstanding fact of all was the total absence of men between the ages of 17 and 40. It was a land of women, children and old men.'[45]

In many other parts of Europe entire generations of young women were doomed to spinsterhood, for the simple reason that most of the local young men were dead. In the Soviet Union, for example, there were over 13 million more women than men by the end of the war. The loss of men was felt most harshly in the countryside, where 80 per cent of the collective farm workers were women. According to the census of 1959, a third of all Soviet women who had reached the age of twenty during the decade 1929–38 remained unmarried.[46]

If Europe had become a continent of women, it was also a continent of children. In the chaotic aftermath of the war, many children had been separated from their families and were living together in gangs for safety. In 1946 there were still some 180,000 vagrant children living in Rome, Naples and Milan: they were forced to sleep in doorways and alleys, and kept themselves alive by theft, begging and prostitution. The problem was so great that the Pope himself appealed to the world for help for Italian children 'wandering aimlessly through towns and villages, forsaken and exposed to many dangers'.[47] In France they were often found sleeping in haystacks by farmers. In Yugoslavia and eastern Slovakia partisans found half-starved groups of them living in woods, caves and ruins. In the summer of 1945 there were 53,000 lost children in Berlin alone.[48]

One such child was found by British Lieutenant-Colonel William Byford-Jones living inside a crack in the Kaiser Wilhelm monument in Berlin. When he asked her what she was doing there she told him that it was the safest place she could find to sleep: 'No one can find me. It is warm here, no one comes up.' When the German Social Welfare Office came to fetch her it took hours of patient enticement to coax her out.[49]

Such stories point to another devastating absence in the fabric of Europe – the absence of parents. The problem was particularly bad in those parts of Europe that had been most devastated by the war. In Poland, for example, there were well over a million 'war orphans' – a term that in British and American official jargon meant those children who had lost at least one parent.[50] In Germany there were probably a million more: in the British quarter alone there were 322,053 registered war orphans in 1947.[51] The lack of fathers, or indeed any male role models, was so common that it was considered quite normal by the children themselves. 'I can only remember one boy who had a father,' says Andrzej C., a Pole from Warsaw, who lived in a succession of displaced persons camps immediately after the war. 'Men were very strange creatures, because there were hardly any of them about.'[52] According to UNESCO, a third of all children in Germany had lost their fathers.[53]

This lack of parents, and of parental supervision, could sometimes have unexpected perks. Andrzej C., for example, acknowledges the hardship of his childhood, but remembers with relish some of the games that he and the other boys used to play in and around the displaced persons camps of southern Germany. Andrzej himself had the opportunity to play with toys that most children today could only dream of.

> We children were like feral dogs. Life was very interesting then! The fear was gone, the sun was shining, and there were interesting things to find . . . Once we found an unexploded artillery shell. We knew that was dangerous, so we kept it in a stream for a time because we didn't know what to do with it . . . Eventually we put the shell in another bonfire and ran to the opposite side of the valley to see what happened. There was a massive explosion. We never thought that maybe someone might come along at the wrong time – we were completely thoughtless. Another time we found some German machine gun ammunition, lots of it. So we put it in a metal stove someone had thrown away in the forest, put some wood in and lit the stove. That was fantastic! It blew holes in it until it was like a sieve!

On other occasions Andrzej and his friends built bonfires out of jerry-cans full of petrol, burned their eyebrows off by setting fire to smokeless powder, threw mortar shells at one another, and even found and fired a Panzerfaust anti-tank rocket: 'That was also very good!' His greatest fear throughout all this was not that he might be seriously injured, but that his mother might find out what he had been up to.

Once he even walked across a minefield in order to pick wild raspberries that were growing alongside some abandoned German army bunkers. 'This was a few years after the war,' he explains, 'and the mines were visible. So we decided that we could walk across – after all, we could see them, so we were safe . . . We were stupid, and lucky. If you haven't got brains, you've got to have luck. But they were lovely raspberries . . .'[54]

Andrzej was lucky in more ways than one. Not only did he avoid serious injury, but he still had his mother with him. Some time after the war his father, who had been fighting with the Polish 2nd Corps in Italy, also turned up. This was a luxury denied to some 13 million other European children.[55] A significant proportion had lost both parents, and by September 1948 there were some – around 20,000 in total – who were still waiting to see if *any* relatives could be traced.[56]

Psychological studies of orphans show that they are often, understandably, far more susceptible to anxiety and depression than other children. They are more prone to erratic and anti-social behaviour, they are more likely to contemplate suicide, they have higher rates of drug and alcohol abuse, lower self-esteem and poorer health.[57] For young children, parents represent the solidity of the world and the way it works: when their parents are suddenly removed, they lose the foundations on which their understanding of the world is built. In addition to the normal process of bereavement, such children have to cope with the fact that the world, in their eyes, has become a place that is essentially unstable.

There is a sense in which the same process occurred in Europe as a whole during the war. The sombre atmosphere of absence changed the psychology of the continent on a fundamental level. Not only had tens of millions of individuals experienced the loss of friends, family and loved ones, but many regions were forced to cope with the extermination of entire communities, and all nations with the death of large slices of their populations. Any notion of stability was therefore lost – not only for individuals, but at every level of society.

If bereaved individuals are prone to act erratically, then the same is true of communities and even whole nations. If, in the coming pages, the reader begins to wonder why I am going into so much detail about what was lost during the war, it is worth keeping this in mind. Europe had suffered many upheavals before, but the sheer scale of the Second World War dwarfed anything that had happened for centuries. It left Europe not only bereft, but bewildered.

3

Displacement

If the Second World War killed more Europeans than any other war in history, it was also the cause of some of the biggest population movements the world has ever seen. Germany was awash with foreign workers in the spring of 1945. The country contained almost 8 million forced labourers at the end of the war, who had been brought to German farms and factories to work from every corner of Europe. In western Germany alone, UNRRA, the United Nations Relief and Rehabilitation Administration, looked after and repatriated more than 6.5 million displaced persons. Most of them came from the Soviet Union, Poland and France, although there were also significant numbers of Italians, Belgians, Dutch, Yugoslavs and Czechs. A large proportion of these displaced persons were women and children. One of the many aspects of the Second World War that make it unique among modern wars is the fact that vast numbers of civilians were taken prisoner along with the traditional military captives. Women and children, as well as men, were effectively treated as war booty. They were enslaved in a way that had not been seen in Europe since the time of the Roman Empire.[1]

To make the situation in Germany even more complicated, millions of Germans were displaced within their own country. By the beginning of 1945 there were an estimated 4.8 million internal refugees, mostly in the south and east, who had been evacuated from bombed cities and a further 4 million displaced Germans who had fled the eastern reaches of the Reich in fear of the Red Army.[2] When we add the nearly 275,000 British and American prisoners of war, this makes a grand total of at least 17 million displaced persons in Germany alone.[3] This is a fairly conservative estimate, and other historians have placed the figure far higher.[4] In Europe as a whole, according to one study, over 40 million people were forcibly displaced for varying periods during the war.[5]

As the end of hostilities approached, huge numbers headed out onto the roads to begin the long journey home. Derek Henry, a British sapper with the Royal Engineers, first began to encounter such groups near Minden in mid-April 1945.

> We had been told to be on the lookout for pockets of German troops still putting up a fight but fortunately all we came across were thousands of DPs and refugees of every nationality, all heading towards us and the West: Bulgarians, Rumanians, Russians, Greeks, Yugoslavs and Poles – you name it, they were there, some in small groups of two or three each with their pitiful bundle of belongings heaped on to a pushbike or in a farm cart, others in large groups, piled onto overcrowded buses or on the backs of lorries, it was never ending. Whenever we stopped they would descend on us, hoping for some food.[6]

Later, according to US intelligence officer Saul Padover, 'Thousands, tens of thousands, finally millions of liberated slaves were coming out of the farms and the factories and the mines and pouring onto the highways.'[7] Reactions to this huge torrent of displaced people differed widely, depending on the person who witnessed it. For Padover, who had little time for Germans, it was 'perhaps the most tragic human migration in history', and simply more evidence of German guilt. For the local population, who were understandably nervous of such large groups of disgruntled foreigners, they represented a threat. 'They looked like wild creatures,' wrote one German woman after the war, 'one could be afraid of them'.[8] For those overwhelmed military government officers whose job was to gain some sort of control over them, they were merely a 'swarming mass'.[9] They filled the roads, which were already too damaged to accommodate them, and were only able to feed themselves by looting and robbing shops, stores and farmhouses along the way. In a country where the administrative systems had collapsed, where the local police force had all been killed or interned, where shelter was non-existent, and where food was no longer being distributed, they represented an impossible burden and an irresistible threat to the rule of law.

But this is to view these people from the outside. To the displaced themselves, they were simply people trying to find their way to safety.

The lucky ones were gathered up by French, British or American soldiers, and transported to displacement centres in the west. But in a huge number of cases there were simply not enough Allied soldiers to deal with them. Hundreds of thousands were effectively abandoned to look after themselves. 'There was nobody,' remembers Andrzej C., who was just nine years old when the war came to an end. He, his mother and his sister had been forced labourers on a farm in Bohemia. In the last weeks of the war they were rounded up and taken to the Sudeten town of Carlsbad (modern Karlovy Vary in the Czech Republic), where the last of their German guards finally deserted them. 'We found ourselves in a vacuum. There were no Russians, no Americans, no British. An absolute vacuum.'[10] His mother decided to head westwards towards the American lines because she thought it would be safer than handing themselves over to the Soviet troops. They spent several weeks walking into Germany, crossing the American lines repeatedly as the US troops fell back towards their designated zone of occupation. Andrzej remembers this as an anxious time, far more stressful even than being a prisoner of the Germans.

> That was a really hungry time, because there was nothing. We begged, we stole, we did whatever we could. We dug potatoes from the fields . . . I used to dream about food. Mashed potatoes with bacon on top – that was the highest of the high. I couldn't think of anything better. A heap of golden steaming mashed potatoes!

He travelled in a whole stream of refugees, made up of separate groups that did not seem to mix with one another. His group had about twenty people in it, most of them Poles. The local people they passed on the way were far from sympathetic to their plight. When Andrzej was given the task of grazing a horse that one of the men in his group had acquired, a German farmer shouted at him to 'Bugger off!' At other times they were refused water, had dogs set on them and, as Poles, were even blamed for starting the war and bringing this whole misfortune upon Germany – an accusation that must have felt doubly ironic, given the huge disparity in their relative predicaments.

The sights Andrzej encountered during his month-long trek towards safety were branded into his memory. He remembers walking past a German field hospital in a forest, where he saw men with broken arms in wire cages, some who were bandaged from head to foot, others 'stinking like hell, decaying alive'. There was nobody there to help them, because all the medical staff had run away. He remembers arriving at a Polish prisoner-of-war camp where the inmates refused to come out, despite the fact that the gates were now wide open, because nobody had given them an order to do so. 'They were soldiers and they thought somebody was going to give them orders to march somewhere. Who – where – they had no idea. They were absolutely lost.' He saw groups of prisoners in pyjama uniforms, still working the fields under German civilian guards. Later on he entered a valley where thousands upon thousands of German soldiers were sitting quietly, a few bonfires dotted between them, guarded by just a handful of American military police.

When they finally passed through the American checkpoints at Hof in Bavaria they were directed to a building with a red flag flying over it. This caused a few moments of panic because his mother thought they were being sent to a Soviet camp, until she realized that this was the flag of UNRRA – a red flag with white lettering on it. They had reached safety at last.

The dangers and difficulties that refugees like Andrzej had to over-come should not be underestimated. These might not have been immediately apparent to a nine-year-old boy, but they were all too obvious to the older generation. Mr and Mrs Druhm were Berliners in their late sixties when the war ended. After spending a short time surrounded by the lawlessness of the Red Army they decided to risk travelling to their daughter's house on the other side of the Elbe, ninety miles away. It was a decision not taken lightly, and their journey was beset with problems from the very beginning, especially once they reached the countryside outside Berlin.

> In places there were still skirmishes going on. We heard shooting and often had to stop until it was quiet. In these remote parts the soldiers didn't know the war was over. Then there were often bridges gone and roads so damaged that we had to go back and find another route . . . We had many heart breaking incidents, like trudging miles and then not getting any further and having to go back. Once we went along quite a deserted wide main road. We saw a big board up with Russian writing and went on but not feeling very safe. Suddenly we were shouted at. We couldn't see anyone but then a shot whizzed by my ear and scraped my collar. We realised that we were not meant to be there, so turned back and had miles to go round to get to where we wanted.

The devastation they encountered along the way hinted of recent violence, both of the war itself and of the occupying Soviet troops.

> In the woods were sofas and feather beds and mattresses and pillows, often burst or cut open and feathers all over the place, even on the trees. There were babies' prams, glasses of conserved fruit, even motor bikes, typewriters, cars, carts, bars of soap, a pile of pen-knives and new shoes from a shop . . . We also saw dead horses, some looking and smelling horrible . . .

And finally there were the other displaced persons on the road, who posed just as much of a potential threat to an ageing German couple as the Soviet soldiers did.

> There were many people of all nationalities going in the opposite direction to us, mostly forced labourers going home. Many of them had babies and they were just stealing anything they wanted, horses and carts from the farmers, sometimes a cow tied to the back, and cooking utensils. They looked like wild creatures . . .[11]

The Druhms at least had the advantage of being able to knock on farmers' doors and ask for help from their fellow countrymen. Most of these 'wild creatures' had no choice but to steal from the local population. They were not welcome, and in any case, after years of being brutalized by German guards were not inclined to trust any Germans at all.

Twenty-year-old Polish girl Marilka Ossowska was one such person. By April 1945 she had already spent two years in Auschwitz, Ravensbrück and Buchenwald, before finally escaping from a death march towards Czechoslovakia. After witnessing the brutality of the liberating Soviets, she and a group of other ex-prisoners decided that they might be safer if they made their way towards the American lines. She too was shocked by the sheer volume of people on the roads.

> Germany in 1945 was one huge ants' nest. Everyone was moving. This was how the eastern territories of Germany looked like. There were Germans escaping from the Russians. There were all these prisoners of war. There were some of us – not that many, but still . . . It was really incredible, teeming with people and movement.[12]

She and two Polish friends hooked up with three French labourers, two British prisoners of war and a black American soldier. Together they made their way towards the River Mulde, which at that time marked the border between the Russian and American armies. As they travelled they begged from local German farmers, or intimidated them into handing over some food. The presence of a black man certainly helped in this respect: the American, who was normally quite reserved in Marilka's presence, deliberately played up to German racial prejudices by stripping himself naked, putting a knife between his teeth and dancing at them like a savage. Seeing this, the terrified housewives were only too keen to hand over baskets of food and get rid of him. Then he would put his clothes back on and continue the journey as normal.

In the Saxon town of Riesa, about halfway between Dresden and Leipzig, Marilka and her two friends finally tricked some Russian soldiers into giving them some transport. They met two bored-looking soldiers guarding a store of hundreds of looted bicycles, and immediately turned on the charm. 'Oh, you must be lonely!' they said. 'We can come and keep you company. *And* we know where some schnapps is!' The delighted guards gave them three bicycles so that they could go and fetch this fictitious schnapps, and never saw them again.

After six days of cycling the group finally reached Leipzig, under American control at the time, where the women were loaded into lorries and taken to a camp in Nordheim near Hanover. From here Marilka hitchhiked to Italy, and was finally transported to Britain at the end of 1946. She did not return to Poland for another fifteen years.

These few stories must be multiplied hundreds of thousands of times to give even a snapshot of the chaos that existed on the roads of Europe in the spring of 1945. Swarms of refugees, speaking twenty different languages, were obliged to negotiate a transport network that had been bombed, mined and neglected through six years of war. They congregated in cities that had been utterly destroyed by Allied bombing raids, and which were incapable of accommodating even the local population, let alone the huge influx of newcomers. That the various military governments and aid agencies were able to round up the majority of these people, feed them, clothe them, locate missing relatives and then repatriate most of them within the next six months is nothing short of a miracle.

However, this rapid process of repatriation could not erase the damage that had been done. The population displacements of the war had had a profound effect on the psychology of Europe. On an individual level it was traumatic not only for those who were displaced, but also for those they left behind, who often spent years wondering what had happened to the loved ones snatched from their midst. On a communal level it had also been devastating: the forced conscription of all the young people had deprived communities of their main breadwinners and left them vulnerable to starvation. But it is on the collective level that the wartime displacements were perhaps most significant. By normalizing the idea of uprooting whole sections of the population, they provided a template for the more comprehensive *postwar* population movements. The pan-European programme of ethnic expulsions that would take place after the war was made possible only because the concept of stable communities, unchanged for generations, had been destroyed once and for all. The population of Europe was no longer a fixed constant. It was now unstable, volatile – transient.

4
Famine

One of the few things that united Europe during the war was the ubiquitous presence of hunger. International trade in foodstuffs had faltered almost as soon as war broke out, and ceased altogether when the various military blockades began to take hold around the continent. The first foods to disappear were imported fruits. In Britain, the public attempted to take this with good humour. Signs began to appear in greengrocers' windows, claiming 'Yes, we have no bananas' and in 1943 the feature film *Millions Like Us* began with an ironic on-screen definition of an orange, supposedly for those who could not remember what one looked like. On the continent one of the shortages that made itself most immediately felt was of coffee, which became so scarce that the population was forced to drink a variety of substitutes made from chicory, dandelion roots or acorns.

Other, more serious shortages soon followed. Sugar was one of the first things to become scarce, as well as perishable goods like milk, cream, eggs and fresh meat. In response to such shortages, rationing was introduced in Britain, across most of continental Europe, and even in the United States. Neither were the neutral countries immune to shortages: in Spain, for example, even staple foods such as potatoes and olive oil were tightly rationed, and the huge drop in imported goods forced the people of Switzerland to make do with 28 per cent fewer calories in 1944 than they had before the war.[1] Over the course of the next five years eggs were almost universally powdered in order to preserve them, butter was replaced with margarine, milk was reserved for young children, and traditional meats such as lamb, pork or beef became so scarce that people began rearing rabbits in their back gardens and allotments as a substitute. The struggle to stave off famine was every bit as important as the military struggle, and was taken just as seriously.

The first country to topple over the brink was Greece. In the winter of 1941-2, just six months after being invaded by Axis troops, more than 100,000 people starved to death. The coming of war had thrown the country into administrative anarchy and, coupled with restrictions on people's movement, this had caused a collapse of the food distribution systems. Farmers began to hoard their foodstuffs, inflation spiralled out of control and unemployment soared. There was also a near complete breakdown of law and order. Many historians have blamed the occupying German troops for sparking the famine by requisitioning food stores, but in truth these food stores were often looted by local people, partisans or individual soldiers.[2]

Regardless of what caused the famine, the results were catastrophic. In Athens and Thessaloniki the mortality rate increased threefold. In some of the islands, such as Mykonos, the death rate was as much as nine times its usual level.[3] Of the 410,000 Greek deaths that occurred during the whole of the war, probably 250,000 were due to starvation and related problems.[4] The situation became so parlous that in the autumn of 1942 the British took the unprecedented step of raising their blockade to allow ships carrying food through to the country. By agreement between the Germans and the British, relief flowed into Greece throughout the rest of the war, and continued to do so for almost all of the chaotic period that followed liberation at the end of 1944.

If the effect of war on Greek food distribution was fairly instantaneous, in western Europe the full force of the shortages took much longer to materialize. Holland, for example, did not feel the worst effects of famine until the winter of 1944-5. Unlike in Greece it was not administrative chaos that caused Holland's 'Hunger Winter', but the Nazis' long-term policy of depriving the country of what it needed to survive. Almost from the moment the Germans arrived in May 1940 they had begun to requisition everything: metals, clothing, textiles, bicycles, food and livestock. Entire factories were dismantled and shipped into Germany. Holland had always relied on importing food and fodder for its livestock, but these imports ceased in 1940, leaving the country to struggle on with what little was left after the German requisitions. Potatoes and bread were severely rationed throughout the war, and the people were forced to supplement their diet with sugar beets and even tulip bulbs.[5]

By May 1944 the situation was desperate. Reports coming from inside Holland warned of impending disaster unless the country were liberated soon. Once again, the British raised their blockade to allow aid through, but only to a very limited degree. Churchill was worried that regular food aid would simply end up in German hands, and the British Chiefs of Staff feared that the German navy would use the aid ships as guides through the mined waters of the Dutch coast. So the people of Holland were forced to wait for the liberation and starve.[6]

By the time the Allies finally entered western Holland in May 1945 between 100,000 and 150,000 Dutch people were suffering from hunger oedema ('dropsy').[7] The country was spared a catastrophe on the scale of the Greek famine only because the war ended, and huge quantities of relief were finally allowed in. But for thousands it was already too late. Journalists entering Amsterdam described the city as 'a vast concentration camp' displaying 'horrors comparable to those of Belsen and Buchenwald'.[8] Over 5,000 people had died of starvation or related illnesses in that city alone. The famine death toll for the country as a whole was between 16,000 and 20,000.[9]

The Nazis did not starve Holland out of pure malice. Compared with other nationalities, the Nazis actually felt well disposed towards the Dutch, whom they regarded as essentially 'Germanic' people who needed to be led 'back to the Germanic community'.[10] The problem was that Germany had her own food problems to worry about. Even before the war the German leadership had believed national food production to be in crisis.[11] By the beginning of 1942 grain stocks were all but exhausted, the national swine herd had been reduced by 25 per cent for lack of feed, and rations of both bread and meat had been cut.[12] Even the bumper German harvest in 1943 did not stave off crisis, and while rations were raised temporarily, they soon resumed their decline.

To give some idea of the problem Germany faced, one must consider the calorific needs of the population. The average adult requires about 2,500 calories per day to keep themselves healthy, and more if they are doing heavy work. Crucially, this amount cannot be made up of carbohydrates alone if they are to avoid hunger-related illnesses like oedema – it must also contain vitamins supplied by fresh vegetables, proteins and fat. At the beginning of the war German civilians were consuming a healthy average of 2,570 calories per day. This fell to 2,445 the following year, to 2,078 calories in 1943, and to 1,412 calories by the end of the war.[13] 'Hunger knocks on every door,' wrote one German housewife in February

1945. 'New ration cards are to last for five weeks instead of four, and no one knows if they will be issued at all. We count out potatoes every day, five small ones each, and bread is becoming more scarce. We are growing thinner and thinner, colder and colder and more and more ravenous.'[14]

In order to prevent their own people from starving, the Nazis plundered their occupied territories. As early as 1941 they reduced the official ration for 'normal consumers' in Norway and Czechoslovakia to around 1,600 calories per day, and in Belgium and France to only 1,300 calories per day.[15] The local populations in these countries only prevented themselves from being slowly starved to death by resorting to the black market. The situation in Holland was not substantially different from that in Belgium or France: the main difference was that Holland was not liberated until nine months later. The famine occurred because by that time even the black market had been exhausted, and the Wehrmacht's scorched earth policy had destroyed more than 20 per cent of the nation's farmland through flooding. By the end of the war, the official daily food ration in occupied Holland had dropped to just 400 calories – that is, half the amount received by the inmates of the Belsen concentration camp. In Rotterdam, the food ran out altogether.[16]

As with all aspects of the war, the way the Reich treated its eastern dominions during the war was incomparably harsher than its treatment of occupied territories in the west. When a young American living in Athens questioned German soldiers about the dire food situation in Greece, he received the answer, 'Oh, you have not seen anything yet; in Poland 600 people die every day from starvation.'[17] If food shortages in Holland and Greece were merely a symptom of war, in eastern Europe they were one of Germany's principal weapons. The Nazis had no intention of trying to feed Europe's Slavic population. Almost from the outset they intended to deliberately starve them to death.

The whole purpose of invading Poland and the USSR was to free up living space for German settlers, and to provide farm land to supply the rest of the Reich, and Germany in particular, with food. According to their original plan for the eastern territories, *Generalplan Ost*, more than 80 per cent of the Polish population was to be expelled from their lands, followed by 64 per cent of Ukrainians and 75 per cent of Belarusians. But by the end of 1942 some amongst the Nazi hierarchy were pressing for the 'physical annihilation' of the entire population – not only Jews, but Poles and

Ukrainians as well.[18] The main weapon of this proposed genocide, which dwarfed the Holocaust in the scale of its ambition, was to be hunger.

The starvation of eastern Europe began in Poland. Early in 1940 the ration for Poland's major cities was set at just over 600 calories, although this increased later in the war after the Nazis realized they needed Polish labour.[19] As the conflict spread eastwards, the starvation of civilians became worse. After the invasion of the USSR, Nazi planners insisted that the army should feed itself by requisitioning all local foodstuffs, and completely shutting off Ukrainian cities from supply. Any surplus food gathered in this way was to be sent home to Germany – Kiev, Kharkov and Dnepropetrovsk in the meantime should be left to starve. In the formulation of this plan, army officials openly talked of 20 to 30 million likely deaths through famine.[20] In desperation, the entire population was forced to turn to the black market for food, and often had to trek for hundreds of miles to find it.[21] People in the countryside were generally better off than those in the towns. For example, in Kharkov alone some 70–80,000 people are thought to have starved to death.[22]

In the end, the Nazi plan to starve its eastern territories stopped, or at least slowed, because it made no economic sense to allow so many able-bodied workers to die when the Reich was short of labour. And in any case, it was an impossible plan to implement. Food supplies to Ukrainian cities could not simply be cut off, city dwellers could not be prevented from fleeing to the countryside, and the black market – which kept literally tens of millions of people alive across Europe – was impossible to police. However, for those who were unable to travel to where the food was, starvation was tragically unavoidable. In the winter of 1941 the German army succeeded in starving between 1.3 and 1.65 million Soviet prisoners of war to death.[23] In the ghettos tens of thousands of Jews are thought to have starved, even before the wholesale killing began. During the 900-day siege of Leningrad, approximately 641,000 of the city's inhabitants lost their lives to hunger and hunger-related diseases. In this one city alone almost twice as many people starved as in Greece during the whole of that country's famine.[24]

One might have expected the food situation in Europe to ease once the war was over, but in many places it actually got worse. In the months immediately following the declaration of peace, the Allies struggled desperately and unsuccessfully to feed Europe's starving millions. As I have mentioned, the normal daily ration in Germany fell to just over 1,400 calories by the end of the war; by September 1945 this had fallen still further to 1,224 calories in the British zone of Germany, and by the following March it was only 1,014 calories. In the French zone the official ration fell below 1,000 calories at the end of 1945, and stayed there for the next six months.[25]

Conditions in the rest of Europe were not much better, and in many cases worse. A year after the south of Italy was liberated, and after $100 million of aid had flowed into the country, housewives were still rioting over food prices in Rome, and a 'hunger march' was held in December 1944 in protest over shortages.[26] At the end of the war, according to an UNRRA report, food riots were continuing throughout the country.[27] The official ration in Vienna hovered around 800 calories for most of 1945. In Budapest the ration for December fell to just 556 calories per day.[28] People in the former East Prussia resorted to eating dead dogs they found by the roadside.[29] In Berlin children were seen gathering grass from the parks to eat, and in Naples all the tropical fish from the aquarium were stolen for food.[30] As a consequence of profound and widespread malnutrition there were outbreaks of disease across the continent. Malaria staged a comeback in southern Europe, as did tuberculosis almost everywhere. In Romania cases of pellagra, another disease associated with deprivation, increased by 250 per cent.[31]

The problem was not only that there was a world-wide shortage of food, but also that what food there was could not be distributed properly. After six years of war, Europe's transport infrastructure was shattered. Before food could travel efficiently into Europe's cities the railway network had to be rebuilt, the roads patched up, and merchant shipping restored. Just as crucially, law and order had to be restored. In some parts of Europe food supplies were looted almost as soon as they arrived, leaving aid agencies unable to distribute vital supplies to the places where they were needed most.

Many British and American troops were appalled by what they saw when they arrived in Europe in the aftermath of the liberation. They had expected to see destruction, and perhaps a certain amount of disorganization caused by the war, but few of them were prepared for the levels of deprivation that they encountered.

Ray Hunting was an officer with a British army signals unit when he arrived in liberated Italy in the autumn of 1944. He was used to seeing beggars in the Middle East, but he was utterly unprepared for the mobs

that crowded round the train in which he was travelling. At one junction he was unable to bear the sound of their wailing any longer, and so
he reached into his bags to throw the crowd some of his spare rations.
What happened next shocked him to the core.

> It is a cruel error to throw foodstuffs indiscriminately into the midst of
> hungry people. They turned instantly into a mass of struggling bodies
> fighting for the falling gifts. Men, brutish in their determination, punched
> and kicked each other to gain possession of the tins; women tore food
> from each other's mouths to push into the hands of children who were in
> peril of being trampled underfoot in the violence.

As the train finally pulled away from the junction the crowd were still
fighting over the few scraps he had thrown them. Hunting continued to
watch them from the open window until his thoughts were interrupted by
an officer leaning out of the next compartment. 'What a waste – chucking
all that grub away,' said the officer. 'Don't you know that you could have
had the best looking woman down there for just a couple of those tins?'[32]

Starvation was one of the most difficult and urgent problems in the
immediate aftermath of the war. The Allied governments understood
this as early as 1943, and made the distribution of food their first priority. But even the most enlightened politicians and administrators tended
to regard food as a purely physical need. It was left to those in the front
line, who had direct contact with starving people, to recognize that food
also had a spiritual dimension.

Kathryn Hulme, the deputy director of one of Bavaria's many displaced persons camps, understood this. At the end of 1945 she wrote
with great sadness about the scramble for Red Cross packages at the
Wildflecken camp.

> It is hard to believe that some shiny little tins of meat paste and sardines
> could almost start a riot in the camp, that bags of Lipton's tea and tins of
> Varrington House coffee and bars of vitaminized chocolate could drive
> men almost insane with desire. But this is so. This is as much a part of the
> destruction of Europe as are those gaunt ruins of Frankfurt. Only this is
> the ruin of the human soul. It is a thousand times more painful to see.[33]

It is to this ruination of the human soul that we shall turn in the next
chapter.

5

Moral Destruction

At the beginning of October 1943, shortly after the liberation of Naples, Norman Lewis of the British 91 Field Security Section found himself driving into a square somewhere in the outskirts of the city. Dominating the square was a large, semi-destroyed public building, with several army trucks parked in front of it. One of these trucks appeared to be full of American supplies, and crowds of Allied soldiers were helping themselves to tins of rations. These soldiers were then streaming into the municipal building, clutching their tins before them.

Curious to find out what was going on, Lewis and his fellow soldiers followed them inside and made their way to the front of the crowd. He recorded in his diary what he found:

Here a row of ladies sat at intervals of about a yard with their backs to the wall. These women were dressed in their street clothes, and had the ordinary well-washed respectable shopping and gossiping faces of working-class housewives. By the side of each woman stood a small pile of tins, and it soon became clear that it was possible to make love to any one of them in this very public place by adding another tin to the pile. The women kept absolutely still, they said nothing, and their faces were as empty of expression as graven images. They might have been selling fish, except that this place lacked the excitement of a fish market. There was no solic-iting, no suggestion, no enticement, not even the discreetest and most accidental display of flesh. The boldest of the soldiers had pushed them-selves, tins in hand, to the front, but now, faced with these matter-of-fact family-providers driven here by empty larders, they seemed to flag. Once again reality had betrayed the dream, and the air fell limp. There was some sheepish laughter, jokes that fell flat, and a visible tendency to slip quietly away. One soldier, a little tipsy, and egged on constantly by his friends, finally put down his tin of rations at a woman's side, unbuttoned and lowered himself on her. A perfunctory jogging of the haunches began and came quickly to an end. A moment later he was on his feet and buttoning up again. It had been something to get over as soon as possible. He might have been submitting to field punishment rather than the act of love.

Unsurprisingly, Lewis was not tempted to indulge himself, and five minutes later he was on his way again. 'The tins collected by my fellow travellers were thrown to passers-by who scrambled wildly after them. None of the soldiers travelling on my truck had felt inclined to join actively in the fun.'[1]

What makes this story interesting is not so much the obviously desperate plight of the Italian housewives, but rather Lewis's description of the soldiers' reaction to it. On the one hand they cannot believe their luck: they can do anything they want to these women, and with a truck full of supplies outside, their power over them is seemingly unlimited. On the other hand, the reality of the situation leaves the majority of them profoundly uneasy. There is an understanding that to take part in this transaction is degrading not only to the women but also to themselves, and even to the very act of sex itself. It is also significant that at no point is there even a hint of empathy for these housewives. They are merely objects, as inanimate as 'graven images'.

According to Norman Lewis, such behaviour became increasingly common in the aftermath of southern Italy's liberation. He records being visited by an Italian prince who wanted to know if his sister might be allowed to work in an army brothel. When Lewis explained that the British army did not have any official brothels the prince and his sister left disappointed. On another occasion, when investigating the serious sexual assault of a young Italian girl, her father tried to press the traumatized girl's favours upon him. All he expected in return was a good square meal for his daughter.[2]

Desperation like this was by no means confined to Naples, nor to Italy. A whole generation of young women in Germany learned to think it quite normal to sleep with an Allied soldier in return for a bar of chocolate. In the Dutch town of Heerlen, US rifleman Roscoe Blunt was approached by a young girl who 'matter-of-factly asked me if I wanted to "ficken" or just "kuszen". It took me a few moments for my brain to click into gear and realize what she was asking.' When he asked her age she told him she was twelve.[3] In Hungary there were scores of girls as young as thirteen admitted to hospital for venereal disease. In Greece VD was recorded in girls as young as ten.[4]

Such degradation affected the *Daily Express*'s war correspondent Alan Moorehead far more than the physical devastation he had seen. When he arrived in Naples in the immediate wake of its liberation he wrote despairingly about how he had seen men, women and children beating each other as they scrambled for handfuls of sweets thrown to them by the arriving soldiers; he had seen pimps and black marketeers offering fake brandy and child prostitutes as young as ten; and boys of six selling obscene postcards, their sisters' favours, even themselves.

> In the whole list of sordid human vices none I think were overlooked in Naples during those first few months. What we were witnessing in fact was the moral collapse of a people. They had no pride any more, or any dignity. The animal struggle for existence governed everything. Food. That was the only thing that mattered. Food for the children. Food for yourself. Food at the cost of any abasement and depravity. And after food a little warmth and shelter.[5]

What Moorehead recognized was that food was no longer just a physical issue but a moral one. Across Europe millions of starving people were willing to sacrifice all moral values for the sake of their next meal. Indeed, years of scarcity had changed the very nature of food. What in Britain was regarded as an everyday right had become in the rest of Europe an expression of power, so that a British soldier was able to say of the German woman who slept with him, shopped for him and mended his clothes, 'She was just like my slave.'[6]

When considering stories like these, two things become immediately apparent. Firstly it appears that the moral landscape of Europe had become every bit as unrecognizable as the physical landscape. Those who had grown used to living amidst ruins no longer saw anything unusual about the rubble that surrounded them – likewise for many of Europe's women after the war there was no longer anything unusual about having to sell one's body for food. It was left to those coming from outside continental Europe to express surprise at the wreckage they were witnessing.

Secondly it is obvious that, for the majority at least, sexual morality took a back seat when it came to matters of survival. Even a *perceived* threat to one's survival seemed to be enough for some to justify the abandonment of virtue – but in an atmosphere where threats were both real and abundant, such notions seem to have become almost an irrelevance.

Looting and Theft

The search for food was also a factor in another phenomenon of the war and its aftermath, the huge surge in the crimes of theft and looting. Many Greeks looted their local shops and stores in 1941 because they were hungry, and because they assumed that if they did not steal the food themselves it would only be requisitioned by the occupying troops.[7] Partisans in Belarus requisitioned food from local peasants in order to survive – and peasants who were reluctant to supply them were robbed.[8] In the final days of the war Berlin housewives ransacked stores despite ubiquitous warnings that looting was punishable by death.[9] Since they appeared to be facing starvation anyway they did not have much to lose.

However, it was not only necessity that drove the high rates of theft and looting during and after the war. One of the most important factors in the phenomenon was that the war provided greater opportunities to steal, and also greater temptations. It is far easier to enter a property whose doors and windows have been blown in by bombs than it is to break those doors or windows oneself. And when a property has been abandoned by its owners in a war zone it is easy to convince oneself that the owners are never coming back. The looting of vacant property therefore began long before the war had created any scarcity. In the villages around Warsaw people looted the homes of their neighbours almost as soon as the war began. Andrzej C.'s family, for instance, fled the fighting in September 1939; when they returned a few weeks later they found that even structural parts of their house itself had been dismantled – his parents had to pay their neighbours a series of visits to reclaim their rafters and other bits of their property.[10]

As war spread across the continent, theft and looting spread with it, and not only in those countries that were directly affected by the war. In neutral Sweden, for example, 1939 saw a sudden surge in convictions, which remained high for the rest of the war. In Stockholm cases of theft almost quadrupled between 1939 and 1945.[11] This is worse even than, say, France, where cases of theft tripled during the war.[12] Similarly, in parts of Switzerland, such as the canton of Basle, rates of juvenile delinquency doubled.[13] Why the neutral countries should have suffered a rise in crime during the war has long puzzled social scientists. The only credible explanation seems to lie in the deep sense of anxiety created throughout Europe at the onset of war: social instability appears to have spread across the entire continent like an infection.

In much of occupied Europe theft became so normal that it ceased to be regarded as a crime at all. Indeed, since many of the local gendarmes, policemen and civil authorities had been replaced by Nazi stooges, theft and other crimes were often elevated to acts of resistance. Partisans stole goods from peasants in order to continue the fight on behalf of those same peasants. Farmers sold food on the black market in order to deny that food to the occupiers. Local stores were looted to prevent German soldiers from doing so first. It was possible to justify all kinds of theft and profiteering, especially in retrospect, because there was often a ring of truth to such claims. In effect, the moral world had been turned on its head: acts that had once been immoral had now been elevated to a moral duty.

When the advancing Allies finally began to liberate Europe, the opportunities to steal and loot increased. Many of the local gendarmes and mayors fled. Those who remained were often removed from office almost as soon as the Allies arrived, and replaced with a skeleton staff of inexperienced military officials who had little understanding of local issues. In the resulting chaos all semblance of law and order vanished: the crime wave that swept Europe dwarfed that which had occurred during the war, and has never been equalled since. The old German provinces of Pomerania and Silesia were so lawless that they were known to the incoming Polish administration as the 'Wild West'. Zbigniew Ogrodzinski, one of the first Polish officials to be appointed in Stettin (or Szczecin, as it would come to be known), routinely carried a pistol to protect himself from muggers and bandits, and regularly had to draw it. According to a British medical officer stationed in the same city, 'Murder, rape, robbery with violence were so usual that nobody paid any attention.'[14]

Naples, which after the liberation briefly became the biggest supply port in the world, also became one of the world's centres of organized theft. 'Army cigarettes and chocolates were stolen by the hundredweight and resold at fantastic prices,' wrote Alan Moorehead in 1945. 'Vehicles were stolen at the rate of something like sixty or seventy a night (not always by the Italians). The looting of especially precious things like tyres became an established business.'[15] Makeshift stalls throughout the city openly sold stolen military articles supplied by corrupt officials, mafia gangs, bandits and groups of army deserters who vied with one another to pillage Allied supply trains.[16] Gangs of children would jump onto the backs of army lorries to pilfer anything they could snatch – Allied soldiers resorted to chopping at their hands with bayonets to deter them, resulting in a spate of children seeking medical help for severed fingers.[17]

Postwar Berlin, according to one historian, became the 'crime capital of the world'. In the aftermath of the war 2,000 people were arrested in the city each month, an increase of 800 per cent on prewar figures. By the beginning of 1946 there was an average of 240 robberies each day, and dozens of organized gangs terrorized the city day and night.[18] One Berlin woman recorded in her diary that 'all notions of ownership have been completely demolished. Everyone steals from everyone else, because everyone has been stolen from.'[19] Ruth Andreas-Friedrich, another woman in Berlin, called life there 'a swapping game', where objects passed from one person to another with no one knowing who the owners were.[20] Similar sentiments were felt across Europe, as a Hungarian woman made clear: 'Sometimes the Russians stole from us, sometimes we helped ourselves to this and that of theirs. Or the other way around . . .'[21] The whole concept of private property had become meaningless.

Necessity undoubtedly played a large part in this crime wave, but there were other equally important factors. To start with, once the taboo on stealing had been broken it became much easier to steal again, and again. After six years of war such behaviour had become a way of life for some people: those who had managed to survive by pilfering or illegally trading were not about to stop just because the war was over, particularly when the hardship was still worsening.

However, there is much to suggest that the widespread theft after the war answered a deeper need in many of those who committed it. Many appear to have experienced the desire to steal as a compulsion, even when the items they were taking were of no conceivable use to them. Former displaced persons (DPs) tell frequent stories of stealing restaurant table cloths, or 'something absolutely stupid like a big flower pot'.[22] Maria Bielicka, a Polish woman who had survived four years of prisons and work camps, claims that she experienced the compulsion to take something almost as a physical urge. After the war the Americans housed her and her sister for a while in a German villa, not far from the porcelain factory where she had been forced to work.

> I was sitting with my sister, and Wanda said, 'You know what, I like this picture on the wall. I think I'll take it. For all I've suffered, I think one picture will do.' And I said, 'There is some porcelain there. I like it very much. We slaved so many years to make that porcelain in that factory. I'll take it.'[23]

The next morning, ashamed of themselves, both girls put their loot back.

The Black Market

The most common misdemeanour after the war was buying or selling goods on the black market. Once again, illegal trading during the war had been elevated in the minds of the people to an act of resistance: any goods, and particularly foods, that were sold on the black market were effectively denied to the German occupiers. In France, for example, 350,000 fewer animals were delivered for slaughter each year than were officially recorded: these animals ended up on the tables of French people rather than those of the occupier.[24] Dairy farmers were often forced onto the black market in order to survive: in a continent where the transport systems were so badly damaged they could not rely on daily milk collections, and so were obliged to develop unofficial local networks to make sure they sold their produce. Across western Europe the unofficial networks became almost as comprehensive as the official market. In eastern Europe, where the Nazis were intent on requisitioning as much food as possible, the same was true. Here more than anywhere the black market was essential for survival, and became almost a moral duty for farmers and traders: without it, hundreds of thousands more Poles, Ukrainians and Balts would have starved.

The problem with illegal trading was that it was an inherently unfair system. While rationing was designed to provide a balanced diet for all, and a richer diet for those who did harder physical work, the black market catered only for those who could afford it. Just before the liberation of France, the black market price of butter was five and a half

times the official price, and eggs were four times as expensive on the
black market.[25] As a consequence, eggs and butter rarely made their
way onto the official markets, and everyone but the wealthy was priced
out of buying them. Some farmers and traders were ruthless in exploiting this market and made themselves extremely rich, much to the disgust
of their countrymen. In Greece, food speculators hoarded supplies and
only sold them in quantity when rumours of an improvement in the
situation sent food prices plummeting. 'While the entire world anguished
over the fate of the Greek people,' one foreign observer wrote bitterly,
'the Greeks got rich on the blood of their brothers.'[26] In Czechoslovakia
the postwar government was so scandalized by such behaviour that the
crime of enriching oneself at the expense of the state or its citizens during the war carried a sentence of five to ten years' imprisonment.[27]

While illegal trading might have been inevitable, and even sometimes
justifiable in wartime, it proved a hard habit to break once hostilities
came to an end. Indeed, after the collapse of all the administrative and
transport systems, as well as the collapse of law and order, the problem
actually became much worse. By the autumn of 1946 black marketeering
was so common that for most people it was not even regarded as a crime.
'It is hardly an exaggeration to say that every man, woman and child in
Western Europe is engaged to a greater or lesser degree in illegal trading
of one kind or another,' claimed the chief of UNRRA for western Germany in a letter to the British Foreign Office. 'In large areas of Europe, in
fact, it is hardly possible to support existence without so doing.'[28]

It was impossible to maintain a respect for the law when the entire
population was flouting it on a daily basis. This inevitably had moral
consequences. Even in Britain there was a perception that moral standards had declined because of such activities. In the words of Margaret
Gore, an Air Transport Auxiliary in 1945, 'in Britain the black market
had undermined people's honesty, and I think as a society we were much
less honest afterwards . . . That was when it started.'[29]

Violence

If theft and illegal trading were a serious problem throughout Europe,
the ubiquitous threat of violence was a crisis. As I have already mentioned, extreme violence was for many an everyday occurrence. By the

end of the war, the people of Germany had become accustomed to being bombed day and night: the sight of dead bodies in the rubble was quite normal. To a lesser extent the same could be said of Britain, northern France, Holland, Belgium, Bohemia and Moravia, Austria, Romania, Hungary, Yugoslavia and Italy. Further east, the population had seen their cities pulverized by artillery, and human beings pulverized along with them. For millions of soldiers, too, this was an everyday experience.

Away from the battle zone the violence was equally brutal, and unending, if on a more personal scale. In thousands of forced labour camps and concentration camps across Europe inmates were savagely beaten on a daily basis. Throughout eastern Europe Jews were hunted out and killed. In northern Italy the shooting of collaborators would be followed by an endless cycle of reprisals and counter-reprisals that sometimes took on the atmosphere of vendettas.[30] Across the Reich gossipers were arrested and beaten, deserters were hanged, and anyone whose opinions or whose ethnic background did not match those of the majority of their neighbours could expect to be beaten, imprisoned or even killed. By the end of the war, all of this was a matter of routine. As a consequence, far from being shocking, acts of extreme violence became quite unremarkable across much of the continent.

It does not take much imagination to realize that those who have been the victims of routine violence become much more likely to commit acts of violence themselves, and there are countless psychological studies which demonstrate this. In 1946 Lieutenant General Sir Frederick Morgan, the former director of UNRRA for western Germany, expressed his fears regarding some of the leaders amongst the Jews who had been freed from concentration camps: '[T]hese Jewish leaders are desperate men who will stick at nothing. Practically everything that can happen to a surviving human being has already happened to them and they place no value on human life whatsoever.'[31] The same was true of Germany's slave labourers. According to an UNRRA study into the psychological problems of displaced persons it was quite normal for DPs to exhibit 'lawless aggressiveness', along with a host of other psychological problems, including a 'sense of unworthiness . . . bitterness and touchiness'. A high proportion of DPs showed signs of extreme cynicism: 'nothing that is done even by helpful people is regarded as genuine or sincere'.[32]

If the victims of violence were everywhere, to a certain extent so were the perpetrators. By the end of the war, partisans involved in an increasingly vicious war against the Germans were now in control of most of Greece, the whole of Yugoslavia, Slovakia, much of northern Italy, substantial areas of the Baltic States and vast swathes of Poland and Ukraine. In France the Resistance had liberated at least fifteen *départements* on their own, and were in control of most of the south and west of the country even before the Allies had reached Paris.[33] In many of these places – particularly in Yugoslavia, Italy and Greece – much of the violence of the war had been directed not against Germans but against fascists and collaborators within their own population. The people who had presided over this violence were now in charge.

As for those who had committed atrocities on behalf of the Nazis and their allies, many of them became prisoners of war, but many more either passed themselves off as DPs or simply melted back into civilian life. These people numbered in their tens of thousands, and were in many ways just as psychologically damaged as their victims. It is important to remember that most of the soldiers who committed atrocities had not been psychopaths, but had started the war as ordinary members of society. According to a psychological study of such individuals, in the beginning most had experienced extreme revulsion at the acts they were required to carry out, and many had found themselves unable to continue with their duties for very long. With experience, however, this revulsion at the taking of human life subsided and was replaced with a perverse delight, even euphoria, at their own breaking of moral codes.[34]

For some of these people killing became an addiction, and they carried out their atrocities in ever more perverse ways. In Croatia the Ustashe not only killed Serbs but also took the time to hack off the breasts of the women and castrate the men.[35] In Drama, in northeastern Greece, Bulgarian soldiers played football with the heads of their Greek victims.[36] At Chełmno concentration camp German guards would kill babies who survived the gas vans by splitting their heads against trees.[37] In Königsberg Soviet soldiers tied the legs of German women to two different cars and then drove off in opposite directions, literally tearing the women in half.[38] Ukrainian partisans tortured Volhynian Poles to death by hacking them with farm implements.[39] In response Polish partisans also tortured Ukrainians. 'While I never saw one of our men pick up a baby or a small child with the point of a bayonet and toss it onto a fire, I saw the charred corpses of Polish babies who had died that way,' said one such partisan. 'If none of our number did that, then it was the only atrocity that we did not commit.'[40] Such people were now a part of Europe's everyday communities.

As a side note it is worth mentioning that Himmler himself recognized that committing atrocities could cause adverse psychological effects in his men. He therefore issued instructions to his SS commanders to ensure that the stress of continued killing did not lead their men to become 'brutalized'.[41] It is a measure of how completely the moral order had been inverted that Himmler was able to regard his SS men as the 'victims' of their own atrocities, without ever sparing a thought for the people they were killing.

Rape

There is one subject that ties together many of the themes I have discussed so far, and also anticipates many of those I will go on to explore. The committing of rape in wartime epitomizes the abuse of military power and the gratuitous use of violence against defenceless civilians. In the Second World War it was a phenomenon that grew beyond any previously known proportions: more rapes occurred in this war, particularly in its final stages, than during any other war in history. The prime motivating factor, especially in the immediate wake of battle, was revenge – but the problem was allowed to get out of hand because of institutional failings on the part of each of the belligerent armies. The consequences for the moral and physical health of the people, particularly in central and eastern Europe where rape was most widespread, were dire.

Rape has always been associated with warfare: in general, the more brutal the war, the more likely it is to involve the rape of enemy women.[42] In the closing stages of the Second World War the worst instances of rape certainly happened in the areas where the fighting was the most intense, and there is anecdotal evidence to suggest that even the women themselves noticed that they were in more danger during and just after periods of heavy fighting.[43] Some witnesses at the time even suggested that rape was inevitable, given the ferocity of the battles these soldiers found themselves in: 'What can you do?' claimed one Russian officer. 'It's war; people become brutalized.'[44]

The worst instances occurred in eastern Europe, in those areas of Silesia and East Prussia where Soviet soldiers first set foot on German soil. But rape was not confined to the areas around where the fighting took place. Far from it – in fact rape increased everywhere during the war, even in areas where there was no fighting. In Britain and Northern Ireland, for example, sexual crimes, including rape, increased by almost 50 per cent between 1939 and 1945 – a fact which caused huge concern at the time.[45]

There are no easy explanations for the huge increases in rape that occurred in Europe during the final stages of the war and its aftermath, but there are some definite trends that are common to the whole continent. As always, the problem was far, far worse on the eastern front than it was in the west. While civilian men were occasionally responsible for committing the crime, it was overwhelmingly a military problem: as the Allied armies converged on Germany from every direction, a wave of sexual violence, along with other crimes, accompanied them. Rape tended to be worst where chaotic conditions existed, for example in the aftermath of heavy fighting, or amongst troops with poor discipline. And, importantly, it was incomparably worse in countries that were conquered rather than liberated. This suggests that revenge and a desire to dominate were important factors – indeed, probably the main factors – behind the mass rapes that occurred in 1945.

Studies suggest that wartime rape is particularly brutal, and particularly widespread, where there is a greater cultural divide between the occupying troops and the civilian population, and this theory is certainly borne out by the events of the Second World War.[46] French colonial troops in Bavaria were particularly notorious. According to Christabel Bielenberg, an English woman who lived in a village near the Black Forest, Moroccan troops 'raped up and down our valley' as soon as they arrived. Later they were replaced with other troops from the Sahara who 'came at night and surrounded every house in the village and raped every female between 12 and 80'.[47] In Tübingen girls as young as twelve and women as old as seventy were raped by Moroccan troops.[48] The terror of the women concerned was increased by the foreign appearance of these men, especially after years of racial propaganda by the Nazis.[49]

This cultural divide was also a factor on the eastern front. The contempt that many German soldiers felt for eastern *Untermenschen* when they invaded the Soviet Union certainly contributed to the vicious treatment Ukrainian and Russian women received at their hands. Vasily Grossman interviewed one teacher who had been raped by a German officer who threatened to shoot her six-month-old baby.[50] Another Russian schoolteacher called Genia Demianova described her gang rape by more than a dozen German soldiers after one of them had lashed her with a horse whip: '[T]hey have torn me to pieces,' she wrote, '. . . I am just a corpse.'[51]

When the tide turned and the Red Army advanced on central and south-eastern Europe, they too were influenced by racial and cultural motives. Bulgaria, for example, suffered hardly any rape compared with its neighbours, partly because the army that entered Bulgaria was far more disciplined than some of the others, but also because Bulgaria shared a similar culture and language with Russia, and the two countries had enjoyed a century of friendly relations.[52] When the Red Army arrived here they were genuinely welcomed by the majority of Bulgarians. Romania, by contrast, had a very different language and culture from the Soviets, and had until 1944 been engaged in a very savage war against them. As a consequence, Romanian women suffered more than Bulgarian women.

In Hungary and Austria the plight of women was worse still, and in some areas truly horrific. Again, the cultural differences between the two sides were considerable, but in this case Soviet antagonism was fuelled by the fact that the Hungarians and Austrians, unlike the Romanians, were still at war with the USSR when the Red Army arrived. Many women in the area around Csákvár, just west of Budapest, were raped so violently that their backs broke under the force of the men's attacks. Alaine Polcz, a twenty-year-old Hungarian from Transylvania, received painful but thankfully impermanent spinal injuries in this way. She was raped repeatedly over a period of several weeks, and frequently lost count of the number of men who attacked her during the course of a night. 'This had nothing to do with embraces or sex,' she wrote later. 'It had nothing to do with anything. It was simply – I just now realize, as I am writing, that the word is accurate: aggression. That is what it was.' She was also consumed with the knowledge 'that this was going on throughout the entire country'.[53]

But it was in Germany that the most widespread cases of rape occurred. In East Prussia, Silesia and Pomerania tens of thousands of women were raped and then killed in an orgy of truly medieval violence. Marie Naumann, a young mother from Baerwalde in Pomerania, was raped and then hanged by a mob of soldiers in a hayloft along with her husband, while her children were strangled to death with ropes on the floor beneath her. She was cut down, still alive, by some Polish civilians, who asked her who had done this to her but when she told them it was the Russians they called her a liar and beat her. Unable to bear what had happened she tried to drown herself in a nearby creek, but was unable to complete the job. Soaking wet, she went to an acquaintance's apartment where she came across another Russian officer who raped her again. Shortly after he left her, four more Soviet soldiers appeared and raped her 'in an unnatural way'. When they had finished with her they kicked her into unconsciousness. She came to when another pair of soldiers entered the room, 'but they left me alone as I was more dead than alive'.[54]

Thousands of similar stories have been gathered by German oral history projects, church archives and also the German government. Soviet sources also back up these claims. Memoirs by Russian officers such as Lev Kopelev and Alexander Solzhenitsyn describe scenes of widespread rape, as do several reports of Soviet excesses made by their secret police force, the NKVD, in 1945.[55]

The raping continued as the Red Army advanced through Silesia and Pomerania towards Berlin. In a huge number of cases the women were gang raped, often again and again on successive nights. Vasily Grossman interviewed a woman in Schwerin who told him she had 'already been raped by ten men today'.[56] In Berlin, Hannelore Thiele was raped by 'Seven in a row. Like animals.'[57] Another woman in Berlin was caught hiding behind a pile of coal in the cellar of her building: 'Twenty-three soldiers one after the other,' she said afterwards. 'I had to be stitched up in hospital. I never want to have anything to do with any man again.'[58] Karl August Knorr, a German officer in East Prussia, claims to have saved a few dozen women from a villa where 'on average they had been raped 60 to 70 times a day'.[59] And the list goes on.

Accounts of rape in 1945 become truly sickening, as with accounts of other atrocities during the war, because they are so numerous. The stories documented in the Eastern Archives in Koblenz read with the same monotony as the descriptions of Jewish massacres during the Nuremberg trials – it is the endless repetition of horror that becomes most difficult to bear. In parts of central Europe rape was not a collection of isolated incidents, but a mass experience endured by the entire female population. In Vienna 87,000 women were reported by clinics and doctors to have been raped.[60] In Berlin it was even worse, and about 110,000 women are thought to have been victims.[61] In the east of the country, particularly in those areas near to Soviet barracks, the constant threat of attack continued until the end of 1948.[62] In Germany as a whole almost 2 million German women are thought to have been raped in the aftermath of the war.[63]

Figures for Hungary are harder to find. While the rape of German and Austrian women was meticulously documented after the war, in Hungary the phenomenon was never admitted by the postwar Communist administration. It was not until after 1989 that proper studies could be made, by which time much of the information was difficult to come by. Rough estimates based on hospital records suggest that between 50,000 and 200,000 Hungarian women were raped by Soviet soldiers.[64] The figures in western Europe, though much lower, are still significant. The United States Army, for example, stands accused of raping as many as 17,000 civilian women in North Africa and western Europe between 1942 and 1945.[65]

The consequences of sexual violence and exploitation after the war were huge. Despite the 2 million illegal abortions that were carried out each year in Germany, between 150,000 and 200,000 'foreign babies' were born to German women, some of whom were the result of rape. Many of these children were obliged to suffer the resentment of their mothers for the rest of their lives.[66] A high percentage of women became infected with venereal disease – in some areas as many as 60 per cent. This was generally incurable, since the price of a single injection of antibiotics in Germany in August 1945 was two pounds of real coffee.[67] Along with such physical problems came the emotional and psychological consequences – not only for those who had suffered directly, but for women as a whole. When so many had been reduced to items of war booty, the message that all women received was that they were never safe, and that a male-dominated world valued them for only one thing. Women in huge areas of Europe were therefore forced to live in a permanent state of anxiety.[68]

We must not forget that men were also affected by this mass phenomenon. Many men were forced to watch while their wives, mothers, sisters and daughters were raped. Those who tried to intervene were often shot, but in general Germany's menfolk simply sat by, and tormented themselves ever afterwards for their impotence. Thus, in Hungary, Austria and Germany especially, the experience of mass rape was not only a violent and degrading experience for the women but an emasculating one for the men. Even those men who were away from home during the liberation were affected when they returned home to find their wives and sweethearts irreversibly transformed by their ordeal. Many were unable to cope with the change and left their wives, thus compounding the distress of their womenfolk. The fear of their husband's response led many women to keep their experiences secret, and a huge number concealed the fact that they had contracted venereal disease, had had abortions, or had even given birth to 'Russian babies'.[69] As a consequence of the various stresses on marital relationships, divorce rates doubled in postwar Germany compared with before the war – as indeed they did across Europe.[70]

Finally, it is important to remember the effect that routine rape and exploitation of women had on the soldiers who indulged in this behaviour, especially since the majority of them received absolutely no punishment whatsoever for their actions. The fact that the incidence of rape was high for several years after the war suggests that it was not motivated solely by revenge as many people contend – instead we are confronted with the far more worrying suggestion that many soldiers committed rape merely because they could.[71]

Statements by soldiers at the time betray a belief that they had a right to sex, and would get it by force if necessary: 'We liberated you, and you refuse us a mere trifle?' 'I need a woman! I spilled my blood for this!' '[T]he G. I. and the Tommy have cigarettes and chocolate to give the Frauleins, so they need not rape. The Russian has neither.'[72] In an environment where soldiers had unlimited power over women, where there was little threat of punishment, and where all one's fellow soldiers were indulging in sexual violence, rape became the norm. Thus, for example, when one of Vasily Grossman's fellow war correspondents raped a Russian girl who had come to their rooms to escape the mobs of drunken soldiers outside it was not because he was a monster, but merely because he was unable to 'resist the temptation'.[73]

The men the Americans now call 'the Greatest Generation' were not all the selfless heroes they are often portrayed to be: a proportion of them were also thieves, plunderers and abusers of the worst kind. Hundreds of thousands of Allied soldiers, particularly those from the Red Army, were also serial rapists. As Lev Kopelev argued at the time,

> [N]ever mind the disgrace – what about those soldiers who queue up by the scores for a German woman, who rape little girls, kill old women? They'll be going back to our own cities, our own women, our own girls. Thousands and thousands of potential criminals, and twice as dangerous, since they'll be coming back with the reputation of heroes.[74]

After their military service, these men melted back into the community of Europe, but also returned to Canada, America, Australasia and other countries all over the world. The effect, if any, that these men had on attitudes towards women within their own countries after the war would make a truly interesting study.

Morality and Children

Given the atmosphere that existed in the aftermath of the war, it is unsurprising that there were widespread concerns over how Europe's children were growing up. Not only were they in constant physical danger – we have already heard stories of children playing on ammunition dumps, crossing minefields to get to the raspberries that grew on the other side, or even firing Panzerfausts they had found abandoned by the road – but the moral dangers were just as considerable. The psychological damage they had suffered was evident in the games that they played. Mothers despaired as they watched their children play games of 'air raids', or 'Frau komm' (the phrase used by Russian soldiers when they picked German women they wished to rape).[75] In Berlin, Lieutenant Colonel William Byford-Jones was shocked to see a simple drawing of a man being hanged repeated fifteen times around three sides of a building. According to a worker in a Salvation Army orphanage, the German children he worked with always dressed their dolls in uniforms, while most of the displaced orphans screamed if they saw a man in uniform approach them.[76]

As I have already noted, it was fairly rare for children ever to see a

man out of uniform – indeed, in some parts of the continent it was rare
for them to see any men at all. This lack of male role models, coupled
with the reduction in adult authority figures, had a stark impact on
children's behaviour. In Britain the amount of juvenile delinquency went
up by almost 40 per cent during the war, especially crimes of breaking
and entering, malicious damage and theft (which more than doubled).[77]
In Germany too, according to figures circulated by Martin Bormann,
youth crime had more than doubled between 1937 and 1942, and was
still rising in 1943. In some cities, such as Hamburg, juvenile delinquency tripled during the war.[78] By the middle of 1945 groups of 'child
gangsters' were reported in the Soviet zone mugging and sometimes
killing people for food and money: the lack of parental supervision, and
in some cases the lack of parents altogether, had made them into 'little
savages'.[79]

It was the German children who caused the most concern. Some people believed that they were innately threatening, simply by virtue of
their German blood. In Norway there were massive demands to deport
any children who had been fathered by German soldiers, on the grounds
that they might grow up to become a Nazi fifth column in years to
come. The same eugenic principle that made the Nazis believe they were
the master race was now applied to German children to identify them
as a future threat.[80]

Within Germany itself, the Allies were more worried about teenagers
than infants. The German teenagers of 1945 had been indoctrinated
with Nazi ideology throughout their whole lives, both through twelve
years of schooling, and through compulsory Nazi youth groups like the
League of German Girls and the Hitler Youth. Many feared that this
generation of children might be irredeemable. British soldiers who
fought in 1944 and 1945 often noted that 'the younger the German, the
more arrogant and "masterful" he was'. In an extraordinary article in
the *Daily Express*, Major R. Crisp stated that the ordinary German
soldiers he used to come across had been replaced by an army of fanatical fifteen- and sixteen-year-olds who appeared incapable of anything
but brutality.

There is nothing that is decent, or gentle, or humble to be read in them.
Everything that is beastly and lustful and cruel. This is a generation of men
trained deliberately in barbarity, trained to execute the awful orders of a

madman. Not a clean thought has ever touched them . . . Every German born since 1920 is under this satanic spell. The younger they are the more fiercely impregnated are they with its evil poison. Every child born under the Hitler regime is a lost child. It is a lost generation.

The newspaper article went on to suggest that it was a blessing that so many of these children were being killed in the fighting, and that the remainder should be dealt with similarly for the good of the world. 'But whether you exterminate them or sterilise them, Nazism in all its horribleness will not perish from the earth until the last Nazi is dead.'[81]

The horrors of Nazi rule had at last found a mirror in the thoughts and writings of the Allies. Here, in a mainstream British newspaper, was a proposal of extermination as a *moral* solution to the evil Hitler had unleashed on Europe. There is nothing to separate these ideas from some of Goebbels' most rabid German articles in the *Völkischer Beobachter*. The difference – and it is a huge one – is that in Britain men with such ideas did not hold the reins of power, and such proposals were therefore never carried out. But the very fact that these thoughts could be seriously expressed in the national media demonstrates the damaged morality that existed even in those countries that had not been occupied during the war.

6

Hope

Despite all the destruction to people's lives and physical surroundings, the end of the war also brought with it a great deal of optimism. When the people of Europe looked around themselves in May 1945 they discovered that there was actually much to feel proud of. Not all of the changes that had been thrust upon them were entirely negative ones. The removal of dictatorships had left the continent freer, safer and fairer than it had been before the war, and democratic governments had at last been able to re-establish themselves – even, for a time, in much of eastern Europe. There was a universal sense that whatever the future might bring, it would at the very least be brighter than the period they had just lived through.

The postwar years saw an explosion of activity and idealism at every level of society. Art, music and literature began to flourish once more, and hundreds of new journals and newspapers were established across the continent. New philosophies were born, which envisaged a world of optimism and action, where the human condition was one of being 'totally committed and totally free'.[1] Dozens of new political movements and parties were created, some of which would come to dominate political thought for the next half-century.[2]

These things would have been impossible had the population of Europe been exclusively demoralized, exhausted and corrupt. Hope was at least as important as any of these darker elements of the postwar atmosphere. It was hope that revitalized the continent and allowed it to drag itself back to its feet. And it was hope that softened the inevitable cynicism with which the people viewed the new governments and institutions that were springing up in place of the old. Much of this hope was a natural, spontaneous reaction to the renewal of rights and

freedoms that accompanied Hitler's downfall. But some of it was man-
ufactured by the deep-rooted needs, desires and even the prejudices of
European society.

The Cult of Heroism

After the war was over, Europe seems to have experienced an insatia-
ble demand for stories about the conflict. This was partly because
people needed to make sense of what they had just experienced – but
the types of stories that tended to emerge show that these were not
the only needs being met. The most popular stories were those of
extreme heroism, which appeared by the thousand all over the continent. In almost every case the heroes were local men and women
whose feats of bravery or sacrifice came to represent, in the popular
imagination at least, the *true* spirit of their countrymen. The evils of
the war, meanwhile, were projected onto the villains of the stories,
who were almost always foreign, and usually German. This contrast
between foreign evil and homegrown nobility was hugely important
in the rebuilding of national identities after the war, and one of the
principal ways in which Europe's battered nations chose to lick their
wounds.

Nowhere was this more apparent than in Britain, which was much in
need of positive distractions after the war. Britain in 1945 was a country
prostrate. Not only were the British obliged to nurse their own damaged infrastructure and virtually bankrupt economy, but they were also
expected to shoulder the burden of policing the rest of Europe, as well
as their collapsing empire in Africa and the Far East. The only thing the
British had to compensate them for the decade of hardship and rationing that lay ahead was the thought that they had remained undefeated
by the war, and that they had acted nobly in the face of evil – that they
were, in short, a nation of heroes.

As an antidote to the tales of horror from abroad, and the tales of
misery at home, the British turned out stories of heroism by the score.
The end of the 1940s and the beginning of the 1950s saw a veritable
avalanche of British war stories – *The Great Escape*, *The Cruel Sea*,
The Dam Busters, *Ill Met by Moonlight*, *The Colditz Story*, *Reach for
the Sky*, to name but a handful of the most famous accounts. None of

the protagonists in these stories ever express any doubts about the justness of their cause, their abilities, or the belief that they would succeed despite the seemingly insuperable obstacles before them. This was not merely the recycling of wartime propaganda – this was how the British *needed* to see themselves in the years after the war. The myth that the British never despaired, doubted or even grumbled – a myth that is contradicted by even a short visit to the wartime 'Mass Observation' archives – was a comforting stereotype that endures to this day.

This need to tell positive stories about one's countrymen was universal in the aftermath of the war in Europe. For those countries that had been occupied by the Nazis, such stories were if anything more important: not only did they serve to distract people from the harshness of postwar life, as they did in Britain, they also drew attention away from the unpleasant fact of collaboration.

In Norway, for example, the purge of collaborators from society was accompanied – and eventually overshadowed – by the very public celebration of the nation's war heroes. Dozens of public speeches were made praising the bravery of the Resistance, and medal ceremonies were held to reward those whose stories were most inspiring. In the mid-to-late forties a series of war memoirs were published, detailing the exploits of Norwegian soldiers, agents and saboteurs. Jens Müller's *Tre kom tilbake* told the story of the 'Great Escape' from Stalag Luft III prisoner-of-war camp: Müller was one of only three who made it all the way home. Oluf Olsen's memoirs told the story of how he blew up the Lysaker Bridge after the Nazi invasion, escaped to Britain, and then parachuted back into Norway in 1943 as an agent for the British Special Operations Executive. Knut Haukelid told how he and his fellow agents destroyed the Nazis' heavy water plant in Rjukan – an act that would be immortalized in the British film *The Heroes of Telemark*. Max Manus's extraordinary career involved a series of breathtaking escapes, intrigues and acts of sabotage. His memoirs were published in Norway in 1946, but the story was made into a feature film as late as 2008. At the time of writing this is the biggest-budget movie in Norway's history. It is a testament to the enduring appeal of the country's war heroes.[3]

When repeated often enough, it was easy to imagine that wartime resistance had been the everyday experience of the majority of the country. There were other positive effects of such stories too: by constant reference to the wartime links between the Resistance and Britain, Norway was confirmed as an active player not only in her own liberation but in the liberation of Europe as a whole.

For these reasons, stories of resistance became the dominant narrative of the wartime experience in all the countries that had been occupied by the Nazis. Holland celebrated the bravery of men such as Bram van der Stok, one of the 'Great Escapers' and the most decorated Dutch serviceman of all time. Denmark had people like Mogens Fog, the founder of the Resistance newspaper *Frit Danmark*, who escaped from the Gestapo when, by luck, the RAF bombed their headquarters in Copenhagen. The Czech Communists had heroes like Marie Kudeříková, a student who was executed for protesting against Nazi rule; while the Czech conservatives had the famous spy and saboteur Josef Mašin, whose sons would later follow in their father's footsteps by resisting the Communist regime.

There were hundreds, if not thousands of such stories, in every country that took an active part in the Second World War. Some of them were exaggerated, and some idealized, but in their straightforward portrayal of ordinary people triumphing against extraordinary odds they came to represent the wider struggle of Europe as a whole. Not only were these stories an inspiration to a whole generation who had not always lived up to such high ideals – they also reminded people that, no matter how hard life in postwar Europe might be, it was infinitely better than living under the tyranny they had overthrown.

Brotherhood and Unity

Heroism was not the only aspect of the war that was universally celebrated in its aftermath. On 9 May 1945 the Yugoslav leader Marshal Josip Broz Tito delivered a victory speech in which he paid tribute to the 'heroism' of the Partisans he had led during the war, whose 'matchless exploits' would 'inspire future generations and teach them how to love their homeland'. However, the main emphasis of his speech was not so much a celebration of heroism as a tribute to unity:

Peoples of Yugoslavia!

Serbs, Croats, Slovenes, Macedonians, Montenegrins, Moslems!

The long-awaited day you have yearned for has come! . . . The power
which was intent on enslaving you has been defeated. The German and
Italian Fascist set you against each other so that you might destroy your-
selves in internecine strife. But your best sons and daughters, inspired by
love of their country and its nations, have foiled these diabolical plans of
the enemy. Instead of mutual discord and hostility, you are united today
in a new and happier Yugoslavia . . .

Later in the speech Tito appealed not only to the 'brotherhood and
unity' of his own countrymen, but to that of the Balkans as a whole, the
Allies and their armies, and indeed the whole of the United Nations. VE
Day, he said, was a day of 'common victory' for all, and he hoped that
'in the aftermath of this great victory in the field of battle, the same
unanimity and understanding among the United Nations continues to
prevail in peacetime as in wartime'.[4]

The sentiments in this speech were replicated by virtually every
leader in Europe at various points during the war. Churchill, for
example, not only promised that 'the British Commonwealth and
Empire stands more united . . . than at any time in its long romantic
history', but also repeatedly stressed the 'unity, comradeship and
brotherhood' that existed between the Allies. The war had been won,
he said, because 'almost the whole world was combined against the
evil-doers'.[5] Romania's first post-liberation leader, Constantin
Sănătescu, spoke of a 'spirit of perfect union' across the 'entire country'.[6] Even Stalin spoke of how 'the ideology of friendship among the
peoples has emerged completely victorious over the Hitlerite ideology
of . . . racial hatred'.[7]

The word 'unity' was one of the watchwords of the era – so much so
that Charles de Gaulle even made it the title of his most important
volume of war memoirs. It was an ideal to which everyone aspired, and
which the war had made possible. Across western Europe, partisan
groups of vastly different political persuasions had put aside their differences to form 'national resistance councils'. By 1945 almost every
nation in Europe had formed a 'government of national unity' in which
all the political parties cooperated. At the end of the war, inspired by

the spirit of unity between the Allies, fifty nations came together to draft the charter for a brand-new international institution: the United Nations.

For many ordinary people, the cooperation between different nationalities, and amongst people of differing classes and political persuasions, was one of the most inspiring things about the war. 'Despite all the horrors,' wrote Theodora FitzGibbon in her memoirs, the war 'was not entirely destructive, for it produced a marked change in the attitude of British people to one another. Experiencing common danger made for a friendliness, almost a love, amongst total strangers', regardless of the traditional barriers of class or sex.[8]

For Richard Mayne, a British soldier who had served with Belgians and Norwegians, and shared military hospitals with Frenchmen, Russians and Poles, the war had been 'Une éducation européenne'. Afterwards he would become a European statesman, a colleague of Jean Monnet and Walter Hallstein, and one of the most enthusiastic champions of European union. As he would remember in later years,

> Not all Europe's 'great expectations' were to be fulfilled. But one underlay all the others: the sense of solidarity that so many had glimpsed during the war. Acknowledged or not, it informed most of men's efforts to build a better world, a better Europe, and a better society – more equal, less rigid, less hierarchical, and freed from the artificial barriers that World War II had swept aside.[9]

Unfortunately, as history has shown, this expectation of universal solidarity was short lived. The Cold War would create a chasm between the eastern and western halves of Europe that would not be bridged for more than forty years. In Yugoslavia and other parts of Europe the rhetoric of 'brotherhood and unity' bore very little semblance to reality, and peace between competing groups was more often coerced than voluntary. Every instance of 'friendship between strangers' would be matched by one of hatred or revenge.

And yet, even in the bleakest periods of the postwar years, a core of those wartime ideals was always kept alive. They would eventually form the basis for a formal partnership between the European nations that is still expanding to this day.[10]

A Brave New World

It is important to remember that the hardship and the destruction of the war years did not affect everyone equally. Indeed, some people found themselves better off after the war than they ever could have imagined before it. The war changed the entire social structure in many regions, leaving the way open for new hierarchies and new centres of power to establish themselves.

The biggest winners in this postwar free-for-all were undoubtedly the various Communist parties of Europe, whose membership across the continent increased exponentially. For this reason, many on the left learned to think of the war as a blessing, despite all the destruction it wrought. 'Even for the postwar generation in Yugoslavia,' writes Slavenka Drakulić, a journalist from Zagreb, 'the war was not a futile and senseless blood-letting, but on the contrary, a heroic and meaningful experience that was worth more than its one million victims.'[11]

The revolutionary consequences of the war were felt not only in those countries that would end up under Communist rule, but also in the west. One of the first countries to experience a taste of the changes to come was Britain, during the very earliest stages of the war. The rationing system that was set up in Britain at the outbreak of hostilities was as revolutionary as anything the Communists could have dreamed up. Almost every basic item of food was rationed, as were other essentials such as clothing and household goods. Nobody was entitled to more food if they were richer, or of a higher social standing than their neighbours – the only people entitled to better rations were those in the armed forces, or those in occupations that required heavy physical labour. In other words, food was allocated on the basis of need rather than social or economic privilege. As a consequence the general health of the population actually *improved* during the war: by the late 1940s, infant mortality rates in Britain were in steady decline, and deaths from a variety of diseases had also dropped substantially since the prewar years. From the standpoint of public health, the war had made Britain a much fairer society.[12]

There were other changes in Britain during the war that had a similar effect, such as the introduction of conscription to people of all classes, and both sexes. 'Social and sexual distinctions were swept away,' wrote

Theodora FitzGibbon, 'and when a dramatic change such as that takes place, it never goes back in quite the same way.'[13] The American war reporter Edward R. Murrow, who also witnessed the social changes brought about in Britain, put it more strongly: '[T]his war has no relation with the last one, so far as symbols and civilians are concerned. You must understand that a world is dying, that old values, the old prejudices, and the old bases of power and prestige are going.'[14]

On the continent similar changes occurred during the war, but in a rather different way. Here, because of both greater shortages and the more exploitative way that the Nazis and their allies ruled Europe, the rationing system did not work. Instead the people relied much more heavily on the black market – which meant city dwellers made regular trips to the countryside to barter their belongings for food. The war years saw a vast redistribution of wealth away from urban areas and into the countryside, thus reversing the trend of centuries. In Italy, for example, middle-class city dwellers were abandoned by their servants who preferred to return to their home villages where food was more plentiful. Peasants and shopkeepers, as one signora in northern Italy complained, were 'today's rich people'.[15] In Czechoslovakia, the changes to some rural communities were dramatic. 'The farmhouse would be twice its prewar size,' wrote Heda Kovaly, a political prisoner who returned to Czechoslovakia after the war. 'A refrigerator would be standing in the kitchen, a washing machine in the hall. There would be Oriental carpets on the floor and original paintings on the walls.' Even the Czech farmers themselves were happy to acknowledge these changes: 'No sense denying it – we did very well during the war.'[16]

For those who had been unable to take advantage of the social changes thrust upon them by the war, the liberation provided other opportunities. In Hungary, where 40 per cent of the peasants were either landless or virtually so, the arrival of the Red Army opened the way for some much-needed land reform. According to the Hungarian political theorist István Bibo, 1945 was indeed a liberation of sorts, despite all the violence and unpleasantness, because it sounded the death knell for the antiquated feudal system: '[F]or the first time since 1514 the rigid social system started to move, and move in the direction of greater freedom.'[17] Likewise, the liberation provided opportunities for workers in the industrial areas of Europe, such as France and northern Italy. Since all the major captains of industry and finance had been compromised by their collaboration with the wartime governments, the workers had a perfect excuse to take control of their workplaces in a way that would have been impossible before the war.

Sometimes there were darker reasons for the social changes caused by the war. In eastern Europe especially, the old prewar elites had been swept away as first the Nazis and later the Soviets deliberately decapitated the societies they overran. The removal of the Jews also paved the way for other groups to rise and take their place, both socially and economically. In Hungary many peasants came into possession of decent clothes and footwear for the first time when the property of expelled Jews was shared out in 1944.[18] In Poland, where the Jews had made up a substantial portion of the middle class, a new, *Polish* middle class rose to take their place.[19]

Regardless of how such changes came about, there were many who thought them long overdue. Whether you were an English liberal reformer, a French factory worker or a Hungarian peasant, it was difficult not to come to the conclusion that there had been some very positive aspects to the war and its aftermath. Perhaps not for all, but certainly for some.

The postwar period saw an explosion of political activity and idealism at every level of society. Many of these hopes and ideas would be short lived, particularly in those areas of Europe that were about to see the establishment of new dictatorships. Many more would become compromised by political haggling, economic hardship or stifling bureaucracy. But the very fact of their blossoming at all, in the wake of the most destructive war the world has ever seen, was no mean thing. Europe was on the brink of an economic and spiritual rebirth that would be hailed by generations to come as a 'miracle'.

If people at the time did not experience the approach of this 'miracle' quite as we imagine them to have done today, there was at least a universal sense of relief. It was enough to know that most of the continent's oppressive dictatorships were no more, that the bombs had stopped falling, that the war was at long last over.

7

Landscape of Chaos

In recent years there has been a tendency by some Western historians and politicians to look back at the aftermath of the Second World War through rose-tinted spectacles. Frustrated with the progress of rebuilding and reconciliation in the wake of wars in Afghanistan and Iraq at the beginning of the twenty-first century, they pointed to the success of similar projects in Europe in the 1940s. The Marshall Plan in particular was singled out as the template for postwar economic reconstruction.

Such politicians would have done well to remember that the process of rebuilding did not begin straight away in Europe – the Marshall Plan was not even thought of until 1947 – and the entire continent remained economically, politically and morally unstable far beyond the end of the decade. As in Iraq and Afghanistan more recently, the United Nations recognized the need for local leaders to take command of their own institutions. But it took time for such leaders to emerge. In the immediate aftermath of the war, the only people who had the moral authority to take charge were those with proven records of resistance. But people who are skilled in the arts of guerrilla warfare, sabotage and violence, and who have become used to conducting all their business in strict secrecy, are not necessarily those best suited to running democratic governments.

For a long while, therefore, the only authorities capable of keeping control were the Allies themselves. Only Allied officials were universally recognized as untainted by association with the Nazis. Only the Allied armies had the strength or the credibility to impose some form of law and order. And only the presence of the Allies could provide the stability that was the prerequisite for any return to democracy. Despite the fact that they soon appeared to be outstaying their welcome, there was really no alternative to the maintenance of a huge Allied presence across the continent.

Unfortunately the Allies were completely unprepared to deal with the complicated and widespread challenges that faced them in the immediate aftermath of the war. Their soldiers and administrators were outnumbered by millions upon millions of displaced persons, whom they were required to feed, clothe, house and somehow repatriate. They were expected to distribute food and medicine for tens of millions of indigenous civilians, many of whom had been left homeless, starving and traumatized by the conflict. They had to create and promote civil administrations, in many cases from scratch, in a way that took account of the sensitivities of a population whose language and customs most Allied soldiers did not understand. They were obliged to act as a police force in a continent that had descended into chaos and lawlessness, and where weapons of all kinds were freely available. And, somehow, they were supposed to motivate a demoralized people into clearing away the rubble and rebuilding their shattered lives.

All of this had to be conducted in an atmosphere of resentment and hatred. Germans everywhere were detested for creating the conflict in the first place, but also for the way in which the Nazis had conducted the war. Other national hatreds had been ignited too, or in some cases merely revived, by the events of the previous six years: Greeks against Bulgarians, Serbs against Croats, Romanians against Magyars, Poles against Ukrainians. Fratricidal conflicts were also beginning to flare up within nations, based on differing social and political conceptions of how a new society in the wake of the war should look. This merely added to friction that already existed between neighbours who had kept a close eye on one another's behaviour during the war. Throughout Europe collaborators and resisters still lived side by side in local communities. Perpetrators of atrocities melted into the population even as Hitler's victims were returning from captivity. Communists and fascists were inextricably mixed in amongst populations with more moderate political views, as well as those who had lost all faith in politics altogether. There were countless towns and villages where perpetrators lived alongside those they had directly harmed.

The Allied presence in the midst of all this was often resented by locals, many of whom had different priorities from those of their military occupiers. In the aftermath of the fighting it seems gradually to have dawned on the Allies that they were sitting on a time-bomb. The one phrase that repeats itself in the reports and memos of the Allies in 1945 is that while the war might have been won, the peace could still be lost.

In December 1944, while on a visit to Greece, the US Assistant Secretary of State Dean Acheson wrote a brief memorandum to Harry Hopkins, President Roosevelt's special assistant, warning of the potential bloodbath that awaited Europe if it were not rehabilitated quickly. Liberated peoples, he wrote, 'are the most combustible material in the world. They are fighting people. They are violent and restless. They have suffered unbearably.' If the Allies did not strive to feed them, rehabilitate them and actively help to restore the social and moral structures of their countries, then all that would follow would be 'frustration', 'agitation and unrest' and, eventually, 'the overthrow of governments'. This scenario was already unfolding in Yugoslavia and Greece. Acheson's fear was that such scenes would multiply across the continent, bringing about Europe-wide civil war.[1]

Just a few weeks after the Allied victory, Pope Pius XII also warned how fragile the newly established peace was. In an address to the Sacred College of Cardinals he claimed that the war had created 'mobs of dispossessed, disillusioned, disappointed and hopeless men' who were willing 'to swell the ranks of revolution and disorder in the pay of a tyranny no less despotic than those for whose overthrow men planned'. Although he did not name this despotic tyranny it was clear that he was referring to Stalin's Soviet regime, which was already in the process of engineering the Communist takeover of several central and eastern European states. The Pope supported the right of small nations to resist the imposition of new political or cultural systems, but recognized that the progression to a true and lasting peace between and within nations would take a long time – 'too long for the pent-up aspiration of mankind starving for order and calm'.[2]

Unfortunately, time was one of the many things the Western Allies did not have. Given the huge tasks that faced them they were unable to deal with Europe's postwar problems with anything like the speed that was required to avoid further bloodshed. Their response to the physical devastation was inadequate – unsurprisingly so, given the extent of the damage – and they were forced in the first instance to confine themselves merely to clearing the roads and rebuilding transport links, in order to re-establish supply lines across the continent. Likewise their response to the humanitarian crisis was lacking: the continent would remain desperately short of food and medical supplies for years to come, and displaced persons, particularly the 'stateless' Jews and Poles, would languish in camps of Nissen huts well into the 1950s. But even more inadequate was their response to the moral crisis. It simply was not possible to locate all the war criminals and remove all compromised leaders from positions of power, intern them, gather evidence against them and try them – and to do so promptly – especially given the challenging conditions of 1944 and 1945.

In the violent and chaotic atmosphere that prevailed at the end of the war, it is unsurprising that people decided to take the law into their own hands. They could do nothing to change the physical devastation, nor the human losses – but they believed that it was at least possible to redress some of the moral imbalances. As I shall show in the next section, this belief was generally nothing but a fantasy: it relied on finding convenient scapegoats, and on treating whole sections of the population as communally guilty for the crimes of a few. In this way a new crime would be added to the damaged moral landscape brought about by the war – that of vengeance.

PART II

Vengeance

There are only two sacred words left to us.
One of them is 'love'; the other one is 'revenge'.

Vasily Grossman, 15 October 1943[1]

8

The Thirst for Blood

In October 1944, after more than two years of butchery between the Germans and the Soviets, the Red Army finally crossed the frontier onto German soil. The little village of Nemmersdorf bears the unhappy distinction of being the first populated place they came across, and the name of the village soon became a byword for atrocity. In a frenzy of violence, Red Army soldiers are reputed to have murdered everyone they found here – men, women and children alike – before proceeding to mutilate their bodies. One correspondent for the Swiss newspaper *Le Courrier*, who claimed he came to the village after the Soviets had temporarily been beaten back, was so disgusted by what he saw that he felt unable to relate it. 'I will spare you the description of the mutilations and the ghastly condition of the corpses on the field,' he wrote. 'These are impressions that go beyond even the wildest imagination.'[1]

As the Soviets advanced, such scenes repeated themselves across all the eastern provinces of Germany. At Powayen near Königsberg, for example, the bodies of dead women were strewn everywhere: they had been raped and then brutally killed with bayonets or rifle butt blows to the head. Four women here had been stripped naked, tied to the back of a Soviet tank and dragged to their deaths. In Gross Heydekrug a woman was crucified on the altar cross of the local church, with two German soldiers similarly strung up on either side.[2] More crucifixions occurred in other villages, where women were raped and then nailed to barn doors.[3] At Metgethen it was not only women but children who were killed and mutilated: according to the German captain who examined their corpses, 'Most of the children had been killed by a blow to the head with a blunt instrument,' but 'some had numerous bayonet wounds in their tiny bodies.'[4]

The massacre of women and children had no military purpose –

indeed it was a propaganda disaster for the Red Army, and only served to stiffen German resistance. The wanton destruction of German towns and villages was also counter-productive. As Lev Kopelev, a Soviet soldier who witnessed the burning of German villages, pointed out, it was all very well to seek revenge, 'But where do we spend the night afterward? Where do we put the wounded?'[5] But to look at such events in purely practical terms is surely missing the point. The desire for vengeance was perhaps the inevitable response to some of the greatest injustices ever perpetrated by man. The soldiers who carried out these atrocities were motivated by a deep and often personal bitterness. 'I have taken revenge and will take revenge,' claimed a Red Army soldier named Gofman in 1944, whose wife and two children had been murdered by the Nazis in the Belorussian town of Krasnopol'ye (Polish Krasnopol). 'I have seen fields sown with German bodies, but that is not enough. How many of them should die for every murdered child! Whether I am in the forest or in a bunker, the Krasnopolye tragedy is before my eyes . . . And I swear that I will take revenge as long as my hand can hold a weapon.'[6]

Other soldiers had similar stories, and a similar thirst for blood. 'My life is twisted,' wrote Salman Kiselev after the death of his wife and six children.[7] 'They killed my little Niusenka,' claimed Second Lieutenant Kratsov, a Hero of the Soviet Union who had lost his wife and daughter to the Einsatzgruppen in Ukraine. 'There is only one thing left for me: vengeance.'[8]

In the immediate aftermath of the Second World War the threat, or promise, of vengeance permeated everything. It formed a thread in virtually every event that took place, from the arrest of Nazis and their collaborators to the wording of the postwar treaties that shaped Europe for the decades to come. Leaders from Roosevelt to Tito happily indulged the vengeful fantasies of their subordinates, and sought to harness the popular desire for vengeance to further their own political causes. Commanders in all the Allied armies turned a blind eye to the excesses of their men; and civilians took advantage of the chaos to redress years of impotence and victimization by dictators and petty tyrants alike.

Of all the themes that emerge in any study of the immediate postwar period, that of vengeance is perhaps the most universal. And yet it is a subject that is rarely analysed in any depth. While there are many excellent studies of its legitimate cousin, retribution – that is to say, the legal and supposedly impartial exercise of justice – there is no general study of the role that vengeance played in the aftermath of the war. Mentions of vengeance are usually confined to superficial, partisan accounts of specific events. In some cases its very existence is deliberately played down by historians, or even flatly denied; in other cases it is exaggerated out of all proportion. There are political and emotional reasons for both of these standpoints, which must be taken into account if an impartial understanding of events is ever to be reached.

Many historians have also taken contemporary stories of vengeance at face value, without stopping to question the motives of those who first drew up these accounts. The story of Nemmersdorf is a perfect example. For almost fifty years, while the Cold War was in progress, Western historians accepted the version of events given in Nazi propaganda. This was partly because it suited them – the Russians were the bogeymen of Europe – and partly because they were unable to access Soviet archives for an alternative version of events. But more recent studies show that the Nazis falsified photographs of Nemmersdorf, and exaggerated both the time-frame over which the massacre took place and the number of people killed. Such distortions of the truth were common in the aftermath of the war, when atrocities by both sides were exploited ruthlessly for their propaganda value. The real story of what happened at Nemmersdorf, which is no less horrific than the traditional accounts, is therefore hidden beneath layers of what we today call 'spin'.[9]

In the following pages I shall describe some of the most common forms of vengeance that were carried out in the immediate aftermath of the war, on both an individual and a communal level. I shall show how the *perception* of that vengeance was, and is, just as important as the vengeance itself. I shall demonstrate how a vengeful population was occasionally manipulated by those with ulterior motives who wished to strengthen their own positions. And I shall show how the new authorities in Europe were unable to establish themselves before first bringing the forces of vengeance under control.

Revenge was a fundamental part of the bedrock upon which postwar Europe was rebuilt. Everything that happened after the war, and everything that will be described in the rest of this book, bears its hallmark: to this day, individuals, communities and even whole nations still live with the bitterness born of this vengeance.

9

The Camps Liberated

Of all the symbols of violence and depravity that litter the history of the Second World War, perhaps the most potent is that of the concentration camps. These camps, and all they represented, were used to justify all kinds of vengeance in the aftermath of the war, and so it is important to understand the sense of shock and sheer disbelief that they engendered at the time. There were many kinds of concentration camps, but it was the 'death camps' – the places where prisoners were either starved to death, or more deliberately exterminated in gas chambers or by firing squads – that were most publicized.

Discovery

The first Nazi death camp to be discovered was that of Majdanek, near the Polish town of Lublin, which was taken by the Red Army at the end of July 1944. By this point in the war the Russians were well-acquainted with German atrocities. They had heard of Babi Yar, and countless other, smaller massacres across western Russia and Ukraine, but as one newspaper correspondent at the time claimed, 'all this killing was spread over relatively wide areas, and though it added up to far, far more than Maidanek, it did not have the vast monumental, "industrial" quality of that unbelievable Death Factory two miles from Lublin'.[1]

The Germans had done their best to evacuate Majdanek before the Red Army arrived, but in their hurry to leave they had failed to conceal the evidence of what had taken place here. When Soviet troops drove into the compound they discovered a set of gas chambers, six large furnaces with the charred remains of human skeletons scattered around them and, nearby, several enormous mounds of white ash filled with pieces of human bones. The ash mounds overlooked a huge field of vegetables, and the Soviets came to the obvious conclusion: the organizers of Majdanek had been using human remains as fertilizer. 'This is German food production,' wrote one Soviet journalist at the time. 'Kill people; fertilize cabbages.'[2]

The scale of the killing that had taken place here and in other nearby camps only became apparent when the Soviets opened up some of the buildings that lay between the gas chambers and the crematorium. In one enormous barn-like structure they found hundreds of thousands of pairs of boots and shoes. Another large building was 'like a vast, five-storey department store': here they found shelves and shelves of shaving brushes, pen-knives, teddy bears, children's jigsaw puzzles, and long corridors lined with thousands of overcoats and women's dresses.[3] On the ground floor of this building was the accounts department, which the departing Nazis had not had time to destroy. Here Soviet officials discovered some of the most damning documents of what would later become known as the Holocaust. Majdanek had acted as a central storage depot for a whole network of extermination camps: the belongings of Jews murdered in Sobibor, Treblinka and Belzec were brought here to be sorted and then shipped back to the Reich, where they would be given to German families who had been evacuated or bombed out of their houses. In the first few months of 1944 alone, eighteen railway wagons of goods from this warehouse had been sent to Germany.[4] Later, after speaking to liberated Soviet prisoners of war who had survived the camp, investigators learned of the gruesomely named 'Harvest Festival' killings of November 1943. Survivors led them to a series of mass graves where 18,000 Jews were buried.[5]

The effect of these discoveries was immediate. The Soviet propagandist Konstantin Simonov was sent to Majdanek to write a story on the camp, which appeared in *Pravda* and *Krasnaya Zvezda* at the beginning of August.[6] Foreign journalists were also invited to the camp, and large parties of Russian and Polish soldiers were taken there on guided tours so that they could spread the word of what they had seen throughout the Red Army.[7] On hearing that Majdanek had been captured virtually intact, Hitler was reportedly incensed. Himmler had gone to great lengths to conceal the Holocaust by dismantling and then levelling the main killing centres – but the discovery of Majdanek provided the first concrete proof that the terrifying reports coming out of Poland were all true.[8]

Over the coming months a whole network of slave-labour camps, prisoner-of-war camps and extermination camps were found throughout the territories formerly held by the Nazis. Treblinka was discovered shortly after Majdanek, and escapees and captured guards alike described a 'hell' where 900,000 Jews were murdered and roasted in furnaces 'reminiscent of gigantic volcanoes'.[9] Six months later the Red Army overran Auschwitz, where almost a million Jews, and over 100,000 Poles, Gypsies and Soviet prisoners of war were gassed, shot and worked to death.[10] Even the Soviets, who had long had their own network of slave-labour camps, or gulags, were shocked at the speed, efficiency and comprehensive nature of the murder.[11]

As a side note, it has often been claimed that the Soviets made no mention of the fact that most of the victims of these death camps were Jews.[12] This is not quite true. In December 1944 Ilya Ehrenburg published an article in *Pravda* in which he claimed:

> Ask a captured German why his countrymen destroyed six million innocent people and he will answer: 'They are Jews. They are black or red-haired. They have different blood' . . . All this began with stupid jokes, with the shouts of street kids, with signposts, and it led to Majdanek, Babi Yar, Treblinka, to ditches filled with children's corpses.[13]

Another article in *Pravda* about Auschwitz also specifically mentions its Jewish victims.[14] Nevertheless, the vast majority of Russian newspaper articles, speeches and later the memorials to the dead, referred to Hitler's victims merely as 'Soviet citizens'. Even while the death camps were being discovered the Kremlin was determined to portray the Nazi genocide not as a crime against the Jewish race, but as a crime against the Soviet state.

While these events immediately filled the Soviet press, the reaction in Britain and America was much more muted. The British knew as early as December 1942 that hundreds of thousands of Jews were being 'slowly worked to death in labour camps' and even 'deliberately massacred in mass executions'. But the government was reluctant to publicize the fact too widely in case they might then be expected to do something about it.[15] The British Ministry of Information were still working to instructions issued earlier on in the war that 'horror stuff . . . must be used very sparingly and must deal always with treatment of indisputably innocent people. Not with violent opponents. And not with Jews.'[16] The British public were therefore not nearly as well versed in German atrocities as the Soviet people were.

The American government also seemed unwilling to admit that Jews were worse off than any other persecuted group. Despite regular reports of the threat to European Jewry from as early as 1940, and despite Roosevelt's unequivocal announcement in March 1944 of 'one of the blackest crimes of all history . . . the wholesale, systematic murder of the Jews of Europe', Americans seemed reluctant to believe that the Holocaust was really taking place.[17] Even within Roosevelt's administration there was scepticism, and senior figures like Secretary of War Henry Stimson and his assistant John McCloy regarded 'special pleading' by Jews with suspicion. Such attitudes were not born solely from anti-Semitism. Remembering that many of the atrocity stories of the First World War had turned out to be untrue – such as the 'discovery' of a factory to manufacture soap out of human fat – they were unsure how much of the information about the death camps they should believe.[18]

There was a similar scepticism about the death camps in some of the press. The *Sunday Times* correspondent Alexander Werth visited Majdanek shortly after it was liberated, and saw the gas chambers, mass graves and mounds of human remains for himself. And yet when he submitted the story to the BBC they refused to broadcast it because 'they thought it was a Russian propaganda stunt'.[19] The *New York Herald Tribune* was equally reticent about the story, claiming that 'Even on top of all we have been taught of the maniacal Nazi ruthlessness, this example sounds inconceivable.'[20]

Attitudes changed only when the Western Allies began to discover similar concentration camps for themselves. The first camp to be discovered in the west was the Natzweiler-Struthof camp in Alsace, which the French army entered on 23 November 1944. Natzweiler-Struthof was one of the principal *Nacht und Nebel* camps – those institutions that were designed to make suspected Resistance fighters disappear into the 'night and fog'. Here the French discovered a small gas chamber, where prisoners were hung by their wrists from hooks while Zyklon-B gas was pumped into the room. Many of the victims were destined for the autopsy tables of Strasbourg University, where Dr August Hirt had amassed a collection of Jewish skeletons in order to prove the inferiority of the Jewish race through anatomical study. Others, mostly Gypsies brought here from Auschwitz, were subjected to medical experiments within the camp.[21]

At the beginning of December 1944 the *New York Times* correspondent Milton Bracker visited the camp. Bracker noticed that although many American officers had toured the camp, they still could not bring themselves to accept the full magnitude and detail of the horror. Many seemed to doubt the evidence before their own eyes, and exhibited what Bracker termed 'double vision' – a condition where they simultaneously saw and did not see the results of German atrocities. According to other contemporary reports the disbelief of American soldiers infuriated the local population when their stories of German crimes were doubted, or even scoffed at.[22]

Such 'double vision' came to an end the following April, when the Americans liberated Ohrdruf, one of Buchenwald's sub-camps. Ohrdruf is particularly important because General Dwight Eisenhower, the Supreme Commander of Allied Forces in Europe, visited it on 12 April, just a week after it had been discovered. He brought with him Generals Omar Bradley and George Patton, and insisted on seeing 'every nook and cranny' of the camp, 'because I felt it my duty to be in a position from then on to testify at first hand about these things in case there ever grew up at home the belief or assumption that the stories of Nazi brutality were just propaganda'.[23] Here they observed torture devices, a butcher's block used to smash the gold fillings from the mouths of the dead, a room piled to the ceiling with corpses, and the remains of hundreds of bodies that had been burned in a huge pit, as if on 'some gigantic cannibalistic barbecue'.[24] Patton, a man well used to the horrors of the battlefield, took one look at the 'arms and legs and portions of bodies sticking out of the green water' in the pit, and was obliged to retire behind a shed to throw up.[25]

Shortly after the discovery of Ohrdruf came the discovery of Nordhausen, where the bodies of 3,000 slave labourers who had worked in the subterranean V-1 and V-2 flying-bomb factories were found lying in disordered piles. On the same day 21,000 prisoners were discovered barely alive in Buchenwald, just a few miles north of Weimar. Many of these men, women and children had been force-marched here on what would become known as the 'death marches' from camps in the east, and were now exhausted, emaciated and riddled with disease. The US Psychological Warfare Division estimated that about 55,000 men, women and children had died in this slave-labour camp during the war.[26]

As the news of such discoveries became better known, American troops became increasingly disgusted with the Germans. According to Fred Bohm, an Austrian-born American soldier who helped liberate Nordhausen, most of his fellow GIs 'had no particular feeling for fighting the Germans' and believed that many of the stories they had heard 'were either not true or at least exaggerated'. It was only when they arrived at Nordhausen that the truth about Nazi atrocities properly began to 'sink in'.[27] It was precisely to drum this home that Eisenhower ordered all nearby units who were not on front-line duty to visit the camps at Ohrdruf and Nordhausen. Even if the average GI did not quite know 'what he is fighting for', said the general, he would now, at least, 'know what he was fighting against'.[28] He also invited British and American government officials to come and tour the newly liberated concentration camps, as well as the world's press. The newsreel footage from these visits, which finally reached American cinema screens on 1 May, shocked the nation to its core.[29]

Anger at what the US Army was discovering reached a peak on 29 April, just nine days before the end of the war in Europe, when the 45th Division fought its way through to Dachau. Here they found scenes of utter horror, including piles of naked bodies stacked up in storerooms 'like cordwood'.[30] On the railway sidings they found a train carrying prisoners evacuated from the east. When they opened up its thirty-nine boxcars they found all 2,000 prisoners were dead.[31]

Unlike other camps, Dachau was liberated by troops on the fringes of a major battle. Some of the American soldiers, who were psychologically prepared for fighting, were not willing to accept the atrocities they witnessed here calmly and decided to take the law into their own hands. One of the company commanders in the 157th Regiment, Lieutenant William P. Walsh, took a group of four SS men who had surrendered to him into one of the railway boxcars and personally shot them. One of his men, Private Albert C. Pruitt, then climbed into the boxcar and finished them off with his rifle. Along with another officer, Lieutenant Jack Bushyhead, Walsh then supervised the separation of the German prisoners into those belonging to the Wehrmacht and those belonging to the

SS. The SS soldiers were lined up in a nearby coal yard, where a machine-gun team opened fire on them, killing at least twelve. In the official report that was prepared following an inquiry into this incident, Walsh, Bushyhead and Pruitt were specifically named, as was their battalion commander Lieutenant Colonel Felix L. Sparks. The medical officer who appeared on the scene shortly afterwards, Lieutenant Howard E. Buechner, was also criticized for failing to administer any aid to the German soldiers, some of whom were still alive.[32]

In one of the towers on the perimeter of the camp a crew of about seventeen SS men were also shot as they tried to surrender. Elsewhere in the camp between twenty-five and fifty more were killed by angry inmates, often with the help of American soldiers. Jack Hallett, one of the GIs who witnessed these killings, later remembered how gruesome these revenge killings could be:

> Control was gone after the sights we saw, and the men were deliberately wounding guards that were available and then turned them over to the prisoners and allowing them to take their revenge on them. And in fact, you've seen the picture where one of the soldiers gave one of the inmates a bayonet and watched him behead the man. It was a pretty gory mess. A lot of the guards were shot in the legs so they couldn't move and . . . and that's about all I can say . . .[33]

Although a report on these incidents was commissioned, no American soldiers were ever brought to trial for breaking the Geneva Convention on the rights of prisoners of war.

The British too were beginning to discover the meaning of Hitler's concentration camps. When they arrived at Bergen-Belsen on 15 April they were completely unprepared for the sights, stories and challenges that awaited them. After a fairly civilized surrender by the camp commandant, Josef Kramer, British officers were shown around by the commandant himself. However, what they witnessed within the camp was far from civilized: kapos leaping on prisoners to beat them with heavy sticks, inmates like 'living skeletons with haggard yellowish faces', the 'stench of putrefying flesh', and people defecating openly in the compounds and even on the floors inside their huts.[34] Most disturbing, once again, was the sight of innumerable corpses, some lying singly where they had collapsed, others stacked in rooms, or heaped in piles around the compound. Derrick Sington, one of the first officers to enter the camp, claimed they looked 'like the overladen counter of a butcher's shop': 'Every trick that rigor mortis can play with the human countenance, every freakish posture that a sprawling human skeleton, thrown down at random, can assume, could be studied as one walked among those birch trees in the sunshine.'[35]

Over the coming days, one of the things that shocked the British most was the nonchalant way that the surviving prisoners lived their lives amongst the corpses, as if such sights were perfectly normal. One horrified medical officer described several such vignettes:

> a woman too weak to stand propping herself against a pile of corpses, as she cooked the food we had given her over an open fire; men and women crouching just anywhere in the open relieving themselves of the dysentery which was scouring their bowels; a woman standing stark naked washing herself with some issue soap in water from a tank in which the remains of a child floated.[36]

There were so many dead bodies in various states of decay that it was impossible to estimate how many had died. According to Wilhelm Emmerich, the SS officer in charge of monitoring prisoner numbers, about 16,000 people died there in the two months before the British arrived, but other estimates go as high as 18,000 in the month of March alone.[37] The small crematorium at Belsen had been unable to cope with the numbers, and a lack of fuel had prevented burning many bodies in open pits.

When the British questioned the inmates of this place they began to uncover some of the horror that they had experienced. Typhus and dysentery were raging through the camp. A diet of nothing but thin swede soup had reduced the prisoners to sticks. The hunger and deprivation here had become so bad that scores of people had resorted to cannibalism in an attempt to stay alive. One Czech prisoner, Jan Belunek, told British officers that he had witnessed corpses with their hearts cut out, and that he had seen another inmate 'sitting beside one of such corpses, and he was eating flesh that I have no doubt was human flesh'. This story was confirmed by two other inmates who worked in the infirmary, a doctor from Dresden called Fritz Leo and a Czech doctor called Zdeněk Wiesner. Both reported the regular theft of corpses' livers, which Dr Wiesner personally saw people eating. Dr Leo, who reported about three hundred cases of cannibalism in the camp, often saw people eating human flesh and even 'boiled sexual organs'.[38]

The prisoners also reported countless cases of brutality, murder, medical experimentation and mass execution, both here and at other concentration camps throughout the Reich. An early report on Belsen, made on 27 April 1945, concluded that 'the purpose of the camps was to destroy portions of the population' before going on to reiterate that 'what took place in the concentration camps was not intended to be mere incarceration, but was destruction immediate or delayed'. As for Belsen itself, although it was designated a *Krankenlager* ('sick camp'), it 'was not in any sense a hospital camp, as prisoners do not seem to have been intended to recover'.[39]

British soldiers did not take revenge on their German counterparts quite as violently as the Americans at Dachau, but the circumstances were very different. Unlike at Dachau the British did not enter Belsen keyed up for battle, but were expecting only medical, administrative and guard duties. Unlike at Dachau there was no hint of resistance from the Germans – indeed, they appeared to welcome the British, and their first contacts were fairly cordial. But as the true horror of the camp sank in, relations between the British soldiers and the concentration camp staff quickly deteriorated. The British put SS men to work burying the dead, forcing them to toil in the hot sunshine in full uniform. They were made to use their bare hands to carry the decomposing remains: anyone who tried to protect his hands with rags or pieces of clothing immediately received a jab from a rifle butt. Many of the camp inmates also came to watch them working, and would gather around the mass graves to shout insults at their former tormentors. 'The one thing I saw that pleased me was the SS men being bullied into work,' wrote one of the British medical staff on 22 April:

> They collect dead and infected clothing – push their carts by hand and throw the mixed loads into enormous mass-graves (5,000 each). All the time our armed troops shout at them, kick them, threaten them, never letting them stop for a moment. What horrible types they were – these SS! – with their Hollywood criminal features. They are being shown no quarter – they know what end is in store for them when their work is finished.[40]

Another soldier, BSM Sanderson of 369 Battery, claimed that British vengeance occasionally became more extreme.

We gave the SS starvation rations, and put them to work without a break on the filthiest jobs. Our boys showed no squeamishness at all but struck them with rifle butts and jabbed them with bayonets to keep them working at the double. In one case an SS man was thrown half alive onto a mass grave, and it didn't take long to smother him with corpses. He'd tried to escape, was fired at and wounded. So the men brought him back to a burial pit and treated him as he would have treated any internee.[41]

It is difficult to know, almost seventy years later, whether such an event actually happened or was merely wishful thinking on behalf of the British soldiers. I have been unable to find any confirmation of an SS man buried alive at Belsen, but the fact that such stories were circulating is no less significant. They served an important psychological function: British soldiers needed to feel that some of the very worst SS atrocities were now rebounding upon their perpetrators.

It was not only the camp guards who were treated harshly at Belsen, but all those who had worked at the camp, including the technicians and clerks who made up the majority of the SS men captured here. German civilians from Celle and other nearby towns were also forced to come to Belsen so that they could see for themselves what crimes had been committed in Germany's name. According to one British sapper tasked with collecting the local town mayors, he and his fellow soldiers were not allowed into the camp because of the risk of typhus, but there was no such consideration for their German charges. When they returned, the Tommies showed them 'the sharp end of our anger' by deliberately dropping rifle butts on their feet in an attempt to break their toes. Many of these civilians appeared completely shocked by what they had seen. 'Some were heaving up, some crying unashamedly, but a few just stared into space with an air of disbelief.'[42]

Just as the Russians had done at Majdanek, the British recognized the chance for making propaganda out of Belsen. Army cameramen were sent here almost immediately, and newspaper journalists and photographers were also invited. But what made a bigger impact was the arrival of British Movietone News on 23 April, eight days after the discovery of the camp. Soon images of the mass graves and mounds of bodies were being shown on cinema screens across Britain, and later in other countries as well.

The sight of this and other haunting films, which showed children playing on mounds of corpses, stick-thin wraiths unable to stand up, and bulldozers tumbling hundreds of bodies into mass graves, sealed the world's view of Nazi Germany for ever. Here at last was visual evidence of German atrocities that could not be dismissed as mere propaganda. More importantly, it seemed at the time to implicate the entire German nation. In the words of Colonel Spottiswoode, the military government commander who gave a speech on camera to the German civilians visiting Belsen, the existence of camps like this was 'such a disgrace to the German people that their name must be erased from the list of civilized nations'. It was not only the perpetrators of these crimes who should be punished, but the whole country: 'You must expect to atone with toil and sweat for what your children have committed and for what you have failed to prevent.'[43]

The discovery of the concentration camps changed the moral landscape irrevocably. It seemed to vindicate everything that the Allies had done during the course of the war – the bombing of German cities, the insistence on unconditional surrender, the economic blockade that had brought famine to so much of Europe. It also provided justification for much that the Allies would do in the coming months. Henceforth, regardless of how much they would come to suffer, Germans would be unable to claim much sympathy: injustices against German soldiers and civilians would be ignored, as those at Dachau were, and as they were during the rape of eastern Germany by the Red Army. Occasionally, as we shall see, blind vengeance would even be encouraged by the authorities. As one historian has concluded, the violence and degradation that was uncovered in places such as Majdanek, Dachau and Belsen 'had a way of implicating all, even the liberators'.[44]

The Revenge of Jewish Prisoners

If the soldiers who liberated the camps expressed a desire for vengeance against the Nazis, then so did the prisoners they rescued. 'Sometimes', Israel Gutman, a survivor of Majdanek, Auschwitz and Gunskirchen has written, the 'desire and expectation of revenge' were the 'hope' that kept camp inmates alive 'during the final and most arduous stages of camp life'.[45]

Most historians tend to brush over the
concentration camp survivors for the same rea
at the time tended to turn a blind eye to it: such a
prick in comparison to what the prisoners themselv
They rightly point out that Jewish vengeance was n
pared to the havoc provoked by some other nation   he
American military governor, Lucius Clay himself, admit.   1947:
'[I]n spite of their natural hatred of the German people [Jewish DPs]
have been remarkably restrained in avoiding incidents of a serious
nature with the German population . . . their record for preserving law
and order is to my mind one of the remarkable achievements which I
have witnessed during my more than two years in Germany.'⁴⁶

However, while it is true that only a very small percentage of Jews
indulged themselves in this way, revenge was perhaps more widespread
than is usually admitted. Most concentration camp survivors seem to
have witnessed some form of vengeance, even if they themselves did not
take part. The first targets were the camp guards themselves, and when
they could not be found – because most guards tended to run away
from the camps before the Allied soldiers arrived – then the inmates
would turn on those amongst their own number who had acted as Nazi
stooges, the kapos. If it was not possible to take revenge on those
directly responsible for their own misery, the inmates' frustrations were
taken out on other Germans, particularly SS men, German soldiers or
Nazi officials, but failing that any German at all.

Revenge was committed by men, women and even children. For
example, after the liberation of Theresienstadt in Czechoslovakia, Ben
Helfgott saw two Jewish girls on the road to Leibnitz attacking a German woman with a pram. He told them to stop, but they refused to do
so until he physically intervened. Later, inside the camp, he witnessed a
mob beating an SS man to death. 'I watched this and I felt sick,' he said
decades later. 'I don't hate anything, but I hate mobs. When people turn
into mobs they are no longer human beings.'⁴⁷

Chaskiel Rosenblum, who was also liberated at Theresienstadt, did
not kill any Germans – not out of any particular moral scruples, but
simply because he could not bring himself to do it. However, he knew
a ten-year-old boy who had seen his parents murdered, 'and he was
killing one Nazi after another'.⁴⁸ Pinkus Kurnedz saw one of the former kapos at Theresienstadt murdered by a mob of his friends when

...ed the man lying low in a nearby village. 'He was hiding ...n and we dragged him out. And there were a couple of Russian anks there in the little square. The Russians helped as well. And we literally beat him to death.'[49]

For obvious reasons it is extremely difficult to find accounts by Jews who admit to committing acts of revenge, but a few brave souls have spoken openly about the things they did – either out of a wish to ensure that the historical record is as accurate as possible, or because they remain unashamed of acts which they believe were justified. In 1988, for example, a Polish Jew named Szmulek Gontarz recorded an interview for the Imperial War Museum in London in which he admitted that he and his friends had taken revenge on Germans during the liberation, and had continued to do so for a long time afterwards.

> We all participated. It was sweet. The only thing I'm sorry about is that I didn't do more. Anything: throw them off trains. Wherever I thought I could take advantage, by beating them, we would. There was one particular instance in Austria. We stayed in stables, and there was a German officer hiding there. We found him, and we did exactly the same as they did to us: we tied him to a tree and we shot him. If you say to me now to do it, no way – but at that time it was sweet. I enjoyed it. There was no other satisfaction at that time that any of us could have had. And I'll tell you now: I challenge any person in a similar situation who would not have enjoyed it . . . It was perhaps the only thing that it might have been worth to survive the war, to be able to do that. And the satisfaction was great.[50]

Alfred Knoller, an Austrian Jew who was liberated at Belsen, remembers raiding local farms for food with the explicit permission of the British soldiers. On one occasion he and his friends found a picture of Hitler hidden behind some sacks in the yard beside a barn. Inside the barn they also found some guns. Incensed, they smashed the picture of Hitler and then, despite the somewhat unbelievable protestations of the farmer and his wife that they were anti-Nazis, they shot the pair of them.

> I know it was something quite inhuman that we'd done. But I'm afraid to us it was something that maybe subconsciously we had wanted to do for a long time. We wanted to fight the Germans. We did not fight them, but somehow we did what the next best thing was . . . We wanted revenge. All the time. It was absolutely an act of revenge. It had to come out.

Far from making them feel guilty about what they had done, the event seemed to provide Knoller and his friends with a much-needed emotional release. 'We were quite open about it. We told everybody. When we came back to the camp, we were triumphant about it.'[51]

At first many such attacks were ignored or even encouraged by the Allied soldiers. There is a general feeling amongst camp survivors that they were given carte blanche to act however they liked for a limited period, but that for the sake of law and order, attacks on Germans were eventually forbidden. Arek Hersh, for example, claims that 'The Russians gave us twenty-four hours to do whatever we wanted to the Germans.'[52] Harry Spiro, another survivor liberated at Theresienstadt, also remembers the Russians telling them that they had twenty-four hours 'to do whatever we wanted, even kill Germans'.[53] According to Max Dessau, a Polish Jew liberated at Belsen, the British too 'let you do it for a certain time, to get out your revenge' but 'after a time they said enough is enough'.[54] The Americans were equally willing to let the prisoners have their way. Kurt Klappholz, a Polish Jew who was liberated while on a forced march, was presented with an SS soldier by an American lieutenant who had already beaten the man black and blue. 'What the American roughly said to me was, "Here is one of your torturers, you can take your revenge."'[55] None of these people took advantage of the opportunity offered them, but it is quite clear that plenty of others did.

With time, naturally, the feelings of most of these ex-prisoners began to soften. The desire for revenge often dissolved when they saw the pathetic nature of some of the supposed 'master race' in whose name they had been incarcerated. For example Peter Frank, who was liberated at Nordhausen, ended the war weighing just over four stone. His only wish was 'to exterminate the whole German nation, so this sort of thing couldn't happen again'. But when he was given a German prisoner of war to act as his 'horse' because he was too weak to move about on his own, his anger seems to have turned first to contempt, and eventually to pity. 'He was assigned to me, and he was my property, so to speak. He used to complain to me about how badly he had been done by the war – but he got wise fairly quickly. I mean, he was a poor sod, and there was no point taking revenge on him . . . Once you started dealing with individuals, who were in many ways victims as well, you left it.'[56] Alfred Huberman, a survivor of Buchenwald and Rehmsdorf, agrees. 'When I was first liberated, I thought Germany should be wiped off the map completely. As time went on if I met a German I thought, What could I say to him? Other than feel sorry for him, to have to live with that on his conscience.'[57]

There were, however, some whose anger did not quickly subside, and who believed that the Jews could never rest easy until some monumental revenge was enacted upon the German people. One such group was the so-called 'Avengers', founded by the former Jewish partisan Abba Kovner. This group appears to have arranged the assassination of more than a hundred suspected war criminals, as well as the placement of a bomb inside a prison camp for SS men that killed eighty of its inmates. Their philosophy involved deliberately indiscriminate attacks on large numbers of Germans, and the impersonal nature of their revenge was designed to mirror the impersonal way that Jews had been killed during the Holocaust. Their slogan was 'a German for every Jew', and their express intention, according to one of the group's members, Gabik Sedlis, was that 'six million Germans will be killed'. To achieve this aim they hatched a plot to poison the water supply of five German cities, but were foiled when Kovner himself was arrested trying to smuggle the poison from Palestine back to Europe.[58] An alternative plan to poison the bread of 15,000 SS men in an internment camp near Nuremberg was more successful. At least 2,000 German prisoners indeed fell sick with arsenic poisoning, although it is not clear how many, if any, died.[59]

Such plans relied on the chaos that reigned during the immediate postwar period. The massive movements of refugees provided an excellent cover for those seeking revenge (just as it provided cover for escaping war criminals), and the lack of any form of law and order meant that murders went unreported, uninvestigated and often unnoticed. Eventually, however, conditions changed, and even the 'Avengers' themselves gave up their dreams of reprisal, choosing instead to fight for the future of an independent state for the Jews in Palestine.[60]

Here, perhaps, is a clue that might explain why Jewish vengeance was not more widespread. In the immediate aftermath of the Holocaust most surviving Jews were either too sick or too weak to consider any form of active retribution – to have survived at all was enough of an act of defiance. But more importantly, vengeance is an act committed by those who have an interest in restoring some kind of moral balance. For many Jews, perhaps the majority, there was no such interest. They had decided to turn their backs on Europe altogether and escape to alternative lands where the moral balance had not been compromised: America, Britain and, most importantly, Palestine. Thus their vengeful feelings were expressed symbolically by leaving Europe en masse, as one Jewish writer explained at the end of 1945:

> We sought to take revenge on our enemies through disparagement, rejection, banning and keeping our distance . . . Only by setting ourselves apart from these murderers completely . . . will we be able to satisfy our desire for vengeance which in essence means: doing away with the European exile and building our homeland in the Land of Israel.[61]

Palestine gave them the hope of a Jewish state in which they could not be persecuted, because they themselves were the masters. Accordingly they did whatever they could to smuggle themselves out of mainland Europe and join their brethren in the attempt to found the new land of Israel. It was not in the long-term Jewish interest to seek vengeance on Germany, or to cause trouble with the Allies who had, in the end, saved them from complete extinction. Often, therefore, vengeance was left to other former prisoners whom the Nazis had persecuted. There was certainly no shortage of groups who also had an axe to grind.

10

Vengeance Restrained: Slave Labourers

Given their own particularly gruesome history, it is understandable that the Jews tend to take centre stage in the painful drama of the liberation of the camps. But, as many historians have pointed out, the 'Holocaust' as we understand it today is largely a retrospective construction.[1] At the time, amongst the Allies at least, there was much less distinction between racial groups – indeed, the Allies often deliberately did *not* differentiate between them, choosing instead to group Hitler's victims by nationality. Confronted by the vast array of horror stories, relief organizations like UNRRA did not at first recognize the Jewish story as a special case, but lumped Polish Jews together with other Poles, Hungarian Jews with other Hungarians, and so on. It was not until September 1945 that Jews won the right to be housed separately, and looked after by specifically Jewish relief agencies.[2]

For many Allied soldiers and relief workers on the ground, it was not immediately apparent that Jews had suffered any more than many of the other groups they came across. Suffering was everywhere. Concentration camps were only one kind of camp in a vast network of exploitation and extermination that covered the whole of the Reich. Prisoner-of-war camps, in which Soviet prisoners had been left to starve in their millions, dotted eastern Europe. Slave-labour camps were attached to every major factory, mine, farm and construction site. (For example Dachau might have hit the headlines in British, French and American newspapers, but it was merely the hub of a system that had supplied prisoners of all nationalities to 240 sub-camps throughout southern Bavaria.) In addition there were scores of transit camps that were only supposed to process prisoners as they moved from one area to the next, but which by the end of the war had become dumping grounds for internees who were

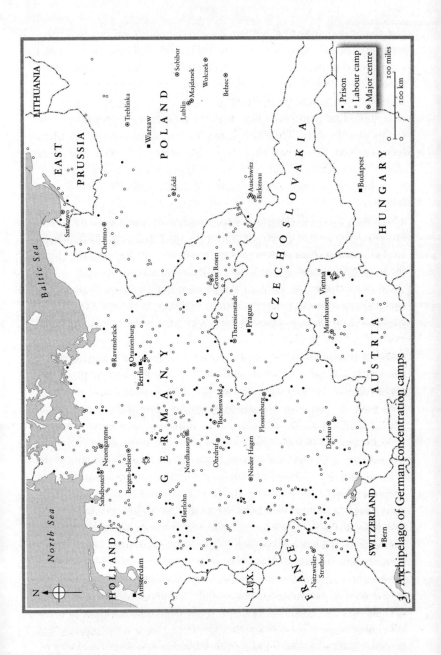

3. Archipelago of German concentration camps

effectively abandoned behind barbed wire without food or care. There were also special camps for orphans and juvenile delinquents, and penal camps for criminals and political prisoners. When taken together these thousands of barbed-wire encampments made up what one historian has described as a 'landscape of terror'.[3]

It should be mentioned here that the treatment of people in these camps varied wildly. While British and American prisoners of war often received Red Cross packages, were fed reasonably well and were allowed to engage in cultural activities, Italians and Soviets were routinely beaten, overworked and starved to death. Similarly, while French labourers on 'obligatory work service' were occasionally paid and fed adequately, Polish *Ostarbeiter* were more often worked to the bone, literally. Even within the concentration camps there were gradations of hardship, with Aryan prisoners being mistreated far less regularly than the supposedly 'inferior' races such as Jews and Gypsies.

To pretend that the German people were not aware of all these foreigners in their midst, or the conditions that they were forced to endure, would be a nonsense – although many Germans in the immediate aftermath of the war tried to do exactly that. At their peak, foreign workers made up around 20 per cent of the workforce in Germany, and in certain industries, such as armaments and aircraft manufacture, often 40 per cent or more.[4] Germans worked alongside these people and saw how they were treated – indeed, many Germans smuggled food to them either out of a wish to help or as a way of making money out of them.

By the end of the war, most Germans were well aware of the situation, and fear of what these millions of foreigners might do once they were liberated began to mount. In Hamburg a special emergency guard was formed by party members at the end of 1944 in case of a rising by foreign workers. In Augsburg there were stories that new labourers had arrived carrying concealed weapons.[5] In Berlin there were rumours that the foreigners were sending information to the enemy, and acting as a 'Trojan horse' within Germany.[6] Many foreign workers deliberately encouraged these fears: French prisoners of war joked that they were the 'advance parachutists' of the invasion force, and Polish workers taunted Germans with the story of 'lists' that had been made of Germans who were to be killed after victory.[7] Given the atmosphere of fear and resentment that existed between Germans and foreign labourers it was only a matter of time before serious confrontations between the two began to materialize.

Revenge of Slave Labourers

The backlash began almost as soon as the Allies entered Germany. In the early days of the invasion British, French and American troops all reported incidents of looting and disorder by liberated foreigners, but were often powerless to stop them. 'Looting is rampant,' claimed Captain Reuben Seddon of the British Civil Affairs Commission after crossing the Rhine in early April 1945. 'Russians, Poles, French and civilians are all having the time of their lives, and it's got to stop, the sooner the better.'[8] Further east the situation was even worse. According to the new military governor in the town of Schwerin in Mecklenburg, 'D.P.s were roaming around in their thousands, murdering, raping, looting – in short, away from the main streets, law did not exist.'[9] In Berlin in May a gang of a hundred DPs held up a train in Anhalt railway station in a scene like something from a Western.[10]

Many put such behaviour down to a combination of high spirits and a wish to express their justifiable frustration and anger at the Nazi regime.[11] But there was a wildness to the celebrations of liberated labourers that frightened both the German population and the Allies. For years they had been mistreated, segregated from the opposite sex, denied adequate food, and kept away from alcohol: many now made up for lost time by embarking on a Bacchic quest for food, alcohol and sex at any cost. Labour camps that had segregated men and women for years soon became a 'shambles' where people 'defecated all over' and began openly 'fornicating in the dorms'.[12] A sapper named Derek Henry later described the scenes he witnessed when he was called to maintain law and order at a former labour camp near the village of Nordhemmern near Minden on 11 April.

> There were both men and women inmates, and as we went into the huts they crowded around us. Most of them were drunk on home-made Vodka which they thrust upon us, some were having sex openly on the bunks, others were singing and dancing. They tried to get us to join in, fortunately we had our rifles with us . . . The DPs were in a filthy state, their huts stank to high heaven but we had to taste their home made vodka which they poured on the table top, then set it alight to prove how strong it was.

Later, according to Henry, a Polish inmate 'offered me his female companion for the night: an offer I declined'.[13]

Alcohol, especially, played a huge part in the disorders that occurred in the wake of the liberation. In Hanau hundreds of Russians drank industrial alcohol which killed at least twenty and left more than 200 semi-paralysed.[14] In Wolfsburg hundreds of labourers who used to work in the city's Volkswagen plant broke into both the city arsenal and the local vermouth factory. As one American company commander who was called in to help disarm the mob remembers, 'Some of them were so drunk they'd stand on dikes or up on buildings and fire a gun and it'd knock 'em flat on their back.'[15] When the journalist Alan Moorehead drove into the village of Steyerberg in the Weser valley, he came across villagers and refugees looting a wine cellar stocked with 'the most beautiful wine I have ever seen'. Most of them were drunk or 'half-demented', and they plundered and smashed bottles until the cellar was empty except for the slush of broken glass and Château Lafite 1891 that lay 'ankle deep' on the floor.[16]

Some of the wildest scenes occurred in Hanover. During the chaos of the liberation, tens of thousands of former forced labourers rampaged through the town looting liquor stores and setting fire to buildings. When the remnants of the German police tried to intervene they were overwhelmed, beaten and hung from the city's lamp posts.[17] Some former forced labourers rounded up German civilians to do the work that they themselves would have been forced to do in previous weeks – such as burying the bodies of 200 Russian officers shot by the SS – and 'lashed them with sticks or beat them with weapon stocks' while they worked.[18] Others sought out the women of the city and raped them in their homes and even in the streets. According to a British battery commander stationed in the town, one group of drunken Russians 'seized an abandoned German 88mm gun, dragged it around and, to their obvious pleasure, loosed off rounds at whatever took their fancy, prominent buildings or houses getting in their way'.[19]

In June 1945, after the city had been under Allied control for ten weeks, the British war reporter Leonard Mosley arrived to find Hanover still in a state of near-chaos. The new military government had managed to get the electricity, gas and water supplies working again, had cleared roads through the rubble and had recruited a German mayor and a makeshift police force, but had still not managed to impose anything close to law and order. 'The problem was too much. No scratch police-force of this kind could keep order among over 100,000 foreign slaves who were tasting their first real freedom for years.'[20]

The extent of the problem was demonstrated when the military governor drove Mosley from the Rathaus to his living quarters a few miles away. On the journey the car was halted five times by full-scale riots that filled the street, which the military governor himself, Major G. H. Lamb, would break up by repeatedly firing his pistol into the air. 'This is the sort of thing that goes on all day,' he reportedly told Mosley. 'Looting, fighting, rape, murder – what a town!'[21]

Much of the looting and violence in Hanover appeared to be occurring just for the sake of it. In one of the most telling eyewitness reports of the postwar chaos Mosley described the frantic looting of warehouses on the outskirts of the city:

> Someone once told me that when the looting fever is in a man he will kill or maim to get something, even if that 'something' isn't worth stealing, and Hanover confirmed it. We saw one crowd on that short journey which had just broken into a storehouse; there were Germans as well as foreign workers among the milling mass of screaming people; they burst through doors and windows and then came out, their arms full – of door knobs! It was a store for door knobs, and what these people could want with such objects, in a city where half the doors no longer existed, is beyond me; yet they not only looted those door knobs, but they fought over them. They kicked and scratched and beat with iron bars those who had more door knobs than themselves. I saw one foreign worker trip up a girl, tear the door knobs from her arms, and then kick her repeatedly in the face and body until she was covered with blood. Then he raced off down the street. Halfway down, he seemed to come to his senses; he looked down at the objects he was carrying, and then with a visible gesture of distaste he flung them all away.[22]

In the early days of the liberation such scenes were ubiquitous. Since most of the German policemen had fled, or been deposed, the local population had no choice but to turn to the Allied soldiers for help, but there were simply not enough to go round. In Hanover the military government enlisted Allied prisoners of war into temporary police forces, but such men were hopelessly inexperienced at police work and often had their own axe to grind against local Germans.[23] In all the major cities German policemen were recruited, but here too there was a lack of experience. For obvious reasons the Allies did not allow them to carry arms – consequently they were not much of a match against rioting DPs and the growing gangs of armed foreigners.[24]

A story told by one British lieutenant demonstrates the powerlessness of Allied soldiers to deal with the highly charged atmosphere that existed at the time, as well as the moral gap between the attitudes of those who had been personally violated by the Nazis and those who had not. In May 1945 Ray Hunting was travelling along a quiet country road near the city of Wesel when he witnessed an event that would stay with him for the rest of his life.

I saw two men ahead: a Russian making his way to Wesel and an old German with a walking stick, moving slowly towards the Station. As we approached, the men stopped, the Russian apparently asking the time, because the old man removed a chained pocket watch from his waistcoat pocket. In a combined movement, the Russian snatched the watch and plunged a long-bladed knife into the German's chest. The old man staggered and fell backwards into the ditch. When we drew up, his feet were in the air and his trouser legs slipped down, showing two thin white calves.

The Russian had pulled out the knife and was calmly wiping the blood from the blade on the old man's coat when I rammed the muzzle of my revolver into his ribs. When the Russian was standing on the road with his hands in the air, I gave the revolver to Patrick whilst I jumped down into the ditch to help the victim. The old man was dead. The Russian, an inarticulate brute, looked down at me kneeling by the body without a trace of emotion or remorse.

I took possession of the knife and watch, then pushed him into the back of the truck and sat facing him with the revolver. We went to the Military Government Office to hand him over to Captain Grubb, but he was out. We took the prisoner to the Kaserne, so he could be dealt with in accordance with Soviet law.

I flung the prisoner into the Leaders' Room by the scruff of the neck, and accused him of murder, producing the knife and watch. One of the Leaders, who identified himself as the Administrator (the Russian word is the same as in English), came forward.

'You say this man killed a German?' he asked with a smile. I showed him the murder weapon. He moved across to a colleague and removed a red star badge from his cap, then pinned it on the murderer's breast and

kissed him on the cheek! The murderer of the old man, wearing his deco-
ration, slipped out of the room and lost himself among the hundreds in
the barracks. I never set eyes on him again.[25]

The Military Control of DPs

In an effort to bring an end to this anarchy, the Allied military governments in each of the zones of Germany were forced to introduce radical
measures. The first thing they did was to round up as many of the newly
freed prisoners and labourers as they could, and put them back under
lock and key – an act that caused anger and consternation amongst
many of those whose only wish was to make their way home to their
own countries. A strict curfew was announced, which in some areas was
as early as 6 p.m., and anyone found leaving their camp at night was
liable to be arrested or even shot. The threat of violence was often the
only way to impose order. For example, when Major A. G. Moon took
control of the military government in Buxtehude he immediately
informed the population of the local DP centres that anyone caught
looting would be shot. As a consequence there was very little trouble in
this area.[26] Later, in August, the British military government in north-
west Germany made the shooting of looters official policy.[27] The
American military government in Hesse also warned that anyone caught
rioting over food shortages would be subject to the death penalty.[28]
There is little difference between announcements like this and those
made by the Nazis themselves, and indeed it was perhaps the semblance
of continuity between the two systems of control which made the
announcement so effective.[29]

Since it was obvious that the threat to law and order would remain so
long as the foreign prisoners were still in Germany, the Allies set about
repatriating DPs as fast as they were able. There was much debate over
who should be given priority. British and American POWs and members
of resistance organizations had a valid claim for special treatment. This
had to be weighed against the impatience of the Soviet authorities to
have their citizens returned to them, especially since there were still
thousands of liberated Allied prisoners being held behind Soviet lines.
Others argued that the most unruly elements should be sent home first,
in order to re-establish law and order. The logistical difficulties of

transporting these people through Europe's destroyed rail networks were compounded by the fact that many of the DPs themselves did not actually want to be repatriated. Many of the Jews, Poles and Balts now regarded themselves as stateless, and therefore as having no home to go to. Other groups, particularly Russians, Ukrainians and Yugoslavs, did not wish to be repatriated because they feared what punishments they might be subjected to once they got home. Many of these people had endured unimaginable hardships, and despite the end of the war appeared to have little to look forward to.

While they waited to be repatriated, DPs were transported to large assembly centres, and funnelled off in their different national groups to DP camps throughout Germany, Austria and Italy. These tended to be either former military barracks or sectioned-off areas of towns. Some of them were specially constructed to house DPs; but others were former labour camps or even concentration camps. In a continent where shelter was in desperately short supply the Allies had to make use of whatever buildings they could find. It was with some dismay that many ex-prisoners found themselves being deloused, shaven and put back into the very concentration camps from which they had so recently escaped.[30]

It is clear from the official reports of the time, as well as the many memoirs and diaries written by ordinary soldiers, that the Allied authorities were far more wary of DPs than they were of the Germans. Over the coming months they began to fear the resentment and desperation of people who, far from being liberated, continued to live in exile, under guard and under military rule. In August the British began to enlist policemen from amongst the Polish DPs to keep their countrymen in order, on the grounds that there were not enough Allied soldiers to control them, and that German police would not be respected.[31] By November both the British and the Americans were considering rearming the German police in areas 'where displaced persons activities have been a menace'.[32] A Joint Intelligence Committee report on possible dangers to the Allies in the coming winter spelled out Allied fears in plain terms: 'If the harder conditions of winter affect the living conditions of the DPs, they are likely to cause more trouble than the Germans as they are banded together in camps and may, unlike the Germans, have access to arms in some quantity.'[33]

There is perhaps an element of alarmism in reports like this. The director of UNRRA in western Germany certainly believed that 'the displaced persons under UNRRA administration are [not] more notable

4. Displaced Persons camps in Germany, Austria and Northern Italy

N

Baltic Sea

North Sea

HOLLAND

POLAND

Flensburg
Eckernförde
Rendsburg ● Kiel
● Itzehoe ● Lübeck
Pinneberg ●
● Emden
● Bremen
BRITISH ● Bergen-Belsen
ZONE
● Meppen
Lingen ● Hanover ● Peine ● Düppel
Gronau ● Minden ● ● Mariendorf
Greven ● Hameln ● Hildesheim ● Braunschweig
● Bocholt ● Detmold SOVIET
Gladbeck ● Lippstadt ● Paderborn ● Goslar ZONE
Mülheim ● Bochum ● Göttingen
● Düsseldorf Hann-Münden ●
Remscheid ● Zigenhain ● Eschwege
Mönchengladbach ● Trutzhain ● Cornberg
● Aachen ● Bad Hersfeld

G E R M A N Y

Wetzlar ●
● Altenstadt ● Wildflecken
Frankfurt-Zeilsheim ●
LUX. ● Babenhausen ● Aschaffenburg ● Schauenstein
FRENCH ● Bensheim ● Lindenfels ● Bamberg ● Bayreuth
ZONE ● Lampertheim Bad ● ● Hersbruck CZECHOSLOVAKIA
Mergentheim ● ● Amberg
● Ansbach ● Fürth
● Heilbronn
● Dinkelsbühl Deggendorf ●
Stuttgart ● AMERICAN
● Heidenheim ZONE Pocking ●
FRANCE ● Leipheim ● Kloster Indersdorf ● Linz-Bindenmichel
FRENCH Augsburg ● ● Braunau- ● Ried im Innkreis
ZONE ● Landsberg ● Munich am-Inn ● Asten
Bad Wörishofen ● ● Gabersee ● Ebensee AUSTRIA
● Bad Aibling ● Ainring ● Salzburg
Mittenwald ● Bad Reichenhall ● Trofaiach
● Mauning ● Fohrenwald ● Hallein ● Kapfenberg
Innsbruck ● Saalfelden ● Admont
● Judenburg
SWITZERLAND ● Bad Gastein
● Lienz-Peggetz ● Leibnitz
● Klagenfurt

YUGOSLAVIA

● Adriatica
Rivoli ●
● ● Turin ● Cremona
Grugliasco ● Carbonara
ITALY
● Praglia
● Reggio Emilia ● Modena
Bologna ● ● Imola
Adriatic Sea
Forlì ● ● Rimini
Ligurian Sea ● Riccione
● Senigallia
● Jesi
0 ● Livorno
100 miles
0 ● Fermo
100 km

for riotous behaviour than other sections of the populace'.[34] There is a huge amount of anecdotal evidence that DPs were frequently blamed for instances of looting that were in fact carried out by the Germans themselves,[35] and official reports indeed show that crime levels remained high long after the majority of DPs had been sent home.[36] In the words of one military government officer, 'DPs were outcasts . . . All and every trouble was put down to DPs.'[37] Now that the war was over, DPs were in danger of becoming characterized as the new enemy.

The 'Liberation Complex'

Given the situation the DPs found themselves in after their liberation, it is hardly surprising that their initial euphoria soon gave way to disillusionment. One of the first people to observe large groups of DPs in Germany was Marta Korwin, a Polish social worker who followed a British military government team into Bocholt in April 1945. According to conversations and assessments she made at the time, many of these people had survived the war by

> counterbalancing the reality that was always extremely hard, and often sordid and horrible, by calling up daydreams of their past life, until they were almost certain that, the moment they were liberated, they would find themselves in the same happy, beautiful world they knew before the war. All their past difficulties would be forgotten, freedom would take them back to a world where nothing had ever gone wrong . . . a paradise in which all people were good . . . and all homes beautiful.

But instead of returning to this 'paradise' they found themselves 'being herded into camps in which, in many cases . . . they found themselves in worse conditions than before their liberation'. Worse still, long periods of inactivity gave them the chance to reflect on the fact that the paradise they had dreamed of no longer existed: in the ruins that surrounded them they saw only 'their hopes for a better future destroyed'.[38]

Marta Korwin's observations were backed up by larger-scale studies conducted by international agencies. In June 1945 an Inter-Allied Psychological Study Group, under the supervision of UNRRA, produced a report on the DPs' state of mind. Far from being glad to be free, the report noted, many DPs were merely bitter and touchy. The gratitude that many Allied soldiers expected was also absent: instead there was an 'increased restlessness', 'complete apathy', 'loss of initiative' and 'a great and sullen suspicion . . . towards all authority'. Indeed, many DPs had become so cynical that 'nothing that is done even by helpful people is regarded as genuine or sincere'. Such attitudes were what some Allied officers began to call the 'Liberation Complex'.[39]

The Allied armies were not exactly blameless in the creation of this complex. Despite the huge strides that British and American military personnel had made in relief work over the previous two years, most army officers still tended to regard DPs more as a logistical than a humanitarian problem. They saw huge numbers of people who needed to be registered, deloused, clothed, fed, categorized into their various nationalities, put to useful work and eventually repatriated. By 1945, all the Allied armies were extremely efficient at doing exactly this sort of work. What they were not good at, however, was what we would now call 'people skills'. In their efforts to process DPs through the system, they often forgot that they were dealing with traumatized human beings.

Humanitarian workers were often dismayed by the insensitivity that military personnel displayed towards DPs. One British employee of UNRRA lost her temper when an American lieutenant ordered a large group of women and children to be moved without any notice whatsoever. 'I hate the army,' she found herself shouting at him. 'Why don't you go and fight someone? Why do you meddle with civilians, with peaceable human beings? They are counters to you – you think you can move mothers and babies and sick people as you move companies and batteries in the war. Why don't you stick to something you understand?'[40]

When DPs were weary or apathetic, the military invariably fell back on an inflexible and heavy-handed authoritarianism to try and goad them into action. In response to the squalid conditions at the Jewish DP camp at Landsberg, for example, one American officer suggested that hygiene rules and regulations should be enforced 'by coercive or disciplinary action'.[41] Such officers did not seem to comprehend that military discipline, while suitable for knocking army recruits into shape, was hardly appropriate for Holocaust survivors recovering from years of dehumanization and abuse.

Similarly, after a series of snap inspections of the Polish DP camp at Wildflecken in September 1945, American generals ordered that the

camp be subject to military discipline. Henceforth any DP caught dropping litter in the streets, hanging washing between trees, or concealing
rubbish in basement corners should be subject to immediate imprisonment. Any Pole who refused to work was to be arrested, and every
woman in the camp was to be given an immediate examination for
venereal disease. The democratically elected Polish camp committee
should be disbanded, and the repatriation of 1,500 Poles each fortnight
– by force, if necessary – should commence immediately.[42]

Needless to say, such edicts were greeted with great bitterness: after
years of similar treatment at the hands of the Nazis, the last thing these
DPs wanted was more of the same. 'The Army's talent for relief work,'
remarked one of the directors of the Wildflecken camp wryly, 'could
hardly be called top flight.'[43]

Relief and Rehabilitation

The Allied governments recognized very early on that military organizations were not best suited to this sort of work. It was for this reason that
the day-to-day care of DPs was taken out of military hands and passed
on to a new international humanitarian agency – the United Nations
Relief and Rehabilitation Administration, or UNRRA. This agency had
been set up in 1943 to coordinate the distribution of food and medical
aid throughout most of liberated Europe. At first its operations were
confined to the Balkans, but by the spring of 1945 it was beginning to
expand into much of the rest of Europe, particularly in the east. One of
its most important responsibilities was the coordination of welfare
amongst refugees and displaced persons throughout the continent.

Between 1945 and 1947 UNRRA tended to the needs of millions of
displaced persons in camps across Germany, Austria and Italy. These
needs were not only physical, but spiritual, social and emotional. Central to the UNRRA ethos was the idea that DPs should be given not only
food, shelter and medical attention, but also opportunities for counsel-
ling, education, recreation and even political activity. This was not
merely an exercise in redirecting their energies towards constructive
ends: it was hoped that such activities would rebuild them as people, by
giving them a renewed sense of self-worth.

UNRRA staff embraced this programme of 'helping others to help themselves' with wholehearted enthusiasm.[44] Almost the first thing that was set up in most DP camps was a school. This not only provided children with the education they had been deprived of, but also gave them a sense of structure and normality, sometimes for the first time in years. According to an American army report in April 1946 attendance rates at DP schools were as high as 90 per cent. Scouting groups and youth clubs also were enormously popular, since they removed children from the unhealthy, aggressive and immoral atmosphere that pervaded in some of the camps.[45]

DPs were encouraged to set up their own churches and religious groups in an attempt to dampen down some of the worst excesses, and also to provide the demoralized men and women with some much-needed spiritual succour. Officials went to great lengths to secure newsprint so that DPs could produce their own newspapers, which UNRRA made a point of leaving uncensored. Cultural activities such as concerts and plays were also encouraged, as was adult education of every kind. DPs created their own apprenticeship schemes, and even started a DP university in Munich.[46]

From the very beginning both the Allied military and UNRRA tried to encourage self-government in the DP camps. Elections were held in most camps, and DPs also set up their own courts and police forces to deal with unruly elements. Such camp institutions were not always wholly trustworthy. In the Polish camp at Wildflecken, for example, UNRRA staff noted the irony of seeing camp councillors make 'impassioned speeches which promised suppression of Black Market, of schnapps stills, of cattle-rustling and hen-house marauding', even while they sat around a table laden with roast beef, chicken and brandy bottles.[47] There was also a worrying trend in some camps of the formation of extremist, and especially nationalist, political groups. But, as camp staff realized, the control of criminal and extremist behaviour was always likely to be a losing battle. What was important was to give DPs something that they had been lacking throughout their ordeal: a sense of direction and self-worth.

Unfortunately UNRRA's generosity was wide open to abuse. DPs often used UNRRA supplies to turn their camps into centres of black-market activity. At the Wildflecken camp the entire Polish police force had to be dismissed and replaced because of corruption – not once, but five times in the first eighteen months.[48] Theft, extortion, illegal distillation of alcohol were so widespread that people began to joke that UNRRA's acronym stood for 'You Never Really Rehabilitate Anyone'.[49]

It was for reasons like this that the agency began to get a reputation as an organization of incompetent do-gooders. Critics appeared at the very highest levels. The British military governor in Germany, Field Marshal Bernard Montgomery, believed from the start that UNRRA was 'quite unable' to do the job, and was only convinced to hand over responsibility for DPs because his government could no longer afford to finance relief work by the British army. American politicians, resentful of the fact that they were providing almost three-quarters of UNRRA's budget, were incensed by the organization's wastefulness, financial mismanagement and corruption. Some even accused it of being 'an international racket', whose main purpose was not the relief of DPs but the 'sustenance of armies or political groups' such as the Communists.[50]

And yet, for all its failings, UNRRA is often remembered with fierce affection by the DPs themselves. UNRRA workers were usually the first non-violent foreigners these people encountered, and they provided the one thing that many DPs craved above all else: compassion. The organization understood, perhaps in a way that the military did not, that kindness and empathy were sometimes also an effective way to prevent former forced labourers from taking their revenge.

The people who understood this most instinctively were probably the children, many of whom were given their first taste of a brighter future in UNRRA's DP camps. In a continent where many children were afraid of men in uniform, the reaction of one French child on seeing an UNRRA uniform speaks volumes. Yvette Rubin was a thirteen-year-old Jewish girl who had been deported to Germany in 1942. After witnessing many horrors, including the brutal murder of her mother, she returned to Paris three years later. Back home, she recounted her terrible story to her family, but her eyes only lit up when she suddenly noticed the clothing her uncle was wearing:

> *Tonton*, you are not a soldier. You are UNRRA. I know them. I was with them for more than two weeks after I was liberated by the British armies. They are wonderful. They have saved my life. They saved me from typhus, which I was still sick with. They fed me and gave me this dress I am now wearing . . . I love them so much. They were the first people to be nice to me.[51]

The Issue of Personal Power

It is difficult to know how best to characterize the behaviour of former forced labourers in Germany after the war. To a degree, their conduct was merely an extreme form of the same lawlessness that was sweeping the whole of the continent. However, their motivations were not merely criminal. After years of pent-up frustration, they saw violence, drunkenness and sexual licence as a legitimate and long-overdue form of self-expression. There was also a strong element of anger in their actions. Many believed that a certain amount of looting and even violence was justified as a way to put right what had been done to them. They were thirsty for what they saw as collective retribution, but what might more accurately be described as revenge.

All of these motivations were tangled up in a chaos of conflicting emotions that even the DPs themselves did not properly understand. The genius of humanitarian organizations like UNRRA was to recognize that what much of it boiled down to was an issue of personal power. During their wartime ordeal many forced labourers had been abused and dehumanized: they had had every aspect of their lives brutally regulated, sometimes for years. Having been denied *any* form of power for so long, at liberation the pendulum had swung the other way: for a brief time they were not only free, but allowed to act with utter impunity. If they lost control of themselves at this time it was often simply because they *could*, and the new-found sense of power was intoxicating. In the words of UNRRA's psychological report, 'the brakes have been taken off'.[52]

While some military agencies sought to curb this violent energy by reintroducing harsh constraints, UNRRA officials wanted to return these people to some sort of equilibrium. Their policy of giving DPs a measure of control over their own lives was undoubtedly the more enlightened approach: given unlimited time, and an unlimited budget, it was far more likely to rehabilitate individuals than mere discipline. But in the chaotic conditions of the war's aftermath it was also hopelessly idealistic. Camp populations were often too transient to see any benefits from such a programme, individuals too traumatized and UNRRA staff too overstretched. In too many cases, particularly in the early days after the war, returning power to DPs simply increased their opportunities for revenge. As a consequence, UNRRA staff were obliged to walk a difficult line between granting DPs responsibility and keeping them in check.

If, after the initial days of the liberation were over, vengeance by former slave labourers did not occur on a large scale, this is largely because DPs in Germany never found themselves in a position of real power. Had they been put in charge of camps in which the Germans had become prisoners – as occurred elsewhere in Europe – the situation might have been different.

As it was, the only people to achieve real domination in Germany – indeed, whose power in some circumstances could be said to be *absolute* – were the Allied military. The occupying armies had far greater opportunities for revenge in the aftermath of the war than DPs ever did.

How Allied soldiers and their leaders reacted to these opportunities has been the subject of controversy ever since.

German Prisoners of War

In wartime the worst atrocities do not generally occur in battle, but after the battle is over. A soldier might be able to avenge his fallen comrades by fighting ferociously, but he is in a much better position to do so once his enemy is defeated, disarmed and at his mercy. It is when a soldier finds himself in charge of prisoners of war that he is at his most powerful, and his enemy is at his most impotent.

It was to prevent the abuse of this power differential that the international community drew up the Third Geneva Convention in 1929. The convention not only forbade the violent or humiliating treatment of prisoners of war, but stipulated the conditions under which they should be housed, fed and cared for. During the Second World War, however, these rules were flouted with such regularity by all sides that they very soon became a nonsense. The German army executed, degraded and starved their prisoners of war, particularly on the eastern front – and when the tables turned, it is not surprising that there was a desire to treat captured Germans in much the same way.

In his multi-volume history of the conflict, Winston Churchill told a story that demonstrates the prevailing attitude towards prisoners of war at the time, which reveals a tendency to vengeance even at the very highest levels. The episode occurred at the first conference of the 'Big Three' in Tehran at the end of 1943. Churchill was having dinner with Stalin and Roosevelt on the second day of the conference when Stalin proposed a toast to the liquidation of 'at least 50,000, and perhaps 100,000, of the German Command Staff'. Churchill, who knew all about the mass shootings of Polish officers at Katyn at the beginning of the war, was disgusted by this remark, and stated baldly that the British people would never tolerate mass executions. When Stalin still insisted that

50,000 'must be shot', Churchill could stand it no longer. 'I would rather be taken out into the garden here and now and be shot myself,' he said, 'than sully my own and my country's honour by such infamy.'

In an ill-judged attempt to lighten the tone, Roosevelt interjected at this point with a suggestion that they compromise on a smaller number to be shot, say, 49,000. It appears he meant this as a joke, but given what he also knew about Stalin's past it was in very poor taste. Churchill was unable to make a reply before Roosevelt's son Elliott, who was also present at the dinner, added his twopenn'orth. 'Look,' he said to Stalin, 'when our armies start rolling in from the West, and your armies are still coming on from the east, we'll be solving the whole thing, won't we? Russian, American and British soldiers will settle the issue for most of those fifty thousand in bat-tle, and I hope not only those fifty thousand war criminals will be taken care of but many hundreds of thousands more Nazis as well.'

At this, Stalin rose to his feet, embraced Elliott and clinked glasses with him. Churchill was dismayed. 'Much as I love you, Elliott,' he said, 'I cannot forgive you for making such a dastardly statement. How dare you say such a thing!' He got up and stormed out of the room, leaving Stalin and his Foreign Minister, Vyacheslav Molotov, to hurry after him with claims that he was taking things too seriously – they had all only been 'playing'.[1]

This anecdote has been repeated by many historians, and has been interpreted variously as proof of Stalin's ruthlessness, a demonstration of Roosevelt's naivety and an illustration of Churchill's growing power-lessness in the shadow of the other two.[2] It is certainly President Roosevelt's comments that are the most revealing, since they are the most unexpected. He does seem to have been taken with the idea of executing 50,000 German prisoners, since it was virtually the first thing he mentioned when the three men met again at their second conference, in Yalta just over a year later.[3] If one takes Roosevelt's comments at face value, and factor in the President's well-known anti-German prejudice, then he begins to appear every bit as ruthless as Stalin.

The treatment of German prisoners of war in 1945 has always been controversial because it calls into question the very values that the Allies claimed to be fighting for. What Stalin, Roosevelt and Churchill were discussing was the necessary flip side of the liberation: a process in which millions of Europeans would not be set free, but incarcerated;

and many thousands not saved, but led to their deaths. Churchill, who always had an eye for posterity, understood that this was not a subject to be taken lightly. It was one thing for released slaves to be seen pursuing vengeance, but quite another for powerful world leaders.

In the aftermath of the war, the fate of German prisoners rested entirely on the whims of their captors. Whether their helplessness invited pity, contempt or merely indifference was not just a matter of luck – it would depend on the prevailing attitudes that existed in the different Allied armies, at every level of command.

American-held Prisoners of War

During the course of the war more than 11 million German soldiers were taken prisoner by the Allies. Given the vast scale of the battles that took place on the Russian front, one would expect the most prisoners to have been taken by the Soviets, but in fact under a third of the total – only about 3,155,000 – were captured by the Red Army. More prisoners were taken by the Americans (some 3.8 million) and by the British (3.7 million). Even the French managed to capture almost a quarter of a million men despite only being involved in the business of taking prisoners for less than a year and having a comparatively tiny army.[4]

This disparity in numbers says less about the relative prowess of the Soviets than it does about the German fear of them. In the final days of the war German soldiers did whatever they could to avoid being taken prisoner by the Red Army. Many units continued fighting long after it was sensible to surrender simply because they were afraid of what might happen to them if they fell into Soviet hands; others did their best to disentangle themselves from the eastern front so that they might be able to give themselves up to the British or Americans instead. In the run-up to the capitulation this became a priority at all levels of the German army: when the German Chief of Staff, General Alfred August Jodl, arrived at Eisenhower's headquarters to sign the capitulation agreement he deliberately stalled for two days in order to give German troops as much time as possible to fight their way westwards.[5] In Yugoslavia, Germans and Croatians defied orders to surrender on 8 May and continued fighting their way towards the Austrian border for another whole week.[6] Thus, while there was an explosion in the numbers of soldiers surrendering to the Western Allies at the very end of the war – the Americans took some 1.8 million men in April and May 1945 alone – there was no corresponding increase in the east.[7]

The sheer number of German soldiers giving themselves up to the Western Allies seems to have taken the British and Americans by surprise. As a temporary measure they corralled these prisoners into sixteen vast enclosures just inside western Germany, collectively known as the *Rheinwiesenlager* ('Rhine meadow camps'). Most of these camps were capable of holding 100,000 men, but by the time of the capitulation many of them were forced to take significantly more. For example, over 118,000 prisoners were crammed into the enclosure at Sinzig, and the number at Remagen quickly exceeded 134,000. Some of the smaller camps were even more overcrowded. Böhl, for example, had a capacity of 10,000 but was housing more than three times that number.[8] It soon became obvious that the Allies were struggling to cope, and a flurry of memos passed between Allied commanders requesting the urgent supply of extra resources.[9]

Contemporary photographs and eyewitness reports gathered by academics and German government agencies after the war give an idea of the kinds of conditions these prisoners were subjected to.[10] The camps were not 'camps' in the traditional sense, because they contained few if any tents or huts: they were simply areas of countryside enclosed within a barbed-wire cordon. Prisoners had no shelter, and were subjected to the elements all day and every day. 'I usually lie on the ground,' wrote one prisoner, who kept a diary written on toilet paper during his time at the vast Rheinberg enclosure.

> During the heat I crawl into a hollow in the ground. I wear a coat and boots, with my forage-cap pulled down over my ears; my field bag, in which I have a silver spoon and fork, serves as my pillow. During a thunderstorm one wall of my hollow falls in on me. My coat and socks are wet through and through . . . How long will we have to be without shelter, without blankets or tents? Every German soldier once had shelter from the weather. Even a dog has a doghouse to crawl into when it rains. Our only wish is finally after six weeks to get a roof over our heads. Even a savage is better housed.[11]

The lack of shelter was compounded by a lack of blankets or proper clothing. Prisoners wore only what they had been wearing when captured, and in most cases had been separated from their standard army equipment. What they had left was 'often beyond primitive. No coats, no caps, no jackets, in many cases only civil clothes and street shoes.' In Heidesheim there were children of fourteen who had nothing to wear but their pyjamas. They had been arrested during the night as potential 'Werewolves' – the term used for fanatical last-ditch resisters – and taken straight to the camp in their nightclothes.[12]

If the lack of clothing and shelter was dire, then so was the lack of hygiene. Prisoners had nowhere to wash, and only an insufficient number of earth pits to use as toilets. According to those imprisoned at Rheinberg the camp 'was nothing but a giant sewer, where each man just shat where he stood'. Parts of the camp at Bad Kreuznach were 'literally a sea of urine', in which soldiers were forced to sleep. Toilet paper was in such short supply that prisoners often used German banknotes instead, an act that caused few prisoners any consternation, since there were already rumours that German currency was to be taken out of circulation anyway.[13]

One of their greatest concerns was the lack of food. The huge concentration of prisoners meant that when the camp in Remagen was first opened daily rations were just a single loaf of bread between twenty-five men. This later rose to a loaf between ten, but it was still not enough to sustain life. In Bad Kreuznach there was no bread for six weeks, so that when it finally arrived it caused a sensation. Until then, the daily ration consisted of 'three spoonfuls of vegetables, one spoon of fish, one or two prunes, one spoonful of marmalade and four to six biscuits'. In Bad Hersfeld the prisoners survived on only 800 calories per day, until a fifth of them became 'skeletons'. To supplement their meagre diet prisoners were forced to forage for whatever edible weeds they could find growing in the camp, and reports of men cooking soups out of stinging nettles and dandelions over tiny camp fires are common. Many dug through the earth with tins in search of turnips, which they would then eat raw, leading to an outbreak of dysentery.[14]

The lack of water was an even greater problem. 'For three and a half days we had no water at all,' claimed George Weiss, a tank repairman.

We would drink our own urine. It tasted terrible, but what could we do? Some men got down on the ground and licked the ground to get some moisture. I was so weak I was already on my knees, when finally we got a little water to drink. I think I would have died without that water. But the Rhine was just outside the wire.[15]

At Bad Kreuznach there was only a single water tap for more than 56,000 men, and water had to be delivered to the perimeter fence each day by truck. In Büderich the five taps that served over 75,000 prisoners were turned on for only an hour each evening. When the American commander of the camp was asked why the prisoners were suffering such inhumane conditions, he allegedly answered: 'So that they will lose their joy of soldiering once and for all.'[16]

It is unsurprising that such camps had a high mortality rate, especially amongst men already wounded and exhausted by battle. But exactly *how* high has been a subject of debate ever since. In his controversial book *Other Losses* James Bacque suggested that Roosevelt's tasteless jokes about killing Germans were symptomatic of a culture of revenge throughout the US administration. He claimed that 800,000 German prisoners died in US captivity – a number that would put American vengeance on a par with some of the worst Soviet and Nazi atrocities of the war. This absurdly high figure has since been comprehensively discredited by academics in several countries, as have many of Bacque's other claims.[17] The official figure is more than 160 times smaller: according to the German government commission chaired by Erich Maschke, just 4,537 are supposed to have died in the *Rheinwiesenlager*.[18] Other academics entertain the possibility that the true number of deaths *might* have been substantially higher, especially when one takes into account the chaos of the time, which was never conducive to accurate record-keeping. But it is generally agreed that the figure cannot have exceeded 50–60,000 at the very outside.[19]

This does not mean to say that losses on the scale that Bacque suggests did not happen, only that Bacque was attributing them to the wrong theatre. The true horror, as usual, occurred not in the west but in the east.

Soviet-held Prisoners of War

If conditions for prisoners of the Western Allies were bad, those experienced by prisoners in the east were atrocious – so atrocious, in fact, that the comparison is hardly worth making. Everything that POWs experienced in the *Rheinwiesenlager* also happened in Soviet prison camps, but on a greater scale and for longer periods of time. In addition, German prisoners were usually force-marched to their places of captivity. These 'death-marches' often lasted for a week or more, during which time the prisoners were regularly denied food and water.

Of the 3 million prisoners taken by the Soviets during the war, more than a third died in captivity. In Yugoslavia the situation was proportionally even worse: around 80,000 prisoners of war were executed, starved, denied medical care or force-marched to their deaths – that is about two prisoners in every five. Such figures would have been inconceivable in the west. A glance at Table 1 on page 122 confirms that German soldiers were right to be so wary of capture by the Red Army or their associated partisans. Prisoners taken in the east were ninety times more likely to die than those taken in the west.

There are numerous reasons why the death toll amongst prisoners of war in the east was so high. To begin with, resources were far scarcer: the Soviets and their allies had relied heavily on the western powers to supply them with food and materials throughout the war, and it was to be expected that they should use these scarce supplies for their own people, and specifically their army, before getting round to feeding prisoners on the scraps that were left over. Transport and infrastructure were far more heavily damaged in the east than in the west, and the distances that had to be walked were far greater: tens of thousands of Axis prisoners died on forced marches across the vast Soviet and eastern European landscape. When one considers how bitter the Russian winters could be, it is unsurprising that more prisoners died from exposure in Soviet camps than in Western ones. But all of this is skating around the main issue. The principal reason why so many German prisoners died in Soviet captivity was because virtually no one who looked after them cared whether they lived or died.

Absolute hatred of Germany, and of Germans, was endemic in Soviet society during the war. Up until the spring of 1945 Soviet soldiers had been subjected to the most strident hate propaganda, which demonized Germans and Germany in every possible way. The Soviet army newspaper *Krasnaya Zvezda* carried poems by Alexei Surkov with titles like 'I Hate', whose last line claimed 'I want to strangle every one of them.'[20] *Pravda* printed poems by Konstantin Simonov such as 'Kill Him!', published on the day that Voroshilovgrad fell, which exhorted Russian soldiers to

> ... kill a German, kill him soon –
> And every time you see one, kill him.[21]

Other writers such as Mikhail Sholokhov and Vasily Grossman also wrote vitriolic stories and reports which were designed to increase Soviet hatred for all things German. But it was Ilya Ehrenburg who occupied a special place in the hearts of the Soviet soldiers. Ehrenburg's inflammatory chants in *Krasnaya Zvezda* were printed and repeated so often that most soldiers knew them by heart.

> The Germans are not human beings. From now on the word 'German' is for us the worst imaginable curse. From now on the word 'German' strikes us to the quick. We shall not get excited. We shall kill. If you have not killed at least one German a day, you have wasted that day . . . If you cannot kill your German with a bullet, kill him with your bayonet. If there is calm on your part of the front, or if you are waiting for the fighting, kill a German in the meantime . . . If you kill one German, kill another – there is nothing more joyful than a heap of German corpses.[22]

The dehumanization of Germans was a constant theme of Ehrenburg's writings. As early as the summer of 1942 he claimed,

> One can bear anything: the plague, and hunger and death. But one cannot bear the Germans . . . We cannot live as long as these grey-green slugs are alive. Today there are no books; today there are no stars in the sky; today there is only one thought: kill the Germans. Kill them all and dig them into the earth.[23]

These 'grey-green slugs' were at other times portrayed as scorpions, plague-carrying rats, rabid dogs and even bacteria.[24] Just as Nazi propaganda had dehumanized the Slavs as *Untermenschen*, so had Soviet propaganda reduced all Germans to vermin.[25]

The bloodthirsty tone of such writings was not markedly different from some of those propagated in other countries, such as Philippe Viannay's exhortation to kill Germans, collaborators and policemen in occupied France.[26] But unlike the majority of Frenchmen, the Soviets possessed the capability to put their words into action on a vast scale. It has often been pointed out that such propaganda was a major cause of the 'orgy of extermination' that took place once the Red Army reached German soil.[27] But it also contributed greatly to the treatment of German soldiers captured during battle. Since the Germans had shown so little humanity towards their own prisoners, many Russians felt they had the right to repay them in kind. Countless Germans were shot while or after surrendering, despite orders to the contrary, and countless more were killed by drunken Red Army soldiers who saw revenge as part of their victory celebrations. Occasionally Soviet soldiers took pot shots at the columns of German prisoners for fun – just as the Germans had done to Soviet prisoners in 1941.[28] In Yugoslavia too, German prisoners were shot for the slightest misdemeanours, for their clothes and equipment, for revenge, or just for sport.[29]

We should remember that it was not only German soldiers who paid this price, although German prisoners were certainly the most numerous. Seventy thousand Italians were also taken prisoner by the Red Army, many of whom never returned.[30] More than 309,000 Romanian soldiers went missing on the eastern front, though how many survived long enough to become prisoners is still not known.[31] Nor were all the prisoners fighting men – indeed, it is often impossible to separate civilians and soldiers in the official statistics. In the aftermath of the war at least 600,000 Hungarians, civilians and soldiers alike, were scooped up by the Red Army for no better reason than that they were of the wrong nationality, and were sent to labour camps across the Soviet Union.[32]

The indignities endured by these hapless prisoners were every bit as bad as those experienced by forced labourers in Nazi Germany. The first thing that happened to them was that they were robbed. Watches, wedding rings and other valuables were most highly prized by Soviet soldiers, but successive groups of looters also took their military kit and even their clothes. 'Woe betide anyone who wore riding boots,' wrote Zoltan Toth, a Hungarian doctor who was captured after the fall of Budapest in February 1945. 'If the Russians spotted a prisoner with usable boots, they took him out of the line, put a bullet through his head and pulled off his boots.'[33]

The looting of their few belongings signalled the beginning of a period of deprivation that would kill a third of them. Moreover, this deprivation was often deliberate. If prisoners of the Americans did not receive proper rations, this was usually only because of a failure of supply. Prisoners of the Soviets, by contrast, were often purposely denied food and water, first by the troops who captured them, then by the guards who transported them and finally by the staff of the camps where they ended up. A perfect example of this is given by Hans Schuetz, a soldier who was captured in east Germany by the Soviets at the very end of the war. During his long march eastwards into captivity many of the local people turned out with boxes of sandwiches or pitchers of milk. 'However, the guards gave strict instructions not to touch anything. They shot into the pots and cans and into the sandwich piles. The milk and water soaked into the ground and the sandwiches burst into the air and fell into the dirt. We did not dare touch anything.'[34]

If the prisoners of the Americans had to queue for their water, prisoners of the Soviets occasionally had to steal it, or in winter make do with eating snow.[35] While the Americans were unable to supply enough medicines to deal with outbreaks of sickness, Soviet doctors sometimes denied what medicines they had to prisoners, and, according to some, even used them as bargaining tools for extortion.[36] No one in American camps was reduced to eating stray dogs and cats, as they were in Soviet gulags, or to using their bread as bait to catch rats for food.[37] The starvation diet in Soviet camps was far worse than anything that prisoners of the Americans were forced to endure, and lasted not just days or weeks, but months. Zoltan Toth, who worked in a makeshift gulag medical centre in 1946, regularly saw bodies in the mortuary that had been cut open and their organs stolen – presumably to be eaten – just as they had been in Bergen-Belsen. When he reported this to the chief doctor his concerns were dismissed with the words, 'If you had seen what went on here a year ago . . .'[38]

Some lucky prisoners of war were sent home as early as 1947, but most remained in Soviet gulags until 1950, when Stalin issued an 'amnesty' for those Germans who had been 'good workers'.[39] Some of those who had not managed to keep out of trouble, however, had been redesignated as political prisoners, and were not released until Khrushchev granted further amnesties after Stalin's death in 1953. The last ones to return to Germany did so in 1957, some twelve years after the war was over. After years of working in remote Soviet mines, forests, railways, tanneries, collective farms and factories, many of them were broken men. Count Heinrich von Einsiedel later described the people he returned home with on one of the earliest transports. 'But the cargoes those trains carried! Starved, emaciated skeletons; human wrecks convulsed with dysentery due to lack of food: gaunt figures with trembling limbs, expressionless grey faces, and dim eyes which brightened up only at the sight of bread or a cigarette.' Einsiedel, once a devout Communist, found his faith well and truly shaken by the sight. Each of these prisoners, he said, was 'a living indictment of the Soviet Union, a death sentence to Communism'.[40]

The Cost of Bad History

The treatment of German prisoners of war was exponentially worse under the Soviets than it was under the Americans – a fact that is confirmed not only by the internationally accepted casualty figures but also by the testimonies of hundreds of former prisoners themselves. However, this has not deterred some writers from claiming otherwise. When James Bacque published *Other Losses* in 1989 he tried to convince the world that it was the Americans rather than the Russians who had presided over the deaths of hundreds of thousands of German prisoners. He placed responsibility for these supposed deaths firmly at the feet of the American leadership, whom he accused of pursuing a deliberate policy of revenge, and then concealing the 'truth' beneath layers of creative accounting. Bacque's claims not only called into question the strongly held American belief that they had fought a moral war, but effectively accused American leaders of crimes against humanity.

This was a classic conspiracy theory, and would not be worth mentioning were it not for the controversy the book caused when it was published. Academics from around the world queued up to rubbish Bacque's historical methods, his misrepresentation of documents, his dismissal of a vast body of methodical research, and above all his complete misunderstanding of statistics.[41] On the other hand some American veterans who had worked as prison guards after the war came to Bacque's defence. Conditions in their camps *were* abysmal, they pointed out, and a culture of neglect, even of passive revenge, did exist at many of them. Even Bacque's detractors were obliged to admit that such points were valid.

If an air of controversy still lingers around this subject, decades after it should have become one of history's footnotes, it is because there always has been a small seed of truth in Bacque's claims. Perhaps what Bacque should be most criticized for is not his misreading of the facts, but that he distracted attention away from the real story. This might not have been as sensational as the story that he wanted to find, but it is nevertheless shocking.

From the official figures drawn up by the Maschke Commission, set up by the German government in 1962 to investigate the fate of German prisoners of war, it appears that the American military government, as well as that of the French, does indeed have a case to answer. The loss rate in American camps, though not as high as in the Soviets', was still more than four times as bad as that in POW camps run by the British (see Table 1). Worse still were the camps run by the French, where, despite housing fewer than a third as many prisoners as the British camps, almost twenty times the number of deaths (24,178 in total) were recorded. We must remember that these are conservative figures: even the official historians concede that thousands of deaths probably went unrecorded.

Table 1: Deaths amongst prisoners of war[42]

Holding Country	POWs	No. of deaths	%
Britain*	3,635,000	1,254	<0.1
USA*	3,097,000	4,537	0.1
France*	937,000	24,178	2.6
USSR*	3,060,000	1,094,250	35.8
Yugoslavia	194,000	80,000	41.2
Poland	70,000	5,400	7.7
Czechoslovakia	25,000	1,250	5.0
Belgium, Holland, Lux	76,000	675	0.9
Totals	11,094,000	1,211,544	10.9

Note: *Figures include camps run in mainland Europe.

The high losses in French camps can at least be explained by the food crisis in France at the time. By the autumn of 1945 the supply situation was so bad that the International Committee of the Red Cross were warning of a possible 200,000 deaths amongst prisoners if the situation did not change. As a consequence a relief operation was launched: American supplies were diverted to French camps to raise the rations above starvation levels, and further disaster was averted.[43]

The discrepancy between British losses and American ones, however, is more difficult to explain. There is no reason the Americans should not have been able to supply their prisoners of war at least as well as the

British did – indeed, the Americans were easily the best supplied of all the Allied armies. Some have suggested that the Americans lost more prisoners because they were the ones in charge of the infamous *Rheinwiesenlager*, but it is not clear why these camps should have been substantially more difficult to supply than any of the others, and in any case some of them were turned over to British control shortly after the end of the war.[44] During the critical period in the war's immediate aftermath the Americans were in charge of more prisoners than the British, but not excessively so: 2.59 million, as opposed to 2.12 million. If one compares this to the relative sizes of the British and American armies, the British were actually responsible for proportionally more prisoners.[45]

The only substantial difference between the British and American figures is in the speed with which their prisoners were released. While the British had released more than 80 per cent by the autumn of 1945, the Americans held on to most of theirs through that winter.[46] The reason for this was that Roosevelt had insisted on trying German soldiers for war crimes all the way down to the lowest ranks: American-held prisoners therefore had to stay longer in the camps so that they could be screened.[47]

Perhaps here we have a clue as to why the Americans recorded higher losses amongst their prisoners than the British did. As I have already hinted, the official attitude towards Germans was always much harsher in America than it was in Britain. At the Tehran conference, while the British advocated the splitting of defeated Germany into three administrative regions, Roosevelt wanted to break up the country even further. 'Germany,' he said, 'was less dangerous to civilization when it was in 107 provinces.'[48] During the Anglo-American conference in Quebec in 1944, the US Treasury Secretary Henry Morgenthau put forward a plan to dismantle Germany's entire industrial infrastructure, effectively returning the country to the Middle Ages. While Roosevelt approved this plan, the British only went along with it under duress.[49] And while both nations agreed to use prisoners as forced labour long after the war was over – the British actually for rather longer than the Americans – it was only the Americans (and the French) who proposed using them for clearing minefields.[50]

Such policies were bound to result in a higher death rate, but for the most part they were never implemented: in the end, British and American policy towards prisoners was very similar. However, official attitudes can affect conditions just as much as official policies. A constant stream of bitter words from above can give the impression at the lower levels that harshness towards prisoners will not only be tolerated but encouraged. If a culture of active hostility is allowed to flourish then prisoners will end up being badly treated. In extreme circumstances this can lead to atrocity, but even in milder circumstances it can lead to unnecessary hardship for prisoners who might already be exhausted by defeat.

Whether there is any correlation between American attitudes towards German prisoners and their death rate is a moot point, and requires much more extensive research. The same applies to the French. If James Bacque had confined himself to investigating this, rather than inventing more elaborate theories, his book might have been rather better received by the academic community. But until such research is carried out it remains a very real possibility that when Roosevelt joked about killing prisoners of war, his words, however humorously meant, ended up having exactly that effect.

1. *Top* The ruins of Warsaw, January 1946: 'something . . . so vicious I can't believe it'. Poland's capital was just one of thousands of towns and cities devastated by the war.

2. *Bottom* The war created a catastrophic housing shortage throughout Europe. This woman and her children have set up home in a cave in Naples along with hundreds of others. The UNRRA poster on the panel behind her promises 'Food, health and hope'.

3. *Above* Former forced labourers return home after the war. The mixed feelings of these Greek men, as their transport ship approaches Piraeus, are evident in their faces.

4. *Right* The fate of sixty-year-old Filip Paluch was all too common after the war. On his return to Poland from a concentration camp he found his home gone, and his family all killed. He is pictured here on the road outside the village of Potworów, where he has been begging for food.

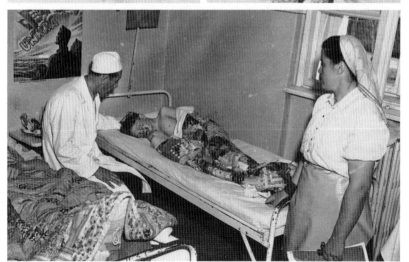

THE EFFECTS OF WAR ON EUROPE'S CHILDREN

5. *Top left* Bosnian partisan Bogdan Belaković, aged about ten. The last of an extended family of fifty-five, Bogdan was killed fighting in the final stages of the war.

6. *Top right* A survivor of the famine in Greece.

7. *Bottom* March 1946: Doctors in Yugoslavia tend to a nine-year-old boy. Four hours earlier the boy had been playing in a field near his home when a land mine exploded. He lost both arms and was blinded.

8. *Top left* The plight of women after the war: American sailors in Naples take advantage of impoverished local girls.

9. *Top right* Soviet soldiers molest a German woman in Leipzig, 1946.

10. *Bottom* In the aftermath of the war, no one in Germany could afford to be fussy about where he found shelter. UNRRA used this building in Heilbronn to house displaced persons.

11. Postwar Europe saw the almost complete breakdown of law and order. Here, freed slave labourers loot a German marshalling yard.

12. *Right* Revenge: the bodies of German men hanging from lamp-posts and trees in Roudnice nad Labem, a Czech town just a few miles from Theresienstadt concentration camp.

13. *Below* At Dachau, liberated prisoners taunt one of their former guards. In the background is the wall against which captured Germans were shot by American soldiers.

14. *Top* August 1944: a French collaborator receives a beating after the liberation of Rennes in Brittany.

15. *Bottom* Fascists summarily executed by partisans in Milan, April 1945. Around 15,000 Italian Fascists met a similar fate.

APPALLING CONDITIONS FOR GERMAN PRISONERS OF WAR

16. *Top* In this temporary enclosure at Remagen in the final week of the war, just a few hundred American soldiers guarded more than 100,000 captured Germans.

17. *Bottom* At Sinzig, after the war was over, German prisoners were still obliged to live in holes in the ground.

12

Vengeance Unrestrained: Eastern Europe

If vengeance is a function of power, then true vengeance is achieved only when the power relationship between perpetrator and victim is completely inverted. The victim must become the perpetrator. The powerless must become all-powerful; and the misery inflicted must in some way be equivalent to that suffered.

This did not happen on a large scale inside Germany, because the presence of the Allies prevented it. Released slave labourers could not preside over the enslavement of their former masters. Concentration camp survivors did not find themselves in charge of German prisoners. But there were other countries where such circumstances did indeed arise, at both an individual level and a communal one.

In Poland and Czechoslovakia especially, but also in Hungary, Romania, Yugoslavia, the Baltic States and even Russia, there were large and long-established populations of expatriate German speakers, collectively known as the Volksdeutsche. These people, who had received all kinds of privileges during the war, now found themselves the target of popular fury. They were forced to flee their homes, denied rations and humiliated in direct emulation of Nazi measures during the war. Hundreds of thousands were conscripted as slave labour in factories, coal mines and farms across the region, just as their former neighbours had been by the Nazis. The remainder were either sent to prison or herded into transit camps pending expulsion to Germany.

This chapter is about the millions of German-speaking civilians who refilled the prison camps, transit camps and concentration camps of Europe once they had been emptied of their wartime inmates. Some of these places have been compared with the most notorious Nazi camps. While it is important to make it clear at the outset that the atrocities that took place here were on nothing like the scale of the Nazi war crimes, it is equally important to acknowledge that they did occur, and that they were barbarous enough.

Extremes of sadism are always difficult to stomach, no matter who the victims are, but the fact that the victims in this case were *German* provides another layer to our discomfort. In every country in Europe, and indeed across the world, the Germans have always been regarded as the perpetrators, not the victims, of atrocity. The world likes to believe that if there was some small measure of vengeance after the war this was no more than the German people deserved – and furthermore, we like to believe that the vengeance that was meted out upon Germans was in any case fairly mild, especially given the circumstances. The notion that the Germans were also treated to some horrific forms of torture and degradation – not only practising Nazis but ordinary men, women and children – and the realization that our own countrymen were also capable of such crimes – these are subjects that mainstream Allied culture has always instinctively shied away from.

Such stories must be confronted if we are ever to learn the truth about the past, or gain a proper understanding of the world we live in today. In recent decades extremists and conspiracy theorists have thrived on the fact that this subject is still treated by the rest of us as something of a guilty secret. New myths and exaggerations have begun to take root, some of which are quite dangerous. Uncomfortable though it is, therefore, it is important to shine a light on both the unpleasant truth and the myths that have fed off it.

Germans in Czechoslovakia

The parts of Europe that saw the greatest levels of enmity towards German civilians were those where Germans and other nationalities lived side by side. The Czech capital of Prague was a paradigm case. Prague had been home to both Germans and Czechs for hundreds of years, and resentments between the two communities dated back to the time of the Austro-Hungarian empire.[1] Not counting Vienna, Prague was the first foreign capital to be taken by the Nazis, and the last to be liberated – its Czech citizens therefore suffered the occupation longer than any in

Europe. Many of them regarded their German neighbours as traitors who had paved the way for the German invasion in 1938.

It is not surprising, therefore, that when the population of Prague rose up against the Nazis in the last week of the war, these long-standing resentments finally gave birth to violence. Captured German soldiers were beaten, doused in petrol and burned to death.[2] Dozens were hung from the city's lamp posts with swastikas carved into their flesh. Guerrillas broke into the cellars where German men, women and children were hiding and beat, raped, and occasionally slaughtered them.[3] Thousands of Germans were taken from their homes and interned in schools, cinemas and barracks, where many were subjected to brutal interrogations in an attempt to discover their political affiliations.[4]

The atmosphere in the city during these few days was thick with fear. Some residents of Prague spoke later of an 'infectious' panic that reminded them of the feeling in the German trenches during the First World War. One German civil servant described Prague at this time as a succession of 'barricades and frightened people'. As he tried to make his way home he repeatedly ran into groups of outraged men, cursing mobs, screaming women, German soldiers surrendering, and in amongst it all a lad selling pennants and badges with the Czech colours. 'Shots are being fired from every house,' he wrote afterwards:

> Czech teenagers, often a revolver in each hand, demand to see identification papers. I hide in the porch of a house; from upstairs I can hear hair-raising screams, then a shot, and then silence. A young man with a face like a bird of prey comes down the stairs, quickly hiding something in his left trouser pocket. An old woman, obviously the caretaker, shouts: 'Did you let her have it, that German slut? That's right, that's how they all must perish!'

Germans across the city were hiding in their cellars, or at the houses of Czech friends and acquaintances, in order to avoid the wrath of the mob.[5]

At the beginning of the uprising, on 5 May 1945, there were some 200,000 Germans in Prague, most of them civilians.[6] According to Czech reports, just under a thousand of them were killed during the rising, including scores of women and at least eight children. This is certainly an underestimate, especially considering the scope and nature of the violence that took place in and around the city, and doesn't take into account official attempts to play down the violence against civilians. For example, a mass grave was later discovered in a cemetery in the suburb of Břevnov containing 300 Germans who had been 'killed during the fight westwards'. The majority of the victims were in civilian clothing, and yet the Czech report assumed that three-quarters of them had been soldiers, and so listed them as military rather than civilian deaths.[7] Given such unreliable reporting, and an unknown number of Germans whose deaths went unrecorded, it is impossible to determine the true number of German civilians killed in Prague during the uprising.

In the days after the war was over, thousands more Germans were interned in Prague, first in makeshift detention centres, then in large collection centres such as the sports stadium in Strahov, and finally in internment camps on the outskirts of the city. According to eye-witnesses, the German inmates of these internment centres were routinely beaten, and occasionally executed without trial. A civil engineer called Kurt Schmidt, for example, found himself interned in Strahov after being force-marched from Brno to Prague at the end of May. 'Hunger and death ruled in the camp,' he later claimed:

> We were even more forcibly reminded of death by the executions which took place in full public view inside the camp. Any SS member who was discovered in the camp was killed in public. One day, six youths were beaten until they lay motionless, water was poured over them (which the German women had to fetch) and then the beating continued till there was no sign of life left. The terribly mutilated bodies were deliberately exhibited for several days next to the latrines. A 14-year-old boy was shot together with his parents because it was alleged that he had tried to stab a Revolutionary Guard with a pair of scissors. These are only some examples of the executions which took place almost daily, mostly by shooting.[8]

According to Schmidt the supply of food was sporadic and always insufficient, and recent Czech research certainly backs this impression up.[9] Hygiene was primitive at best, and the buckets in which the food had to be fetched were used 'for different purposes' during the night. An epidemic of dysentery raged through the camp, and Schmidt lost his fifteen-month-old son to a combination of this and starvation. The absence of sanitation and sufficient rations are subjects which come up again and again in statements of all those interned after the war.

The women at Strahov had a particularly bad time of it, and were constantly subjected to the depredations of Czech guards and Russian soldiers. As Schmidt explained, he and the other men were powerless to protect them:

> If any man had tried to protect his wife, he would have risked being killed. The Russians, and the Czechs as well, often did not even trouble to take the women away – amongst the children and in view of all the inmates of the camp, they behaved like animals. During the nights one could hear the moaning and whimpering of these poor women. Shots rang out from every corner and bullets passed over our heads. The presence of so many people created an incessant noise. The darkness was lit up by search lights and the Russians continuously fired flares. Day and night there was no peace for our nerves and it was as if we had entered hell.[10]

In an effort to escape such conditions many Germans volunteered for work outside, particularly for the repair work that was needed in the city, including the dismantling of the barricades thrown up by the insurgents during the uprising. But if they believed that they would be treated better outside the prisons they were sorely mistaken. Schmidt describes being beaten, spat at and pelted with stones by the crowds that accumulated around such work parties. His description is corroborated by a woman from another prison camp, who had served in the German Women's Signal Corps in Prague during the war.

> The mob in the streets behaved even worse [than the guards]. Especially the older women excelled themselves and had armed themselves for this purpose with iron rods, truncheons, dog leashes, etc. Some of us were beaten so badly that they collapsed and were unable to get up again. The rest, including myself, had to remove barricades at the bridge. Czech police cordoned off the place where we worked, but the mob broke through and we were again exposed to their maltreatment without any protection. Some of my fellow sufferers jumped into the Moldau in their desperation, [where] they were immediately fired at . . . One of the Czechs had a pair of large scissors, and one after another of us had her hair cut off. Another Czech poured red paint over our heads. I myself had four teeth knocked out. Rings were torn by force from our swollen fingers. Others were interested in our shoes and clothes, so that we ended up by being almost naked – even pieces of underwear had been torn from our bodies. Young lads and men kicked us in the abdomen. In complete desperation, I also tried to jump into the river. But I was snatched back and received another beating.[11]

It is unsurprising that some Germans preferred to commit suicide rather than endure such treatment. In Prague's Pankrác prison, for example, two young German mothers strangled their children to death and then tried to kill themselves. When they were revived they claimed that they had done this because the guards had threatened to 'gouge their children's eyes out, torture them and kill them, just as the Germans had done with Czech children'.[12] There are no reliable statistics for suicides in the immediate aftermath of the war, but Czech reports from 1946 list 5,558 amongst ethnic Germans in Bohemia and Moravia. Once again, the real figure must have been even higher.[13]

The situation for Germans in Prague is broadly representative of the rest of the country, although in many areas the worst excesses did not happen until later that summer. Perhaps the most famous massacre occurred in Ústí nad Labem (formerly known to Germans as Aussig), where over a hundred Germans were killed at the end of July – although shocked eyewitnesses later exaggerated the numbers to ten or even twenty times that number.[14] Much worse but less well known was the massacre in the northern Bohemian town of Postoloprty, where a zealous Czech army detachment carried out orders to 'cleanse' the region of Germans. According to German sources, 800 people were killed in cold blood. Czech sources agree: two years after the event the Czech authorities uncovered 763 bodies buried in mass graves around the town.[15] In Taus (known to the Czechs as Domažlice), 120 people were shot behind the station and buried in mass graves.[16] In Horní Moštěnice, near the Moravian town of Přerov, a Czech officer named Karol Pazúr stopped a train full of Slovakian Germans, ostensibly to conduct a search for former Nazis. That night his soldiers shot 71 men, 120 women and 74 children – the youngest of them an eight-month-old baby. Once again, they were buried in mass graves. Pazúr later justified the killing of the children by saying, 'What was I supposed to do with them after we'd shot their parents?'[17]

This behaviour was by no means sanctioned by the new Czech authorities, who often condemned such excesses.[18] However, this does not quite absolve them of any responsibility. On his return to Czechoslovakia President Edvard Beneš issued a series of decrees that singled out Germans for punishment, including the appropriation of their land, the confiscation of their property and the deprivation of Czech citizenship along with the dissolution of all German institutions of higher education. The rhetoric used by Beneš and others in the new government was hardly designed to pour oil on troubled waters. For example, in his first speech in Prague after his return from exile Beneš did not blame just the Nazis for the moral crimes of the war but the whole German nation, which deserved 'the limitless contempt of all mankind'.[19] His future Justice Minister, Prokop Drtina, went further, claiming openly that 'There are no good Germans, only bad and even worse ones,' that they were a 'foreign ulcer in our body' and that 'the whole German nation is responsible for Hitler, Himmler, Henlein and Frank, and the whole nation must bear the punishment for the committed crimes'.[20] In July 1945 Antonín Zápotocký, the future Czech president, wrote an article in *Práce* claiming that the authorities should not bother to follow the law when punishing suspected collaborators, on the grounds that 'When you chop wood, the splinters fly' (a Czech expression that means something along the lines of 'You can't make an omelette without breaking eggs').[21] Similar sentiments were voiced by Prime Minister Zdeněk Nejedlý, Deputy Prime Minister Josef David, Minister of Justice Jaroslav Stránský and many others.[22]

If such figures of authority were content to heap invective upon all Germans, they were also quick to pardon their own people for the vengeance they had taken. On the first anniversary of the end of the war a law was drawn up that excused all acts of 'just reprisal' against the Nazi authorities or their 'accomplices', even if such acts would normally be considered a crime. Significantly, this amnesty applied not only to reprisals carried out during the war, but also to those committed between 9 May and 28 October 1945.[23]

It is difficult to say just how many Germans died in Czechoslovakia as a result of the chaotic events in the aftermath of the war, but the figure is certainly in the tens of thousands. The subject is still so controversial, and provokes such strong emotions on both sides, that all statistics relating to the number of deaths are contested. German sources name 18,889 people who died before and during the expulsions from Czechoslovakia, 5,596 of them violently – but these figures do not take into account those whose deaths went unrecorded.[24] Sudeten Germans often claim that the true figure is more like 250,000, but this is almost certainly a wild exaggeration.[25] Conversely, some Czech historians claim that any violence in the aftermath of the war is a mere fiction created by Germans who still want to claim compensation today.[26] The most reliable and impartial estimates have been compiled by the Czech historian Tomáš Staněk, who cautiously suggests that between 24,000 and 40,000 Germans died as a direct result of their treatment during the postwar chaos in Czechoslovakia.[27] Even this figure does not take into account those who died prematurely in the following years because their health was wrecked by what they had been through.

Staněk also gives figures for the numbers of Germans imprisoned in the aftermath of the war. Even before the wholesale internment began in the run-up to the official expulsions, Czech records list 96,356 German prisoners – although Staněk argues that the real figure is at least 20,000 higher. In fact, in mid-August 1945, more than 90 per cent of *all* the prisoners held in Bohemia and Moravia were of German nationality. This was ostensibly because they were supposed to represent a threat, and yet perhaps as many as 10,000 of them were children under fourteen.[28]

There is no doubt that some of these prisoners were guilty of the crimes that they were collectively blamed for. But the main reason they were kept in camps for so long after the war – and we must remember that many were not released until 1948 – was that they were a useful supply of free labour, particularly in the important agricultural and mining industries.

In principle, this use of conscripted German labour was not markedly different from what was going on in the rest of Europe, including Great Britain, where 110,000 German prisoners of war were still working at the beginning of 1948.[29] Indeed, the use of forced German labour was endorsed by the international agreements between the Big Three at Yalta and Potsdam. But whereas in Britain only military prisoners were used as forced labour, most of those conscripted in Czechoslovakia were civilians. There was also a huge difference in the way such labourers were treated. In Britain, according to the International Committee of the Red Cross, German labourers were fed the same as British workers, and subject to the same safety rules. In the Czech lands, where the Red Cross were often not even allowed access, many prisoners were fed less than 1,000 calories a day – under half what is necessary in order to maintain health – and were forced to do all kinds of dangerous work, including clearing minefields.[30]

Forced labourers in Czechoslovakia were also routinely humiliated in ways that deliberately emulated the Nazi treatment of Jews. Thus they were made to wear swastikas, white armbands, or patches of material painted with the letter 'N' (for Němec, meaning German).[31] When taken outside the internment camps on work duties they were frequently forbidden from using public transport, entering shops or public parks, or even walking on the pavement.[32] The spectre of Nazism was often

CITIZENS OF VINOHRADY!

The praesidium of the Local National Committee for Prague XII has decided to solve the questions of Germans, Hungarians and traitors as follows:

1. The term 'German' in all its inflections will hitherto be written only with small letters, likewise the term 'Hungarian'.

2. To Germans, Hungarians and traitors apply in future these provisions –

a) all persons from fourteen years of age who come under the category German, Hungarian, traitor or collaborator will wear on the left side visibly on white canvas, size 10x10cm, a Swastika together with the number under which they will be registered. No person marked with the Swastika will receive normal ration cards. The same applies to persons who entered 'D' in column 6 (nationality) of their Registrations Certificate;

b) no person marked with the Swastika is allowed to use tramway cars except when they go direct to work, at which time they must do so in the trailer; seats must not be used by these persons;

c) no person marked with the Swastika is allowed to use the pavement – they may move only on the roadway;

d) no person marked with the Swastika is allowed to buy, subscribe to, or read daily or other newspapers; this applies also to subtenants, if any, of such persons;

e) no person marked with the Swastika is allowed to stay in, or proceed through, public gardens or parks, or woods, they are not allowed to call at or use barbers' shops, restaurants, places of amusement of any kind, especially theatres, cinemas, lectures etc; likewise they are not allowed to use laundries, cleaners' shops and rolling-presses. Shopping time for these persons is exclusively between 11 a.m. and 1 p.m., and between 3 and 4 p.m. For disregarding the times so defined both buyer and seller will be liable to the same punishment. For dealings with authorities the time between 7.30 and 8.30 is exclusively fixed for these persons in all offices;

f) no person marked with the Swastika is allowed to be away from his or her home after 8 p.m.;

g) all persons over 14 years of age with the entry 'D' in their Registration Certificate report at once, at the latest within two days, to the Control and Report Commission of the L.N.C. for Prague XII for the issue of their badges and for registration. Those who fail to report in the set time, and who are found without the proper badge as prescribed, will be severely punished in the way the Nazi authorities adopted in similar cases. The same punishment will also be meted out to those who abet these persons in any way or associate with them for any purpose whatsoever;

h) all persons with the entry 'D' in their certificates must appear without delay before the said Investigation Commission irrespective of whether they have perhaps received a provisional certificate concerning freedom of movement, etc. At the same time they [must] submit a proper list of all their property and hand it over, together with all valuables, to the Trustee of National Property of the N. C. XII, likewise also savings books and bank or other deposits, if any; they must report whether and in what way they have any capital interests, submitting proper evidence; further, they surrender at the same time all wireless sets together with their licences. Any financial transactions are forbidden and void; the Germans are not entitled to tobacco supplies, and they are not allowed to smoke in public or while working.

Citizens, workers and toiling people! We will, in accordance with the principles of our Government, carry out a proper purge and establish order at least in our district. Therefore help us, you too, to make Vinohrady national and ours as soon as possible.

These measures are only temporary, pending the deportation of all these people.

Given in Prague, 15 June 1945
Local National Committee for Prague XII
Oldrich Hlas, Chairman

Translation of a poster displayed in a district of Prague, June 1945[36] invoked during beatings and other 'punishments', particularly when the camp guards had themselves been victims of Nazi cruelty. For example, one German civil servant remembers his tormentor shouting, 'I have got you at last, you sons of bitches! Four long years you tortured me in the concentration camp, now it is your turn!'[33]

According to Hans Guenther Adler, a Jew who had been imprisoned in Theresienstadt, there was very little difference between his own treatment and the treatment of Germans when they were imprisoned in that very same camp after the war:

> Many amongst them had undoubtedly become guilty during the years of occupation, but in the majority they were children and juveniles, who had been locked up merely because they were Germans. Merely because they were Germans . . . ? This sentence sounds frighteningly familiar; only the word 'Jews' had been changed to 'Germans'. The rags the Germans had been clothed with were smeared with swastikas. The people were abominably fed and maltreated, and they were no better off than one was used to from German concentration camps. The only difference was that the heartless revenge at work here was not based on the large-scale system of extermination carried out by the SS.[34]

Adler's moral argument is incontrovertible: the maltreatment of innocent Germans is every bit as wrong as the persecution of innocent Jews. However, he is wrong to belittle the difference in scale between the two events. He also glosses over the fact that while Germans suffered at the hands of individuals, their torture and murder was never part of official government policy: the Czech authorities wanted merely to expel Germans, not to exterminate them. This, surely, constitutes a whole world of difference.

However, there are others who claim that while the wholesale extermination of Germans might not have been on the agenda in Theresienstadt it certainly was in other places. When millions of bruised and destitute refugees began flooding into Germany in the autumn of 1945, they brought with them some disturbing stories of places they called 'hell camps', 'death camps' and 'extermination camps'. In these places, they said, Germans were routinely worked to death, starved to death and subjected to mass executions. The sadistic methods used by the camp guards were every bit as bad as, and perhaps worse than, those used by the SS at Auschwitz. In some camps, it was claimed, 'only about five per cent' of the inmates survived.[35]

Such allegations were taken extremely seriously by the German government, and were embraced by large sections of the population who preferred to see themselves as victims, rather than perpetrators, of atrocity. These beliefs would have political consequences long into the twentieth century and beyond.

Since the most notorious of these camps were not in Czechoslovakia but in Poland, it is to that country that we must turn our attention next.

The New 'Extermination Camps'

In February 1945, after the Red Army had driven deep into German territory, an abandoned labour camp was discovered at Zgoda, near Świętochłowice, a small provincial town in what today is south-western Poland. Eager for retribution, the Polish paramilitary Public Security Service (Urząd Bezpieczeństwa Publicznego or UBP) decided to reopen it as a 'punishment camp'.[37] Thousands of local Germans were arrested and sent there for labour duties. While the local population was told that Zgoda was a camp only for committed Nazis and German activists, in reality almost anyone could end up there, and alongside the former Nazi prisoners were people who had been arrested for belonging to German sports clubs, for not having their papers on them, or occasionally for no reason at all.

Such prisoners might have guessed what was in store for them as soon as they arrived. The camp was surrounded by a high-voltage electric fence, with ominous signs on it displaying a skull and crossbones and the words 'Danger of death'.[38] According to several witnesses, these messages were reinforced by the sight of dead bodies hanging on the wire.[39] Prisoners were met at the gates by the camp director, Salomon Morel, who told them that he would 'show them what Auschwitz meant';[40] or he would taunt them by saying, 'My parents and siblings were gassed by the Germans in Auschwitz, and I will not rest until all Germans have had their rightful punishment.'[41] Zgoda had been a satellite camp of Auschwitz during the war: to reinforce this link, someone had scrawled the inscription 'Arbeit macht frei' above the gate.[42]

The torture began immediately, especially for anyone suspected of being a member of a Nazi organization. Members of the Hitler Youth were told to lie on the ground while the guards trod on them, or they were forced to sing the Nazi Party anthem, the 'Horst Wessel Song', with their arms raised while guards beat them with rubber truncheons.[43] Sometimes Morel would throw prisoners on top of each other until their bodies formed a huge pyramid; he would beat them with a stool, or he would order prisoners to beat each other for the guards' entertainment.[44] Occasionally prisoners were sent to the punishment chamber, an underground bunker where they were made to stand for hours in freezing chest-deep water.[45] Special occasions were marked with extra beatings. On Hitler's birthday, for example, the guards entered Block No. 7 – the barracks reserved for suspected Nazis – and set about beating them with chair legs.[46] On VE Day, Morel took a group of prisoners from Block No. 11 for another celebratory beating.[47]

The conditions in which these prisoners were forced to live were deliberately subhuman. The camp was built for a capacity of only 1,400 inmates, but by July it already had more than three and a half times this number. At its peak, 5,048 prisoners were interned here, all but sixty-six of them either Germans or Volksdeutsch.[48] They were packed into seven wooden barrack buildings crawling with lice, where they were denied adequate food or access to proper washing facilities. Rations were routinely withheld by greedy camp staff, and food packages sent by concerned relatives outside the camp were confiscated.[49] Two-thirds of the men were sent daily to the local coal mines, where they were sometimes literally worked to death.[50] The suspected Nazi prisoners in Block No. 7 did not go to work, but were kept under the constant attention of the UBP guards inside the camp. When an epidemic of typhus struck, sick prisoners were not isolated but forced to stay in their overcrowded barracks. As a consequence the death rate accelerated rapidly – according to one prisoner tasked with burying the dead, up to twenty people died daily.[51]

Anyone who tried to escape this hell was immediately singled out for special treatment. Gerhard Gruschka, a fourteen-year-old German boy imprisoned in the camp, witnessed the punishment meted out to one escapee who had the misfortune to be recaptured. His name was Eric van Calsteren. Once he had been brought back to the barracks, a group of guards repeatedly beat him to the ground with fists and clubs, while the rest of the prisoners were made to watch. According to Gruschka, it was one of the most brutal beatings he ever saw.

Eric . . . suddenly tore himself away from the militiamen and clambered onto one of the plank beds. The four rushed round behind it and dragged it into the centre of the room. They were obviously extremely irritated by such an attempt at resistance. One of them fetched an iron bar from the corner of the room where we kept the vat used for fetching our food. When pushed through both handles of the vat this bar made it easier to carry the full container. Now however it became an instrument of torture. The militiamen took it in turns to strike Eric's legs with unrestrained rage. Whenever he fell to the ground they worked him over with kicks, pulled him up again and beat him again with the steel bar. In his desperation Eric begged his torturers, 'Just shoot me, just shoot me!' But they beat him even harder. It was one of the most terrible nights at Zgoda. Every one of us believed that our fellow prisoner was going to be killed.[52]

Miraculously, van Calsteren somehow survived this beating. Like Gruschka, he was only fourteen years old. He was also a Dutch citizen, and so should never have been imprisoned in Poland in the first place.

These were the kinds of events that took place daily in Zgoda. It is not surprising that parallels are often drawn between this camp and Nazi concentration camps, especially since the camp commander himself appears to have been consciously trying to resurrect the atmosphere of Auschwitz. Such parallels were also drawn by outsiders at the time. A local priest passed on information about the camp to British officials in Berlin, who in turn forwarded it to the Foreign Office in London. 'Concentration camps have not been abolished, but have been taken over by the new owners,' reads the British report. 'At Schwientochlowitz, prisoners who do not die of starvation or are not beaten to death, are made to stand up to their necks, night after night until they die, in cold water.'[53] German prisoners who were released from Zgoda also made comparisons with Nazi camps. One, a man named Günther Wollny, had had the misfortune to have experienced both Auschwitz and Zgoda. 'I'd rather be ten years in a German camp than one day in a Polish one,' he later claimed.[54]

For all the torture that took place in Zgoda, it was the lack of food and the arrival of typhoid that proved to be the biggest killers. For those who survived, however, the epidemic proved to be their salvation. Details of the outbreak leaked to the Polish newspapers, and finally to the Polish government department in charge of prisons and camps. Morel was formally reprimanded for allowing conditions in the camp to deteriorate so badly, as well as for being too ready to use weapons on the prisoners, and one of the camp's head administrators, Karol Zaks, was sacked for withholding rations.[55] The authorities then set about releasing prisoners or transferring them to other camps. By November 1945, on the condition that they never spoke about what they had experienced, the majority of prisoners had been set free and the camp was closed down.

According to official figures, of the estimated 6,000 Germans who had passed through Zgoda 1,855 died – almost one in three. Some Polish and German historians have concluded that, despite being officially downgraded from a punishment camp to a work camp, it always functioned as a place where German prisoners were deliberately denied food and medical care in order to bring about their deaths.[56]

It would be tempting to dismiss Zgoda as the individual vengeance of a single, brutal camp commander, were it not for the fact that similar conditions prevailed at many other Polish camps and prisons. At the Polish Militia prison in Trzebica (German Trebnitz), for example, German inmates were regularly beaten for sport, and often had dogs set on them by the guards. One prisoner claimed he had been forced to crouch down and hop around his cell while his warder beat him with an iron-tipped stick.[57] The prison at Gliwice (or Gleiwitz) was run by Jewish Holocaust survivors who used broomsticks, clubs and spring-loaded truncheons to beat confessions out of German prisoners.[58] Survivors from the prison at Kłodzko (or Glatz) tell stories of prisoners who had their 'eyes beaten out with rubber cudgels', and all kinds of other violence, including straightforward murder.[59]

Women suffered just as much as men. At the work camp of Potulice women were routinely raped, beaten and subjected to sexual sadism by camp staff. Perhaps worse, their children were separated from them, and were only allowed to see their mothers on Sundays for an hour or two. One witness even claims that this was part of a wider policy of removing children to Polonize them, just as the Nazis had tried to Germanize Polish children during the war – although it is likely that this is an emotional response to the pain of being separated from her own child for a year and a half.[60] Other inmates of Potulice claim to have been made to undress while on work parties and buried in liquid manure, and even to have witnessed a guard catch a toad and shove it down a German prisoner's throat until he choked to death.[61]

Perhaps the most notorious Polish camp, however, was that at Łambinowice – or Lamsdorf, as it was known to its German occupants.

This former POW camp was reopened in July 1945 as a forced-labour camp for German civilians awaiting expulsion from the new Poland. It was run by the twenty-year-old Czesław Gęborski, 'a depraved-looking Pole, who only made himself understood with kicks'.[62]

According to one of the first prisoners, the atrocities began almost immediately. On the evening after they arrived, he and forty others were woken and hounded out of their barracks into the camp yard, where they were forced to lie on the ground while the militiamen jumped on their backs. They then had to jog around the yard while being beaten with lashes and rifle butts. Anyone who fell to the ground was immediately set upon by groups of militiamen. 'The next morning we buried fifteen men,' claims this witness. 'For several days afterwards I could move only with the greatest pain, my urine was mixed with blood, my heartbeat irregular. And fifteen men were in the ground.'[63]

When the first large transport of prisoners arrived a couple of days later, the atrocities continued. It was not only the Polish militia who indulged in the beatings, but also their German henchmen, particularly the 'Camp senior', a sadistic Volksdeutsch prisoner from Lubliniec (or Lublinitz in German) called Johann Fuhrmann. 'Before my eyes he struck a baby dead, whose mother had pleaded for some soup for the child, which at Lamsdorf was supplied for the smallest children. Then he chased the woman, still clutching the tiny bloody body in her arms, lashing her across the yard . . . then he retired to his room with his "assistants" and polished off the meal soup meant for the infants.'[64]

According to the same witness, the camp guards became gradually more and more inventive in their sadism. For entertainment the camp commandant forced one of the men to climb a tree that stood in the yard and call out, 'I'm a great big monkey', while he and his guards laughed and took potshots at him until he eventually fell to the ground. Perhaps the most disgusting allegation by this witness is the description he gives of what happened to the women of the nearby village of Grüben (now Grabin in Poland). They were sent to exhume a mass grave that was discovered near the camp, in which the bodies of hundreds of Soviet soldiers had been buried by the Nazis after they had died in their prisoner-of-war camp. The women were not given gloves or any other protective clothing. It was summer, and the bodies, which were in an advanced state of decay, gave off an unbearable stench.

As the corpses lay out in the open, the women and girls were forced to lie face-down on top of these slimy and disgusting corpses. With their rifle butts the Polish militiamen shoved the faces of their victims deep into the hellish decay. In this way human remains were squashed into their mouths and noses. Sixty-four women and girls died as a consequence of this 'heroic' Polish deed.[65]

The validity of accounts like this is impossible to verify, and it is quite likely that some aspects have been greatly exaggerated. However, photos survive of the exhumation, and even Polish historians concede that the women were forced to undertake it without gloves or protective clothing.[66] Many of the details are also corroborated by other survivors of the camp. A female prisoner claimed that her son Hugo was also forced to exhume dead bodies with his bare hands, and that the decay was so bad that its slime soaked through his shoes.[67]

That a culture of casual sadism existed at Łambinowice is undeniable. Several witnesses attest to having seen people being beaten to death, or shot in reprisal for escape attempts.[68] Punishments were certainly meted out for the most trivial of transgressions, such as expressing a desire to flee to the American zone of Germany (for which one teenager was allegedly beaten to death), or speaking to a member of the opposite sex.[69] One woman claims that she cried out in joy when she discovered her husband alive in the camp, and as a consequence the two of them were tied down facing the sun for three days as a punishment.[70]

Alongside this culture of violence, prisoners were forced to endure the most terrible physical conditions. As in other camps they were given very little food – usually just a couple of boiled potatoes twice a day, and thin broth at lunchtime. Hygiene was non-existent, and even the sheets that were used to wrap the dead had to be reused, as did the palliasses in the hospital.[71] According to one of the camp gravediggers, the lice on the corpses he buried were sometimes '2cm thick'.[72] Unsurprisingly, as elsewhere the biggest killers in the camp were the twin evils of sickness and malnutrition. According to Polish sources, 60 per cent of the deaths here were caused by typhus, with many more brought about by spotted fever, dysentery, scabies and other diseases.[73]

For those who survived the camp, its memory was like a vision of hell. By the time they were released and transported to Germany, they had lost their homes, all their possessions, their health, and sometimes up to half their body weight – but it was the psychological burden of bereavement that weighed on them most. As one woman explained a couple of years after her ordeal:

> In the camp I lost my ten-year-old daughter, my mother, my sister, my brother, two sisters-in-law and a brother-in-law. Near death myself, I managed to join a transport to West Germany with my other daughter and my son. We spent fourteen weeks in the camp. Over half of the people of my village were dead . . . Full of longing, we awaited the arrival of my husband. In July 1946 the terrible news reached us that he too had become a victim of that hell-camp, as had so many after our departure . . .[74]

Such stories have since become part of Germany's collective memory. Whole libraries of books have been written using them as a basis – as a consequence our view of the Polish work camps has remained impressionistic. As I hope to show next, despite the best efforts of the German government to gather statistics, good, hard facts on precisely how many people were interned in these camps, and how many died in them, are extremely hard to come by.

The Politics of Numbers

One of the most famous incidents at Lamsdorf was the fire that broke out in one of the barracks in October 1945. Nobody knows exactly how the blaze started, but the chaotic events that ensued have been well documented. According to German eyewitnesses, the camp guards used the occasion as an excuse to begin a massacre. They opened fire indiscriminately, killing many of those who were merely trying to put the blaze out, and then began to throw prisoners headlong into the flames. In the aftermath of the blaze the prisoners were forced to dig mass graves. The bodies of patients who had been recovering in the sick ward were also buried around this time: some of them were shot first, but many were merely beaten unconscious and buried alive.[75]

When the Polish Communist government was presented with these stories in 1965 they flatly denied them. According to their version of events, after the fire had broken out the prisoners had taken the opportunity to start an uprising, which the Polish guards had been obliged to suppress with force. The government steadfastly supported the camp commandant, Czesław Gęborski, and claimed that he was innocent of all the charges raised against him. Furthermore, they claimed that such stories were merely propaganda created by a German political lobby whose only aim was to discredit Poland and force the return of those lands that were granted to Poland in the Potsdam Agreement in 1945.[76]

The argument about how many people had died during and after this fire was equally fierce. The lowest number given is just nine (according to a man who buried their bodies, and conceded even by the postwar Polish Communist authorities).[77] However, some German witnesses claim that this is a massive underestimate. The German camp doctor, Heinz Esser, claimed that Gęborski deliberately made him move the bodies to three separate locations in order to prevent them being counted properly, and that women and children were made to dig graves for them away from the official gravedigging parties. Esser kept a secret list of the fire victims according to different categories: those killed in the fire itself, those shot around the fire, those buried alive during the aftermath, and those who died of their injuries in the following days. He gives the final death toll as 581. Unfortunately, this number contradicts the figure apparently given by Esser several years earlier, when he claimed that only 132 people died.[78] Given the unreliability of first-hand accounts, the absence of proper documents and the highly charged political atmosphere that prevailed after the war, it is impossible to say how many people actually did die at Lamsdorf on that day. The difference between nine deaths and over five hundred is huge. (At the trial of Czesław Gęborski, the camp commandant, in 2000 the number of people said to have died in and around this fire was forty-eight.[79])

The same dispute occurred over the *total* number of deaths during the year when the camp was open. According to Heinz Esser's figures, 6,488 prisoners died there in 1945 and 1946. The Communist administration in Poland again dismissed this, claiming that only 4,000 prisoners had ever been interned at Lamsdorf, and that Esser's figures were therefore impossible.[80] According to the latest Polish research, it seems likely that there were about 6,000 prisoners, and that about 1,500 of them died. The names of 1,462 of them are known.[81]

This bickering over numbers is not merely an academic disagreement – there are intense emotions involved, both on a personal and a national level. Nine people killed accidentally in a fire is an unfortunate event, but scores, perhaps hundreds, deliberately burned and buried alive is an atrocity. A few hundred deaths from typhus is perhaps an unavoidable tragedy, but the deliberate starvation and denial of medical care to thousands is a crime against humanity. The numbers are all-important, because they themselves tell a story.

When one looks at this issue on a national scale, the disparity between the German figures and the Polish ones becomes vast. In a study by the Ministry of Expellees, Refugees and War Victims that was presented to the German parliament in 1974, it was claimed that 200,000 people had been imprisoned in Polish labour camps after the war, including Lamsdorf, Zgoda, Mysłowice and the NKVD prison at Toszek. The overall death rate was estimated to be between 20 and 50 per cent. This meant that somewhere between 40,000 and 100,000 people died in such camps, although the report claimed that 'certainly more than 60,000 people perished there'.[82] By contrast, a Polish report by the Ministry for Public Security (Minsterstwo Bezpieczeństwa Publicznego) claimed that only 6,140 Germans died in labour camps – a number that the report's compilers must surely have known was far too low, even at the time.[83] The German figure was therefore almost ten times the Polish figure.

Once again, the numbers are important to both sides. For the Poles it was a matter of retaining the moral high ground. The Second World War was the culmination of decades of tension between Germany and Poland: after the devastation and dismemberment of their country at the hands of the Nazis (and later the Soviets), the Poles were understandably indignant about being expected to accept any guilt for the brief period of chaos that occurred during the aftermath. It was therefore in their interest to keep these embarrassing figures as low as possible. There are some blatant examples of manipulation in the official documents of the time, where mortality rates are impossibly low.

Germany, by contrast, had a vested interest in exaggerating the figures. Not only did stories of Polish crimes against humanity feed into all the racial prejudices that some Germans had held during the war, but they also helped to alleviate some of the sense of national guilt: such stories showed that Germans were not only perpetrators but also victims of atrocity. The greater the tragedy that Germany had itself endured, the further it could distance itself from its own guilt – in a sense, the wrongs that were done to the eastern European Germans partly 'cancelled out' the wrongs that they themselves had done to the Jews and Slavs. While this has never been the mainstream view in Germany, there are still political groups there today who refuse to acknowledge the Holocaust on the grounds that what Germans in eastern Europe suffered was 'exactly the same'.[84] This is an extremely dangerous point of view. While it is true that the Polish labour camps contained some repugnant examples of extreme sadism towards Germans, there is absolutely no evidence to show that this was part of an official policy of extermination. Indeed, the Polish authorities sent strict orders to their camp commanders stressing that beating or otherwise abusing prisoners was illegal, and anyone found guilty of doing so would be punished.[85] Those who were found to have mistreated prisoners were disciplined (albeit lightly), and removed from their posts. To equate the atrocities in Lamsdorf or Zgoda with the Holocaust is a nonsense, in terms of both quality and scale.

One of the main reasons this subject cannot be laid to rest is that so few of those responsible for crimes in the postwar prison camps have ever been brought to trial. Czesław Gęborski, the commandant of Lamsdorf, was tried in 1956 by the Communist administration, but found not guilty. After the fall of communism in 1989, the investigation of events at Lamsdorf resumed, and Gęborski was due to be tried in 2001, in Opole. However, the trial was repeatedly postponed due to the poor health of both Gęborski and the witnesses against him, and was finally called off in 2005. Gęborski died a year later.

Salomon Morel, the commandant of Zgoda/Świętochłowice, has likewise managed to avoid coming to trial. After the fall of communism he moved to Israel, where he has lived ever since. The Polish Ministry of Justice applied for his extradition, but Israel was obliged to turn the application down because, according to their statute of limitations, too much time had elapsed since the crimes were committed.[86]

Both men should have been prosecuted in the 1940s, along with hundreds of others, but they were not, because the authorities had other things on their minds. The Poles, like every other nation that had endured Nazi occupation, were more concerned with restoring their own power than with looking after the rights of German civilians. This might make us indignant, but it should not surprise us. Justice in the aftermath of the war was in any case a highly subjective affair, and rarely exercised within what we would now consider a normal legal framework.

None of these events were unique to Poland or eastern Europe. As I shall show next, the same themes exist throughout the continent: the only difference is that elsewhere it was not Germans who were punished, but rather those who had collaborated with them.

13

The Enemy Within

At the height of the war, Germany directly or indirectly controlled more than a dozen countries across Europe, and exercised enormous influence in half a dozen more. For all their military might, the Nazis could not have done this without the help of tens of thousands, perhaps *hundreds* of thousands, of collaborators in those countries. No matter how much the people of Europe hated Germans in the immediate aftermath of the war, they hated collaborators more. Germans at least had the excuse that they were part of a foreign culture, a foreign power: collaborators, by contrast, were traitors to their own countries, and in the fiercely patriotic atmosphere that permeated Europe at the end of the war, this was an unforgivable sin.

The dehumanization of collaborators in the aftermath of the war is difficult for modern generations to understand. In the European press they were portrayed as 'vermin', 'mad dogs', or 'inferior' elements that needed to be 'cleansed' from society.[1] In Denmark and Norway they were depicted in popular art as rats, while in Belgium the collective animosity towards them, according to British observers, was akin to 'a religious fervour'.[2] In such an atmosphere, it was hardly surprising that some people became violent towards them. As Peter Voute, a doctor who worked with the Dutch Resistance, noted after the war,

> Deep hatred of the collaborators and a desire for revenge were so widespread that some kind of punishment was inevitable. Though it was on everyone's mind, no one really knew what form this retaliation would take. There were rumours of a 'day of the axes', when the mob would take the law into its own hands.[3]

This 'day of the axes', or what the French would call '*l'épuration sauvage*', was repeated to some extent in every country. The list of those who were targeted is seemingly endless: not only wartime leaders and politicians but also local mayors and administrators; not only members of Europe's far-right militias but also those ordinary policemen and gendarmes who had enforced repressive laws; not only prominent industrialists who had made money from Nazi contracts but also the owners of cafés and shops who had made money by serving German soldiers. Journalists, broadcasters and film-makers were vilified for disseminating Nazi propaganda. Actors and singers were attacked for entertaining German troops; as were priests who had given succour or encouragement to fascists, prostitutes who had slept with German soldiers, and even ordinary women and girls who had smiled at Germans a little too readily.

Every form of vengeance shown to Germans in Czechoslovakia and Poland was also visited upon collaborators and fascists across Europe. During the chaos of the liberation, Dutch and Belgian collaborators were summarily executed and their houses burned down 'while the police looked on with indifference or even approbation'.[4] In Italy the bodies of Fascists were displayed in the streets where they could be kicked or spat at by passers-by – even Mussolini's corpse was treated like this, before being suspended from the roof of a petrol station in Milan's Piazzale Loreto.[5] In Hungary, members of the far-right Arrow Cross party were forced to exhume Jewish mass graves in very hot weather while local people threw sticks and stones at them.[6] In France clandestine prisons were set up where suspected collaborators were subjected to various forms of sadism, including mutilation, rape, enforced prostitution and every type of torture imaginable.[7]

The incoming authorities and the Allies alike witnessed these events with horror. Even the Resistance themselves found such stories distressing. 'The terrible thing is,' reported *La Terre Vivaroise* newspaper on 29 October 1944,

> that we are repeating some of the most heinous procedures carried out by the Gestapo; it would seem that Nazism has intoxicated a number of individuals to the point where they believe that violence is always legitimate, that they can do what they please to those they consider to be their adversaries, and that everyone has the right to take another person's life.

What was the point in triumphing over the Barbarians if only to imitate
them and become like them?[8]

It was clear that such a state of affairs could not be allowed to continue.
The Allies could not afford any suggestion of anarchy behind their own
lines, particularly while the war was still going on. Neither could the
incoming governments permit local people to take the law into their
own hands, since this challenged their own authority. 'Public order is a
matter of life and death,' claimed Charles de Gaulle on his return to
Paris in August 1944. In a radio broadcast to the people, he insisted that
the Provisional Government was now in charge, and that 'absolutely all
improvised authorities must stop'.[9]

The new governments of western Europe attacked the problem from
several angles at once. Firstly, recognizing that part of the problem was
the people's lack of faith in the police, they did whatever they could to
bolster the position of the police force as the most important pillar of
law and order. In some areas, particularly in Italy and Greece, they
merely relied on the massive Allied presence to provide support. But in
other areas they tackled the problem head-on by purging suspect officers from the force. Within a year of the liberation of France, for
example, one policeman in every eight had been suspended, and one in
five French detectives had lost their jobs.[10] Other countries followed
suit: the purge of the police in Norway and Denmark was equally
impressive, although perhaps less so in the rest of western Europe. The
important thing was to restore the legitimacy of the police so that they
could stand up to the vigilantes who had taken control of many towns
and neighbourhoods.

Secondly, the new authorities set about trying to disarm the groups
of former resisters who were committing most of the violence. This was
often easier said than done. In Paris, for example, the Patriotic Militia
continued to conduct armed patrols in open defiance of the authorities.
In Valenciennes they maintained huge secret arms caches, which
included grenades, anti-aircraft machine-guns and anti-tank rifles.[11] In
Brussels, where members of the 'Secret Army' were given two weeks to
disband, a protest demonstration degenerated into a minor riot: the
police opened fire, wounding forty-five people.[12] In Italy and Greece
thousands of partisans refused to give up their weapons for the simple
reason that they did not trust the authorities, which still, even after the

bloodshed of the liberation, contained countless people who were tainted with connections to the old regime.

In an attempt to coax former partisans back into civilian life many countries announced amnesties for crimes committed in the name of the liberation. In Belgium, for instance, the authorities were willing to turn a blind eye to almost any Resistance activity that occurred in the forty-one days after the Germans had been ejected. In Italy the amnesty on revenge killings covered the first twelve weeks after the end of the war, and in Czechoslovakia it lasted an astonishing five and a half months.[13] But if crimes of passion, committed in the heat of the liberation, were regarded with leniency, those committed much later, when power was supposed to have been returned to the state, were punished extremely harshly. In France, for example, a series of arrests of former *maquisards* in the winter of 1944–5 was widely interpreted as a warning to the Resistance to bring an end to lynch justice.[14]

Such measures, however, were little more than a sticking plaster. The real problem, and the main reason why lynch mobs were so common, was that many people believed vengeance to be their only real recourse to justice. In the words of the British ambassador to Paris, Duff Cooper, who wrote several reports on lynchings in France, 'So long as people believe that the guilty will be punished, they are prepared to leave them to the law but when they begin to doubt this is so, they will take the law into their own hands.'[15] In the aftermath of the war, such doubts were everywhere. The only real way to stop revenge attacks was to convince the people that the state was capable of administering what the Belgian newspapers called '*justice sévère et expéditive*'.[16]

Accordingly, every incoming government in Europe made a show of reforming the law and its institutions. New courts were set up, new judges appointed, and new prisons and internment camps opened to cope with the sudden flood of arrestees. New treason laws were enacted to replace outdated and irrelevant ones. Because of the scale of the collaboration, new concepts of justice had to be devised and applied retrospectively. In western Europe the new punishment of 'national degradation' was introduced for minor crimes, which deprived collaborators of a range of civil rights, including the right to vote. For more serious crimes the death penalty, which had long been consigned to history in Denmark and Norway, was reinstated.[17]

Some parts of Europe were convinced by this show far more easily than others. In Belgium, Holland, Denmark and Norway, the Resistance were on the whole quite happy to turn collaborators over to the proper authorities and be done with them. In parts of France, however, as well as large parts of Italy, Greece and much of eastern Europe, the partisans – and indeed the people in general – were much more keen to take the law into their own hands. There was a whole range of reasons for this, many of them political, as will become clear later on. But the most important reason was a lack of trust in the authorities. After years of fascist rule, the people of Europe took a very dim view of official 'justice'.

Perhaps the best example of such mistrust was provided by Italy. This country was certainly an extreme case: while the rest of Europe sought retribution for a relatively short period of collaboration, many Italians had been storing up resentment against the Fascists for over twenty years. The process of liberation had been more protracted here than anywhere else – lasting almost two years – and the north of the country had been involved in a bitter civil war throughout the whole of this time. Many events that occurred in other parts of Europe also happened here, but in exaggerated form. As a consequence Italy provides a stark demonstration of many of the themes that were causing popular discontent across the continent.

The Italian *Epurazzione*

In 1945, Italy was a nation divided. For much of the last two years of the war this divide had been physical: the south had been occupied by the British and Americans, while the north had been occupied by the Germans. But the divide was also political, especially in the north. On one side were the Fascists, whose atrocities against their own people had only accelerated after the Germans had invaded; on the other side were the opposition groups, many of them Communist, many of them not, who were united only by their common hatred of Mussolini and his followers.

When the Fascists were finally defeated in April 1945, the partisans embarked on a frenzy of revenge. Anyone who had anything to do with the Fascists was targeted – not only fighting members of the Black Brigades or Decima Mas, but also members of the Women's Auxiliary

Service, or even ordinary secretaries and administrators from the Fascist Republican Party. According to Italian sources, the regions of Piemonte, Emilia-Romagna and Veneto were the most violent, with thousands of shootings taking place in each area.[18] British sources claimed that some 500 people were executed in Milan in the run-up to VE Day, and a further 1,000 in Turin, although, as liaison officers reported to the British ambassador in Rome, 'no one had been shot who didn't deserve it'. These figures were, if anything, an underestimate.[19]

The Allies evidently felt powerless to intervene in this bloodbath, at least in the early days. In Turin, the president of the local liberation committee, Franco Antonicelli, was reportedly told by the head of the Allied mission, Colonel John Stevens: 'Listen, president, clear things up in two, three days, but on the third day, I no longer want to see dead on the streets.'[20] Many ordinary partisans also claimed that the Allies allowed them to administer their own forms of justice. 'The Americans allowed us to do it,' said one former partisan after the war. 'They saw us, let us torture them a little, then took them away from us.'[21]

As a consequence of factors like this, the postwar violence that took place in northern Italy was far worse than anywhere else in western Europe. The statistics tell the story. The number of collaborators killed during the liberation of Belgium was around 265, and in Holland only around 100.[22] France, which suffered a more protracted and violent liberation, saw around 9,000 Vichyites killed during the course of several months, although only a few thousand of these happened *after* the liberation.[23] In Italy the final death toll is even higher: somewhere between 12,000 and 20,000, depending on whose figures one believes.[24]

In other words, for every 100,000 people in each country, Holland saw only a single suspected collaborator killed in vengeance, while Belgium had more than three, France more than twenty-two, and Italy somewhere between twenty-six and forty-four.

One of the striking things about the revenge in northern Italy is not so much the scale of the killings as the urgency with which they were carried out. According to the Italian Interior Ministry in 1946, some 9,000 Fascists or their sympathizers were killed in April and May 1945 alone.[25] Some historians have portrayed it as an orgy of violence, more or less uncontrolled in character – but while crimes of passion certainly took place in abundance, there was also a strongly organized element which was more dispassionate, and more systematic in its approach. Specific individuals were sought out and executed by military-style firing squads, and in some cases the partisans even held brief improvised trials before executing their captives.

Rather than waiting for the Allies to arrive and handing over their prisoners to the conventional justice system – as most resisters did in most other western European countries – these partisans were making a conscious decision to take the law into their own hands. The reason for this is that few of them believed that the Fascists would receive the sentences they deserved if left to the Italian courts. In the words of Roberto Battaglia, the former commander of a partisan division, 'We have to conduct the purge now because after the liberation it will not be possible, because in war you shoot, but when the war is finished you can't shoot any more.'[26]

The widespread cynicism about the quality of Italian justice was not without cause. The partisans in northern Italy had already witnessed the sort of purge they could expect by watching what had happened in the south of the country over the previous eighteen months. Here, under the tainted leadership of Pietro Badoglio, former Fascists continued to rule at every level of society. In some areas the Allies had insisted on ejecting Fascists from their posts – but many of these had been reinstated as soon as control of the liberated areas was returned to the Italian authorities. Policemen continued to harass Communists, and indeed anyone with overtly left-wing sympathies, and the singing of Fascist anthems in public remained fairly commonplace. In 1944 there was something of a Fascist revival in parts of Calabria, and even a brief spate of Fascist terrorism and sabotage. More than a year after their liberation, many communities in southern Italy were still being run by the same mayors, police chiefs and landowners, who used the same violent and repressive measures to oppress them as they had done during the Fascist years.[27]

By the time the north of the country was liberated, the failure of the purge in the south was already well established. The problem was that to be a Fascist per se was never considered a crime – it could not be, since the Fascist government in Italy had been internationally recognized as legitimate since long before the war. In the north, however, things were slightly different. Here the Fascists, now based at Salò, had imposed their government upon the people despite the fact that they had been removed from power in 1943. More importantly, they had supported and facilitated the German occupation of their country. As a consequence, anyone who had held a position of authority in the Salò Republic could potentially be prosecuted both as a Fascist and as a collaborator.

On the face of it, the prospects for a proper purge in the north of Italy looked much more promising than they had done in the south. In practice, however, the political will to bring about such a change was missing from the start. When the Allies arrived, many officials and civil servants successfully pleaded their case to remain in office: in the chaos of the liberation their experience would be needed if the situation was ever to be brought under control. Likewise, many policemen and carabinieri (military police) were kept on because the Allies were understandably nervous about handing police powers over to the partisans. Businesses that had collaborated were allowed to keep trading, so as to avoid destroying workers' jobs, and their owners and managers were kept in place for fear of further damaging the economy. In fact, apart from in those areas where the partisans *imposed* change, the default position was to keep the current power structures in place.

The purge, when it came, was delegated to the courts – but no real attempt was made to reform the legal system first. Despite calls for new laws, new courts, new judges and legal professionals, the general atmosphere within the legal structure was one of continuity rather than change. Some new laws were enacted, but the Fascist Penal Code of 1930 was not repealed – indeed it is still in use today. New courts were set up to hear cases of collaboration – the Extraordinary Courts of Assize – but these were generally staffed by the same judges and lawyers who had served under Mussolini. Thus many collaborators who went to court in Italy found themselves in the absurd situation where they were being tried by men who were at least as guilty as they were. Their sentences, when they were not acquitted, were scandalously lenient – judges simply could not enforce sanctions against other civil servants without also bringing their own roles into question.[28]

For all their faults, the Extraordinary Courts of Assize did at least condemn crimes of violence, such as the murder or torture of civilians by the infamous Black Brigades. But even these sentences could be overturned by appealing to the highest court in Italy, the Court of Cassation in Rome. The judges who served in this court were unashamedly close to fascism, and apparently keen to defend the actions of the previous regime. By continually annulling the sentences handed down by the Assize Courts, and by pardoning, ignoring and covering up some of the worst atrocities committed by the Black Brigades, the Court of Cassation systematically undermined all attempts to bring Fascist criminals to justice.[29]

Within a year of the end of the war the official purge had become something of a farce. Of the 394,000 government employees investigated up to February 1946 only 1,580 were dismissed, and the majority of these would soon get their jobs back. Of the 50,000 Fascists imprisoned in Italy, only a very small minority spent much actual time in jail: in the summer of 1946 all prison sentences under five years were cancelled, and the prisoners set free. Despite having witnessed some of the worst atrocities in western Europe, Italian courts handed out proportionally fewer death sentences than any other western European country – no more than ninety-two out of a postwar population of more than 45 million. This is twenty times fewer executions per head than in France.[30] Unlike their German partners, no Italian was ever brought to trial for war crimes committed outside Italy.

In the face of such a spectacular failure of justice, it is unsurprising that popular frustrations began to resurface. Once people had concluded that any purge was impossible if left to the authorities, it was only a short step to deciding to take the law back into their own hands. In the months after the end of the war a second wave of popular violence swept parts of the country, as people demonstrated their distrust of the official purge by breaking into prisons and lynching the prisoners there. This occurred in towns across the provinces of Emilia-Romagna and Veneto, but also in other northern regions.[31] The most famous instance was at Schio, in the province of Vicenza, where former partisans broke into the local prison and massacred fifty-five of its inmates. The words of some of the people who were present during this crime show how bitterly the people resented the failure of the purge at the time. 'If only they had held two or three trials,' claimed one, 'if only they had tried to do something, it might have been enough to release the tension that was felt by the people.' 'I have always defended the act,' claimed another, when interviewed more than fifty years later, 'because for me it was an act of justice that they were killed . . . I have no compassion for those people, even if they are dead.'[32]

The Failure of the Purge Across Europe

The Italian experience was an extreme example of something that occurred all over western Europe. The postwar purges were at least a partial failure everywhere. In France, for example, praised by the Allies for the 'thoroughness' and 'competence' of its purge, disillusionment with the courts was widespread.[33] Of more than 311,000 cases that were investigated in France only about 95,000 resulted in any kind of punishment at all – just 30 per cent of the total. Less than half of these – only 45,000 people – received a prison sentence or worse. The most common punishment was the loss of civil rights, such as the right to vote, or the right to be employed in any kind of public office. However, most of these punishments were reversed after an amnesty in 1947, and the majority of those imprisoned were set free. After a further amnesty in 1951 only 1,500 of the worst war criminals remained in prison. Of the 11,000 civil servants who were removed from their jobs in the first days of the purge, most of them were back at their posts within the next six years.[34]

Half of those punished in Holland suffered only the removal of their voting rights, and while most of the other half were imprisoned, their sentences were generally short. In Belgium the punishments were slightly harsher, with 48,000 prison sentences being handed out, 2,340 of them for life. But this still only represented about 12 per cent of the total number of cases investigated. Belgian judges also gave out 2,940 death sentences, but of these all but 242 were commuted.[35]

Many people across the continent regarded such sentencing as hopelessly lenient. They certainly made their frustrations known. In May 1945 a series of demonstrations took place across Belgium in which collaborators were lynched, their families humiliated and their houses sacked.[36] In Denmark, where serious collaboration was almost unknown, some 10,000 people took to the streets of Aalborg to demand harsher treatment for collaborators, and a general strike was called. Smaller demonstrations occurred in other parts of the country.[37] In France, as in Italy, there were numerous attempts by mobs to break into prisons and lynch the inmates.[38]

Perhaps the only place in north-west Europe where the people showed any satisfaction with the purge was Norway, where the trials

were rapid and efficient, and the punishments harsh. Out of a population of just 3 million, 90,000 cases were investigated, and more than
half of these received some kind of punishment. In other words, more
than 1.6 per cent of the entire population was punished in some way
after the war; and this does not include the unofficial punishments that
were meted out on women and children, which shall be the subject of
the next chapter.[39]

The fact is that justice varied wildly from one nation to the next. The
country where an individual was most likely to be investigated was, needless to say, Germany, where the denazification process necessarily
demonized an entire people. More surprisingly, however, the country
where an individual was most likely to be imprisoned was Belgium, with
Norway coming close behind. The country where an individual was most
likely to be executed was – just as surprisingly – Bulgaria, where more than
1,500 death sentences were carried out. (As in the rest of eastern Europe,
however, many of these executions had more to do with the Communist
seizure of power than with punishment for actual crimes.)

This discrepancy between the way collaborators were treated in different countries is perhaps best illustrated by what happened in central
Europe. Austria and Czechoslovakia, though neighbours, had vastly differing results to their respective purges. In Austria, collaboration was
overwhelmingly treated as a minor crime, to be punished with fines or
the loss of civil rights. More than half a million people were punished in
this way. These sanctions would not last long, however: in April 1948
an amnesty restored civil rights to 487,000 former Nazis, and the rest
were allowed back into the fold in 1956. Some 70,000 civil servants
were dismissed but, as in other countries, their exit proved to be via
something of a revolving door.[40]

In the Czech lands, by contrast, collaboration was taken much
more seriously. The Czech courts handed out 723 death sentences for
crimes committed during the war, and because of their unique policy
of conducting executions within three hours of the sentence, a
higher percentage were actually carried out here than anywhere else in
Europe – almost 95 per cent, or 686 in all. While the absolute number
of executions does not appear much worse than, say, France, one must
remember that the Czech lands had only a quarter of France's population – their execution rate was therefore four times that of France's.
Czechs were twice as likely to be executed for collaboration as Belgians,

six times as likely as Norwegians, and eight times as likely as their Slovak cousins in the eastern half of the country. But the comparison with Austria is most telling of all. Of the forty-three death sentences in Austria, only thirty were ever carried out, making Austria one of the safest places in Europe for collaborators. Czechs were over sixteen times more likely to be executed for 'war crimes' than their Austrian neighbours.

Of course, there are all kinds of cultural, political and ethnic reasons for the differences between these two countries. The Czechs wanted revenge for the dismemberment of their country, and their marginalization by the German minority in their midst – a minority that they were in the process of expelling, even while the trials were going on. The Austrians, by contrast, had largely welcomed the *Anschluss* in 1938, and felt a natural affinity with their fellow German-speakers – all of which made a mockery of their official status as Hitler's 'first victim'. It was precisely *because* Austrian collaboration had been so universal that the authorities felt unable to punish it properly.

Whether the difference between the way collaborators were treated in the two countries was *fair* or not is a completely different matter. From an international viewpoint it is impossible simultaneously to justify the severity in one and the leniency in the other.

Table 2: The judicial punishment of collaborators in western Europe[41]

	Norway	Denmark	Belgium	Holland	France	Italy	Czech.	Austria
Population 1945	3.1m	4m	8.3m	9.3m	40m	45.4m	10.5m	6.8m
Executions*	1	0.7	3	0.4	3.8	0.2	6.5	0.4
Prison sentences*	573	33	582	553	110	110	208	200
Milder sanctions*	1,083	—	378	663	188	—	234	7,691
Total punished*	1,656	33	963	1,216	309	—	449	7,892

Notes: *Figures per 100,000. Despite the precise nature of some of the figures above, they should be considered estimates only, as many of the absolute numbers are disputed. For the purpose of comparison between countries, however, they give a broadly accurate picture.

The differing treatment of collaborators in different countries is just one of the many inconsistencies that hampered the pursuit of justice in Europe after the war. The courts everywhere tended to be harsher on the poor and the young, who were less well connected, less articulate and less able to afford expensive lawyers. (This was true even in eastern Europe in the months before the purge was hijacked by the Communists for their own political purposes.) They were also harsher on those who were tried in the early days of the purge, when emotions were still running high: many crimes that were punishable by death in 1944 were only punishable by a few years in prison after the war was over.[42] Different categories of collaboration were also treated differently. Military and political collaborators, for example, were punished harshly everywhere, as were informers. Those who worked in the media were perhaps punished most severely of all, given the relatively minor nature of their crimes, since there was ample documentary evidence of their guilt and it was easy to make an example of them.[43] Economic collaborators, by contrast, were barely punished at all, at least in the western half of Europe. Not only was it difficult to prove a case against most businessmen, but they were much more likely to be able to afford lawyers who could string out their trials until an acquittal was more likely. Besides, the political will to try businessmen was not there: the abysmal conditions of postwar Europe meant that they were needed, no matter how unpopular they were.

One cannot entirely blame the courts for this state of affairs. Putting aside the emotional demands of the people, some of the dilemmas that the courts had to grapple with were genuinely baffling. For example, the legal arguments surrounding the issue of what exactly constituted 'collaboration' were impossible to unravel. Was it really treason, for example, if the defendant truly believed himself to be acting in the best interests of his country? Many politicians and administrators claimed that they had only gone along with the Nazis because it was better than the massive repression that would have resulted if they had collectively resisted. Similarly, economic collaborators often claimed that if they had shut off production in their factories the people would have starved, and their workers would have been conscripted into forced labour and deported to Germany. By collaborating with the Germans they had prevented their country from experiencing a much worse fate. Others pointed out that the new laws against collaboration were being applied retroactively – in other words, since their actions had not been against any law *at the time*, how could they be considered a crime? Could someone 'collaborating' under duress be held responsible for their actions? And how could the postwar authorities proclaim membership of far-right political parties illegal – again, retrospectively – while at the same time espousing the universal right to freedom of association?

In France, Slovakia, Hungary, Romania and Croatia prosecutors grappled with the additional problem that the state itself had collaborated with Germany. While the leaders of these states could certainly be accused of working for the Germans, most of the ordinary bureaucrats and administrators had had nothing to do with Germany or the Nazis. Could one be a traitor if one was simply following the instructions of one's apparently legitimate government?[44]

The subtleties of such legal arguments were lost on the general population, who cared less about level-headed justice and more about their own emotional need to see people punished. Inevitably, many trials got bogged down in details. Far from being '*justice sévère et expéditive*', it was often lukewarm and painfully slow. In Belgium, for example, six months after the liberation, 180,000 cases had been opened, but only 8,500 brought to trial. As one Allied observer noted wryly, 'If this slow rate of progress were maintained it would take ten years before the last case came before the courts.'[45]

The only way to speed things up was to take short cuts, or to write off cases before they ever came to court. In the end this is exactly what happened in Belgium. Of the 110,000 charges of economic collaboration that were laid, only 2 per cent ever ended up in court.[46] In the rest of Europe, too, the great majority of cases were dropped before they came to trial.

The Construction of Convenient Myths

The main reason Europe's purges ended up being such mild affairs is because, in the end, the political will for anything stronger simply was not there. Harsh and rigorous retribution was not in any nation's interest. De Gaulle's expatriate government, for example, had spent most of the war portraying the French as a people united in their struggle against both the Germans and the tiny elite at Vichy. When de Gaulle came to power after the liberation it did not make sense to drop this myth of unity, especially since the French people were apparently united behind *him*. And besides, France would need to be united if it were ever to have the strength to rebuild itself. Collaborators and resisters still had to live together in the same communities after the war. To promote enmity between them would only store up trouble for the future.

Other governments and Resistance groups across Europe played exactly the same game. The Norwegian, Dutch, Belgian and Czech expatriate governments also wanted to ease national tensions by portraying their respective peoples as united against the Nazis. The Resistance were happy to have their wartime exploits repeated like a mantra after the war, even if it gave the impression that *their* behaviour, rather than that of petty everyday collaboration, had been the norm. The Communists, especially, were keen to pretend that the people stood as one behind them, since it gave greater legitimacy to their seizure of power in eastern Europe. The illusion of unity was far more important to all the postwar governments than the purge ever was. In general, therefore, the purge was only ever pursued vigorously in order to remove those who threatened that unity – to justify the expulsion of hostile ethnic groups, for example, or to remove outspoken political opponents from power in eastern Europe.

This insistence on unity was the source of one of the most potent myths of the postwar period – the idea that the responsibility for all the evils of the war rested exclusively with the Germans. If it was only 'they' who had perpetrated atrocities upon 'us', then the rest of Europe was released from all accountability for the injustices it had perpetrated upon itself.[47] Better still, the bulk of Europe would be able to share in the 'victory' over Germany. The loathing that all Europeans expressed towards Germany and Germans in the aftermath of the war was therefore only partly a reaction to the things Germany had actually done – it was also a way for each country to heal its own wounds.

As a defeated nation, Germany had little choice but to take this on the chin. Germany had, after all, started the war. It had enslaved millions of forced labourers from all over Europe, and had presided over the Holocaust. And yet, even in Germany it was possible to dodge any feeling of accountability for these crimes. The stereotypical image of the German who continually apologizes for the war is largely a creation of the 1960s: before then, Germans were just as likely as any other nation-ality to deny both personal and collective responsibility for the events of 1939–45. The majority of Germans saw themselves as victims, not per-petrators – victims of Nazism, of their leaders' failure to win the war, of bombing, of Allied revenge, of postwar shortages, and so on. Blame was easily shifted elsewhere.

In general, the denazification trials yielded the same results as the purges elsewhere, with all the same inconsistencies. Some zones of Ger-many pursued Nazis more vigorously than others; some categories of prisoner were treated more harshly than others; and many prominent Nazis got off scot free while their 'fellow travellers' were punished.[48]

The single trial that overshadowed all the others was that of the Nazi leaders at Nuremberg in 1946. The blaze of publicity that accompanied this event was designed to educate the nation in the horrors of Nazism – but it also gave the impression that the guilt of the nation resided in these men *alone*. Once the trial was over, it was easy to imagine that justice had been done.

The continued rooting out of Nazis in the following years, particu-larly in the American zone, was universally resented. It did not come to an end until 1949, when the new Federal Republic was established in West Germany. As elsewhere in Europe, at the same time that the purge was officially brought to a close, many of the punishments that had been doled out to former Nazis were formally annulled or reversed. On 20 September that year the new West German Chancellor Konrad Aden-auer announced in his first official address to parliament that it was time to 'put the past behind us'.[49] The nightmare of the war would be deliberately forgotten, in favour of new dreams of the future.

It is tempting to imagine that such postwar myth-making was fairly benign. If the myth of unity brought about a *real* unity of sorts, then what harm could it do? And if forgetting the facts of wartime guilt and collaboration allowed Europe to move on and forge a better future, then surely that too was for the best? Unfortunately, however, there have been some significant side-effects to this particular medicine. Attempts to rehabilitate the political right in western Europe have not only resulted in a whitewash: in some cases, absurdly, it has allowed right-wing extremists to portray themselves as the injured party.

As the myth that responsibility lay *exclusively* with Germany began to take hold, the harsh treatment of collaborators began to look less like rough justice and more like a slaughter of the innocents. In France, by the 1950s, hundreds of lurid stories began to emerge in the popular press giving graphic details of the torture and abuse perpetrated by *maquisards* upon civilians. In all of these stories the innocence of the victims was either assumed or overtly stressed. Many focused on the treatment of women, who were stripped, shaved, insulted, beaten with iron bars, sexually mutilated and raped. These things did indeed happen after the war – but the stories in the press were often based on hearsay rather than fact, and exaggerated accordingly.[50]

Along with the stories came bogus statistics. Many writers in the 1950s claimed that around 105,000 collaborators were executed by the French Resistance in the months after the liberation. This figure was based on a casual remark supposedly made in November 1944 by Adrien Tixier, who was Minister of the Interior at the time – but Tixier himself died in 1946, and there has never been any documentary evidence to back this figure up. The real number, repeatedly confirmed by government agencies and independent academic studies, was less than a tenth of this total.[51]

In Italy, too, the political right lost no time in painting themselves as victims. Ever since the 1950s they have portrayed the immediate aftermath of the war as a bloodbath, in which anything up to 300,000 people were murdered.[52] These frankly absurd claims, if repeated often enough, begin to attain an air of authenticity. More importantly, they dwarf the number of partisans killed by the Fascists during the war – a mere 45,000 – making it seem as if the resisters had been the greater villains.[53] In reality, the number of people killed by partisans after the war was nowhere near 300,000, but at least twenty times smaller.[54]

The myth of the innocence of the right is just as strong in Italy as it is in France. Indeed, in recent years it has been gaining strength. One of the most controversial books to have been published in Italy at the beginning of the twenty-first century was Giampaolo Pansa's *Il Sangue dei vinti*, which attacked the heroic idea of the Italian resistance movement by describing in detail the murders that they carried out during and after the liberation. Pansa's book concentrated heavily on the innocence of many of those killed, often citing a 'not guilty' verdict from the courts as proof of that innocence. The book caused outrage on the left because it lacked the subtlety of other studies, which took much more account of the context in which these killings took place, the popular anger felt towards fascism at the time, and the often understandable lack of trust in the judgement of the courts. But what really angered the left was the popularity of the book, which sold over 350,000 copies in its first year.[55] Pansa had tapped into the mindset of a newly confident Italian right wing, which happily latched on to his well-argued polemic – as well as the works of more dubious historians – as a way of rehabilitating their past.

Since the fall of communism in the early 1990s, and the subsequent rise of right-wing parties everywhere, a similar process has been taking place across Europe. Figures who were once universally reviled are now being resurrected as role models simply because they opposed the 'greater evils' of communism and the Soviet Union. In the popular imagination, the crimes of wartime dictators like Mussolini or Romania's Ion Antonescu have been excused or even ignored in favour of their supposed virtues. Ultra-nationalists in Hungary, Croatia, Ukraine or the Baltic States – men who indiscriminately murdered Jews, Communists and liberals both during and after the war – are now being rehabilitated as national heroes. These are more than benign myths: they are dangerous distortions of the truth that need to be exposed as such.

While we might understand the widespread collaboration with despotic regimes during the war, this does not mean we should condone it. When the conduct of those collaborators crossed a moral line, this cannot be excused just because the broad political outlook of those collaborators might chime with our own. Likewise, we should not condone the brutal vengeance committed by partisans in the aftermath of the war. But neither can we judge their actions by modern-day standards. Injustices *did* occur. Innocent people *were* killed. But for the European people, brutalized by years of repression and atrocity, to be capable of avoiding such excesses would surely have been asking too much.

14

Revenge on Women and Children

In most of western Europe, vengeance on collaborators tended to be a small-scale affair. It was usually committed by individuals or by small groups of partisans with particular grudges to settle. Mass vengeance – that is, vengeance committed by whole towns or villages *communally* – was actually fairly rare, and generally confined to those areas where the process of liberation had been particularly violent. On the whole, as I have shown, the communities of western Europe were more or less content to turn their collaborators over to the proper authorities. In those areas where they did not trust the authorities, and tried to take the law into their own hands, the police or the Allied armies stepped in fairly quickly to restore order.

The only major exception, which occurred throughout western Europe, was the way in which women who had slept with German soldiers were treated. Such women were universally regarded as traitors – 'horizontal collaborators', to use the French term – but they had not necessarily committed any crime that could be legally prosecuted. When their communities turned on them after the war, very few people were willing to come to their defence. Policemen or Allied soldiers who were present almost always stood aside and allowed the mob to have their way: indeed, in some towns the authorities *encouraged* the abuse of these women because they regarded it as a useful pressure valve for popular anger.[1]

Of all the revenge that was carried out upon collaborators in western Europe, this was by far the most public and the most universal. There are many reasons why women were singled out in this way, not all of which relate to the actual betrayal they were supposed to have committed. Their punishment, and the subsequent treatment of their children, is worth looking at because it says a great deal about the way that European society had come to view itself after the war.

The Shearing of Women

In the autumn of 1944 a young girl from Saint-Clément in the Yonne *département* of France was arrested for having 'intimate relations' with a German officer. When questioned by the police she openly admitted to her affair. 'I became his mistress,' she said. 'He sometimes came to the house to help my father when he was ill. When he left, he left me his *Feldpost* number. I wrote to him and had my letters taken to him by other Germans because I could not use the postal services in France. I wrote to him for two or three months but I do not have his address anymore.'[2]

Many women across Europe embarked on such relationships with Germans during the war. They justified their actions by saying that 'relationships based on love' were 'not a crime', that 'matters of the heart have nothing to do with politics', or that 'love is blind'.[3] But in the eyes of their communities, this was no excuse. Sex, if it was with a German, *was* political. It came to represent the subjugation of the continent as a whole: a female France, Denmark or Holland being ravished by a male Germany. Just as importantly, as I have already mentioned in Chapter 4, it also came to represent the emasculation of European men. These men, who had already shown themselves impotent against the military might of Germany, now found themselves communally cuckolded by their own womenfolk.

The number of sexual relationships that took place between European women and Germans during the war is quite staggering. In Norway as many as 10 per cent of women aged between fifteen and thirty had German boyfriends during the war.[4] If the statistics on the number of children born to German soldiers are anything to go by, this was by no means unusual: the numbers of women who slept with German men across western Europe can easily be numbered in the hundreds of thousands.[5]

Resistance movements in occupied countries came up with all kinds of excuses for the behaviour of their women and girls. They characterized women who slept with Germans as ignorant, poor, even mentally defective. They claimed that women were raped, or that they only slept with Germans out of economic necessity. While this was undoubtedly the case for some, recent surveys show that women who slept with

Vichy leader François Darlan throws the key to
'her' room to a German

German soldiers came from all classes and all walks of life. On the whole European women slept with Germans not because they were forced to, or because their own men were absent, or because they needed money or food – but simply because they found the strong, 'knightly' image of the German soldiers intensely attractive, especially compared to the weakened impression they had of their own menfolk. In Denmark, for example, wartime pollsters were shocked to discover that 51 per cent of Danish women openly admitted to finding German men more attractive than their own compatriots.[6]

Nowhere was this need more keenly felt than in France. In a nation where the huge, almost entirely male German presence was matched by a corresponding absence of French men – 2 million of whom were prisoners or workers in Germany – it is unsurprising that the occupation itself was often seen in sexual terms. France had become a 'slut', giving herself up to Germany with the Vichy government acting as her pimp.[7] As Jean-Paul Sartre noted after the war, even the collaborationist press tended to represent the relationship between France and Germany as a union 'in which France was always playing the part of the woman'.[8]

Even those who still felt patriotic in the face of this were obliged to register a sense of sexual humiliation. Writing in 1942, Antoine de Saint-Exupéry suggested that all Frenchmen were tainted by an unavoidable feeling of being cuckolded by the war, but that they should not allow this shame to destroy their innate sense of patriotism:

> Does a husband go from house to house crying out to his neighbours that his wife is a strumpet? Is it thus that he can preserve his honour? No, for his wife is one with his home. No, for he cannot establish his dignity against her. Let him go home to her, and there unburden himself of his anger. Thus, I shall not divorce myself from a defeat which surely will often humiliate me. I am part of France, and France is part of me.[9]

Such emotions were experienced not only by Frenchmen, but also by men in all the occupied nations. As an airman fighting on behalf of the Free French, Saint-Exupéry was at least doing something to help liberate his country. For those who were stuck at home without any realistic means of fighting back, the frustration was more difficult to bear.

The liberation was an opportunity to put some of this right. By taking up arms once more, and participating in the invasion of their own country, French men had a chance to redeem themselves both in the eyes of their womenfolk and in the eyes of the world. This is perhaps one reason why Charles de Gaulle became such an important symbol for the French during the war. In contrast to the effeminate supplication of Vichy, de Gaulle had never surrendered his martial spirit, and stubbornly refused to bend to anyone else's will, including that of his allies. The speeches he broadcast on the BBC were littered with masculine references to 'Fighting France', the 'proud, brave and great French people', the 'military strength of France' and the 'aptitude for warfare of our race'.[10] In a speech to the Consultative Assembly in Algiers in the run-up to the D-Day landings, de Gaulle praised

> The work of our magnificent troops . . . the ardour of our units as they prepare for the great battle; the spirit of our ships' companies; the prowess of our gallant air squadrons; the heroic boys who fight in the Maquis without uniforms, and nearly without arms, but animated by the purest military flame . . .[11]

Such words are often used by generals who wish to appeal to the martial spirit of their troops. But they are significant here because they contrast so strongly with the defeatist, 'effeminate' way that Vichy portrayed French military hopes.

The rehabilitation of French masculinity began in earnest after the D-Day landings in June 1944, when de Gaulle and his 'Free French' troops finally returned to France. In the following months, they won a series of military scoops. The first was the liberation of Paris, which was conducted exclusively by French troops under General Philippe Leclerc (despite American attempts to hold Leclerc in check while they organized a more coordinated assault with US divisions). The second was the arrival in Provence on 15 August of French troops, who fought all the way through to Alsace and eventually crossed into Germany to capture Stuttgart. On the way, they liberated Lyon, France's second city – again, without American help. Slowly but surely they were beginning to redeem themselves for the military embarrassment of 1940.

However, perhaps the greatest boost to French pride was the formation of something that the British and Americans did not have – a separate army within France itself, which rose up and fought the Germans from the inside. The Forces Françaises de l'Intérieur (FFI) – or *les fifis* as they were affectionately and disparagingly known – were an amalgamation of all the most important French Resistance groups under the nominal leadership of General Pierre Koenig. During the summer of 1944 they took control of town after town, often fighting alongside regular British and American forces. They liberated almost all of south-west France without any outside help, and likewise cleared the region east of Lyon for Allied troops driving north from Marseilles (see Map 8, p.282).

The exploits of the FFI gave a huge psychological boost to French morale, and particularly to the morale of young French men, who flocked to join up in great numbers: between June and October 1944, the ranks of the FFI swelled from 100,000 to 400,000.[12] While seasoned *résistants* tended from habit to keep a fairly low profile, these new recruits were enormously keen to flaunt their new-found virility. Allied soldiers often reported seeing them appear with 'bandoleers of ammunition strung all about them' or with 'grenades hanging from shoulder and belt', as they kept 'letting off round after round into the air'.[13] According to Julius Neave, who served as a major in the British Royal Armoured Corps, they were perhaps more of a nuisance than they were worth: 'They roar round in civilian cars knocking each other down and fighting pitched battles with everyone, including themselves, ourselves and the Boche.'[14] Even some of the French villagers characterized them as 'young men . . . parading with FFI amulets and posing as heroes'.[15] But if they appeared a little too keen to prove themselves, this was only because, unlike British and American men, they had for years been unable to take up arms against Germany. Now, for the first time, they were presented with a chance to fight properly, openly – like *men*.

Unfortunately, this new-found display of virility also had its darker side. The sudden influx of young men into the ranks of the Resistance pushed out many much more experienced female *résistantes*. Jeanne Bohec, for example, who was a well-respected female explosives expert in Saint-Marcel, suddenly found herself sidelined. 'I was told politely to forget about it. A woman isn't supposed to fight when so many men are available. Yet I surely knew how to use a submachine gun better than lots of the FFI volunteers who had just got hold of these arms.'[16] During the last winter of the occupation women were phased out of active participation in the Resistance, and the Communist Francs-Tireurs et Partisans (FTP) issued orders to phase out women altogether. This is in direct contrast to countries like Italy and Greece, where significant numbers of women continued to fight for the partisans on the front line right to the end of the war.[17]

If 'good' women were pushed aside by this sudden reassertion of French masculinity, then 'bad' women who had 'cuckolded' the nation were treated much more harshly. In the immediate aftermath of the liberation, the FFI turned upon these 'horizontal collaborators' en masse. In most cases the punishment they meted out was head shaving, which was often conducted in public in order to maximize the humiliation for the women involved. After the liberation, head-shaving ceremonies were carried out in every *département* of France.

A British artillery officer described a typical ceremony when he wrote about his experiences in northern France after the war:

> At St André d'Echauffeur, where people showered us with flowers as we passed, others proffering bottles, a grim scene was being enacted in its market place – the punishment of a collaborator said to be *une mauvaise femme*. Seated in a chair while a barber shaved her head to the crown, she attracted a crowd of onlookers, among them, as I learned later, some Maquis and a Free French officer. The woman's mother was also present and as the barber cropped her daughter, she stamped, raved and gesticulated frantically outside the circle of watchers. The woman was of some spirit. For, with her head fully cropped, she jumped to her feet and cried '*Vive les Allemands*,' whereupon someone picked up a brick and felled her.[18]

Lieutenant Richard Holborow of the Royal Engineers witnessed a similar scene at the hands of a mob in a small town near Dieppe, 'many of whom had obviously been celebrating their liberation all day, mostly from the neck of a bottle'. About eighteen women and girls were paraded to a makeshift stage, where each of them was made to sit before the local barber:

> Drawing a cut-throat razor from his pocket, he opened it, pulled up the woman's hair and, with a few deft strokes, cut it off and threw the severed ends into the crowd. She gave out a scream as the barber proceeded to dry-scrape her scalp until it was completely bald, and then she was lifted up and displayed to the now howling and jeering mob.

This was not the end of the women's ordeal. A couple of days later, as his unit moved out of the same town, Holborow witnessed the second part of their punishment when he was delayed in the main street by yet another chanting crowd.

> They were watching with considerable glee a group of shaven women, all with placards tied round their necks, who were busily engaged in filling

buckets of horse shit with their bare hands. As a bucket was filled so it was kicked over and the process ordered to be started again. It was evident that the women of the town were still getting their own back on the girls who had misbehaved with the German soldiers.[19]

In dozens of towns women were forced to undergo their ordeal either partially or completely naked. According to an article in *La Marseillaise* in September 1944, a group of young men in Endoume forced a woman to 'run through the streets completely naked in front of innocent children playing outside their houses'.[20] Likewise in Troyes, the FFI rounded up women, stripped them and displayed them before the crowd while they were having their heads shorn. According to a leaflet of the local Comité Départemental de la Libération:

> With hardly any clothes on, branded with the sign of the swastika and smeared with a particularly sticky tar, after having received cutting jibes, they would go and have their heads shaved in the regular way and would then look like so many strange convicts. Begun on the evening before, this merciless hunt would go on throughout the day, much to the great pleasure of the local people who would form ranks in the streets to watch these women walk past wearing Wehrmacht caps.[21]

According to Fabrice Virgili, probably the foremost expert in this field, women were stripped in at least fifty major towns and cities across France.[22]

Such scenes were by no means unique to France. Similar events took place all over Europe. In Denmark and Holland a combination of wounded national pride and sexual jealousy at the behaviour of local women resulted in thousands of women having their heads shaved.[23] In the Channel Islands, the only small corner of the British Isles that Germany had managed to invade, there were several cases of women having their heads shaved because they had slept with German soldiers.[24] In northern Italy they even sang songs about shaving the heads of women who slept with fascists, such as this one sung by partisans in the Veneto:

E voi fanciulle belle	And all you beautiful misses
Che coi fascisti andate	Who with fascists misbehaved
Le vostre chiome belle	All your beautiful tresses
Presto saran tagliate	Will presently be shaved[25]

The immense popularity of such punishments, as well as the ritual that surrounded them, seems to point to a deep need amongst the liberated people to express their disgust for collaboration. Historian Peter Novick, who pioneered the objective study of this period in France, makes the point that the shearing of these women gave local communities an emotional outlet that helped to prevent widespread bloodshed of more serious collaborators, almost as if they were a 'sacrificial offering'.[26] Often during the first weeks of the liberation the sight of shorn women in the market square resulted in a perceivable drop in local tension, and a reduction of bloodshed against other collaborators.[27] While some historians have questioned this notion, the shearing of women undeniably brought communities together – as a relatively safe and non-permanent form of violence, it was the single act of vengeance in which everyone could be involved.[28] The practice may now be seen as a shameful episode in European history, but at the time it was celebrated with pride. Resistance newspapers in 1944 describe a carnival air at shearing ceremonies, where spontaneous renditions of patriotic songs were sung by the crowds. In at least one area of France, the local people presented those who carried out the ceremony with knives and razors as a 'souvenir' of their day's work.[29]

With hindsight, it is obvious that patriotic vengeance was only one side of the story. The shearing of women's hair is not a new phenomenon – even before the war it was a time-honoured punishment for adulteresses – but at no other time in European history has this punishment been meted out on such a comprehensive scale. It is therefore significant that the majority of French women who were punished for sleeping with Germans were not married: their 'adultery' was not to their menfolk but to their country. In a subtle way, therefore, France was being rebranded from an effeminate, submissive entity to a masculine, vengeful one.

The sexual nature of the rituals themselves is also significant. In Denmark the women were frequently stripped naked during their head-shaving ceremonies, and their breasts and backsides painted with Nazi symbols.[30] In many areas of France women also had their bare bottoms spanked, and their breasts daubed with swastikas.[31] The fact that these rituals took place in market squares or on the steps of town halls sent a very clear message to the whole community: the FFI were reclaiming these women's bodies as public property. They were also reclaiming them as *male* property – the hundreds of photographs taken during these punishments show that they were conducted almost exclusively by men.

Some French women were all too aware that they were being used in this symbolic way. They were also indignant that they should be condemned for a *private* act that they believed had nothing to do with the war. When the French actress Arletty was imprisoned in 1945 for her wartime liaison with a German officer, she reputedly justified herself at her trial by saying, 'My heart belongs to France, but my vagina is mine.'[32] Unsurprisingly such protestations fell on deaf ears. According to recent research, about 20,000 French women had their heads shaved as a punishment for collaboration, the largest proportion of them for sleeping with German soldiers.[33]

It is difficult to judge, at a distance of some seventy years, whether these women deserved to be punished in this way, in an alternative way, or not at all. Allied soldiers and administrators certainly did not feel qualified to judge: in the words of Anthony Eden, the British Foreign Secretary of the day, those who had not been through the 'horrors of occupation' had 'no right to pronounce upon what a country does'.[34] What is undeniable, however, is the fact that these women were scapegoats: shaving their heads was a symbolic way of cutting away not only their own sins, but the sins of the whole community. All of western Europe had, in the words of French journalist Robert Brasillach, 'slept with Germany', through the thousands of everyday actions that had made the German occupation possible. But in many communities it was only the women who had slept with actual Germans who were punished for it.[35]

The only consolation for the women concerned was the thought that it could easily have been much worse. We have seen how, in eastern Europe, the reassertion of a national sense of masculinity was partly carried out through widespread rape. In western Europe the cutting of women's hair represented a much less vicious form of sexual violence to achieve the same political end.

The Ostracism of Children

If proof were ever needed of the widespread 'horizontal collaboration' that took place across Europe, then it exists in the form of the children who were born as a result of it. In Denmark 5,579 babies were born with a registered German father – and undoubtedly many more whose German paternity was concealed.[36] In Holland the number of children born to German fathers is thought to have been anything between 16,000 and

50,000.[37] In Norway, which had only a third of the population of Holland, between 8,000 and 12,000 such children were born.[38] And in France the number is thought to be around 85,000 or even higher.[39] The total number of children fathered by German soldiers in occupied Europe is unknown, but estimates vary between one and two million.[40]

It is safe to say that these babies were not exactly welcomed by the communities they were born into. An indiscreet relationship might be ignored, hushed up or forgotten, but a child was a constant reminder of a woman's shame – and by extension the shame of the whole community. Shorn women might comfort themselves that their hair would soon grow back. A child, by contrast, could not be undone.

In some cases the local children of Wehrmacht soldiers were considered such an embarrassment that it was thought best to try to dispose of them straight away. In Holland, for instance, some eyewitnesses claim to know of many instances where children were killed shortly after birth, usually by the parents of the particular girls who strayed. Such actions were taken, presumably, to restore the 'honour' of the family – but occasionally they were more overtly political acts, made by people outside the family, in order to restore the honour of the wider community. According to an account by Petra Ruigrok, for example, a baby in northern Holland was snatched from its cradle by a member of the Resistance and dashed to the floor.[41]

Such events were thankfully rare, but they reflected a very strong feeling in European society that local children born with German fathers during the war were an affront to the nation in which they were born. Such strong feelings are summed up in an editorial in *Lufotposten*, a Norwegian daily newspaper, on 19 May 1945:

> All these German children are bound to grow up and develop into an extensive bastard minority in the Norwegian people. By their descent they are doomed in advance to take a combative stance. They have no nation, they have no father, they just have hate, and this is their only heritage. They are unable to become Norwegians. Their fathers were Germans, their mothers were Germans in thought and action. To allow them to stay in this country is tantamount to legalizing the raising of a fifth column. They will forever constitute an element of irritation and unrest among the pure Norwegian population. It is best, for Norway as well as for the children themselves, that they continue their lives under the heavens where they naturally belong.[42]

The study of Norwegian attitudes towards what they termed the 'war children' of German soldiers is a particularly rich area because, unlike in other countries, these attitudes are so well documented. In the aftermath of the war the Norwegian authorities set up a War Child Committee to consider what to do with such children.[43] For a short time, therefore, the problem was openly discussed here in a way that it was not anywhere else in Europe. The subject has also come under intense scrutiny more recently. In 2001, under political pressure from war child groups, the Norwegian government funded a research programme to discover exactly how these people had been treated in the aftermath of the war, what the effect had been on their lives, and what might be done to redress any potential injustice. The findings of this research programme constitute the most complete study of war children in any country to date.[44]

In the immediate aftermath of the war, Norwegians were extremely bitter about the behaviour of some of their women and girls. In the early summer of 1945, thousands of women accused of sleeping with Germans were rounded up and put into jails and prison camps – some 1,000 of them in Oslo alone.[45] As we have already seen, many had their heads shaved during the liberation, and some were publicly humiliated by mobs. Perhaps more worrying, however, were the calls from people in authority to have them stripped of their Norwegian citizenship and deported to Germany. Such an action would have been extremely difficult to justify, since sleeping with German soldiers was not against the law. In any case, the national body for trying war criminals and traitors had already begun to establish that stripping people of their citizenship should not be used as a punishment.[46] As a consequence, calls to deport women who had slept with Germans were gradually dropped.

Women who had gone so far as to marry Germans, however, would not escape so easily. In August 1945 the Norwegian government resurrected a law from twenty years earlier stating that women who married foreigners automatically took on the nationality of their husbands. In order to limit this law, an amendment was made stating that it should apply only to those who married a citizen of an enemy state – in effect, Germans. Against all the principles of Norwegian justice, the law was to be applied retrospectively. Almost overnight, therefore, hundreds – perhaps even thousands – of women who had believed themselves to be acting within the law lost their citizenship. They were now designated

'German', and as such they faced the possibility of deportation to Germany, and along with them their children.[47]

The position regarding the children of German soldiers was even simpler to establish. According to the same law, the nationality of war children was defined by their paternity. Even without the law these children had few if any champions, and a consensus developed across the country that they should be considered unequivocally German. As a consequence, they too faced the prospect of immediate deportation. There were many people, including those in authority, who believed that such deportations should be carried out irrespective of whether their mothers were allowed to stay in the country.

Naturally such a proposal opened up all kinds of moral and political problems. While few people were likely to oppose the deportation of 'German' orphans, the expulsion of children who had living, still-Norwegian mothers was much more difficult. When the War Child Committee was set up at the beginning of July 1945 it was specifically asked to investigate the changes in the law that needed to be made in order to expel children and their mothers. If this was not possible, it was to consider what other measures should be put in place, both to protect the children from a resentful society, and to protect society from a potentially dangerous group of children.

The War Child Committee considered these problems for the best part of five months at the end of 1945. Their findings were, and still are, extremely controversial. On the one hand they suggested that the government should mount a public campaign to get local communities to accept these children, while on the other hand they suggested that, if local communities so wished, children should be taken from their mothers and sent to other areas of Norway, or even abroad. The Committee also recommended that neither the children nor their mothers should be forcibly deported; and yet its chairperson, Inge Debes, reportedly offered all 9,000 war children to an Australian immigration delegation, apparently without regard to what the children's mothers would think of such a move. (The offer was eventually turned down on logistical grounds, but also because the Australians decided in the end that they did not want 'German' children either.)[48]

Since it was looking increasingly unlikely that the government would be able to deport these children, the Committee began to look into the consequences of keeping the children in Norway. One of the things that

worried Norwegians most was the possibility that these children might
be mentally substandard. There was a widespread belief in Norway, as in
other countries, that any woman who allowed herself to be seduced by a
German soldier was probably feeble minded. Similarly, any German who
would take such a mentally deficient partner must himself also be feeble
minded. Following this circular logic to its inevitable conclusion meant
that their children would almost certainly possess the same defects. To
assess the problem, the Committee appointed an eminent psychiatrist
named Ørnulf Ødegård to give a statement regarding the mental condition of war children. Based on a sample of a few dozen patients, Ødegård
suggested that as many as 4,000 of the 9,000 war children might be
mentally retarded or otherwise hereditarily inferior. While the Committee did not fully accept this statement, it did not stop one of its members
writing in a newspaper about the likelihood of both mothers and children being mentally deficient.

Consequently, many war children were labelled retarded on no evidence whatsoever, and some of them, particularly those in the old
German-run orphanages, were damned to spending the rest of their
lives in institutions. According to a doctor who looked after one such
group during the 1980s, had they been treated the same as other, 'non-
German', orphans they would probably have gone on to lead perfectly
normal lives.[49] The War Child Committee did, in fact, recommend that
all war children should be psychologically assessed in order to determine the state of their mental health, but this never happened because it
was deemed far too expensive.

The branding of children as feeble minded by their nation, their communities and even sometimes their schoolteachers merely added another
possible layer of persecution for a group that was already vulnerable.
Some later told stories about being routinely taunted by their classmates
at school, being excluded from the anniversary celebrations of the end
of the war, being prevented from playing with 'pure' Norwegian children, and having swastikas painted on their schoolbooks and satchels.
Many were rejected by their wider families, who regarded them as a
source of familial shame. When their mothers later married, many suffered verbal, mental and physical abuse at the hands of stepfathers who
resented them on the grounds that they were 'children of the enemy'.[50]

Some even suffered rejection from their own mothers, who saw them
as the source of all their own suffering. Six-year-old Tove Laila, for

example, who was taken away from her mother by the Nazis during the war to be raised as a German girl, was returned to her family in Norway in 1947, by which time the only language she knew was German. Her mother and stepfather managed to beat the German out of her in just three months, and forever afterwards mistreated, humiliated and bullied her. In the absence of the sort of social services now taken almost for granted in Norway, this unfortunate girl spent the rest of her childhood being called a 'damned German swine' by her own mother.[51]

The most common experience of war children was that of a shameful silence about their paternity. This silence existed at both a national level and a personal one. After their initial interest in the fate of war children, particularly when it looked as though they might be able to get rid of them, the Norwegian government pursued a policy of trying to erase all traces of the children's German heritage. They did not pursue German fathers for child maintenance, and actively discouraged paternal contact. When a child had a German-sounding first name, the government claimed the right to change it to something more traditionally Norwegian.[52]

On a personal level, such silence could be even more damaging. The children's mothers often both refused to talk about their paternity and forbade them from talking about it themselves. Some children did not learn about their father's nationality until they went to school and found themselves being taunted in the playground. It seems that silence on the subject rarely prevented the children from being verbally abused outside the family.[53]

The devastating effects that such universal rejection had on these children have only recently come to light. According to the study sponsored by the Norwegian government in 2001, war children suffer higher death rates, higher divorce rates and worse health than the rest of Norway's population. They are typically less well educated, and earn lower incomes than other Norwegians. They are also significantly more likely to commit suicide than their peers. The worst mortality rates occurred in those born in 1941 and 1942 – a tendency that the authors of the study partly ascribe to the fact that these children were old enough at the end of the war to understand what was happening to them. The immediate postwar years were the time when bitterness towards these children was at its strongest.[54]

War children in Norway would remain outcasts for years to come. In some crucial ways they were treated even more harshly than their mothers. In 1950 a new Citizenship Act gave those women who had married Germans the right to reacquire their Norwegian citizenship; war children, by contrast, were denied this right until they reached eighteen years of age. Every year, right up until the start of the 1960s, these children and their guardians had to undergo the annual humiliation of applying to the local police office for permission to remain in the country.

Broadly speaking, the experiences of Norwegian war children are fairly representative of the experiences of those across the whole of western Europe. Children with German fathers were threatened, teased and shunned wherever they were born. Sometimes they were physically abused, but more often the abuse was verbal – derogatory nicknames like *bébés boches*, *tyskerunger* or *moeffenkinder*. War children from every country speak of being bullied by other children, teachers, neighbours and sometimes members of their own family. They were often ignored in classrooms and shunned in their communities.

As in Norway, a culture of shameful silence followed these children wherever they went, both in their private lives and in their dealings with officialdom. War children in Denmark, for example, later claimed to have been 'born into an atmosphere of pain, shame and lies'.[55] Those Danes who wanted to discover information about their German fathers were often actively obstructed from doing so.[56] Governments across Europe consistently under-reported the numbers of 'German' children in their midst – indeed, in Poland the official number of war children is still zero: realistic estimates of the phenomenon did not sit happily alongside the newly established national myths about 'universal resistance' to occupation.[57]

Of course, this is not the only story – there were many children who suffered little or no discrimination at all because of their paternity. Indeed, in one study by the University of Bergen almost half of the war children questioned claimed that they had had no problems because of their background. However, that still means that more than half *had* had problems.[58]

In the vast majority of cases there was nobody to stand up for these children but their mothers, who were themselves often the objects of contempt. One can only applaud the bravery of the French mother who confronted a schoolteacher who had called her daughter a '*bâtard du Boche*' with the words: 'Madame, it was not my daughter who slept with a German, but me. When you want to insult someone, save it for me rather than taking it out on an innocent child.'[59]

15

The Purpose of Vengeance

Vengeance is a much-condemned but little-understood aspect of the immediate postwar period. Much as we might now deplore vengeance in all its forms, it is important to acknowledge that it served several purposes, not all of which were entirely negative. For the victors, it underlined the defeat of Germany and its collaborators, and established beyond any doubt who now held the reins of power. For Hitler's victims it restored a sense of the moral equilibrium, even if it did so at the expense of relinquishing some of the moral high ground. And for the European community as a whole it at last gave expression to some of the frustration that had built up throughout the years of Nazi repression.

Acts of vengeance certainly gave individuals, as well as communities, a sense that they were no longer passive bystanders to events. Rightly or wrongly, the mobs who lynched German soldiers on the streets of Prague or Black Brigade members on the streets of Milan were collectively satisfied by what they had done: not only had they struck a blow at fascism, but they had taken power back into their own hands. Likewise, the millions of foreign slave labourers who were released from captivity in Germany usually took delight in stealing food and valuables from German houses, and occasionally also mistreated the German families they found there. They saw this as their right after years of their own hunger and mistreatment.

In some parts of Europe, where the people had lost all faith in their institutions of law and order, the recourse to vengeance at least gave them the sense that some kind of justice was possible. In other parts, the less violent forms of revenge were sometimes thought to have had quite positive effects on society. The most common form of vengeance in

western Europe – the shaving of women's heads – was credited at the
time with reducing violence and giving occupied towns and villages a
new sense of pride. Though we now find such events reprehensible, it is
undeniable that they brought communities together and made them, at
last, feel re-empowered. Acknowledging such facts does not mean that
we have to condone vengeance – but if we fail to acknowledge them we
will never have a proper understanding of the violent forces that drove
events during this chaotic period.

The issue of vengeance has always been an extremely controversial part
of the aftermath of the Second World War, and is still used as a political
football today. The most graphic indication of this is the repeated use
that has been made of bogus statistics. Exaggerated and emotional
claims have been made both by people who genuinely suffered in the
aftermath of the war and by certain groups who wish to capitalize on
that suffering. For example, writers from the French political right
claimed for decades that over 100,000 suspected collaborators were
murdered by the Resistance during and after the liberation – a figure
that is on a par with the number of *résistants* killed during the war. The
true number of collaborators killed was probably a tenth of that, and
only one or two thousand can realistically be categorized as revenge
attacks. The French right wing was effectively trying to deflect attention
from its own role during the war, and perhaps even gain absolution for
it, by fiddling the figures.

Likewise, Germans who were expelled from their homelands at the
end of the war often make exaggerated claims about the most famous
atrocities that occurred in eastern Europe. They say that 2,000 civilians
were killed in Aussig, and 6,500 at Lamsdorf prison camp (when in fact
the figures are more likely to be 100 and 1,500, respectively). Words like
'genocide' and 'Holocaust' are deliberately used in an attempt to reclaim
the concept of victimhood for Germany. And to drive the point home,
the most gruesome stories are repeated again and again, despite the fact
that some of them are little more than hearsay. Such exaggerations are
unnecessary and counter-productive: the true figures, and the verifiable
stories, are terrible enough without having to embellish them.

To our collective discredit, historians have sometimes failed to question these claims, either because of a dearth of reputable source material
or, in some cases, because the exaggerations happen to suit our own

political points of view. This is a problem that plagues postwar history, just as it plagues the history of the Second World War itself. (As another example, books and articles are regularly published today claiming that as many as 100,000 people died during the bombing of Dresden in 1945, despite the fact that most reputable sources of the past ten or fifteen years, including an official German government commission in 2009, have put the figure at around 20,000.) The issue of such exaggerated numbers will come up again and again in the following chapters.

However, if some people overstate the extent of postwar vengeance, then sometimes the opposite is also true. Many Jews are quick to point out that vengeance was actually fairly uncommon. 'We couldn't take vengeance, or we'd be the same as them,' claims Berek Obuchowski, who was liberated at Theresienstadt. 'Out of all those people who survived I doubt there was more than five per cent that took vengeance on the Germans.'[1] Even at the time Jews made such claims. 'We do not want revenge,' declared Dr Zalman Grinberg, in a speech delivered to an assembly of his fellow Jews at Dachau at the end of May 1945. 'If we took this vengeance it would mean we would fall to the depths and ethics and morals the German nation has been in these past ten years. We are not able to slaughter women and children! We are not able to burn millions of people! We are not able to starve hundreds of thousands!'[2]

Most historians would agree with such claims – vengeance *was* only the path of a minority. There were many areas across Europe where soldiers, partisans and ex-prisoners showed remarkable restraint, and the rule of law was more or less intact. In Norway and Denmark, for example, there was very little violence after the war. But even in these countries, which had not suffered nearly as much physical and moral destruction as other areas further south and east, vengeance did take place, especially against women who had slept with German soldiers. The fact that it was a relatively mild form of vengeance does not make it any less present.

It is also true that Jews were probably far less guilty of vengeance than any other group in postwar Europe. But those who did choose the path of vengeance embraced it wholeheartedly, to the point where they were willing to risk both their own lives and those of innocent people. The fact that Dr Grinberg spoke so forcefully about the subject in his speech at Dachau shows that the desire for revenge was very much alive amongst Jews there. And, as we know, this desire was acted upon at Dachau, both by camp inmates and by American troops.

The issue of Jewish vengeance is still an extremely sensitive subject. At the time, most Jews were quick to reject the temptation for the reasons spelled out in Dr Grinberg's speech – they did not want to sink into the same moral cesspool as the Nazis themselves. Today, however, Jews play down the existence of vengeance for slightly different reasons: they are worried about how the world might *perceive* their actions. People of other faiths cannot possibly understand this anxiety that Jews feel about their image. Having suffered centuries of anti-Semitic slurs and conspiracy theories, of which the Nazi hate campaign between 1933 and 1945 was merely the apogee, Jews are understandably determined to avoid any kind of unnecessary controversy. Studies show that whenever any controversy does arise, such as over the issue of Israel, the traditional anti-Semitism immediately surfaces once again throughout Europe, as is evidenced by the spate of attacks on Jews that occurred after the Israeli war in southern Lebanon in 2006.[3]

It is unsurprising, therefore, that when journalist John Sack published a book about Jewish vengeance in the 1990s it caused an uproar in the Jewish community, particularly in America. Sack interviewed several Jews who became prominent in Poland's prison camp system after the war, and who admitted to torturing German prisoners. His work, though sensational in style, was backed up by documentary evidence, and all his interviews were taped and made publicly available. Nevertheless his agent refused to represent the book, and his American publishers, having paid Sack an advance, belatedly decided to cancel it. Likewise, a magazine that had bought serial rights pulled their article two days before publication. Despite being Jewish himself, Sack was accused both in print and on television of anti-Semitism and Holocaust denial. There was similar controversy over his book in Europe, where Sack's Polish publisher cancelled publication for fear of bad publicity, as did his German publisher. Sack's book was insensitive and badly written – and, like James Bacque's book about German POWs, was considered dangerous precisely because it did contain seeds of truth.

The acknowledgement of postwar vengeance is an extremely uncomfortable issue for any historian, even when it is not clouded by national or religious sensitivities, and it is probably impossible to discuss it without stepping on somebody's toes. Firstly, there is the worry that by characterizing an action as retributive, the historian partially legitimizes it. So, for example, when the rape of German women by Soviet soldiers is described as revenge, it thereby becomes more understandable, and perhaps to a degree more acceptable. German women, so the argument goes, were part of the Nazi regime just as much as German men, and rape was therefore something that they had brought upon themselves. This was the argument that many Soviets used at the time.

Conversely, the act of vengeance might be deemed so terrible that it overshadows the original offence: so, to use the same example, the mass rapes in Germany might be considered so repugnant that modern readers will forget that many of the women who were raped were also part of an evil regime. In our minds the atrocities that were committed in the name of Nazism – even crimes as vast as the Holocaust – might be at least partially 'cancelled out' by the suffering that German people endured once the war was over. This is certainly the worry that many academics in Germany have. When a groundbreaking documentary about the mass rape was broadcast in 1992, for example, it caused a furore in the German press: outraged commentators argued that the documentary should never have been broadcast, because if Germans began to see themselves as victims of atrocity, they would lose sight of the fact that they were also perpetrators.[4]

In order to avoid weaving a path between these two extremes, many historians cheat. Most histories of the Second World War, for example, make no mention of the revenge that came after the war was over; likewise, most books that describe the rape and murder of Germans after the war do so without so much as a peep about the wartime atrocities in eastern Europe that first created this seemingly unquenchable desire for revenge. The problem with divorcing vengeance from its wider context is that it makes it impossible to understand *why* people acted the way they did in the aftermath of the war. From a modern, political point of view it also creates a competition over victimhood.

Sooner or later the arguments tend to break down along national or political lines. Poles and Czechs understandably feel aggrieved when historians begin to speak about the suffering of ethnic Germans, since they themselves were forced to endure years of savage occupation at the hands of many of those Germans. French Communists become indignant when right-wingers highlight their excesses, since it was the French right that presided over the capture, torture and execution of tens of thousands of Communist Resistance fighters. Russians dismiss the anger over how Romanian and Hungarian civilians were treated after the war by arguing that Romania and Hungary should never have gone to war against the Soviet Union in the first place. And so on.

The truth is that the moral morass produced by the war spared nobody. All nationalities and all political persuasions were – to vastly differing degrees, of course – both victims and perpetrators simultaneously. If historians still struggle to see these issues in the many varying shades of grey that are necessary to understand them properly, then perhaps it is inevitable that most people at the time, still raw from the events of the war, were usually only able to see things in black and white. The political and national polarization we still occasionally see today was, in 1945, both intense and ubiquitous.

But the fact that the arguments about postwar violence so often get bogged down in issues of race or politics is not an accident. It points to some of the deeper themes that lay behind both the war itself and its immediate aftermath. Regardless of how prominent vengeance was in the thoughts and motivations of people across Europe, it is not on its own an adequate explanation of the violence that occurred in the aftermath of the war. There were also other, more ideological forces at play. Sometimes the violence was not a *reaction* to the sweeping changes that had been brought about by the war, but a continuation of them. Sometimes vengeance was not an end in itself, but merely a tool for achieving more radical goals.

The pursuit of these goals, and the intense racial prejudice that often lay behind them, are the subject of the next section.

PART III

Ethnic Cleansing

You should create such conditions . . . that they want to escape themselves.

Josef Stalin[1]

16

Wartime Choices

The Second World War was never merely a conflict over territory. It was also a war of race and ethnicity. Some of the defining events of the war had nothing to do with winning and maintaining physical ground, but with imposing one's own ethnic stamp on ground already held. The Jewish Holocaust, the ethnic cleansing of western Ukraine, the attempted genocide of Croatian Serbs: these were events that were pursued with a vigour every bit as ardent as the military war. A vast number of people – perhaps 10 million or more – were deliberately exterminated for no other reason than that they happened to belong to the wrong ethnic or racial group.

The problem for those pursuing this racial war was that it was not always easy to define a person's race or ethnicity, particularly in eastern Europe where different communities were often inextricably intermingled. Jews who happened to have blond hair and blue eyes could slip through the net because they did not fit the Nazis' preconceived racial stereotype. Gypsies could and did disguise themselves as members of other ethnic groups just by changing their clothes and their behaviour – as did Slovaks in Hungary, Bosniaks in Serbia, Romanians in Ukraine, and so on. The most common way of identifying one's ethnic friends or enemies – the language they spoke – was not always an accurate guide either. Those who had grown up in mixed communities spoke several languages, and could switch between one and the next depending on whom they were speaking to – a skill that would save many lives during the darkest days of the war and its aftermath.

In an effort to categorize the population of Europe, the Nazis insisted on issuing everyone with identity cards, coloured according to ethnicity. They created vast bureaucracies to classify entire populations by race. In Poland for example, a racial hierarchy was devised which put

Reich Germans at the top, ethnic Germans next, then privileged minorities such as Ukrainians, followed by Poles, Gypsies and Jews. The classifications did not stop there. Ethnic Germans, for example, were broken down into further sub-categories: those who were so pure that they were eligible to join the Nazi Party, those who were pure enough for Reich citizenship, those who were tainted by Polish blood or Polish influences, and finally those Poles who were to be considered as ethnically German only because of their physical appearance or way of life.[1]

Those who did not have their ethnicity chosen for them had to make the decision for themselves. This was not always easy. Many people had multiple options, either because they had mixed-race parents or grandparents or because they saw no contradiction in being simultaneously, say, Polish by birth, Lithuanian by nationality and German by ethnicity. When forced to make a choice, their decision was often naively random at best, perhaps inspired by a parent, a spouse, or even a friend. The more calculating chose an identity according to what benefits it might offer. Claiming German ethnicity, for example, could confer exemption from labour round-ups and eligibility for special rations and tax breaks. On the other hand, it could also mean liability for military conscription: the decision sometimes boiled down to whether the Russian front was preferable to a slave-labour camp.

The choices that people made regarding their ethnicity would have implications far beyond the end of the war. While hostilities in Europe officially ended in May 1945, the various conflicts over race and ethnicity continued for months, sometimes years, afterwards. Sometimes these conflicts were intensely local, even personal – people in small towns and villages knew the ethnicity of their neighbours, and acted accordingly. Increasingly, however, the conflict would be conducted on a regional, or even a national level. In the aftermath of the war entire populations would be expelled from areas where they had lived for centuries – purely on the basis of what was written on their wartime identity cards.

The fascist obsession with racial purity, not only in those areas occupied by Germany but elsewhere too, had a huge impact on European attitudes. It made people aware of race in a way they never had been before. It obliged people to take sides, whether they wanted to or not. And, in communities that had lived side by side more or less peacefully for centuries, it made race into a problem – indeed, it elevated it to *the* problem – that needed solving.

As the war had taught people, some of the solutions could be radical, and final.

17

The Jewish Flight

At the beginning of May 1945, an eighteen-year-old Polish Jew named Roman Halter was liberated by the Russians. He and two other Jews had been hiding with a German couple near Dresden who had taken them in after they escaped from a death march. Having survived various labour camps, including Auschwitz, he was weak and emaciated – but he was alive, and knew himself to be extremely lucky.

The day after his liberation, Halter said goodbye to the couple who had sheltered him. He wanted desperately to find out if anyone else in his family had survived the Holocaust, so he acquired himself a bicycle, tied to the handlebars a few glass jars of preserved meat that he had found in a deserted farmstead and set off on the road back to Poland.

He had not been travelling long when he came across one of his Russian liberators, who was driving a motorbike. Halter was enormously grateful to the Russians for rescuing him. He thought of them as friends to the Jews, liberators, 'good people' – he even spoke a little Russian himself, which he still remembered from his childhood. Unfortunately, as he would find out, his fraternal feelings were not reciprocated.

I was pleased to see him . . . I still remembered the Russian words which I had learned from my parents. 'Ruski, ja cie lublu!' I said ('Russian, I love you'), and then added, 'Zdrastvite towarisz' ('Hello friend'). He looked at me strangely and began speaking Russian very fast. I smiled and said in Polish that I was unable to understand him. He looked me up and down. Then he looked at my bike and said, 'Dawaj czasy' ('Give me watches'). I understood that. He pulled up his shirt sleeves and showed me his forearms full of watches and then repeated the two words again. 'Dawaj czasy.'

I glanced at his eyes, they were stern and cold. I began speaking to him in Polish. I said that I hadn't got watches and showed him both my thin forearms. He pointed to the bulging blanket fixed to my bike's crossbar and said something in Russian. I went up and took out one jar and handed it to him. 'Mieso,' I said. 'Towarisz, mieso' ('Comrade, meat'). The meat was visible through the glass. He looked at it and then at me. 'Towarisz, you have it, please take it and enjoy it.'

He lifted the glass jar and held it above his head for a second or so and then smashed it on to the ground. The glass and the meat spattered in all directions. I looked at the Russian soldier and fear entered my heart. What could I say to make him leave me alone? I felt momentarily numb. 'Lower your trousers,' he said in his language. I stood there shaken and didn't quite know what he meant. He repeated his command and by gestures showed me what he wanted me to do.

. . . I put my bike carefully on the ground so as not to break the glass jars in the pouch and began lowering my trousers. 'Why is he making me do this?' I thought. Perhaps he thinks that I carry a belt with watches around my waist. I must tell him that I am not a German who just speaks Polish. So, as I was lowering my trousers and showing him that I am without belt or watches around my waist, I slowly told him in Polish that I am a Jew. I knew the word 'Ivrei'. 'Ja Ivrei,' I repeated. 'Ja Ivrei, ja towarisz' ('I am a Jew, I am a comrade').

I stood before him now naked from my waist down, although my instinct told me not to take off my good lace-up boots in case he took them and left me bare-footed. I could not reach Chodecz bare-footed. So I let my trousers and pants hang over my socks and boots. I glanced at his eyes again. There was a look of contempt in them as he was viewing the exposed part of my body. I saw in them a killer's void.

He took out his revolver from his holster, pointed at my head and pulled the trigger. There was a loud click. Without a word to me he kick-started his motorbike and drove off. I stood there for a time with my trousers and pants down and looked at him disappearing into the distance.[1]

The memory of that meeting would haunt Halter for the rest of his life. Its meaning was ominous. Despite their shared experience as victims of the Germans, and despite Halter's spontaneous offer of friendship, this nameless Russian had treated him exactly as an SS officer might have done: first establishing that he was Jewish by checking to see if he were circumcised, and then putting a gun to his head. Whether Halter's life had been saved by the gun jamming, or merely a lack of ammunition, he would never know.

In the months to come such scenes would be repeated across Europe. Jews of all nationalities would discover that the end of German rule did not mean the end of persecution. Far from it. Despite all that the Jews had suffered, in many areas anti-Semitism would *increase* after the war. Violence against Jews would resurface everywhere – even in places that had never been occupied, such as Britain. In some parts of Europe this violence would be final and definitive: the task of permanently clearing their communities of Jews, which even the Nazis had failed to do, would be finished off by local people.

The Choice to Return Home

In the aftermath of the war, European Jews began to turn their thoughts to the lessons that could be learned from what they had just experienced. Some Jewish thinkers believed that the Holocaust had been possible only because Jews had made themselves too conspicuous before and during the war. They argued that the only way to avoid the possibility of a similar catastrophe in the future was to make themselves invisible, by assimilating completely into the various countries in which they lived.

Zionists, however, claimed that this was nonsense: even well-assimilated Jews had been winkled out by Hitler's henchmen and murdered along with all the others. They argued that the only way to ensure their safety was to leave Europe altogether and set up their own state.

A third group thought that either of these approaches was effectively an admission of defeat. They believed it their duty to return to their countries of origin and try to rebuild their communities as best they could.[2]

The vast majority of Europe's surviving Jews initially tended to agree with this last view – not out of any particular ideology, but simply because they had spent their years of exile and incarceration daydreaming about the possibility of returning home. Most realized, intellectually if not emotionally, that the communities they had left behind no longer existed. But the majority of Jews returned anyway, partly out of an emotional attachment to their home towns and villages, and partly out of a desire to reconstruct the only version of normality they had ever known. Whether they continued to nurture these hopes after they arrived depended a great deal on the welcome they received.

From a Jewish point of view, Europe was a confusing place after the war. Much had changed since the defeat of Germany, but much had also remained the same. On the one hand the organizations dedicated to persecuting Jews had been replaced by organizations dedicated to helping them. The American Jewish Joint Distribution Committee was bringing in millions of dollars worth of food, medicine and clothing, and was helping to rebuild synagogues and Jewish cultural centres across the continent. Non-Jewish aid agencies such as UNRRA and the Red Cross were also providing targeted help, such as the establishment of exclusively Jewish DP camps and the tracing of friends and family members. Even the new national governments had made a start at changing attitudes towards Jews, for example by repealing all anti-Jewish legislation.

On the other hand, years of Nazi propaganda could not be over-turned in a matter of weeks or months, and open anti-Semitism still existed everywhere. Sometimes this expressed itself in ways that are quite shocking. Jews who returned to the Greek city of Thessaloniki in 1945, for example, were sometimes greeted with, 'Ah, you sur-vived?' or even, 'What a pity you were not made into soap.'[3] In Eindhoven, Jewish repatriates were confronted by an official who registered them with the words, 'Not another Jew, they must have forgotten to gas you.'[4] In the German cities of Garmisch and Mem-mingen, cinema newsreels that mentioned the death of 6 million Jews provoked shouts of 'They didn't kill enough of them!' followed by deafening applause.[5]

The greatest fear of returning Jews was that, for all the measures being put in place by governments and aid agencies, the real issue of deep-rooted anti-Semitism would never disappear. Experience had taught them that neither democracy nor apparent equality of rights, nor even their own patriotism was a guarantee against persecution. Their greatest challenge was not to treat every small incident as 'the sign of a future explosion' or proof that 'a new mass murder is being prepared'.[6] If they were to manage this, they needed help from the communities they were rejoining.

On returning home, therefore, what Jews required more than anything else was reassurance. If they were to be able to pick up their lives once more they should be given more than just food and shelter and medical care, most of which was generally provided along the same lines as it was to other returnees. What they needed was to be *welcomed*.

Some Jews, like Primo Levi, did indeed return to 'friends full of life, the warmth of secure meals, the solidity of daily work, the liberating joy of recounting my story'.[7] There are many stories of Jews being reunited, as if by a miracle, with loved ones; of compassion from strangers who spontaneously provided them with food or shelter, or who listened to their stories. Unfortunately, however, such stories are not quite as common as they should have been, and the experience of most was somewhat different.

The Return: Holland

Of the 110,000 Dutch Jews who were deported to concentration camps during the war, only about 5,000 returned. They were amongst the 71,564 displaced Dutch people who returned to Holland in 1945, most of them en route to Amsterdam.[8] On arrival in the city's central station they were interviewed, registered, and given ration cards and clothing coupons. Sometimes they were given advice on where to stay, or where to find help, but sometimes the desks of the various aid agencies were unattended. The official welcome was efficient, but cold: no flags or flowers, no brass bands, just a series of desks and questions followed by a swift dispatch outside into the streets of the city centre.[9]

Right from the beginning there were subtle distinctions made between returnees. It was not the Jews who were discriminated against, however, but those returnees who were deemed to be collaborators. People who had worked in Germany as volunteers (*vrijwilligers*) had their repatriation cards stamped with a V: they were then refused a welcome food parcel and food coupons, and shunned by virtually every institution they came into contact with thereafter.

Of the others, the *onvrijwillig*, the only people to be greeted with any kind of fanfare were those who were deemed to have been part of the Resistance. The benefits for Resistance members were immediate.

They were often sent to special convalescent centres located in luxurious settings, including a wing of Queen Wilhelmina's palace. They were lauded in the press, in the government, and in the streets. 'If you came from the resistance, everything was possible!' claimed one former Resistance member, Karel de Vries. 'You could ask for and get money from anyone. All building materials, for example, were scarce and difficult to get, but if you said, "This is for resistance fighters returning from concentration camps," well, then it was fine, immediately!'[10] Later they were even awarded a special pension in recognition of their Resistance activities.

It quickly became obvious to returning Jews that the only distinction that the Dutch were interested in was the difference between collaborators and resisters. All other categories, including Jews, were simply lumped together as one. This was by no means unique to Holland. When Italian deportees were returned to Italy, they too were all lumped together as 'political prisoners', regardless of whether they had been Jews, forced labourers or prisoners of war.[11] Likewise, French returnees were also put together as a single group – indeed, in most popular histories of the period today they still are.[12] This was not discrimination *against* Jews as such, but it was almost as bad: it was an attempt to ignore them altogether. As one Dutch camp survivor put it, 'Where there should have been pity, I encountered the dry, difficult to approach, repellent, amorphous mass known as officialdom.'[13]

There were many reasons why the Dutch authorities did not give returning Jews the specific help they needed and deserved. To begin with, they took their lead from the Allies, specifically the British, whose official policy was *not* to treat Jews as a distinct category. Jews made up only a small proportion of the returnees, and so were not regarded as a priority. The authorities also had to prepare for the return in something of a rush, since Holland was one of the last countries in Europe to be liberated.

If they had thought about the situation more carefully they would have seen that Jews, more than any other group, were entitled to special treatment – on both moral and humanitarian grounds. They had certainly endured incomparably more suffering than any other group in Dutch society: of the 210,000 Dutch casualties of the Second World War half had been Jewish – and this despite the fact that Jews had only made up just over 1.5 per cent of the prewar population.[14] In most areas the community had been entirely wiped out, and even in Amsterdam only a small fraction had survived. While other returnees had communities to welcome them and to fall back on, many Jews had no one – not even family.

It was not only 'officialdom' that ignored these facts. Ordinary people also tended to be quite astonishingly insensitive. The historian Dienke Hondius has gathered together a whole series of examples showing the attitude of ordinary Dutch people to returning Jews. For example, Rita Koopman was greeted by a former acquaintance with the words, 'You're lucky you weren't here. We suffered such hunger!' When Ab Caransa returned to his former job he was denied an advance from his employer on the grounds that in Auschwitz, 'You had a roof over your head and food the whole time!' Most Jews did not try to explain the horrors they had been through but, like Gerhard Durlacher, merely 'bought acceptance' by listening to the stories of others and maintaining a 'discreet silence' about their own plight. 'People didn't understand,' explains another Dutch Jew, 'or else they didn't believe you.'[15]

Many of these comments were born of pure ignorance. Unlike in eastern Europe, where the Holocaust took place right under the noses of the people, in the west many were completely unaware of what had happened to the Jews after they had been deported. Before the films from the concentration camps were released, stories of industrial mass-murder were often dismissed as exaggerations; but even after the films had been shown in cinemas there was a complete lack of understanding of what they actually meant to the people who had survived.

More important than people's ignorance, however, was the sense of discomfort that such stories inevitably provoked. According to Frank Keizer, people in Holland reacted to his story of incarceration at Theresienstadt by saying, 'I don't want to know. That's all over now; be glad you survived.'[16] Jews who returned to other countries reported similar reactions. In France too, according to Auschwitz survivor Alexandre Kohn, 'there was a general indifference', and Jews were urged to draw a line under their experiences.[17] In Hungary returning Jews were beaten if they dared to suggest that they had suffered more than their Christian neighbours.[18] Even in America, Jewish survivors who immigrated were often treated with impatience: 'the war was over: "enough already!"'[19]

One must remember that ordinary Europeans had also suffered terribly during the war, particularly in the final year – but there was at least some comfort in the thought that they had all been through it together. After the liberation the whole continent began constructing myths of unity in adversity. These myths suited pretty much everybody, from former collaborators who wanted a chance to be brought back into the

— *Vous savez, jeune homme nous avons terriblement souffert des restrictions, nous aussi*

A well-nourished French couple greet a returning concentration-camp prisoner: 'You know, my dear boy, we too suffered terribly from the restrictions' (*La Marseillaise*, 13 June 1945)

fold, to an exhausted public that was eager to put the war behind them, to the politicians who wanted to rebuild a sense of national pride. Even at an international level, the idea that all the different peoples of Europe had suffered together under Nazism was a convenient way to rebuild a common sense of brotherhood between battered nations. But the presence of the Jews made a mockery of such myths. Not only had they suffered much, much more than everyone else, but none of the other groups had come to their aid: the comfortable thought that Europeans had been 'all in it together' was demonstrably untrue.

Here perhaps is the key to why the plight of returning Jews was so commonly ignored in the aftermath of the war, not only in Holland but all over western Europe. While stories of resistance gave people the chance to feel good about themselves, and reassure themselves that they too had produced their fair share of heroes, the stories of the Jews had the opposite effect. They were a reminder of former failings at every level of society. Their very presence was enough to create discomfort, as though they might at any moment reveal an embarrassing secret. It was far easier, therefore, simply to pretend that what had befallen the Jews was really just the same as what had happened to everyone else. Far from being welcomed, they were ignored, sidelined, silenced.

The Fight over Jewish Property

Sometimes there were darker reasons why the Jews were not welcomed home. In the aftermath of the war, there was a joke doing the rounds in Hungary. It went something like this: A Jew who survived the camps returned to Budapest, where he ran into a Christian friend. 'How are you?' the friend inquired. 'Don't even ask,' the Jew replied. 'I have returned from the camp, and now I have nothing except the clothes you are wearing.'[20]

The same joke could have been told in virtually any city in eastern Europe – plus a good many in the west – and it would have been understood. The plunder of Jewish property during the war had taken place in every country, and at every level of society. The comprehensive nature of this plundering was sometimes quite astounding. In the old Jewish quarter of Amsterdam, for example, the houses were stripped of everything right down to the wooden window and door frames.[21] In Hungary, Slovakia and Romania, Jewish land and property was often divided up amongst the poor.[22] Sometimes people did not even wait until the Jews had gone. There are examples in Poland of acquaintances approaching Jews during the war with the words, 'Since you are going to die anyway, why should someone else get your boots? Why not give them to me so I will remember you?'[23]

When handfuls of Jews began to come home after the war, their property was sometimes returned to them without any fuss – but this tended to be the exception rather than the rule. The historiography of this period in Europe is littered with stories of Jews trying, and failing, to get back what was rightfully theirs.[24] Neighbours and friends who had promised to look after valuable items for Jews while they were away frequently refused to return them: in the intervening years they had come to regard them as their own. Villagers who had farmed Jewish land during the war saw no reason why returning Jews should benefit from the fruits of their labours. Christians who had been granted empty apartments by the wartime authorities considered those apartments rightfully theirs, and they had papers to prove it. All these people tended to regard Jews with varying degrees of resentment, and cursed their luck that, of all the Jews that had 'disappeared' during the war, *theirs* had to be the ones who came back.

A good example of how Jewish property ended up being dispersed during the war – and the frightening consequences this could have – occurred in Hungary, in the small town of Kunmadaras. At the beginning of the war 250 Jews had lived here, out of a population of about 8,000. All had been deported in April 1944 – some to Auschwitz, some to Austria – and only seventy-three of these unfortunates survived. While they were away their property was 'confiscated' by local officials, who used it firstly to enrich themselves, but also to distribute to the poor. Some homes and businesses were looted wholesale by the community, with the implicit blessing of the authorities. Others were taken over by the various armies that passed through, and items of furniture and so on were dispersed amongst the local community. When the Red Army arrived they in turn plundered the homes of the upper and middle classes, where many of the more valuable items had ended up. Some of the property they acquired was used to barter for food, or simply abandoned when they moved on, and thus – by a circuitous route – it found its way into the possession of local peasants. To complete this tangled web, the incoming Communists also requisitioned property for their own use or for the good of the Party, and this too was occasionally traded locally.[25]

Thus, through a combination of confiscation, plunder, theft and resale the property of Jews was dispersed all over the town. In larger cities like Budapest the confusion often rendered it impossible for returning Jews to trace their property. But in a small town like Kunmadaras finding one's property was not difficult – it was getting the new owners to return it that was the problem. Some people refused outright, and thereafter regarded the presence of the Jews as both a reproach and a potential threat. Others were ordered to return property by the police, but even those who complied voluntarily did so reluctantly, and were resentful ever after. The poor felt especially aggrieved, particularly if they were forced to return property to previously wealthier Jews. 'When the Jews returned they had nothing,' said one Kunmadaras woman when interviewed by a local newspaper, 'but now they are eating white bread and even though I plough the fields with my nose, I still have nothing.'[26]

Through the winter and spring of 1946 a tense, anti-Semitic atmosphere began to build in Kunmadaras. It came to a head towards the end of May when a group of women attacked a Jewish egg vendor named Ferenc Kuti at the Kunmadaras market, and smashed all the eggs on his stand. The woman who led the attack was Eszter Toth Kabai, who invoked blood libel to justify her actions – that is, the ancient myth that Jews sacrificed Christian children in their rituals. Absurd rumours had been circulating the region that Jews had been abducting and killing children, and then selling 'sausage made from human flesh'. As she beat Kuti with her wooden shoe, Kabai began shouting, 'My sister's child has been taken away by the Jews.' Some of the other, non-Jewish stall holders came to Kuti's aid, but when they too were attacked Kuti abandoned his stall and fled home.[27]

Kuti's house quickly became surrounded by a mob. For a while the crowd refrained from entering because they were afraid he might have a gun. But when the police went in and discovered that he was in fact unarmed – and made the mistake of announcing this to the crowd – the rabble surged inside. Kuti apparently begged the intruders for mercy but was killed by a man named Balázs Kálmán, who beat him to death with an iron bar, shouting 'I'll give you sausages made out of the flesh of Hungarian children!'[28]

The attack on Ferenc Kuti marked the beginning of a pogrom in which at least one other Jew was murdered, and fifteen more seriously injured.[29] Jewish homes were broken into and plundered, and Jewish shops were also looted. The rumours of child abduction and blood libel were invoked again and again during the pogrom, and rioters were heard to shout a variety of slogans along the lines of, 'We must beat the Jews because they will steal our children!' The real motive behind the rioting, however, appears to have been to loot Jewish property. When the crowd broke into a clothes shop they demanded the return of three children who were supposedly imprisoned there – but rather than look for the missing children they immediately began helping themselves to the stock of clothes. One Jewish woman, a Mrs Rosenberg, was attacked by a woman called Sara Kerepesi, who bore her a special grudge because she had been forced by the courts to return Mrs Rosenberg's belongings to her after the war. Mrs Rosenberg remembered her attacker shouting, while beating her, 'This is for the eiderdown!'[30]

What happened at Kunmadaras is a particularly violent example of a phenomenon seen all over Europe in the aftermath of the war. It was not only returning Jews who had trouble regaining and retaining their property – but the anti-Semitism that existed throughout the continent made them much more vulnerable than any other group. In other parts of Hungary the courts ruled that horses and other livestock plundered from Jewish farms should remain with those who had 'saved' them.[31] In Italy the authorities not only hesitated to return Jewish businesses to their rightful owners, but then tried to charge a 'management fee' for 'looking after' them during the war.[32] In Poland, any 'abandoned' property formerly owned by Jews was taken into local authority control – in other words, the local authorities had a vested interest in making sure that Jews who returned after the war were driven away again.[33] Such examples can be found in almost every European country.

Jews had been fair game during the war, and their property regarded as a resource that could be shared by everyone. It is quite clear that many people, and some governments, still viewed them the same way once the war was ended.

Jews as Capitalists, Jews as Communists

The pogrom at Kunmadaras was only one of many such incidents that took place across Hungary in the immediate postwar years. Anti-Semitic violence included the looting of homes and shops (for example, in the mining town of Ózd), lynchings and murders (as in Miskolc), and the burning down of Jewish buildings such as synagogues (as in Makó). Alongside the violence, Jews were obliged to suffer all the usual forms of non-violent anti-Semitism: discrimination, intimidation, verbal abuse and so on. The level of racial hatred was so high, and so universal, that it clearly cannot be explained away as a mere squabble over property. Something much deeper was going on.

To begin with, the people who indulged in such excesses were often themselves suffering from unbearable hardship. The economy of the whole region was close to meltdown in 1946, but it was especially bad in Hungary, where the rate of inflation reportedly rose to a peak of 158,486 per cent *per day*.[34] In his memoirs, the writer György Faludy gives an indication of what this meant to ordinary people: when his publisher printed a new edition of one of his books in 1946 Faludy was paid 300 billion pengős – an amount that in 1938 would have been equivalent to around 60 billion US dollars. And yet, after collecting this bounty he was obliged to race directly to the market, knowing that the money would have devalued by at least 90 per cent by the time he got there. He spent the entire amount on just a single chicken, two litres of olive oil and a handful of vegetables.[35] Inflation like this had a devastating effect on the lives of ordinary people, who were obliged to barter possessions for food. Workers often relied on the meals they received in the factory canteens, because their wages were effectively worthless. Eventually some employers abandoned money altogether and began paying their workers in food.

The blame for this state of affairs was, generally speaking, aimed at two groups of people. Firstly, the Soviets were blamed – for the destruction they had wrought, for their widespread looting and for the punitive sums they had demanded in reparation for the war. The Communists were guilty by association, and in the minds of the people the Communists were almost universally regarded as Jews. This was not unique to Hungary – the Communist Party was regarded as the 'party of the Jews' across eastern Europe, and not entirely without justification.[36] But since the Communists were widely hated, this did not reflect well on the Jews. For example, when the Jewish leader of the Communist Party, Mátyás Rákosi, came to Miskolc to deliver a speech on the economic situation, graffiti appeared on the factory walls calling him 'the king of the Jews' and the man who 'sold the country to the Russians'.[37]

The second group of people to be blamed for the desperate economic situation in Hungary were the black marketeers and speculators who hoarded foodstuffs in the hope of driving up prices. Popular opinion also considered *these* people Jewish. When the women of Kunmadaras started beating up the Jewish egg vendor in the market place, for example, one of the accusations they hurled at him was that he was charging excessively high prices for his eggs. Jews everywhere were accused of overcharging customers, exploiting the economic disaster, and hoarding food and gold. Such claims appealed to a stereotype that was centuries old – the Jew as miser.[38]

The Communists, who were keen to shake off their image as 'the party of the Jews', saw this latter stereotype as an opportunity to win some much-needed popularity. In the summer of 1946 they began to make speeches against the black market which condemned Jews in veiled terms as 'speculators'. When they printed posters about the subject, these 'speculators' were depicted with exaggerated Semitic features: in fact, there was very little difference between these posters and the images of 'Jewish parasites' from the Nazi era. There is even compelling evidence that the Communists orchestrated the lynching of Jews in Miskolc, as an experiment in directing popular anger.[39]

In the political and economic turmoil of 1946, Jews in Hungary had very few places to turn. Mór Reinchardt, a Jew from Jánoshalma, summed up their plight in a letter to the president of the Hungarian Jewish Bureau that August:

> Regrettably, following the events in Miskolc and other similar occurrences it is obvious that Jews are hated equally by the Communist Party and the Smallholders Party. The slogan and posters of one say 'Death to the Communists and the Jews' and the slogans and posters of the other say 'Death to the Smallholders and the Jews!' Jews are universally hated and all political parties are ready to annihilate every one, whether guilty or innocent . . . In my view there is no other possibility but to seek protection from the occupying forces. We need to seek their help. Here – that is in Hungary – it is impossible for a Jew to exist. Therefore, we need to leave. We need to emigrate. We need to petition the Soviet military authorities to allow us to leave the country . . . and while the emigration takes place . . . the Red Army should continue to occupy the country in order to afford us their protection.[40]

This letter is a perfect expression of the sentiments held by hundreds of thousands of Jews all across Europe, who believed that the continent would never again be a safe place for them to live.

The Kielce Pogrom

If anti-Semitism in Hungary was bad after the war, it was even worse in Poland. In the summer of 1945, having survived a series of Nazi labour camps, sixteen-year-old Ben Helfgott and his cousin travelled back to Poland from Theresienstadt. While they were changing trains at Częstochowa, however, they were stopped by two armed and uniformed Poles who asked for their papers. They examined the documents, then told the boys to come with them to the police station for a routine check. The pair had no reason to suspect that anything was wrong, and so followed them into the city. For a while Helfgott tried to make conversation with the strangers, but then one of the men turned to him violently and said, 'Shut your fucking mouth, you fucking Jew.' The boys knew immediately that they were in trouble.

The men did not take them to a police station but to a dark apartment, where they were made to open their suitcases. After taking everything they could find of any value, the men took them back out into the night, again claiming that they were going to the police station. The boys no longer believed them, of course, but since the men were armed they had no choice but to comply. They were led to a derelict and deserted area of town, where the two men drew their revolvers and told the boys to walk towards the nearest wall. Ben Helfgott immediately started pleading with them, appealing to their patriotism, exclaiming that they were all fellow Poles who had suffered together during the war, and should be helping each other now that the war was over. Eventually one of the men took pity on them, saying to his partner, 'Let's leave them. They're only boys.' So they put away their revolvers, laughed, and walked away, leaving the cousins to find their own way back to the railway station.[41]

Poland was easily the most dangerous country for Jews after the war. At least 500 Jews were murdered by Poles between the German surrender and the summer of 1946, and most historians put the figure at around 1,500.[42] It is impossible to be sure because individual incidents like the one described by Ben Helfgott were rarely reported, and even more rarely recorded – even when they resulted in murder. Jews were thrown from trains. They were robbed of their possessions and taken to the forests to be shot. Letters were sent to Jews by local nationalist groups warning them to get out or be killed. Corpses were left with notes in their pockets reading, 'This will be the fate of all surviving Jews.'[43]

As in Hungary, the ancient calumny of blood libel was invoked again and again. In Rzeszów there were rumours that 'Jews who needed blood after returning from the camps' were performing ritual murders. These murders supposedly included the killing of a nine-year-old girl named Bronisława Mendoń, whose 'blood was sucked out for ritual purposes' in June 1945. During the riot that followed these rumours several Jews were beaten up, Jewish properties were looted, and one or two Jews possibly also killed.[44] In Kraków a full-blown pogrom broke out after stories circulated that a Christian child had been killed inside a synagogue. Polish police and militiamen were amongst a mob that descended upon the synagogue and pursued Jews through the town. In the resulting violence dozens of Jews were wounded, and possibly as many as five were killed. Those Jews who ended up at hospital were beaten again, while nurses looked on and called them 'Jewish scum' who 'should be shot'.[45]

The most famous postwar pogrom, however – and easily the worst – occurred at Kielce in southern-central Poland.[46] It began on the morning of 4 July 1946, after an eight-year-old boy named Henryk Błaszczyk falsely accused a local Jew of abducting him and imprisoning him in the basement of the Jewish Committee's building at 7 Planty Street. The particular Jew accused by the boy was immediately arrested and beaten up. A lynch mob was assembled to break into the building and rescue the other children who were supposedly being held there, waiting to be ritually sacrificed. Rumours quickly spread throughout the community that children were being kidnapped, and that the Jews had 'killed a Christian child'. Attempts by the head of the Jewish Committee to calm things down fell upon deaf ears.

When the police came to search the building in question an hour later, they discovered that it did not contain any Christian children – in fact it did not even have a basement. They told the boy off for lying and sent him home, but the damage had already been done. By now a large crowd had gathered outside the building, which began to throw stones at the windows. Shortly afterwards more than a hundred soldiers arrived, supposedly to re-establish order – but after a gun was fired (it is unclear by whom) these soldiers joined policemen in storming the building, grabbing hold of men and women they found there and forcing them out into the arms of the baying mob outside.

Baruch Dorfman was on the third floor of the building, where he and a group of twenty others had barricaded themselves in a room.

But they started shooting at us through the door, and they wounded one person, who later died from the injuries. They broke in. These were soldiers in uniform and a few civilians. I was wounded then. They ordered us to go outside. They formed a double row. In the staircase there were already civilians and also women. Soldiers hit us with rifle butts. Civilians, men and women, also beat us. I was wearing a uniformlike vest, perhaps that's why they did not hit me then. We came down to the square. Others who were brought out with me were stabbed with bayonets and shot at. We were pelted with stones. Even then nothing happened to me. I moved across the square to an exit, but I must have had such a facial expression that they recognized that I was a Jew who'd been taken out of the building, because one civilian screamed, 'A Jew!' And only then did they attack me. Stones flew at me, I was hit with rifle butts, I fell and lost consciousness. Periodically I regained consciousness; then they hit me again with stones and rifle butts. One wanted to shoot me when I was lying on the ground but I heard somebody else say, 'Don't shoot, he'll croak anyway.' I fainted again. When I came to, somebody was pulling me by the legs and threw me onto a truck. This was some other military, because I woke up in a hospital in Kielce.[47]

Some witnesses remember Jews being thrown from the windows into the street below. The head of the Jewish Committee was shot in the back while he was phoning for help. Later, when 600 workers from the Ludwików foundry arrived shortly after midday, some fifteen or twenty Jews were beaten to death with iron bars. Others were stoned, or shot by policemen or soldiers. The list of dead included three Jewish soldiers who had won the highest combat decorations fighting for Poland, and also two ordinary Poles who had apparently been mistaken for Jews. Also killed that day were a pregnant mother and a woman who had been shot along with her newborn baby. In total, forty-two Jews were killed at Kielce, and as many as eighty others injured. A further thirty or so were killed in related assaults on the local railways.[48]

The striking thing about this massacre was the fact that the entire community had taken part, not only men but also women; not only civilians but also policemen, militiamen and soldiers – the very people who were supposed to be keeping law and order. The racist myth of blood libel had been invoked, but the Catholic Church did nothing to refute this myth, or to denounce pogroms. Indeed, the Cardinal-Primate of Poland, August Hlond, claimed that the massacre had not been racially motivated, and that, in any case, if there *was* some anti-Semitism in society this was largely the fault of 'Jews who today occupy leading positions in Poland's government'.[49]

Local and national Communist leaders responded a little more helpfully – by prosecuting some of the main participants and by providing protection and a special train to take the wounded away to Łódź – but on the day itself they remained mute. The reason given by the local party secretary was that he 'didn't want people to be saying that the [Party] is a defender of Jews'.[50] The Interior Minister, Jakub Berman, who was himself Jewish, was informed of the pogrom while it was still going on, but also rejected suggestions that radical measures should be taken to stop the mob. Thus even the highest authority in the land proved himself unable, or unwilling, to help. Just as in Hungary, the Polish Communists – even the ones who were Jewish – were keen to distance themselves from any possible association with the Jews.

The Flight

The reaction to the anti-Semitic violence in eastern Europe was dramatic. Many survivors who had gone back to Poland after the war now returned to Germany on the grounds that it was safer in the country that had originally persecuted them than it was at home. The stories they told dissuaded others from making the same journey. 'Whatever you do, don't go back to Poland,' was the advice given to Michael Etkind. 'The Poles are killing all the Jews returning from the camps.'[51] Harry Balsam was told the same thing: 'They said that we must be mad to want to go back as they were still killing Jews in Poland . . . They told us the Poles were doing what the Germans could not manage, and that they had been lucky to come out alive.'[52] As early as October 1945, Joseph Levine of the Joint Distribution Committee was writing to New York that 'everyone reports murder and pillage by the Poles and that all the Jews want to get out of Poland'.[53]

Fortunately for many Polish Jews, and indeed Jews from several other countries in eastern Europe, an escape route had been set up for them. In the aftermath of the war, groups of determined Jews had set up an organization called Brichah ('Flight'), which had begun to secure a whole series of safe houses, methods of transport and unofficial border crossing points in Poland, Czechoslovakia, Hungary and Romania. At first they had been a very clandestine organization, smuggling truckloads of Jews across borders by bribing guards with money and alcohol, but by 1946 they had attained a semi-official status amongst the governments of eastern Europe. In May that year the Prime Minister of Poland, Edward Osóbka-Morawski, stated openly that his government would not stand in the way of Jews who wished to emigrate to Palestine – an assertion he repeated after the Kielce pogrom.[54] In the aftermath of the pogrom, a formal border crossing point was negotiated between one of the commanders of the Warsaw ghetto uprising, Yitzhak 'Antek' Zuckerman, and the Polish Defence Minister Marian Spychalski. Other prominent people associated with Brichah organized similar border crossings with the Hungarians, the Romanians and the American authorities in Germany, and the Czechs agreed to supply special trains for the transport of Jewish refugees across the country.[55]

The numbers of Jews fleeing westwards were significant, but they increased dramatically in the aftermath of the Kielce pogrom. In May 1946 Brichah organized the flight of 3,502 people from Poland. This rose to approximately 8,000 in June. But in July, after the pogrom, the figures more than doubled to 19,000, and then almost doubled again to 35,346 in August, before falling back to 12,379 in September. These figures do not include the 10–20,000 who fled Poland by other means, including putting themselves in the hands of private speculators and smugglers. In addition, the Joint Distribution Committee in Bratislava reported that some 14,000 Hungarian Jews had fled through Czechoslovakia in the three months after Kielce. In total, between 90,000 and 95,000 Jewish refugees are thought to have fled from eastern Europe in July, August and September 1946.[56]

The total number of Jews who fled west in the two years after the end of the war is probably in the region of 200,000 from Poland, 18,000 from Hungary, 19,000 from Romania, and perhaps a further 18,000 from Czechoslovakia – although most of this last group were forced out not because they were Jewish but because the Czechs considered them German.[57] When one also factors in the 40,000 or so Jews who fled the same countries in the years 1948–50, we reach a grand total of almost 300,000 people who were forced to leave their countries because of anti-Semitic persecution. This is, if anything, a slightly conservative estimate.[58]

Where did all these Jews go? In the short term they aimed for the displaced persons camps in Germany, Austria and Italy; but the irony that it should be these former Axis countries that would provide them with salvation did not escape them. Their long-term aim was to leave mainland Europe altogether. Many wanted to go to Britain or parts of the British Empire; many more wanted to get to the United States; but by far the majority wanted to go to Palestine. They knew that Zionists were pushing for a Jewish state there, and considered such a state the only place where they might realistically be safe from anti-Semitism.

They were helped in this aim by just about every nation apart from Britain. The Soviets, who were perfectly happy for their Jews to flee Europe, did not place obstacles in their way and opened their borders for Jews – but only Jews – to exit. The Poles and the Hungarians, as we have seen, did whatever they could to make life for Jews uncomfortable, and again encouraged them to leave by any means possible. The Romanians, Bulgarians, Yugoslavs, Italians and French all provided ports for Jews to embark on ships bound for the Holy Land, and rarely made any effort to stop them. But it was the Americans who helped the Jews most of all – not by allowing them to come to the United States, but by facilitating their journey towards British-controlled Palestine. They exercised considerable diplomatic pressure on the British to get them to accept 100,000 Jews in Palestine, despite the fact that they themselves officially allowed only 12,849 Jews into America under President Truman's special DP directive.[59]

The British were the only ones who tried to stem the flow of Jews from the east. They pointed out that the vast majority were not survivors of Hitler's concentration camps, but Jews who had spent the war in Kazakhstan and other areas of the Soviet Union. Since it was now supposedly 'safe' for them to return to their home towns, the British did not see why they should be the ones to provide sanctuary for them – the Soviet Union and the countries of eastern Europe should also be doing their fair share. While they were happy to provide shelter for Hitler's victims in Germany, they drew the line at welcoming a new wave of Jewish refugees that had little to do with the war. Unlike the Americans, they refused these new Jews entry to the DP camps under their control.

The British believed – wrongly, as it turns out – that this new wave of Jewish refugees was inspired not by fear of anti-Semitism but by Zionists who had travelled from Israel to eastern Europe in order to agitate for recruits to their cause. In fairness to the British, the Brichah movement was indeed made up mostly of Palestinian Zionists – but they were entirely mistaken in their assumption that the new desire to flee to Palestine had originated with them. As historians like Yehuda Bauer have conclusively shown, the impetus to flee came exclusively from the refugees themselves: all the Zionists were doing was providing them with a place to aim for.[60]

The British also argued passionately that it was morally wrong, particularly in the aftermath of the Holocaust, to allow the flight of European Jews towards Palestine. According to the Foreign Office, it was 'surely a counsel of despair . . . indeed it would go far by implication to admit that [the] Nazis were right in holding that there was no place for Jews in Europe'. The British Foreign Secretary himself, Ernest Bevin, strongly believed that 'there had been no point in fighting the Second World War if the Jews could not stay on in Europe where they had a vital role to play in the reconstruction of that continent'.[61]

For all their appeals to moral philosophy, the real reasons behind British reluctance were political: they did not want to create a potentially explosive situation between Arabs and Jews in the Middle East. But without the robust cooperation of any of their partners in Europe there was not really much they could do to prevent the westward flight from continuing. Their efforts to prevent Jews from arriving in Palestine were a little more successful, and ships in the Mediterranean carrying tens of thousands of Jewish immigrants were boarded by the Royal Navy and redirected to special DP camps in Cyprus.

5. The Jewish flight to Palestine

But this was merely a case of King Canute trying to hold back the tide – in the end there was little the British could do to stop the course of events. In the summer of 1946, Zionists began a campaign of terror against the British in Palestine (a campaign that was the main cause of the rise of anti-Semitism in postwar Britain). The following year the British started to scale down their military presence in Jerusalem. At the end of November 1947, after intensive lobbying by Zionists, the United Nations voted to award part of Palestine to the Jews for the formation of their own state. And finally, in 1948, after a close-run civil war between the Jews and Arab Palestinians, the state of Israel was consolidated. The Jews were free to make one small corner of the world their own.

This is not the place to embark on a discussion of the brutal conflict that has existed between Israelis and Arabs ever since that time, and which continues to fill our newspapers today. Suffice it to say that the Jews were presented with an opportunity that was too great to pass up. Given their recent history, one can hardly blame them for wishing to create their own state, even if, in the words of one Palestinian historian, the Arabs 'failed to see why they should be made to pay for the Holocaust'.[62] For better or worse, huge numbers of European Jews at last found themselves in a country where they themselves were the masters, where they could not be persecuted, and where they would be allowed to follow their own agenda. Israel was not only the promised land, but a land of promise.

As a result of this process, however, the areas of Europe where the Jews had once lived were irrevocably changed. Poland in particular was almost unrecognizable from the cultural and ethnic melting pot it had been before the war. To a lesser extent, the same was true of the whole of eastern Europe.

By 1948 much of the region had become, even more than in Hitler's time, *Judenfrei*.

18

The Ethnic Cleansing of Ukraine and Poland

The Jews were not the only people to be chased out of their home towns in the aftermath of the war. Nor were they the only ones to suffer violence from mobs, policemen and armed militias. If the survivors of the Holocaust were correct to insist that they had been singled out during the war, this was no longer the case after the war was over. Jews were certainly mistreated, as I have shown, but after the liberation the true focus of nationalist violence now fell on other minorities.

One need only compare the events at Kielce with what happened in other parts of Poland that same year. At the end of January 1946, soldiers from the Polish 34th Infantry Regiment under Colonel Stanislav Pluto surrounded the village of Zawadka Morochowska (or 'Zavadka Morochivska' in Ukrainian), near Sanok in south-east Poland. The village was inhabited entirely by ethnic Ukrainians, and it was their ethnicity that was the sole reason for the events that took place there. According to eyewitnesses, the arrival of the army heralded a massacre that was every bit as bloody as anything that had happened during the war:

They came to the village at dawn. All the men began to run to the woods, and those who remained attempted to hide in the attics and cellars but to no avail. The Polish soldiers were looking everywhere so that not a single place was left unsearched. Whenever they captured a man, he was killed instantly; where they could not find a man, they beat the women and children . . . My father was hidden in the attic and the Poles ordered my mother to climb up the ladder to search for him. These orders were accompanied by severe rifle-butt blows. When mother started to climb, the ladder suddenly broke and she fell down, breaking her elbow. Five Poles began to beat her again with rifle-butts and when she could not lift herself, they kicked her with their heavy boots. I ran to her with my four-year-old daughter and wanted to shield her, but the soldiers began to beat me and my child. I soon fell unconscious and awoke to find my mother and child killed and the entire village afire![1]

When Ukrainian partisans arrived in the area the next day they discovered a scene of utter devastation: 'nothing but smouldering ruins and a few moving shadows that looked more like ghosts than human beings'.[2] Apart from looting the village comprehensively, and stealing most of the livestock, Polish soldiers had killed dozens of the villagers, most of them women and children. Worse than the fact of their murders was the manner in which they were committed. Many were beaten to death, disembowelled, or set on fire. Some women had their breasts sliced off while others had their eyes gouged out or their noses and tongues removed. According to one of the Polish soldiers who took part in the massacre, 'there were some among us who were enjoying this butchery'.[3]

Most of the historical sources for this massacre come from the Ukrainian side, which had a vested interest in portraying Polish brutality, but even allowing for a certain degree of embellishment it was an undeniably horrific event. Neither did it end there. Two months later the army returned to Zawadka Morochowska and instructed all the surviving inhabitants of the village to gather their things and cross the border into Soviet Ukraine. All the remaining buildings apart from the school and the church were torched and, as a warning of what awaited the villagers if they stayed, a group of eleven men were shot. Finally, in April, after several more villagers had been killed, the church and the school were also destroyed, and the entire population was rounded up and forcibly expelled from the country. During the course of these operations some fifty-six people had been murdered, and many others horribly wounded. The village was all but wiped from the map.[4]

The difference between the massacres at Zawadka Morochowska and the pogrom in Kielce is that the former were carried out by the army, rather than by an unruly mob. The harassment and murder of Jews in Poland was a popular phenomenon inspired by widespread anti-Semitism. It was a consequence not of government action, but of government *in*action: anti-Semites felt free to attack Jews because they were confident that they would not be punished for doing so. In the event, several of the perpetrators of the Kielce pogrom were tried and even executed for their crimes. The massacre of Ukrainian speakers at Zawadka Morochowska, by contrast, followed on directly from official government policy. The army had been sent to south-east Poland specifically to get rid of the Ukrainian population there. Unlike the Jews, who were merely 'encouraged' to flee, Ukrainians were deliberately chased out – and when they refused to go, were killed or forcibly removed. If, as at Zawadka Morochowska, the army was somewhat over-zealous in its actions, it was not, generally speaking, sanctioned for them. The most important thing, from the government's point of view, was that they were successful.

Zawadka Morochowska was just one event in thousands. The persecution and expulsion of ethnic minorities occurred throughout Europe, especially in central and eastern parts of the continent. But events in Poland were particularly important – partly because this was the country where the most comprehensive ethnic cleansing took place, but also because the Polish/Ukrainian problem had such huge consequences for the rest of Europe. It was the nationalist tensions unleashed here that finally brought the Soviets round to the idea of harnessing nationalism for their own ends – not only in Poland but in the whole of the Eastern Bloc. And it was the mutual expulsion of Poles and Ukrainians that would provide the template for ethnic cleansing throughout the continent.[5]

However, before one can truly understand events in villages like Zawadka Morochowska, it is necessary to go right back to the beginning. As many historians have pointed out, the ethnic cleansing of Poland did not occur in isolation, but in the aftermath of the greatest war of all time. Poles did not remove Ukrainians simply for the sake of it: it was only the huge events of the war that made such a radical move either desirable or possible.[6]

The Origins of Polish/Ukrainian Ethnic Violence

The borderlands of eastern Poland were invaded not once, but three times during the war: first by the Soviets, then by the Nazis, and finally by the Soviets again. The different ethnic communities that lived in this richly diverse area reacted to each invasion in different ways. Most of the Polish population resisted the Nazis and the Soviets alike, in the hope that Poland might somehow be able to return to its prewar status quo. The Ukrainian population, by contrast, was more divided. Almost all of them feared and hated the Russians because of the brutal way that they had ruled the Soviet part of Ukraine during the 1930s; but many welcomed the Germans, at least at first, as liberators. The Jews, meanwhile, did not know where to place their faith. Many hoped that the Soviet invasion might deliver them from Polish and Ukrainian anti-Semitism; later, some seemed to hope that the German invasion would save them from Soviet persecution. By the time the region was invaded for a third time at the end of 1943, the handful of Jews who still survived had lost faith in all outsiders, whatever their nationality.

Both the Soviets and the Nazis played these different ethnic groups off against one other. The Nazis especially sought to harness the nationalist sentiments of the Ukrainians, in order to suppress the rest of the population. Even before the invasion they had made contacts with Ukrainian far-right political groups, particularly the Organisation of Ukrainian Nationalists (OUN). This was an illegal ultra-nationalist movement, akin to the Ustashas in Croatia or the Iron Guard in Romania, which embraced the use of violence to achieve its aims. The Nazis dangled the promise of Ukrainian independence before them in return for their collaboration. While the most powerful factions of this shady organization never trusted German intentions, other factions enthusiastically allowed themselves to be exploited – partly because they thought the Nazis would give them what they wanted, but also because they shared some of the Nazis' darker intentions.[7]

The most shameful collaboration between the OUN and the Nazis was the way in which they worked together to eradicate the Jews. The OUN had for years been speaking of ethnic purity, of a 'Ukraine for Ukrainians', and of the benefits of revolutionary terror. The implementation of the Final Solution, particularly in the region of Volhynia, showed followers of the OUN that the slogans were not mere rhetoric. These massacres, which occurred in full view of the general population, would provide the template for all future ethnic cleansing in the region. What once would have been unthinkable now became eminently possible.

During the course of 1941 and 1942, about 12,000 Ukrainian policemen became intimately acquainted with the tactics the Nazis used to kill over 200,000 Volhynian Jews. As collaborators, they were involved in the planning of operations. They gave assurances to local populations in order to lull them into a false sense of security. They were employed in the sudden encirclement of Jewish villages and settlements, and even took part in some of the killing itself. The slaughter of the Jews was the perfect apprenticeship for what would come later.[8]

At the end of 1942, when it first became obvious that German power was waning, these same Ukrainian policemen deserted their posts en masse. They took their weapons and went to join the OUN's new, armed partisan group, the Ukrainian Insurgent Army (Ukrains'ka Povstans'ka Armiia, or UPA). They used the skills they had learned under the Nazis to continue their campaign against their ethnic enemies – not only the region's few remaining Jews, but this time also its large Polish population.

The massacre of Poles began in the same areas where Ukrainian policemen had been most intimately connected to the massacre of Jews: Volhynia. There were many reasons why the ethnic cleansing began here – the area contained extensive forests and marshes, and so was particularly suited to partisan activity, and the isolated Polish communities were much less well defended than in other areas – but the previous actions against the Jews certainly played their part. The taboos had already been broken: young Ukrainian men here had become both trained to kill, and inured to mass killing. When they embarked on their cleansing of the region at the end of 1942 they were therefore relatively free of both external and personal constraints.

In the frenzied massacres that were to take place over the next few years, Polish communities were murdered in their entirety, from old men and women right down to newborn babies. The village of Oleksięta, for example, was torched during the Easter of 1943 in an operation deliberately designed to create terror amongst the Polish population.[9] In Wysocko Wyżne thirteen children were locked in a Catholic church which was then set on fire.[10] In Wola Ostrowiecka the entire Polish community was rounded up in the local schoolyard. While the men were taken off five at a time to be hacked to death in a nearby barn, the women and children were driven into the school, which was blown up with hand grenades and then set on fire.[11]

In the village of Podkamień a campaign of night-time raids on remote farmsteads and outlying hamlets drove the villagers out of their homes. At first they took to sleeping in the fields in order to avoid surprise attacks, but eventually they sought sanctuary in the local monastery. On 12 March 1944, however, the monastery itself was besieged by UPA troops. Apart from a few people who managed to escape by jumping out of windows, the entire community – including the monks – was slaughtered. Their bodies were hung by the legs around the monastery as a warning to the rest of the Polish community of what lay in store for them if they stayed in the region.[12]

These are just a handful of examples that must stand for the hundreds of Polish villages affected by ethnic violence in 1943 and 1944. According to not only Polish sources but German and Soviet ones, Ukrainian partisans indulged in beheading, crucifying, dismembering and disembowelling their victims, and often displayed bodies in a conscious attempt to strike terror into the remaining Polish community. They burned homes and churches, razed villages and looted whatever they could lay their hands on. This took place throughout eastern Poland/western Ukraine. Any Ukrainians who attempted to shelter their Polish neighbours were also killed.[13]

Even UPA reports themselves confirm that they set out to exterminate Poles as thoroughly as the Jews had already been exterminated, and in many areas succeeded. One of UPA's commanders-in-chief, Dmytro Kliachkivs'kyi, advised his commanders to 'liquidate the entire male [Polish] population between 16 and 60 years', and ordered that 'villages in the forests and villages adjacent to forests should be razed to the ground'. The local commander of the Zavykhost region, Iurii Stel'mashchuk, admitted that he had been given an order for 'the total physical extermination of the Polish population in all western provinces of Ukraine. Fulfilling this order of the OUN leaders, a formation consisting of several UPA bands slaughtered more than 15,000 Poles in August 1943.'[14]

In reaction to such events, some local Poles began to set up their own militias for the purpose of self-defence. The Polish underground also diverted resources away from resisting the occupation in order to protect Polish communities from the UPA. Some Volhynian Poles turned to the Germans for jobs as policemen so that they might have opportunities for revenge. (The Germans certainly appeared happy to recruit them, and a new wave of collaboration was born – ironically in the name of controlling *former* collaborators who were now running amok.) When the Soviets arrived in 1944, many Poles joined the Red Army or the NKVD – again, with the purpose of exacting revenge for all they had suffered. Ukrainian villages were burned, and thousands of Ukrainian peasants killed, in both official and unofficial reprisals for the actions of UPA.[15]

These reprisals, naturally, were used by Ukrainian partisans as further justification for their targeting of Poles and Polish villages. And so the situation degenerated into a vicious cycle. During the final year of the war, and in its immediate aftermath, the entire region was engulfed in what was effectively a civil war. What began in Volhynia spread to Galicia and central Poland. Poles and Ukrainians slaughtered one another and burned each other's villages with an enthusiasm that far exceeded any of their actions against the German or Soviet occupiers. Waldemar Lotnik, a Polish partisan at the time, put this conflict in stark terms:

> They had killed seven men two nights previously; that night we killed sixteen of theirs . . . A week later the Ukrainians responded by wiping out an entire Polish colony, setting fire to the houses, killing those inhabitants unable to flee and raping the women who fell into their hands . . . We retaliated by attacking an even bigger Ukrainian village and this time two or three men in our unit killed women and children . . . The Ukrainians in turn took their revenge by destroying a village of 500 Poles and torturing and killing all who fell into their hands. We responded by destroying two of their larger villages . . . This was how the fighting escalated. Each time more people were killed, more houses burnt, more women raped. Men become desensitised very quickly and kill as if they know nothing else.[16]

It is in this context that we must see the massacre at Zawadka Morochowska that I described at the beginning of this chapter. When viewed in isolation, it would be easy to come to the conclusion that it was a cold-blooded, purely Polish crime, committed in the name of ethnic cleansing. When one widens the time-frame slightly, and discovers that the units involved in the massacre had suffered casualties during an attack by UPA partisans only the day before, it no longer seems quite so cold-blooded.[17] And when one widens the time-frame still further, and discovers that some of those involved in the massacre were veterans of the civil war between Poles and Ukrainians in Volhynia, revenge begins to look like a much stronger motive.[18] This context in no way justifies what occurred at Zawadka Morochowska, or indeed the attacks on any of the other Ukrainian villages in south-east Poland in 1946 – but it does go part of the way towards explaining it.

Even the most conservative estimates suggest that around 50,000 Polish civilians were killed by Ukrainian partisans in Volhynia, and a further 20,000 to 30,000 in Galicia. In total it is thought that up to 90,000 Poles were killed throughout the borderland areas during the civil conflict. Ukrainian deaths also number in the thousands, but since the Poles did not enter the conflict with an explicit plan to commit genocide, the Ukrainian faction lost far fewer people than they killed – perhaps 20,000 in all.[19] As with so many other areas of wartime European history, these numbers are controversial, and subject to an ongoing argument between Polish and Ukrainian historians over who owns the rights to victimhood. In one sense, the absolute numbers do not really matter – it is enough to register that a violent civil war took place and that thousands died on both sides. But in another sense the numbers are desperately important, especially in a climate where nationalism is on the rise once more across Europe. Ukrainians, naturally, are reluctant to admit to the role of the OUN and UPA in starting the cycle of violence, and in their attempts to minimize the numbers of Polish dead occasionally distort the figures. Some Poles, on the other hand, wield statistics like a weapon in a historiographic rerun of the civil war itself.[20] In such a highly charged atmosphere, it is unlikely that any agreement over figures will be reached – the ones I have given above are the most impartial estimates available.

The Soviet Solution

When the Soviets reinvaded Ukraine and Poland in 1944 and discovered the extent of the ethnic conflict there, they were alarmed. They certainly could not allow such chaos to disrupt their supply lines while the war was still going on – and since the UPA had also begun to attack Soviet formations, something had to be done to stabilize the situation.

Their solution was simple: if the different nationalities could not be made to live together peacefully on the same territory, then they should be separated. This separation was to be done on a state-wide scale: the Poles should live in Poland, and the Ukrainians should live in a Ukrainian Soviet Socialist Republic.

The demarcation line between the two would not be the old Polish border from the 1930s: it would be moved westwards, so that most of what Ukrainians regarded as 'Western Ukraine' would be reunited with 'Eastern Ukraine'. This would not only extend Soviet territory, but would steal the thunder of the OUN/UPA by giving Ukrainians the very thing they had been fighting for. Any Poles living on the wrong side of this border would be expelled into Poland; and likewise, Ukrainians on the other side of the border would be 'repatriated'.

To say this was a controversial solution at the time would be a gross understatement. For the Polish government in exile in London the idea of changing the Ukrainian/Polish border so far westwards was virtually unthinkable. The border that the Soviets proposed was the so-called Curzon Line, which would see an area the combined size of all three Baltic States – Estonia, Latvia and Lithuania – severed from eastern Poland. The Polish city of Lwów would be awarded to Ukraine, Brest-Litovsk given to Belarus, and Wilno (modern-day Vilnius) handed over to Lithuania. To agree to such a border would be effectively to endorse the Soviet invasion of Poland in 1939.

On the face of it the Western Allies were also opposed to such a solution. Both Churchill and Roosevelt had previously expressed outrage at any suggestion that the Soviets should be allowed to hold on to this territory.[21] And yet both politicians were realists, and knew that it would be virtually impossible to oppose Soviet plans now that they already occupied the whole region. The price of challenging Stalin over the issue was not one that either premier was willing to contemplate. 'Do you want me to go to war with Russia?' said Roosevelt sharply when his ambassador to Poland suggested that America should stand firm on the subject.[22]

As early as November 1943, when Churchill and Roosevelt met Stalin for the first time at Tehran, they both indicated to him that they would not oppose his plans to incorporate the eastern borderlands of Poland into the Soviet Union. Churchill made no secret of this, and tried soon after to convince the Polish Prime Minister, Stanisław Mikołajczyk, to accept this as a fait accompli – something that Mikołajczyk steadfastly refused to do. Roosevelt was more calculating, however, and did not make his position clear until after he was re-elected the following year, because he was relying on the support of millions of Polish-American voters. The final blow to Polish hopes on the subject came at the next meeting of the Big Three at Yalta in February 1945, when they jointly and formally declared that the eastern frontier of Poland should follow the Curzon Line.[23]

The tragic thing about this process is that it was pushed through without any reference to the wishes of the Polish people themselves. Not even their elected representatives were consulted until *after* the deal had been struck in Tehran. For Poles the world over this was nothing short of an Anglo-American betrayal. When Churchill and Roosevelt had signed the Atlantic Charter in 1941 they had promised never to endorse any territorial changes 'that do not accord with the freely expressed wishes of the peoples concerned'; by agreeing to Soviet demands at Tehran and Yalta they had explicitly broken that promise. There were many within the British and American establishment who shared these feelings. Arthur Bliss Lane, the US ambassador to Poland, openly called it a 'capitulation' to Stalin, a policy of 'appeasement' that was similar to the appeasement of Hitler before the war, and a 'betrayal' of America's Polish allies.[24] In Britain, the Labour MP John Rhys Davies stated bitterly in the House of Commons, 'We started this war with great motives and high ideals. We published the Atlantic Charter and then spat on it, stomped on it and burnt it, as it were, at the stake, and now nothing is left of it.'[25]

Forced 'Repatriation'

Very little thought was given at Yalta to just what this change of borders would mean for the population of the region: it was regarded as Stalin's own business, and not something that the Western Allies could realistically influence. In fact, the Soviets had already started to arrest and deport people according to their usual methods almost as soon as they had arrived in the area. But Stalin remained cautious, and the wholesale deportation of Poles did not begin in earnest until the Yalta Agreement was signed.

This was something quite new, as far as the Soviets were concerned. The Soviets were well acquainted with deporting whole populations from one region to another for reasons of nationality. Throughout the 1920s and 30s entire communities in the Soviet Union had been moved like pieces on a chessboard.[26] The most recent such move had been the deportation of the Tatars from the Crimea (which at the time was not a part of Ukraine) in May 1944.[27] However, until now such deportations had always been carried out for political or military rather than purely ethnic reasons. Moreover, they had only ever been conducted within Soviet territory – the Soviets had never before *expelled* an ethnic minority from their territory into another country. The population exchange that was to take place between Ukraine and Poland therefore reflected a marked change in Soviet policy.[28]

Between 1944 and 1946 some 782,582 Poles were removed from Soviet Ukraine and resettled in Poland. A further 231,152 were expelled from Belarus, and 169,244 from Lithuania – giving a total of almost 1.2 million.[29] Many of these people were harassed into leaving by the authorities. But many were also encouraged to leave of their own accord in order to escape the continuing ethnic violence which raged throughout 1945 and even into 1946. In a peculiar way the Soviets and the UPA seemed to be working in tandem to achieve their common goal. Maria Józefowska and her family, for example, were forced out of their home village of Czerwonogród when the UPA burned it down in July 1945. Immediately after the attack, the Soviet authorities laid on a special train to transport them out of Ukraine to Jarosław in Polish Galicia, almost as if the opportunity were too good to miss.[30]

With the blessing of the Soviets, the Poles replied in kind by 'repatriating' over 482,000 Ukrainians, mostly from Galicia in the south-east of the country.[31] The massacre at Zawadka Morochowska was part of this process, and shows how brutally it was carried out. Once again, the official actions of the Polish government were accompanied by unofficial actions by nationalist groups and members of the underground Armia Krajowa ('Home Army'). Atrocities were carried out on innocent civilians, and even people who did not consider themselves Ukrainian at all. The Łemkos, for example, were an ethnic group belonging to the Beskidy ranges of the Carpathian Mountains who had no historical interest in Ukraine or any other kind of nationalism, and wanted only to keep their own lands intact. Yet they were targeted and deported along with other Ukrainian speakers. Attempts by local leaders to explain the difference between Ukrainians and Łemkos fell on deaf ears.

Unsurprisingly, some Ukrainians and Łemkos turned to the UPA for protection against deportation. The UPA in Polish Galicia was not nearly so indiscriminately brutal as it was across the border in Ukraine, but was still not above murder, torture and the mutilation of its enemies. One former Polish soldier from this time, Henryk Jan Mielcarek, writes passionately about fellow soldiers who were beaten to death by UPA partisans, had their eyes and tongues cut out, or were tied to trees and left to die.[32] But, given that nobody else was willing to help them, many Ukrainians saw no alternative to joining such partisan groups, or at least to providing them with support. This increasing popularity of the UPA in Galicia only inflamed the situation: it gave the army and the authorities even more justification for their policy of expelling these communities.

The Polish 'repatriation' campaign in 1945–6, brutal as it was, ended up being fairly successful. It did, however, encounter a major problem: towards the end of 1945 some of those Ukrainians who had already left Poland voluntarily started to come back. Many of these people had discovered that life in Ukraine was far worse than it was in the areas they had left, even factoring in Polish harassment. Not only was Ukraine much less well developed than south-east Poland, but the way it had repeatedly changed hands during the war had left it desolate. To make things even worse, the Soviets were not allowing many Polish Ukrainians to settle in the very country they were supposed to be 'returning' to: in order to prevent the OUN/UPA problem escalating, more than 75 per cent of Polish Ukrainians were settled in other parts of the USSR. As a consequence, thousands of Ukrainians returned to Poland in 1945 and 1946 to warn their fellow villagers not to go. This goes part of the way towards explaining why so many Ukrainians resisted deportation even in the face of increasingly violent racist attacks against them.[33]

At the end of 1946 time finally ran out for the Polish authorities who wished to expel Ukrainian speakers from the country in their entirety. To bring the repatriations to an end, the Soviets closed the border between Ukraine and Poland. This did not suit the Polish authorities at all, since they estimated that there were still some 74,000 Ukrainians in the country who had evaded repatriation. In fact the numbers were much higher – about 200,000 in total. The Polish government petitioned the Soviets to allow the process to continue a little while longer, but to no avail.[34]

Given the impossibility of expelling any more Ukrainians, it is conceivable that the matter might have ended there. Perhaps if the terrorist activities of the UPA had stopped, the Polish government would have felt confident enough to leave the remaining Ukrainians and Łemkos alone. Plans to continue the displacements on an internal basis, which already existed at the beginning of 1947, might have been dropped, and centuries of Ukrainian culture in Galicia might have been allowed to remain. Perhaps.

Such speculation is moot, however, because tensions between the Poles and their Ukrainian-speaking minorities did not relax – indeed they escalated. The tipping point came on 28 March 1947, when the Polish Deputy Minister of Defence, General Karol Świerczewski, was assassinated by the UPA. This killing proved to be a disaster for Poland's Ukrainians, and was used as justification for a whole range of repressive measures against them. The following day, Polish officers began to speak openly of 'the complete extermination of the remnants of the Ukrainian population in the southeastern border region of Poland'.[35] The Polish administration immediately launched another sweep of the region to root out all the remaining Ukrainian speakers.

The operation was to be called Akcja Wisła – Operation Vistula. Its objectives were not only to destroy the UPA in Poland, but to bring about what its architects called, rather chillingly, a 'final solution' to the Ukrainian problem.[36]

Forced Assimilation

Operation Vistula began at the end of April 1947 and continued through to the late summer. Its intention was not only to 'destroy the UPA bands' but to work with the State Office of Repatriation to conduct 'an evacuation of all persons of Ukrainian nationality from the region to the northwestern territories, resettling them there with a dispersion as sparse as possible'. Historians who claim that the only purpose of the operation was to remove support for the UPA are ignoring these clear statements, issued by the Office of State Security itself, declaring ethnic cleansing of the country as an overt, and separate, objective.[37]

The operation was intended to root out all the remaining Ukrainian speakers in the country to the last man, woman and child, and was to include even mixed Polish–Ukrainian families. These people were to be given a few hours to pack their things, and then taken to transit hubs to be registered. From here they were to be transported to diverse locations throughout the areas in the west and north that had once been German, but which were now part of Polish territory. In theory, families were to be transported together, but in practice all deportees were given a number and were displaced along with those who registered at the same time. In this way, family members who registered separately were often sent to towns and villages miles apart unless they could convince (or bribe) officials to let them stay together. Families were also supposed to be allowed to take clothes and valuables with them, and even a certain amount of livestock, in order to sustain themselves in their new homes. In reality they were rarely given enough time to pack properly, and were often forced to abandon important items at home to be looted by their Polish neighbours. Many also complain of being robbed by unscrupulous guards or gangs of local people during their journey.

There was nothing especially unique about the rounding up of entire villages and their displacement to another part of the continent – the war had made this practice commonplace, and by 1947 the specific displacement of Ukrainians had already been going on for more than two years. Nor was the *scale* of it unique – indeed, it was a relatively minor event compared to the continent-wide expulsion of Germans that I shall describe in the next chapter. What made this particular displacement different from all the others was its purpose: the Polish authorities did not merely want to eject this ethnic group, but to compel it to give up all claims to a separate nationality. They were to be forced to change the way they spoke, the way they dressed, the way they worshipped and the way they were educated. The authorities would no longer allow them to be Ukrainians or Łemkos – 'Because they wanted us all to become Poles.'[38]

The whole process was deeply distressing, as interviews with Ukrainian-speaking Poles in recent times clearly show. For Anna Klimasz and Rozalia Najduch, Łemkos who were deported from their village of Bednarka in Galicia, the most distressing event was the expulsion itself, and especially the behaviour of their Polish neighbours. Far from supporting or helping them, local Poles seemed only too keen to be rid of them, and looted their homes and property enthusiastically even before they had left. Fellow villagers who refused to allow looters into their homes were beaten, while others had to stand by and watch while their houses were ransacked before their eyes. Some even had things stolen from the carts they were loading up to take with them, with the words, 'Don't take this, don't take that. You won't need this any longer . . .'[39]

For others, the most stressful time was the period of uncertainty that came after they had left their villages and were forced to wait in shabby transit camps to see where they would be displaced to. This period could last anything from a few days to several weeks. Olga Zdanowicz, a Ukrainian from Grąziowa in Galicia, had to sleep in the open at the transit camp in Trzcianiec for three weeks.[40] The villagers from Bednarka were forced to stay in a camp at Zagórzany for two weeks, also without shelter, and with little food to eat but that which they had brought with them. Rozalia Najduch was reduced to stealing fodder from local peasants to feed her animals. Anna Szewczyk and Mikołaj Sokacz remember sleeping underneath their carts alongside the livestock as the only way of escaping the elements.[41] During this time all deportees were questioned by Polish officials, the implication being that their very ethnicity made them potential UPA terrorists.

It was at the transit camps that those who were most suspected of partisan involvement were arrested. For these people the stress of displacement now became a nightmare. They were sent to prisons and internment camps, the most infamous of which was Jaworzno, an ex-Nazi prison camp that had been taken over by the Polish authorities. Here they were beaten, robbed and subjected to a regimen of poor food, poor sanitation and poor treatment. One of the several commandants of the camp was the infamous Salomon Morel, who was transferred here after his time in charge of the camp for Germans at Zgoda (see Chapter 12). As at Zgoda, prisoners were tortured by sadistic prison guards, who hung them from pipes, pierced them with pins, force-fed them various liquids and beat them with metal bars, electric cables, rifle butts and a variety of other implements. In the Ukrainian sub-camp at Jaworzno 161 prisoners died as a direct result of malnutrition, five from typhus, and two women committed suicide.[42]

For the majority of Ukrainians, meanwhile, the next stage was their journey to their new homes. Friends and acquaintances were split up and loaded onto trains along with their livestock – four families and their animals to each boxcar – and transported to the former German provinces of East Prussia, Pomerania and Silesia on the opposite side of Poland. While the journey was nothing like as terrifying as the ordeal awaiting those who were sent to Jaworzno, there was a brief moment of panic when the trains passed within a few kilometres of Auschwitz. The journey could take anything up to two weeks, during which time the deportees became filthy and covered in lice.[43]

For all the uncertainty and discomfort of the journey it was sometimes not nearly so unpleasant as their arrival in a new and unknown land. The way the system was supposed to work was as follows: each family would be given a destination, and would be expected to report to the local State Office of Repatriation when they got there. They would be allocated a property to live in, or sometimes they would be awarded this property in a lottery. Having been abandoned by their former German owners, these properties were supposed to be furnished – the idea was that the furniture that the displaced Ukrainians and Łemkos had had to leave behind would be replaced by furniture in their new homes. In reality, however, anything of use or value had long since been looted, or confiscated by corrupt officials. By 1947 all the best properties had been taken by displaced Poles, leaving only derelict buildings, ransacked apartments or broken-down farms with desperately poor soil. Families who arrived here often abandoned the places they had been allocated and roamed the countryside looking for something better.[44]

Their welcome was usually far from warm. Since the purpose of removing these people from their communities was to disperse them, families from the same village were not supposed to be housed in the same area. Indeed, often only nuclear families were allowed to stay together – extended families were to be split up in the same way as the whole community was. In most cases, therefore, families found themselves completely isolated, without any of the community they had grown up with to support them. Worse than this, they regularly found themselves surrounded by hostile people who actively despised them. Many of the Poles who had recently been deported from Volhynia and other parts of Soviet Ukraine had also been relocated in these areas. Having survived the savage civil war in their own homelands, the last people these Poles wanted as neighbours were more Ukrainians. Some of those deported in Operation Vistula speak of being beaten by Poles in the towns where they were rehoused, others were merely shunned – almost all found it difficult to find work or make friends.

Anti-Ukrainian prejudice was everywhere. Mikołaj Sokacz remembers being arrested and beaten by militiamen who were convinced that he was a member of the UPA. He had no choice but to take it in his stride for, as he explains, 'Łemkos were beaten a lot.' Those who were sent to Jaworzno remember having stones thrown at them and being spat at by local people, because they were supposedly the ones responsible for the assassination of General Świerczewski.[45] Teodor Szewczyk remembers overhearing a Polish smallholder he worked for claiming, 'I won't pay those f . . . ing Ukrainians! They can work for food.'[46] And so on.

Where Ukrainians and Łemkos did come across others like them, opportunities for mutual support, or even basic socializing, were rare. Official paranoia about the UPA had led to rules banning Ukrainian speakers from gathering in groups of more than a few people. Anyone caught speaking Ukrainian to someone else was automatically suspected of conspiracy. The Orthodox and Uniate churches were also banned, obliging Ukrainians to worship in a foreign tongue, in Catholic churches, or not at all.

Since the point of Operation Vistula was to assimilate Ukrainians into the Polish Communist state, children were in some ways the main focus of the authorities' attentions. All children were forced to speak Polish at school, and Ukrainian literature was banned. Boys and girls caught speaking Ukrainian were reprimanded and sometimes punished. They were often given compulsory classes in Catholicism, as well as the usual Stalinist Communist indoctrination that was a part of every child's education. Anything that revealed an alternative identity to the official Polish one was forbidden.[47]

And yet, for all this, assimilation was impossible because their classmates often would not let them forget that they were *not* Polish. Children laughed at their accents, taunted them, and sometimes physically bullied them. 'Ukrainian' children were not invited to Polish children's houses. Their difference from their classmates, and their isolation from any other children like themselves, made their situation quite similar to that of the 'German' children in Scandinavia. While there do not yet appear to have been studies into the life chances of these children compared with others, as there have been in Norway, it would be reasonable to assume that they probably suffered similarly high rates of anxiety, stress and depression in later life. Even more than the children of Germans in Norway, today many Ukrainians once again openly speak of themselves as a distinct group in Polish society – something that would have been unthinkable in the early 1950s.

The one experience that united all these people – and indeed all of the millions of others who were displaced from their lands after the Second World War – was a desire to return 'home'.[48] This was, however, the one act that was forbidden above all others. Those who tried to return to their villages in Galicia found themselves faced with angry militiamen, and were threatened with violence or imprisonment. For others, there was simply no point. In the absence of the communities they had grown up with, their villages were no longer the idealized places they remembered. When Olga Zdanowicz tried to visit Grąziowa many years later she found nothing there. 'The village had been burnt – it didn't exist any more.'[49]

The ethnic cleansing of Poland in 1947 is not something that can be considered in isolation. It was a product of many years of civil war, and more than seven years of racial violence that had begun almost as soon as the Germans had invaded the west of the country in 1939. It saw its foundation in the Holocaust of Polish Jews, particularly in the massacres in Volhynia, and the collaboration of Ukrainian nationalists in these and subsequent atrocities. After the war, the expulsion of Poland's ethnic minorities was carried out with the explicit help of the Soviet Union, but the subsequent displacement and assimilation of Ukrainians and Łemkos was something that Poles conducted on their own initiative. Operation Vistula was effectively the final act in a racial war begun by Hitler, continued by Stalin and completed by the Polish authorities.

By the end of 1947 there were barely any ethnic minorities left in Poland. Ironically, given that Ukrainians had been responsible for much of the initial impetus, the country was far more ethnically homogeneous than its neighbour. The 'Ukraine for Ukrainians' espoused by the OUN was never achieved – particularly in the eastern parts of the republic, which kept a large Polish and Jewish minority even while western Ukraine was busy exchanging populations with Poland. 'Poland for the Polish', by contrast, was by the end of the 1940s not merely an aspiration, but a fact.

This process, which destroyed centuries of cultural diversity in just a few short years, was accomplished in five stages. The first was the Holocaust of the Jews, brought about by the Nazis but facilitated by Polish anti-Semitism. The second was the harassment of Poland's returning Jews, which, as I discussed in the last chapter, caused them to flee not only Poland but Europe as a whole. The third and fourth were the ejection of Ukrainians and Łemkos in 1944–6, and their assimilation during Operation Vistula in 1947.

The final piece of the ethnic jigsaw in Poland, and one that I have not yet touched on, was the expulsion of the Germans. This, along with similar actions across the whole of Europe by other countries, is the subject of the next chapter.

19

The Expulsion of the Germans

The eastern border of Poland was not the only one to move in 1945. When the Big Three met at Tehran they also discussed what would happen to Poland's western border. Churchill and Roosevelt were keen to compensate the Poles for what they would lose to Stalin by giving them parts of Germany and East Prussia instead. Churchill explained this proposal in a late-night session on the first day of the conference. 'Poland might move westwards,' he said, 'like soldiers taking two steps "left close". If Poland trod on some German toes, that could not be helped . . .' To demonstrate what he meant, he placed a row of three matchsticks on the table and moved them each to the left. In other words, what Stalin took on the eastern side of Poland, the international community would give back on the western side.[1]

Stalin was delighted with this idea, not only because it legitimized his seizure of Poland's eastern borderlands, but because it pushed the demarcation line between Moscow and the Western Allies even further westwards. The only nation to lose substantial amounts of territory would be Germany, for whom it was regarded as a fitting punishment.

Once again, there was no consultation of the 'freely expressed wishes of the peoples concerned', as promised by the Atlantic Charter. Such a consultation amongst the people of eastern Germany was naturally impossible while the war was on – but none of the superpowers considered it necessary to wait until after the war was over before pushing ahead. As the British Foreign Secretary stated to Parliament in justification of these plans, 'There are certain parts of the Atlantic Charter which refer in set terms to victor and vanquished alike . . . But we cannot admit that Germany can claim . . . that any part of the Charter applies to her.'[2] Discussions about the borders between Poland and Germany therefore continued at Yalta at the beginning of 1945, and were concluded – as far as they would ever be concluded – at Potsdam the following summer.

As a result of these discussions, everything east of the Oder and Neisse rivers would become Polish, including the ancient German provinces of Pomerania, East Brandenburg, Lower and Upper Silesia, most of East Prussia (apart from a portion that Russia would keep for herself), and the port of Danzig. All of these areas had been considered German for hundreds of years, and were populated almost exclusively by German people – more than 11 million of them, according to the official figures.[3]

The consequences for these people would be momentous. Given the history of German minorities within other countries, and the way that these minorities had been used by Hitler as an excuse to foment war, it was unthinkable that 11 million Germans would be allowed to continue living within the borders of the new Poland. As Churchill put it, when discussing the subject at Yalta, 'it would be a pity to stuff the Polish goose so full of German food that it got indigestion'.[4] It was understood by all parties that these Germans would have to be removed.

When concerns were raised at Yalta about the practicality, and the humanity, of expelling such large numbers of people from their ancestral homelands, Stalin remarked blandly that most of the Germans in these regions had 'already run away from the Red Army'. Broadly speaking, he was correct – the bulk of the populations in these areas *had* fled in fear of Soviet vengeance. But by the end of the war there were still some 4.4 million Germans living there, and in the immediate aftermath of the war, a further 1.25 million would return – mostly to Silesia and East Prussia – in the belief that they would be able to pick up their old lives. According to Soviet plans *all* these people would either be conscripted as forced labour to pay off German war reparations, or be removed.[5]

Strictly speaking, the Soviets and the Poles were not supposed to start expelling Germans from these areas until after the borders were finalized. Even the provisional borders were not agreed upon until the Potsdam conference in the summer of 1945. It was expected that the final borders would be drawn once a peace settlement with Germany was signed by all the Allies. But because of the breakdown of relations between the Soviets and the West during the Cold War, and the consequent partition of Germany, such a peace treaty would not actually be signed for another forty-five years.

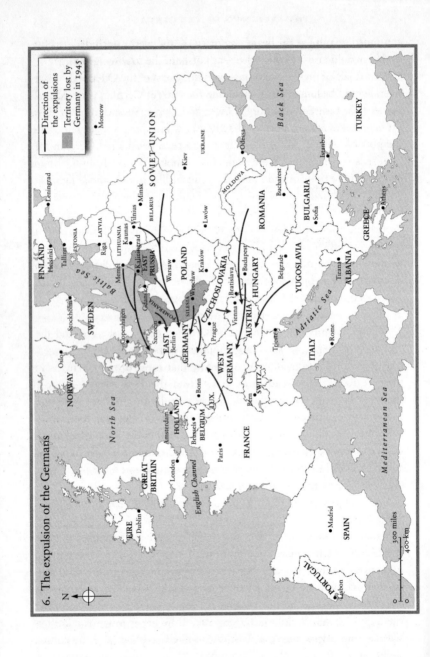

6. The expulsion of the Germans

In the meantime, the Poles and the Soviets would embark on their programme of expulsions regardless of international agreements. This became evident to the American ambassador, Arthur Bliss Lane, when he visited Wrocław in the early autumn of 1945. Wrocław, which until just a few months before had been the German city of Breslau, was already in the advanced stages of Polonization:

> Germans were being forcibly deported daily to German territory. It was obvious that the Poles did not consider that they were occupying Wrocław temporarily, subject to final approval by the peace conference. All German signs were being removed and replaced by those in the Polish language. Poles were being brought into Wrocław from other parts of Poland to replace the repatriated Germans.[6]

In fact, expulsions across the region had already been taking place for months by this time. Almost as soon as the war was over Poles began evicting Germans from their homes and claiming their property for themselves. It was not only the Red Army that raped and robbed Germans with abandon, but Poles too. In the cities, such as Szczecin (Stettin), Gdansk (Danzig) and Wrocław, Germans were herded into ghettos – partly so that Poles could take over their properties without a fuss, but also for their own protection.[7] In many areas Germans were rounded up and put into camps, either for use as slave labour or to be held until they could be officially deported. Some Poles were too impatient to wait for official permission, however, and began to hound whole communities of Germans across the border. According to official Polish records, in the last two weeks of June 1945 alone, 274,206 Germans were unlawfully deported across the Oder into Germany.[8]

Such actions were by no means unique to Poland. In the spring and summer of 1945 the Czechs were busy driving hundreds of thousands of Sudeten Germans over their borders in a similarly frenzied way. The suddenness with which these 'lightning' expulsions were carried out demonstrates their popular nature, especially in Czechoslovakia: they were not events organized by the central authorities, but spontaneous expulsions sparked by local hatreds.[9] The urgency that characterized them implies that Poles and Czechs alike were eager to get rid of their German minorities before any outside agency stepped in to stop them doing so.

It was for this reason that the Big Three felt obliged to make a formal declaration on the way that the transfer of Germans was to be carried out. At Potsdam, in July and August 1945 they demanded a halt to all expulsions from Poland, Czechoslovakia and Hungary until such time as they could be undertaken 'in an orderly and humane manner'. It was not only the brutal way that these people were being expelled that was the problem – it was also the inability of the Allies within Germany to cope with the huge influx of refugees. They needed time to organize a system for integrating these newcomers, and dispersing them equitably throughout the different zones of Germany.

Although this declaration managed to slow the transfer of Germans, it signally failed to bring it to a halt. The Poles especially refused to stop expelling Germans from Silesia and Szczecin.[10] Furthermore, in its recognition that the expulsions would 'have to be undertaken', the Potsdam declaration provided all the countries involved with an official endorsement for their actions – if not immediately, then at least in the very near future. As a consequence, the expulsion of Germans from across Europe would not be confined to a spontaneous but temporary phenomenon that might fizzle out over time. It now had the potential to become an official, permanent and total removal of German men, women and children from every other corner of Europe. It was for this reason that Anne O'Hare McCormick of the *New York Times* called it 'the most inhuman decision ever made by governments dedicated to the defence of human rights'.[11]

The Human Reality of the Expulsions

On Sunday, 1 July 1945, at around half past five in the evening, the Polish army came to the village of Machuswerder in Pomerania and told the people that they had thirty minutes to gather their things and leave. Almost the entire population of this village was German, and since most of the men had long since been lost to the war, it consisted mainly of women, children and old people. Bewildered and afraid, the villagers began to gather up their valuables, family photos, clothes, shoes and any other essential items they could fit into their bags and handcarts. They gathered outside their houses, and on the road that ran through the village. Then, under the supervision of the Poles, they began to walk in the direction of the new Polish/German border sixty kilometres away.

Amongst them was a farmer's wife and mother of three named Anna Kientopf. Later, in a sworn deposition for the German government, she described the ordeal that she and the rest of her village had to endure.[12] The journey, she said, lasted six days, and passed through a blasted landscape still covered in the detritus of war, and the remains of previous treks to the border by other refugees. They came across their first dead body just beyond Landsberg – a woman, who was blue in the face and whose body was swollen with decay. Thereafter, corpses became a common sight. In a forest they passed through they could see the dead bodies of both animals and human beings, whose heads and feet were poking through the earth of their shallow graves. Occasionally members of her own trek succumbed to exhaustion. Some, including her own daughter Annelore, became sick from drinking contaminated water from troughs and wells along the way; others succumbed to starvation:

> Most of the people of the trek lived solely from what they found in the fields or ate unripe fruit on the side of the road. We had very little bread. The result was that many people got ill. Small children under one year of age almost all died on the trek. There was no milk, and even if the mothers made them a thick meal soup, the journey was too long for them. Then the changes in the weather, first a scorching sun, and then showers of cold rain, which were fatal. Every day we got a bit further, sometimes we did 9 kilometres, on one day perhaps only three, then 20 or more . . . I often saw people lying at the side of the highway, blue in the face, and struggling for breath, and others who had collapsed from fatigue, and never got onto their feet again.

They spent the nights in bombed-out houses or in barns, but since these tended to be filthy Anna herself preferred to remain in the open air. Sleeping away from where the others were congregated also saved her from the depredations of some of the Poles, who used the cover of darkness to come and rob the refugees. She often heard shots in the night, as those who tried to defend their possessions were dealt with by their assailants.

The precariousness of her situation was brought home to her one day when she and her party were stopped by a group of armed men,

> ... and a terrible scene was enacted before our eyes, and touched us most deeply. Four Polish soldiers tried to separate a young girl from her parents, who clung in desperation to her. The Poles struck the parents with their rifle-butts, particularly the man. He staggered, and they pushed him across the road down the embankment. He fell down, and one of the Poles took his machine pistol, and fired a series of shots. For a moment there was a deathly silence, and then the screams of the 2 women pierced the air. They rushed to the dying man, and the four Poles disappeared in the forest.

Anna Kientopf suspected that the men had intended to rape the young girl, though it is possible that they merely wanted to conscript her into some form of forced labour. Of course, this does not mean that she would not have been raped in any case, as happened to hundreds, perhaps thousands of others. Many of those who gave their stories to the German Ministry for Expellees, Refugees and War Victims in the late 1940s and early 1950s attest to having been sexually assaulted in similar circumstances, often repeatedly. They were effectively kidnapped during their trek to the border in order to be put to work on farms or in local factories – but once they no longer had their families around them they became easy targets for the soldiers or foremen who were responsible for them.

It was probably one such round-up for forced labour that Anna Kientopf witnessed when she arrived at Tamsel, although she had no idea about this at the time:

> We had to pass through a lane of Polish soldiers, and people were taken out of the column. These had to drop out, and go to the farms on the highway with their carts, and all that they had with them. No-one knew what this meant, but everyone expected something bad. The people refused to obey. Often it was single individuals, particularly young girls, who were kept back. The mothers clung to the girls and wept. Then the soldiers tried to drag them away by force and, as this did not succeed, they began to strike the poor terrified people with rifle-butts and riding whips. One could hear the screams of those who were whipped, far away. I shall never forget it in my life.
>
> Polish soldiers also came to us with riding whips in their hands. With flushed faces, they ordered us to get out of the column, and to go to the farms. Else and Hilde Mittag began to weep. I said: 'Come, it is no use

resisting. They will beat us to death. We will try to escape afterwards.'
Russians were standing there looking on cynically. In our desperation we
begged them for help. They shrugged their shoulders and indicated to us
that the Poles were the masters. Just as everything already seemed to be
hopeless, I saw a senior Polish officer. I pointed to my 3 children, and asked
what I could do, as I had three children. I can no longer remember all that
I said in my desperation, but he answered: 'Go to the highway.' We got
hold of our cart and got away as quickly as we could . . .

Anna and her children finally arrived at Küstrin (or what was now
called Kostrzyn Odrzański) on 6 July. They tried to cross the Oder, but
the border guards refused to let them onto the bridge and sent them
away. In desperation they headed southwards in the direction of Frank-
furt-an-der-Oder. That night a terrible thunderstorm broke. They spent
the night beside the river, without shelter, with nothing to eat or drink,
and no guarantee that after their long trek they would be allowed to
cross over into Germany after all.

In the end, Anna Kientopf was fairly lucky. Despite being robbed
repeatedly – the last time by the Russian border guards on the bridge
where they were finally allowed to cross – she made it over the border
relatively quickly, and relatively unscathed. Many of those who were
driven out of their villages were more actively prevented from crossing
the border: alarmed by the massive overcrowding in their zone of Germany, the Russian guards had been instructed not to let any more
refugees cross the river. One witness speaks of being expelled on 25
June 1945 and escorted towards the border by Polish guards, only to
have those Polish guards disarmed later by Soviet troops, and told to
return the expellees to their village. The following week he had to go
through exactly the same process again. Thousands of German civilians
were forced to march backwards and forwards throughout the border
areas, 'driven on like cattle', because nobody was willing or able to offer
them sanctuary.[13]

The vast majority of eyewitness accounts stress the absolute lawlessness that surrounded them as they travelled: 'Every day Germans came
to me in tears and told me that the Poles had robbed them of all their
possessions'; 'The Poles behaved like vandals . . . looting, ransacking,
raping'; 'The Poles robbed us of anything they found in our possession,
swore at us, spat in our faces, and flogged and beat us'; 'We were

molested and robbed by the rabble again and again'.[14] Such criminal behaviour was compounded by an official policy of confiscating anything of value that the Germans tried to take with them. According to rules drawn up by the Polish government, Germans were not allowed to take more than 500 Reichsmarks out of the country, and no other currency at all.[15] No concessions were to be made for those who were actively pro-Polish, or who had opposed the Nazis during the war. Antifascists and German Jews were treated exactly the same as any other Germans – they were to be defined by their 'Germanness', not their war record or political outlook.[16]

In the beginning the expulsions were spontaneous, extremely disorganized, and often conducted simply to clear villages in order to make them easier to loot. Communities were force-marched towards the borders because other forms of transport were not available. It was not until later in 1945 and into 1946 that an element of proper state organization was introduced, and transport by train could finally be arranged.

To be fair, the Polish authorities were not only aware of what was going on, but deeply concerned by it – at least in some quarters. In an attempt to make the transfer more 'orderly and humane', the government drew up a list of rules at the beginning of 1946. It was stated, for example, that unaccompanied children, the elderly and the sick should be deported only during the summer months, on trains that contained medical supplies. Heavily pregnant women should not be allowed to travel until after they had safely given birth. German-speaking medical staff should accompany every transport, and adequate food and water must be provided. For a basic (if inadequate) measure of security, each train would be protected by ten Polish guards.[17]

In a further agreement between the Polish authorities and the British army, a provisional timetable was drawn up, and it was again agreed that only healthy people who were capable of enduring the arduous journey would be allowed to travel.[18] This was in response to the dozens of international press reports the previous summer revealing that orphanages and hospitals in East Prussia had been emptied straight onto trains without adequate supplies or medical facilities.[19] However, while such blatant abuses were curbed, it proved impossible to enforce the new rules fully. Germans keen to leave the country would do their best to conceal sickness, infirmity and pregnancy in order to get themselves onto the transports. Some Polish repatriation officials, meanwhile, were complicit in letting them go. Not only were these officials hopelessly overstretched, but the Polish establishment as a whole had a vested interest in keeping hold of the young and the fit for work in Poland: the elderly and the sick were the first to be deported, because these were the people nobody had any use for. As a consequence, the National Committee for Repatriation often complained to local officials that the repatriation rules were not being followed.[20]

From the German point of view, conditions on the trains were appalling in the extreme. A German priest who witnessed the arrival of the expellees at the border described what he saw:

> The people, men, women, and children all mixed together, were tightly packed in the railway cars, these cattle wagons themselves being locked from the outside. For days on end, the people were transported like this, and in Görlitz the wagons were opened for the first time. I have seen with my own eyes that out of one wagon alone ten corpses were taken and thrown into coffins which had been kept on hand. I noted further that several persons had become deranged . . . The people were covered in excrement, which led me to believe that they were squeezed together so tightly that there was no longer any possibility for them to relieve themselves at a designated place.[21]

Deportees were told to carry four days' worth of food with them, but sometimes their trains would be stopped in sidings for days or even weeks while they waited for clearance to pass into the Soviet zone of Germany. One refugee from Neisse, who was deported at the depth of winter at the beginning of 1946, claimed that his train was halted near the border for three weeks. After his food ran out he was reduced to bartering his belongings with local villagers for something to eat. Every day Polish militiamen entered the trucks to rob his fellow travellers of their valuables. Sometimes it was only their money and wristwatches that were taken; other times it was their shoes and boots, or even the food they had only recently managed to obtain.

> But these raids on the part of the Poles were nothing compared to the sufferings we endured as regards hunger and cold. For three weeks we lived in the trucks, and the icy wind, the rain and the snow came through the chinks. The nights were dreadful and seemed endless. There was hardly enough room for us to stand, let alone sit down or lie down . . . Every

morning at dawn the doors of the trucks were unlocked by the Polish guards and the dead who had not survived the night were carried out. Their number increased alarmingly from day to day. Sometimes there were as many as ten.[22]

Owing to the appalling weather and the lack of facilities for refugees on the other side of the border, the Soviets did their best to deny entry to trainloads of Germans – but Poles, who were keen to keep up the process of 'repatriation', carried on deporting them anyway. Another expellee tells how his group was made to get out of the train near the border and walk the rest of the way into the Russian zone. Along the way they had their suitcases and shoes stolen. 'When we arrived at Forst at three o'clock in the afternoon . . . the Russians refused to let us enter the town and tried to make us turn back. It was not until eight o'clock in the evening that they finally allowed us to seek shelter from the cold.'[23]

The cruelty of refusing to allow German refugees to cross the border, and denying them shelter when they got there, is perhaps more understandable when one takes into account the fact that the Soviet zone along this stretch of the border was already saturated with refugees. One Silesian factory owner, who spent the summer of 1945 travelling back and forth across the River Neisse in an attempt to salvage something of his property, came across notices fixed to the telegraph poles outside Görlitz warning of a local blockade. The authorities here had banned the entry of refugees in order to prevent conditions from degenerating beyond their control. 'There is a famine in Görlitz,' the notice read. 'All local attempts to solve the problem of the refugees have failed. All persons returning home and all refugees are herewith advised to make for places where the food problem is not acute. If you disregard this warning you will probably starve to death.'

According to notes he made at the time, the situation was just as bad all the way along the river. Refugees had crossed the border in the hope that their suffering would end:

> But now that they have at last reached the Neisse their hopes are dashed to the ground. There is no one who can help them. There is no one who can tell them where to find refuge or who can provide them with a temporary shelter. They are left to their own fate, and are driven on pitilessly from place to place like lepers.[24]

Some refugees managed to make it deeper into Germany, but wherever they went they were greeted by similarly desperate conditions. In the summer of 1945 Lieutenant Colonel William Byford-Jones witnessed a trainload of refugees arriving from the east. 'The train was a mixture of cattle and goods trucks, all of which were so packed that people lay on the tops, clung to the sides or hung on the bumpers. Children were tied by ropes to ventilator cocks, heating pipes, and iron fittings.' As the train came to a halt, they were not welcomed. The platforms were already packed with refugees that had arrived earlier, and who had nowhere to go. According to Byford-Jones the crowds were so dense that a full minute elapsed before anyone was able to disembark from the train.

> The people who had arrived days before pressed back to make room, and looked on in silence. Soon the platform was filled with cries of disillusionment as the newcomers learned how they had been deceived, or had deceived themselves. They stood in groups, clutching or sitting on their belongings. Their hair was matted. They were filthy, covered with soot and grime. Children had running sores, and scratched themselves continually, and with seeming pleasure. Old men, unshaven, red-eyed, looked like drug addicts, who neither felt, nor heard, nor saw. It is certain that if one half of these people had been asked why they had come to swell the ranks of the army of the dispossessed of Berlin, they would not have been able to say.[25]

After witnessing dozens of similar scenes in stations across Germany, British and American observers began to urge their respective governments to do something about it. The American Political Adviser for Germany, Robert Murphy, wrote to the State Department recommending that America 'should make its attitude as expressed at Potsdam unmistakably clear' to the Polish and Czech governments. 'The mind reverts to other recent mass deportations which horrified the world,' he wrote. 'Those mass deportations engineered by the Nazis provided part of the moral basis on which we waged war and which gave strength to our cause . . . It would be most unfortunate were the record to indicate that we are *particeps* to methods we have often condemned in other instances.'[26]

The State Department did indeed instruct their diplomatic staff to express American displeasure to the Poles, but both the American and the British ambassadors in Warsaw resisted such calls because they did not want to come across as 'pro-German'. At the time they were under attack from the Communists, who were making considerable gains by branding the western governments as 'fascists'. Cruel as it may seem, British and American diplomatic staff did not want to increase that perception by championing the cause of German refugees – particularly since they believed that any complaints were unlikely to be heeded.[27]

More effective was the dispatch of British medical teams to Szczecin early in 1946 to supervise train arrangements and prevent sick people and unaccompanied children from getting on the trains in the first place. When the temperature dropped at the end of the year, the western military authorities also managed to convince the Czech and Polish governments to cancel some train movements. In this way they prevented a repetition of some of the worst instances of exposure that had happened the previous winter. The International Committee of the Red Cross also had some success with postponing deportations when conditions dropped below an acceptable level in January 1947.[28] But the situation in general only really improved because, with the passage of time, more efficient systems evolved on both sides of the border. Proper transit camps and refugee camps were built, train lines repaired and heating installed in train carriages. The Poles became better at transporting large numbers of people in shorter periods of time and the Soviets, British and Americans became better at receiving and dispersing them once they arrived at the other end.

This was all that the Big Three had requested at Potsdam – a pause, so that the authorities on both sides would be able to organize themselves efficiently. Most of the tragedies occurred because that pause was not observed. In their impatience to be rid of their German minorities, the Poles and Czechs who conducted the expulsions were simply not interested in the consequences of their actions. As a result, an unknown number of German refugees – but certainly many, many thousands – died needlessly in some of the most squalid conditions imaginable.[29]

'Home' to the Reich

The statistics associated with the expulsion of the Germans between 1945 and 1949 defy imagination. By far the greatest number of them came from the lands east of the Oder and Neisse that had been incorporated into the new Poland – almost 7 million, according to the German government figures. Almost another 3 million were removed from Czechoslovakia, and more than 1.8 million from other lands, making a total of 11,730,000 refugees altogether.[30]

Each of the different zones of Germany coped with this massive influx of people in its own way. Probably the worst prepared was the Soviet zone, whose towns and cities were amongst the most comprehensively destroyed by the war, and which was in the process of being stripped of everything of value for Soviet war reparations. A flood of refugees arrived in the aftermath of the war, mostly from the new Poland, but also from Czechoslovakia. By the end of November 1945 there were already a million of them trying to scratch a living here, disoriented and virtually destitute. During four years from the end of the war at least 3.2 million refugees settled in the zone, and possibly as many as 4.3 million. A further 3 million or so paused there temporarily before moving on to other parts of Germany.[31]

The British zone, which bordered none of the deporting countries, had a little more time to prepare. In the autumn and winter of 1945 the British organized an operation to take in millions more refugees, codenamed Operation Swallow. Between February 1946 and October 1947 eight trains plied their way back and forth between Szczecin and Lübeck, each composed of covered freight wagons with a total capacity of 2,000 people. Other trains took refugees from Kaławska to Mariental, Alversdorf and Friedland; and from April 1946, refugees were also transported to Lübeck by sea. In this way some 6,000 'eastern' Germans were transported into the British zone almost every single day for a full year and a half.[32] By the end of the decade more than 4.25 million new people had settled here.

Further south, the Americans continued to receive refugees from Czechoslovakia, Hungary, Romania and Yugoslavia – more than 3.5 million of them in total. The authorities there struggled to cope, and hundreds of thousands were still languishing in refugee camps at the start of the 1950s. According to General Lucius D. Clay, the American military governor in West Germany, the influx of refugees increased the population of the British and American zones of West Germany by over 23 per cent. In East Germany, according to its first president, Wilhelm Pieck, the increase in population was as much as 25 per cent.[33] The effect this had on all parts of Germany (with the

exception of the French zone, which received relatively few refugees)
was verging on the catastrophic. Most of the cities had been reduced
to rubble by Allied bombing during the war, and the country's shattered infrastructure simply could not cope. Even after their arrival
refugees continued to die in their thousands because they were unable
to find the shelter, the medical aid or the food to sustain them after
their westward odyssey.

For those who were least able to find work or integrate themselves
into German society – mostly the sick, the elderly, or widowed women
with children – several years in refugee camps was all they could look
forward to. Conditions in these camps were sometimes not much better than finding shelter in ruined buildings. A report on the camp at
Dingolfing by the Bavarian Red Cross, for example, described a high
number of invalids and people with tuberculosis living in overcrowded conditions. They had no proper shoes, clothing or bedding.
In another camp in Sperlhammer cardboard had to be pasted to the
walls of the barracks as protection against the water that leaked
through.[34]

Worse than this, however, were the social and psychological problems experienced by the refugees. People from the east or the Sudetenland
were sometimes regarded as foreigners by other Germans, and tensions
often rose up between them. As General Clay wrote in 1950,

> Separated from Germany through many generations, the expellee even
> spoke in a different tongue. He no longer shared common customs and
> traditions nor did he think of Germany as home. He could not persuade
> himself that he was forever exiled; his eyes and thoughts and hopes turned
> homeward.[35]

According to one man deported from Hungary, it was difficult for his
fellow expellees to forge a new life for themselves, 'Not only because
they had lost their homelands and practically all their material possessions, but also they had lost their identity.'[36] The social democrat
Hermann Brill described the refugees he saw as suffering from a deep
state of shock. 'They have fully lost the ground from under them. That
which is taken for granted by us, a sense of security from life experience,
a certain personal feeling for their individual freedom and human
worth, that is all gone.'[37] In July 1946, a Soviet report on politics in

Leipzig described the refugees as still 'deeply depressed' and 'the most indifferent to politics of any group of the Leipzig population'. Unable to adjust to their new circumstances, they did little but dream of returning to their ancient homelands across the border.[38]

Total Expulsion

The right to return was the one thing that these Germans would be denied. Their expulsion was designed from the outset to be permanent, and with this in mind ever stricter border controls were set up: Germans would be allowed to leave, but they would not be allowed to come back.

Furthermore, their deportation was only the first stage of a much larger operation: after they were gone, attempts were also made to erase all traces of their existence. Even before the Germans had been driven out of Poland and Czechoslovakia, towns, villages and streets were being renamed. In the case of villages that had never had Polish or Czech names before, new ones were invented for them. German monuments were torn down and new Czech or Polish ones erected in their place. Swastikas were taken down everywhere, although their shadow could still be seen on many walls for years to come. The speaking of the German language was banned, and the few Germans who were allowed to stay (by renouncing their German nationality) were advised to speak Polish or Czech even in private.[39]

Schools were banned from teaching the German history of areas like the Sudetenland or Silesia. Instead, Germans were portrayed as invaders on lands that had historically always been Polish or Czech. The new areas of Poland were referred to as the 'Recovered Territories', and Polish children there were taught nationalist slogans, such as 'Here we were, here we are, here we stay', and 'These regions are reclaimed property'. Students in the border areas were not permitted to study German, even as a foreign language – in contrast to other parts of Poland where it was allowed.[40]

It was not only in schools that this new, nationalist mythology was taught – the adult population was also fed propaganda on a prodigious scale. In Wrocław, for example, an 'Exhibition of the Recovered Territories' was held, and was visited by some 1.5 million people. Amongst all the obligatory political exhibits stressing Polish–Soviet brotherhood there was a huge historical section, largely devoted to the relationship between Poland and Germany. This emphasized the thousand-year conflict between the two countries, the return of Poland to its 'Piast Path' (in reference to a medieval Polish dynasty who defied German kings to create an independent Poland centred around Silesia), and an exhibit entitled 'Our Immemorial Right to the Recovered Territories'.[41]

This was not merely the claiming, or even the reclamation, of territory: it was the rewriting of history. In the new, nationalist Poland, any trace of an indigenous German culture had to be eradicated: this was to be a Poland for Poles only. As official policy at the time recognized, the reclamation of territory was the easy part: 'We are aiming for a much harder and more complicated target: the removal of age-old traces of Germanization in these lands. It is more than just the removal of signs or memorials, it is purging the sap of Germanization from every part of life, the removal of Germanization from the people's psyche.'[42] The same was true in Czechoslovakia, where President Beneš called for not only 'a definitive clearance of Germans' but also of 'German influence from our country'.[43]

In this way the return of Sudeten, Silesian, Pomeranian or Prussian Germans to their homelands was made not only more difficult, but ultimately quite pointless. The places they had left behind no longer existed. Their communities, their culture, their history, their language and sometimes even, given the destruction caused by the war, their very fabric had been entirely erased. All this had been replaced by something wholly alien: a new society peopled almost entirely by members of a different ethnic group.

It is easy to condemn the Poles or the Czechs for their racist attitudes towards their German minorities in 1945. One must remember, however, that these attitudes did not appear from nowhere: they were largely a reaction to the cruel treatment that they themselves had suffered under German racial policy during the war. While the methods used by Poles and Czechs were undeniably brutal, the ideology behind them was mild compared to the ideology of the Nazis. Neither country pursued a policy of genocide towards the German race, whatever some of the more extreme literature about the expulsions might claim: their purpose was only ever to remove the German minorities, not to annihilate them. Neither was the removal motivated purely by revenge: it was initially conceived as a practical measure to prevent future conflict arising between nationalities. Though today we would abhor the idea of uprooting millions of people for the sake of a flimsy nationalist ideology, in the aftermath of the war – when the deportation of huge numbers of people had become commonplace, and when the whole of Europe was teeming with millions of displaced persons – the idea was perhaps more acceptable than it ever was before, or has been since.

What happened in Poland and Czechoslovakia was not unique. A similar process would take place in other countries, particularly in Hungary and Romania, where the German-speaking Danubian Swabians were also ejected towards Germany and Austria. In Romania especially this was done with little enthusiasm – there was no real enmity towards Germans here.[44] But the feelings of the people were irrelevant, since the expulsion of Germans was part of official policy. In the years after the war, the only place in Europe that welcomed Germans would be Germany itself.

A Cleansed Landscape

It was not only the German minorities who suffered such treatment in countries where they were not wanted. This was in effect the opposite of what was attempted in the aftermath of the First World War: rather than trying to move borders to suit the people who lived in the region, the governments of Europe now decided to move the people to suit the borders.

A typical example of what was happening all over Europe was the treatment of the Hungarian minority in Slovakia, who were hated just as much as the Germans. Slovaks could not forgive the way that Hungary had seized parts of their country in the run-up to the war; as soon as these lands were returned to Slovakia, therefore, they went about expelling all 31,780 Hungarians who had moved to the area since 1938.[45] But for the majority of Slovaks this was not enough. Government officials called for the 'total expulsion' of Hungarians – all 600,000 of them.[46] They spoke in chilling terms of finding a 'final solution' to the Hungarian problem, while stating baldly that 'we do not recognize national minorities'. The popular press agreed: 'Slovakia and its southern borderlands can only be Slovak and nothing else.'[47]

In 1946 government forces removed some 44,000 Hungarians from the Slovak borderlands and, in an operation that was similar to Poland's forced assimilation programme, dispersed them around the rest of Czechoslovakia.[48] Soon afterwards, some 70,000 Hungarians were sent to Hungary as part of a population exchange programme (which saw a similar number of Slovaks 'repatriated' to Czechoslovakia). And a further 6,000 Hungarians fled the country to avoid varying degrees of persecution.[49] At the Paris Peace Conference the Czechoslovak delegation tried to finish the job, and requested the right to deport a further 200,000. On this occasion, perhaps having learned their lesson from the deportation of Germans, Britain and America refused to give their permission. As a consequence Czechoslovakia was not quite allowed to become the homogeneous nation-state it wanted to be. Their only other course of action was their policy of 're-Slovakization' – a programme that restored civil rights to Hungarians, but only on the condition that they renounced their Hungarian identity and declared themselves officially Slovaks. Needless to say, this programme did nothing to integrate Hungarians into Czechoslovakian society, and a great deal to alienate them further. They understandably began to see themselves as scapegoats whom the Slovaks were using to divert attention from their own collaborationist behaviour during the war.[50]

These were the kinds of actions that were taking place all across Europe. Hungarians were also expelled from Romania, and vice-versa. Albanian Chams were expelled from Greece; Romanians were expelled from Ukraine; Italians were expelled from Yugoslavia. A quarter of a million Finns were forced to leave western Karelia when the area was finally ceded to the Soviet Union at the end of the war. As late as 1950 Bulgaria began expelling some 140,000 Turks and Gypsies across their border with Turkey. And so the list goes on.[51]

As a result of all this forced population movement, eastern Europe became far less multicultural than it had been at any time in modern history. In the space of only one or two years, the proportion of national minorities more than halved. Gone were the old imperial melting pots where Jews, Germans, Magyars, Slavs and dozens of other races and nationalities intermarried, squabbled and rubbed along together as best they could. In their place was a collection of monocultural nation-states, whose populations were more or less ethnically homogeneous. Eastern Europe had cleansed itself on a massive scale.[52]

Europe in Microcosm: Yugoslavia

If the transfer and exchange of ethnic populations across eastern Europe was often brutal, it was not the worst that could happen. Indeed, the reason such movements were endorsed by so many governments, including the governments of the Western Allies, was that it was so widely regarded as the *least* worst option. At the beginning of the war, the Germans had used their minorities in other countries as an excuse for invasion: removing those minorities was considered the only practical way to prevent future conflicts from breaking out. In those areas where the war had had a particularly racist flavour, population transfer was considered – not always from cynical motives – as the best method of removing vulnerable populations from harm's way. Even those who were forced to leave their homelands often accepted flight as their only option. Their lives had been made so unbearable that they regarded their successful transfer to another country as a lucky escape.

However, population transfers were by no means the answer to every ethnic question after the war. Some groups could not be driven out, no matter how unpopular they were, because they did not have their 'own' country to go to – Gypsies, for instance, who everywhere were almost as unwelcome as the Jews. Some countries were obliged to integrate separate communities in an effort to cover up the internal splits that had burst open during the war – the Czechs and the Slovaks, for example, or, to a lesser degree, the Flemings and Walloons of Belgium. In the most extreme cases, governments were forced to pretend that ethnic problems did not exist at all, because to acknowledge them would be politically impossible. This was the case in the USSR and Yugoslavia, where the authorities struggled to convince the population that the violence of the war had been the result of class differences rather than ethnic ones.

Yugoslavia requires special mention because it encompasses all these problems and more. Since most of the groups who had been responsible for the violence during the war were not 'outsiders', they could not be expelled – indeed, when some tried to flee the country they were prevented from leaving. Nor could they be separated from one another within the country. There were suggestions at the time that this should be done: 'Some individuals are asking why Serbs shouldn't have their own federal Slavonia', stated one report by Odjel za zaštitu narodna, the Yugoslav intelligence service, 'or why Croats shouldn't move to Croatia and Serbs to Serbia.'[1] But the whole purpose of re-establishing the Yugoslavian federation was to hold these separate nations together under a single banner. How would Marshal Tito be able to speak of 'brotherhood and unity' while at the same time banishing each nationality to separate corners of the country? And how could he allow such nationalist tendencies to thrive while he continued to preach the internationalism of Communist Party doctrine? The different ethnic groups were therefore obliged to continue living side by side despite the fact that each regarded the others with undisguised hatred.

Yugoslavia was the site of some of the worst violence in Europe, both during and after the war. What makes the situation here unique is the many layers that made up the conflict. Yugoslav resistance groups fought not only against foreign aggressors in a war of national liberation, but also against troops of their own government in a war of revolution, against alternative resistance groups in a war of ideology, and against gangs of bandits in a battle to impose law and order. These different strands were so intertwined that they were often indistinguishable from one another. But there was one thread in this tapestry of violence that stood out amongst all the others: the issue of ethnic hatred. The power of this hatred was harnessed by all sides in the war, whatever their alternative agendas. Almost half a century before the civil war that would give the term 'ethnic cleansing' to the world, Yugoslavia was embroiled in the closing stages of one of the most vicious ethnic conflicts of the twentieth century.

Historical Background

The Second World War in Yugoslavia and its aftermath is one of the most complex fields in twentieth-century history, and one strewn with moral and historical booby traps. As in other countries where local atrocities occurred, accounts from the former Yugoslavia itself tend to be extremely biased, with each ethnic group competing for the right to victimhood. Many original documents have been doctored to suit the national or ideological outlook of those who took possession of them. Even without such pitfalls there remain areas of real controversy which even impartial historians of the period find impossible to unravel.[2]

To begin with, the whole concept of 'Yugoslavia' is one that was controversial at the time, and continues to be so today. The country had only existed since 1918, when it was constructed out of the ruins of the First World War. It lay across the fault lines between the remnants of three great nineteenth-century powers – Russia, Austro-Hungary and the Ottoman Empire. It was therefore the meeting point of three great religions – Christian Orthodoxy, Catholicism and Islam (or indeed four, if one also includes the small Jewish minority that was all but wiped out by the war). It was home to more than half a dozen large national and ethnic minorities, all of whom had nursed petty rivalries and jealousies for generations. The two strongest political groups in the interwar period – the Serb monarchists and the Croat Peasant Party – had argued endlessly over whether Yugoslavia should remain a single kingdom, and if so, how much autonomy should be granted to each region.

During the Second World War, these divisions of nationality, ethnicity, politics and religion were inflamed to such a degree that 'Yugoslavs' became just as willing to kill one another as to kill the foreign occupiers. Croats massacred Serbs in the name of Catholicism; Serbs torched Muslim villages in Bosnia and Hungarian villages in Vojvodina; monarchist Chetniks fought pitched battles against Communist Partisans. As if this were not complicated enough, militias often tried to pin the blame for their atrocities on each other. Muslim militiamen donned the uniforms of Serb Chetniks, Croat Ustashas dressed up as Muslims, and Chetniks pretended to be Serb Partisans. It was therefore not always straightforward to identify who was massacring whom.[3] Presiding over the whole were the German, Italian and other occupiers of the country, who not only committed their own war crimes but also encouraged in-fighting between the different groups.

Out of this soup of violent rivalries there emerged two major opponents. The first of these were the Ustashas, a far-right political group that had been installed by the Italians as a puppet government in the new Independent State of Croatia during the war. The Ustashas were one of the most repugnant regimes on the continent. During the war they indulged in ethnic and religious cleansing on a scale surpassed only by the Nazis themselves. They were responsible for systematically murdering hundreds of thousands of ethnic Serbs, and forcing hundreds of thousands more to convert to Catholicism. Their most notorious prison camp, at Jasenovac, saw the murder of around 100,000 people, over half of whom were Serbs.[4] The Ustashas were by no means the only collaborators in Yugoslavia – there were several Serbian, Slovenian and Montenegrin far-right groups and militias – but they were easily the most powerful.

Opposing the Ustashas was the second major force in Yugoslavia, and the one that was eventually victorious: the Communist Partisans. The Partisans had gradually outgrown all the other resistance movements, including Draža Mihailović's royalist Chetniks, to become a huge fighting force with Allied backing. They were made up of men and women of every ethnic minority, but the majority were Serbs fleeing persecution. Later in the war large numbers of Chetniks – also Serbs – defected to the Partisans. This was partly out of a cynical desire to make sure they were on the winning side, but also because their urge to destroy the Croat Ustashas outweighed any political differences they might have with their fellow Serbs. Thus, the end of the war in Yugoslavia had a particularly ethnic flavour. While the Partisan leadership might have been focused on returning the state of Croatia to the Yugoslav fold, much of the rank and file had one overriding priority: vengeance upon Croats in general, and the Ustasha regime in particular.

The 'Bleiburg Tragedy'

During the final six months of the war, German forces conducted an epic withdrawal from the whole of the Balkan peninsula. As they retreated through Yugoslavia in April 1945, they were joined by various local collaborationist groups, soldiers and militias. The intention of all these groups was to fight their way towards British-held territory in Austria and north-east Italy: after the bitter war they had just waged, they reasoned, the British were more likely than Tito's troops to show them mercy when they surrendered.

As the Ustasha regime finally abandoned Zagreb on 6 May a measure of hysteria took hold of the civilian population. There are suggestions that the Ustashas deliberately spread panic in order to provoke a more general exodus. In any case, large numbers of refugees joined the fleeing troops, and some of them were apparently given guns – a fact that would make it very difficult in the coming days to separate the sheep from the goats.[5] This vast crowd, numbering hundreds of thousands, trekked northwards through Slovenia towards the Austrian border. They were determined to reach Austria before they surrendered, and as a consequence continued to fight long after the war was over in the rest of Europe. The battle raged on until 15 May 1945, when the first Croatian units finally arrived on Austrian soil, at Bleiburg. Here they immediately attempted to hand themselves over to British forces. But the British refused to accept their surrender on the grounds that Allied policy stipulated that all Axis forces must surrender to those armies they had been fighting against. Despite the desperate campaign that they had just fought, the Ustashas and their hangers-on would be obliged to hand themselves over to the Partisans after all.

The events at Bleiburg have long been the subject of myth and controversy. In the years after the war Croatian émigrés claimed that the entire Croatian army arrived on Austrian soil, and that the British disarmed them and handed them back to the Partisans to be annihilated. Many maintained that this British 'betrayal' constituted a war crime, on the grounds that their refusal to protect them was a breach of the 1929 Geneva Convention. In reality, however, only a small proportion of Croatian troops and refugees ever made it to Austrian territory – perhaps 25,000 people: another 175,000 or so were spread out in columns some forty-five to sixty-five kilometres long. The British had little choice but to instruct them to give themselves up to the Partisans, because they had no facilities or supplies to accommodate such huge numbers of refugees in this remote part of Austria. And besides, they wanted to keep the area clear in case they themselves needed to conduct military operations against Tito's Partisans, who had already invaded parts of

Austria and north-east Italy and were threatening to annex them to Yugoslavia.[6]

Accusations of betrayal have also been directed at the way that the British treated those who did manage to surrender to them. A few days before the arrival of the Croats, a force of about 10,000 to 12,000 collaborationist Slovenian Home Guards (recently renamed the Slovene National Army) had reached Austria. The British disarmed them and put them in a camp near Viktring (Vetrinje), a small town just a few kilometres south-west of Klagenfurt, but they had no intention of keeping them – instead they planned to return them to Yugoslavia at the earliest opportunity. Realizing that the Slovenes would resist any attempt to send them back, the British pretended that they were transporting them to camps in Italy. Similar deceptions were employed against Cossacks captured in the region, whose officers were told they were being taken to a conference when in fact they were to be handed over to the Soviets. Such blatant dishonesty does nothing to endear the British to those who escaped or survived the massacres that were to follow. It merely adds weight to the body of evidence suggesting that the British knew exactly what lay in store for these prisoners.[7]

For those who were sent back across the Austrian border, or who were captured by Tito's Partisans in the northernmost parts of Slovenia, an epic and often tragic ordeal lay ahead. A large proportion were marched along the Drava river towards Maribor, where the Partisans had set up transit camps. At first these marches were conducted in a fairly orderly and professional manner, but according to survivors they became more dangerous the further away they progressed from the safety of the Allied lines. The prisoners were given neither food nor water by their Partisan guards, and were often stripped of any valuable items such as pens, watches, wedding rings, boots or shoes. When gaps in the column inevitably opened up, those at the rear were ordered to run to catch up. To encourage them to move faster, those who lagged behind were often shot without warning.

In the 1960s the Croatian exile John Prcela gathered together scores of testimonies by those who had experienced the forced marches back into Yugoslavian territory, most of which agree on these details.[8] The testimonies of German soldiers gathered by a German government commission in the 1960s provide further corroboration.[9] Conditions on these 'death marches' were brutal in the extreme. As they trudged towards Maribor, Croatian soldiers and civilians alike were gunned down using any conceivable excuse. Those who tried to escape were, of course, considered fair game, but even stepping out of the column to relieve oneself could prove fatal. In villages along the way some local people had left food and water for them, but anyone who made a move to gather them might also receive a bullet. Running out of energy was not an option: one survivor, a man named Stankovic, tells the story of a fifty-year-old priest who was killed for no better reason than that he was too tired to walk any further.[10]

Sometimes people seemed to be singled out at random:

> A Communist officer, usually a Serb, but sometimes a Slovene, would yell out suddenly, 'Kill that fellow whose head is sticking out above all the rest of the bandits!' Then another would cry, 'Kill that little runt there!' Someone else would order that anyone wearing a beard, or someone who had been stripped of his shirt, should be done away with.[11]

According to another eyewitness, 'the Reds began to shoot whomever they happened to feel like shooting. In the beginning, they took individuals out of the formation and killed them in the nearby woods. Later, they fired directly into the prisoner column. This shooting was entirely indiscriminate.'[12]

However, while some Partisans undoubtedly indulged in indiscriminate murder, there was often much more method to these killings than met the eye. One of the reasons for searching their prisoners, apart from the obvious motive of stealing their valuables, was to ascertain which prisoners were officers or members of the Ustasha elite. Some men were foolish enough to keep papers or photographs on them. Those with more valuable items than the others were obviously of higher rank, and while many officers had dumped their uniforms before surrender, sometimes they could not bring themselves to part with decorations or rank insignia. One such was an Ustasha lieutenant named Mark Stojic, whose sister-in-law tied them to her leg in order to protect him. Unfortunately these came loose and fell into the road. They were spotted by some of the guards, who asked Stojic's sister-in-law whom they belonged to. When she refused to answer, one of them smashed in her skull in full view of the rest of the column.[13]

Many survivors speak of small groups of men being led away into the forest and shot. Since almost all the testimonies come from the victims themselves we cannot be sure how Partisan officers chose who to include in these groups, but in many cases there did appear to be some rudimentary form of selection. One of the few contemporary accounts by a Partisan officer tells how his comrades chose fifty-four officers from amongst their prisoners to be taken out into the woods and murdered. 'To verify what had happened I went up and found 54 bodies which some soldiers were then burying. I saw pools of blood and one corpse that had been knifed, but I reckon that the rest had been knifed also, for I only heard two or three revolver shots and there were 54 dead.'[14]

A prisoner named Franjo Krakaj tells how Ustasha soldiers were also singled out for special treatment. He himself was misidentified as an Ustasha leader, and immediately led off into the forest with a group of other similar men to be shot. He escaped when one of the others ran at the guards to distract them.

Krakaj's story is interesting because he escaped from Partisan hands not once but four times. Each time he was obliged by hunger to give himself up once more. In the first instance he put his brush with death down to the sheer bad luck of falling into the hands of a particularly sadistic group of soldiers – it was not until he was almost executed a second time that he realized that wholesale killing was part of a wider Partisan policy. On this occasion he had his hands bound behind his back, and was loaded onto one of a number of trucks along with his fellow prisoners.

After a ride of about twenty minutes, we were unloaded like sacks of wheat at Maribor Island, which is upstream from the town. As we approached this place, we heard the staccato firing of a machine gun, along with single rifle shots from time to time. So we had no doubt now concerning our fate.

I landed on my feet when I was tossed out of the truck. Thus, I was able to take a good look at a scene of horror that could have inspired a twentieth-century Dante . . . What absorbed my interest were several mass graves which had been dug about three hundred yards apart. Since they were almost filled with bodies, I could not determine how deep they were. I judge that each of them contained perhaps three hundred corpses. On top of these masses of cadavers, I could discern movement; some of the victims were still alive! Out of these grisly holes came screams, 'Brother, kill me! Shoot once more!' I remember that cry being repeated several times. Also, there were unwounded men in the graves who were smothering as bodies were thrown on top of them. They were trying to make themselves heard too. Some intended victims were trying to get away into the woods and the Partisans were shooting at them.

Trucks drove up bringing other groups of prisoners. As the guards started to unload them, the volume of rifle and machine gun fire increased tremendously because these prisoners made a break for it as soon as they hit the ground. Although my hands were still bound behind my back, I also took off at a run. Bullets were whacking into the trees and cutting the shrubbery all around me. I tripped over a fallen branch and fell down headlong. Probably this saved me, because the guards evidently thought that I was accounted for and turned their attention elsewhere.[15]

It is obvious from accounts like this that, far from being the actions of a few isolated individuals, the killing of Croatian prisoners was the work of entire units of men. It was also fairly well organized. Prisoners were executed not only individually and in small groups but on a massive scale: slaughter like this would not have been possible without an element of central organization by authorities high up the Partisan chain of command.

The local headquarters of these authorities appear to have been at the nearby town of Maribor. Here and at other centres in Slovenia, Partisan troops followed a standard process before liquidating their prisoners. First, an elementary form of selection was made, initially to separate out the civilians from the soldiers, then to separate the Ustasha troops from the ordinary *domobrans* or regulars, and finally to sort the officers from the rank and file.[16] The 'least guilty' were then loaded on trains to take them back towards Celje and Zagreb. Tens of thousands were sent on a series of forced marches that could last for days or even weeks to prison camps across the country. Some groups of men were retained locally as forced labour to carry out heavy or unpleasant tasks. But for the rest, this was the end of the road.

Near to the town were long lines of anti-tank trenches, which had been dug by German troops as a last-ditch defence against the Partisans. Prisoners were brought here by the truckload, where they were lined up along the edge of the trench and shot. These prisoners knew precisely what lay in store for them, because they could see the corpses of previous groups of prisoners lying at the bottom of the trenches. Many of them had been stripped of all their clothes. They had their hands bound behind their backs to prevent them trying to escape or lash out at their guards.

The following account is by a Croatian officer who, like many who escaped Yugoslavia but still had relatives there during the Cold War, wished to remain anonymous.

> In the evening the Partisans undressed us, tied our hands behind our backs with a wire, and then tied us two and two. After that we were taken in trucks to the east of Maribor. I managed to untie my hands but was still tied to the other officer. We were brought to huge ditches where there were already dead bodies piled. The Partisans started shooting at our backs. Fast as lightning, I threw myself on top of the dead bodies. More dead bodies fell on me. When the Partisans were through shooting our group, they left. They did not bury us because there was room for more. So they went to Maribor for more victims. I untied myself from my dead partner and crawled out of this mass grave. I was naked, covered with blood of other victims, and so full of fear that I could not walk very far. I climbed a tree not far from the execution place. Three more times Partisans arrived with officers and priests and killed them all. When the sun started to rise, I went away.[17]

The killing at Maribor lasted several days, and when the anti-tank trenches were full special burial squads were detailed to pile earth across the top of them and then level them off. Bodies were also buried in shell holes, bomb craters and specially dug mass graves.

One former Partisan, who later fled Yugoslavia, gave a graphic description of what it was like to work on one of these burial parties.

> As we were performing our grim duty, another group was detailed to dig out a large hole that began where the trenches ended. To my horror I saw that this pit, too, was full of bodies. Since the dead in this hole were quite stiff or already putrefying, they probably had been killed days before . . .
>
> We were still engaged in the task of burial at 5:00PM, when a hundred prisoners were brought to the newly excavated abattoir. We were told that they were going to help us inter the dead. But then these prisoners were lined up at the edge of the hole where the older corpses lay. Next they were looted of what belongings they had. Finally, the hundred prisoners were machine-gunned. I watched this slaughter from a distance of one hundred yards or less. Some of the prisoners threw themselves down flat and escaped the machine gun fire. They pretended to be dead, but the Partisans went

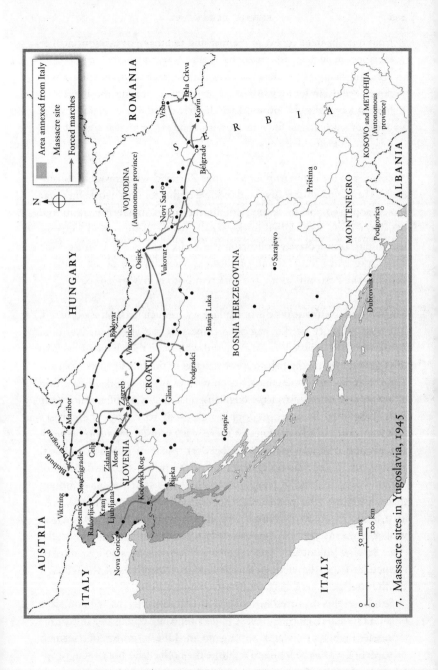

7. Massacre sites in Yugoslavia, 1945

from one apparent corpse to another and ran their bayonets through everyone whom they suspected of being alive. Screams rent the air, providing grim evidence that those who had dodged the machine gun fire had not eluded death for long. All of the new victims were thrown into the hole on top of the old corpses. Then the Partisans directed several more bursts of machine gun fire into the pile of bodies, just to make sure that they had not left anyone alive.[18]

According to the demographer Vladimir Žerjavić, who is widely considered to be the most objective and reliable authority on Yugoslavia's war losses, some 50,000 to 60,000 collaborationists, mostly Croatian and Muslim troops, were killed in the area between Bleiburg and Maribor in the days immediately following the end of the Second World War. This represents around a half of all those Yugoslav troops who surrendered to the Partisans along the Austrian border in May 1945.[19]

Maribor was by no means the only place where such massacres occurred. The vast majority of the 12,000 members of the Slovenian National Army who had escaped to Austria, and who were then handed back to the Partisans by the British, were murdered in the forests near Kočevje. They were taken to the edge of deep ravines in the Kočevski Rog and either shot or thrown over the edge alive. The walls of the ravines were then dynamited in order to topple masses of rock onto the corpses below. According to eyewitnesses there was no discrimination between officers and ordinary soldiers, or between those of differing political persuasion: 'There was no questioning of the prisoners, nor did any of them receive any kind of trial, nor was there any selection made among them. Everyone who was brought to Kočevje was doomed to die.'[20] At least 8,000 to 9,000 Slovenian nationalists were killed in this way, as well as some Croatians, Montenegrin Chetniks and members of the three Serbian Volunteer Corps regiments.[21] There were also a handful of women amongst the victims, and around 200 members of the Ustasha youth movement aged between fourteen and sixteen.[22]

Similar events occurred in an abyss at Podutik, only a few kilometres outside Ljubljana. Here, the mass of decomposing bodies began to contaminate Ljubljana's water supply, so in June a group of German prisoners of war were made to exhume the bodies and bury them properly in freshly dug mass graves.[23] The Partisans used all and any methods

in order to kill their victims. In Lasko and Hrastnik Croatian collaborators were thrown down mineshafts, and hand grenades thrown in after
them.[24] In Rifnik, prisoners were driven into a bunker that was then
blown up with them inside it.[25] In the prisoner-of-war camp at Bezigrad
prisoners were locked inside an enclosed reservoir, which was then
flooded until they were all drowned.[26] In Istria, on the border between
Yugoslavia and Italy, hundreds of Italian prisoners were thrown down
deep pits and ravines to their deaths.[27]

Inevitably, as at Maribor, there were some who managed to survive.
One survivor, who was shot along with hundreds of others at Kamnik,
tells a story that, were it not for the terrifying circumstances, might
seem almost comic. He and his fellow prisoners were told to form a
circle, after which the guards opened fire on them. Despite being hit in
the forehead he somehow survived. As he lay amongst his dead and
dying comrades he heard the Partisans arguing amongst themselves.

> They were quite upset because, when the fools lined us up in a circle and
> began firing they were spread out in a circle too, outside of ours. Thus, in
> effect, they were shooting one another as well as at us. Two Partisans were
> killed and two others severely wounded because of this bit of stupidity.[28]

The sheer wealth of such testimonies is quite staggering. Some of them
are difficult to believe, such as the claim by Milan Zajec that he spent
five days in a mass grave before being able to escape, but the majority
are not only plausible but contain numerous verifiable details.[29] They
are corroborated by similar accounts from German prisoners, members
of the local population where the massacres took place, and even from
various Partisan documents and testimonies.[30] If any further evidence
were necessary, it is provided by the scores of mass graves that have
been located all over the region. Since the fall of communism in Yugoslavia some of these mass graves have been exhumed, and there are now
many memorials across Slovenia and Croatia commemorating the
deaths of Tito's victims.

The biggest question that remains is what motivated these massacres? Was it merely revenge against former military opponents, or rough
justice for a regime that had been responsible for starting the cycle of
atrocity in the first place? Were the killings politically motivated or the
result of ethnic hatred? The simple answer is that all of these motives
existed simultaneously, and are often indistinguishable from one

another. The Ustasha regime in Croatia was built on an ideology of ultra-nationalism and ethnic hatred – the execution of soldiers and officials associated with this regime was therefore simultaneously a political and an ethnic act, and a fitting, if vengeful and often misdirected, punishment for the ethnic cleansing that the Ustashas themselves had carried out during the war.

However, such subtleties were often lost on those who did the killing, as well as their victims. All of the victims I have quoted stress that they were singled out for being Croatian – unsurprisingly, perhaps, given the fiercely nationalist views of many of those victims themselves. However, even Communist sources admit that ethnicity was the deciding factor in much of the unofficial violence after the war. In July 1945, the Yugoslav intelligence service in Croatia reported that 'chauvinistic hatred' had 'so flared up between the Serbian and Croatian villages that they are almost fighting each other'. Reports of murder and violence on purely ethnic grounds after the war are commonplace, particularly by Serb nationalists who, returning to their villages, took out their prejudices on their Croatian and Bosnian neighbours. 'Why don't you kill all Croats?' returning Serbs are supposed to have asked their fellow villagers in Banija after the war. 'What are you waiting for?'[31]

Yugoslavia as a Symbol of Pan-European Violence

All this killing, on both a small scale and a large one, has helped to create a general perception of Yugoslavia as a uniquely cruel place – a perception that has been reinforced by the ferocious civil war that occurred there during the 1990s. The term 'Balkan violence' is used throughout Europe to denote a particularly vicious kind of bloodthirstiness, and various episodes from history are regularly invoked to support this hypothesis.[32]

It is true that the statistics associated with postwar Yugoslavia are worse than in any other country. Some 70,000 collaborationist troops and civilians were killed by the Partisans in the aftermath of the war: when compared to the population as a whole, this is more than ten times as bad as in Italy and twenty times as bad as in France.[33] At first sight, the anecdotes that emerge from the postwar period also appear to support the stereotype of Yugoslavian cruelty. Dusan Vukovic, who joined the Partisans at the tender age of eleven, claims that he saw a Ustasha skinned alive and then hung on a tree branch with his own skin. 'With my own eyes I saw the Partisans cut off noses and ears and gouge out eyes. They cut symbols of various kinds into the flesh of the captives, too, especially when they thought they had Gestapo personnel in their hands.'[34] Other eyewitnesses speak of routine sadism, such as guards killing their victims slowly with knives, riding prisoners like horses, or binding men and women together and throwing them into rivers to watch them drown.[35]

Numbers aside, however, the violence that occurred in Yugoslavia at the end of the war was no more cruel than that which occurred in other countries. On the contrary, the same themes that pervaded here were present throughout the continent. There is no difference between the anecdotes above and the stories of French *miliciens* who are supposed to have arrested Resistance fighters during the German occupation, 'ripped out their eyes, put bugs in the holes and sewn up their sockets'.[36] Czech mobs were just as likely to carve Nazi symbols into the flesh of SS men they caught hold of, and Belgian *maquisards* thought nothing of burning collaborators alive.[37] Despite the stereotypes, therefore, the cruelty that took place in this unfortunate part of the Balkans should not be considered unique – rather it was symbolic of a dehumanization that had taken place across the continent.

Neither does the ethnic dimension to the violence set Yugoslavia apart. Such ethnic tension might have been missing in most of western Europe but, as I have shown, it was an integral part of the war and its aftermath in Czechoslovakia, Poland and Ukraine. There were also numerous smaller, more regional conflicts involving minorities across the continent, some of which were every bit as violent on a local scale.

In fact, the only unique thing about Yugoslavia is how well it simultaneously encapsulates *all* of the themes I have discussed so far in this book. As in the rest of Europe, much of the violence in Yugoslavia was motivated by a simple desire for vengeance. As in the rest of Europe, the rifts caused by the war were deliberately concealed beneath a layer of cosy mythology once the war was over. The postwar breakdown of law and order was no different there than in other badly damaged areas of the continent. Lack of trust in the new police force, whom the people feared 'as they would a plunderous mob', was no different from the fear that Poles, Romanians, Hungarians, Austrians and East Germans felt towards their own militias (or indeed towards Soviet soldiers).[38] Lack of trust in the courts was the same as it was in France and Italy and, as in those countries, often led to people taking the law into their own hands. Clandestine, unofficial prisons were set up for collaborators, just as they were in France and Czechoslovakia; gulags were created for prisoners of war, just as they had been in the Soviet Union. Populations of Germans and Hungarians were expelled, just as they were from other countries across the continent.

It is only the involvement of the Yugoslav state that points the way to a new theme that I have not yet discussed in depth – the idea that much of the violence was politically motivated. Almost all of the events described up to now were brought about by individuals or groups acting outside state control, and who were eventually brought back into line by a combination of the Allied armies and traditional politicians. In Yugoslavia it was the state itself that conducted the violence, the Allies were absent, and traditional politicians had been replaced by revolutionaries. It is perhaps unsurprising that these fighting men took a distinctly unsubtle approach to returning the country to law and order.

Tito's right-hand man, Milovan Djilas, put their methods succinctly in an interview published in a British magazine in 1979: 'Yugoslavia was in a state of chaos and destruction. There was hardly any civil administration. There were no properly constituted courts. There was no way in which the cases of 20–30,000 people could have been reliably investigated. So the easy way out was to have them all shot, and have done with the problem.'[39] While the French and the Italians tried to rid themselves of collaborators through the courts, and bemoaned the inadequacy of their purge ever afterwards, Tito recognized the shortcomings of his legal system and dispensed with it altogether. 'We put an end to it,' he reminisced later, 'once and for all.'[40]

There is no doubt that the massacres that occurred in Yugoslavia after the war were, at least in part, politically motivated. Since the Communists were intent on forcing Croatia and Slovenia to rejoin a Yugoslavian federation, it made no sense to allow tens of thousands of staunch Croatian and Slovenian nationalists to put that reunion in jeopardy. Neither could Tito allow the continued existence of Mihailović's royalist Chetniks to jeopardize his vision of a Communist Yugoslavia. Both groups therefore had to be dealt with one way or another. Those who were not shot were imprisoned for years or sometimes decades.

Politically motivated violence by the state was not unique to Yugo-slavia. Other Communist groups across Europe were perhaps more subtle in their pursuit of power, but equally ruthless, and just as willing to resort to violence when they believed it necessary. For countless millions of people throughout the eastern half of the continent, therefore, the end of the war did not signal 'liberation' at all, it merely heralded a new era of state repression. The Nazi terror was over: the Communist terror was about to begin.

Western Tolerance, Eastern Intolerance

The Second World War and its aftermath ushered in a new and disturbing contrast between the eastern and western halves of Europe. In the west, the atmosphere had become far more cosmopolitan than the pre-war population could ever have imagined. London had been transformed into the diplomatic hub for all Europe's expatriate governments, and the meeting point for the world's armed forces. The cafés of Paris or Berlin had always been frequented by customers from all over Europe: after the war they also thronged with Australians, Canadians, Americans and Africans, black faces and white. Rural parts of Germany that had rarely seen foreigners before the war were now awash with Poles and Ukrainians, Balts, Greeks and Italians. Austrians who had never before seen black faces now had to get used to mixing with black Americans, Moroccans, Algerians and Senegalese tribesmen. Despite some inevitable racism, and much grumbling about 'drunken Poles' or 'lawless Ukrainians', this new cosmopolitanism was generally tolerated.[1]

In the east, by contrast, the cosmopolitanism that had existed for centuries was partly – and in many areas entirely – destroyed. The war had wiped out most of the region's Jews and Gypsies. It had set neighbours against one another to an unprecedented degree – Slovaks against Magyars, Ukrainians against Poles, Serbs against Croats, and so on across the region. As a consequence of these events, entire communities were scapegoated after the war, or designated as collaborators and fascists, simply by virtue of their race or ethnicity. Minorities who had become integrated into eastern European society over the course of centuries were now weeded out and expelled, sometimes over the course of just a few days.

The difference between the two halves of Europe is partly a result of long-term historical processes. The problem of ethnic minorities had always been more of an issue in the east, especially since the breakdown of the old Russian and Austro-Hungarian empires: even before 1939 there were alarming outbreaks of nationalist violence in many parts of eastern Europe. But these problems were brought to a head by the arrival of war. The Nazis and their allies not only brought a new, murderous quality to racial attitudes, but they promoted hatred between rival ethnic groups as a means of dividing and conquering them. Thus groups like the UPA in Ukraine or the Ustashas in Croatia were not only taught how to conduct large-scale massacres through witnessing the Holocaust at close quarters, but were given the opportunity to conduct genocides of their own. None of these things happened in western Europe. Nazi brutality in the west was milder by far, the genocide of the Jews occurred well out of sight of the population, and competing nationalist tensions were rarely an issue.

However, differences in the way the war was conducted are not the only reason why ethnic tension was so much worse in the east than in the west. The *postwar* regimes in each region were also very different, and they too must take their share of responsibility. In the west, the Allies not only imposed a system that required harmony between different ethnic groups, but provided an example of that harmony in action. The Allied armies in the west contained people from dozens of countries and all six continents. Their military governments contained representatives from four of the world's great powers, all of whom were obliged to try to get on with one another. There is also a suggestion that the very cosmopolitanism of the authorities in the west provided a distraction for people's prejudices. The Walloons in Belgium, for example, were far too worried about their daughters being taken advantage of by American soldiers to concern themselves with the much less alarming question of their relationship with their Flemish neighbours.[2]

One would expect the Soviets to have imposed similar attitudes on the eastern half of Europe: their internationalist doctrine required the workers of all nations to unite in pursuit of their common goals. But in fact they promoted the persecution of minorities both within the Soviet Union itself, and within the eastern European countries that would soon become Soviet satellite states. It was the Soviets who pushed through the population exchange between Poland and Ukraine. It was the Soviets who supported Poland's expulsion of Germans from the 'Recovered Territories', and who insisted on similar expulsions of Germans from the rest of eastern Europe. When the British and Americans refused Czechoslovakia the right to expel its Hungarian minority during the Paris Peace Conference, the Soviet delegation were deeply in favour of it, and they supported similar ethnic deportations in all the countries where they had become the dominant power.[3]

Rather than fighting against racial and ethnic hatred in the areas they controlled, the Soviets sought to harness it. There are many ways in which the nationalist and racist policies that swept eastern Europe after the war suited the Soviets. To begin with, displaced people were far easier to control than people who were entrenched in their homelands and traditions. The chaos created by the deportations was also the ideal atmosphere for preaching revolution. The lands and businesses left behind could be parcelled out and redistributed amongst the workers and the poor, thus furthering a Communist agenda. It also created a new loyalty amongst those who received land, who saw the Communist Party as their benefactors. By promoting communism throughout Europe, the Soviets were also promoting loyalty to Moscow, the home of international communism.

Unfortunately, most nationalists were not quite so easily harnessed to the Soviet cause. While they were happy to have a superpower to sponsor their deportation policies, they were not willing to allow the Soviets a free hand. Nor were they willing to relinquish power to local Communists – whom they rightly regarded as Soviet stooges – without putting up a fight.

The Western Allies were equally difficult to convince. After seeing the way that Soviet power was exercised in eastern Europe, they were beginning to suspect that it was not only deported Germans whose 'freely expressed wishes' the Soviets were willing to ignore.

Thus, while the aftermath of the war saw a depressing increase in ethnic violence, a new, bigger conflict was also brewing. On a local scale it would involve a series of power struggles between nationalists and communists in individual countries. But on a European scale it would involve the clash of superpowers, and herald a new era of continent-wide civil war.

PART IV

Civil War

We who saw Europe liberated know that the Communistic fear that men will cling to freedom is well-founded. It is possible that this truth may be the reason for what appears to be an aggressive intent on the part of the Communists to tear down all governmental structures based upon individual freedom.

Dwight D. Eisenhower, 1948[1]

22

Wars within Wars

In the autumn of 1943 a group of Italian partisans was hiding out in the Alpine forests of the Upper Veneto when an event occurred that would severely test their loyalties. The unit was part of a Communist brigade, and was committed to fighting not only the Germans but the Fascist ruling classes who were nominally in charge of northern Italy. The brigade had only recently formed, and was still inexperienced as a guerrilla force.

One day the unit stumbled across three German soldiers who had been convalescing in the area, and who had gone out for a walk in the woods, completely unaware of the danger of 'bandits'. The partisans were obliged to take them captive, and would have been pleased with their catch were it not for the fact that they now found themselves in a dilemma. What should they do with their prisoners? In the normal course of things they would have interned them in some kind of prison camp, but the realities of guerrilla warfare made this impossible. After much debate it was decided that they had no alternative but to shoot them.

The decision immediately threw the unit into turmoil. None of the partisans wanted to carry out this gruesome task, and there were many who voiced serious concerns over the sentence. During interrogation the three Germans had revealed that they had all been ordinary workers during peacetime. Surely it was not right for Communists to kill fellow workers, even if they were German? Furthermore, they were all conscripts, and therefore fellow victims of capitalist forces that had compelled them to fight against their will. After much argument, and further interrogations, the unit held another vote, and it was decided that they would set the German prisoners free.

This story might have been a rare and refreshing example of empathy between enemies, were it not for what happened next. Three days later, acting on intelligence from the freed Germans, the Wehrmacht descended on the entire area and began a comprehensive search. In granting the German prisoners their lives the partisans had not forwarded the cause of international communism, but merely risked their own annihilation. They would never again make the same mistake: from that day on they shot all prisoners without compunction.[1]

From the safety of the twenty-first century, we tend to imagine the Second World War as a single, unambiguous conflict between the Allies on one side and the Axis on the other. In our collective memory the motives and allegiances of each side are transparent: the Nazis and their accomplices fought for the domination of Europe, while the Allies fought for a 'free world'. It was a war of right against wrong or, even more simplistically, good against evil.

The reality was, of course, much more complicated. For the Italian partisans in this story there were at least three simultaneous reasons for fighting: firstly, to drive the Germans out of the peninsula; secondly, to defeat the Fascists, who had been in control of the country since the 1920s; and, lastly, to bring about a social revolution, which would oust their capitalist rulers and institutions and return power to the ordinary workers and peasants of Italy. Just like Tito's Partisans in neighbouring Yugoslavia, therefore, they were fighting three separate wars in parallel: a national war, a civil war, and a class war.[2] As the story demonstrates, it was sometimes difficult for partisan groups to recognize which of these three wars should take priority.

Similar situations were occurring all across Europe both during and after the Second World War. Hidden within the main conflict were dozens of other, more local wars, which had different flavours and different motivations in each country and each region. In some cases they were conflicts over class or other political differences. In other cases, as I have already shown, they were conflicts over race or nationalism. These alternative, parallel conflicts have received little attention in the past because they upset so many of our neat assumptions about the Second World War.

I have mentioned several times that our memories of the war are built upon myths of national unity: it is opportune at this point to explain exactly how flimsy those myths are. France, for example, was in no way unified during and after the war. Physically it was split between those areas in the north and south-east that were liberated by the Allies, those areas in the centre and south-west that liberated themselves and, for a time, various pockets in the east and along the Atlantic coast that remained under German occupation. Politically it was split between those groups who wanted only to restore France to its prewar status quo and those, like the Communists, who wanted a full-blown social revolution. The national force of the Resistance – the Forces Françaises de l'Intérieur – was cobbled together out of various disparate groups who had nothing in common beyond their mutual wish to see Vichy ousted. Once this was achieved there was no longer any strong reason to keep the organization together, and different elements of the Resistance soon returned to fighting amongst themselves.

The main internal conflict in France was between the forces of the left, particularly the powerful Francs-Tireurs et Partisans (FTP), and those of the centre-right followers of de Gaulle. But even within these groups there were violent splits. The left, for example, was riven by competing factions – Communists against Anarchists, Stalinists against Trotskyites, and so on – who often accused each other of spying for the Vichy authorities. To this day it is impossible to tell whether some of those shot as informers were genuine Vichy agents or merely victims of a local internal Communist purge.[3] The Spanish Communists, who had fled to France at the end of the Spanish Civil War, were supposed to be particularly ruthless in this respect. According to one source, about 200 Spanish refugees were assassinated in the last three months of 1944 – not for reasons linked to the occupation, but because Stalinists saw the liberation as a convenient moment to get rid of their non-Stalinist rivals.[4]

Despite the semblance of unity at a national level, therefore, in the regions of France this unity was lacking at every level. The same was true in Italy, where the coalition between Communist partisans and more moderate anti-Fascists quickly broke down as soon as the war was over. It was also true in Greece, where the various resistance groups were violently opposed to each other right from the beginning and even made local pacts with the Germans in order to concentrate on their own private war. It was true again in Slovakia, where the uprising against

German forces in 1944 drew a distinctly mixed response from a population that was not sure if it wanted to throw in its lot with the Soviets,
the Nazis or the Czechs, or to oppose them all. And so the list goes on.

To acknowledge the parallel nature of these local wars-within-the-
war has always been controversial, because it has such huge consequences
– not only for historians but for the wider world in general. Firstly, there
is a political dimension to our stories and myths about the Second
World War. If we remember the war as a simplistic battle between good
and evil then we do so for a reason. Any change in the way it is remembered also changes our perception of ourselves: not only does it tear
apart some of our most cherished notions of who was right and who
was wrong, but it also, for better or worse, allows former 'villains' an
opportunity to rehabilitate themselves. Neo-fascist groups across Europe have always justified their actions during the war by claiming that
they were merely fighting against the 'greater evil' of international communism. Since the break-up of the Soviet Union in the early 1990s their
arguments have been gaining ground.

Secondly, and more immediately, the acknowledgement of these parallel wars challenges our whole concept of what exactly the Second
World War *was*. If the international war against Germany was only one
strand of this conflict, then it stands to reason that the defeat of Germany did not necessarily bring about a cessation of the fighting. Just
because the main war was over, it did not mean that the various sub-
wars had also come to an end. Far from it – sometimes the absence of
an external enemy simply meant that local people could concentrate
their efforts more effectively on killing each other. We have already seen
how this was true on a regional level where there were specific conflicts
between different ethnic groups. But it was also true on a more general
level in the Europe-wide battle between right and left.

In the following chapters I will outline some of the most violent episodes of postwar history, and show how they were not really 'postwar'
at all. Some of them were merely the continuation of political struggles
born during the Second World War but yet to come to a head. Others
were the culmination of tensions that had been simmering for decades,
and which would continue to do so after the war was over.

In each case, to a degree at least, the outcome was a foregone conclusion. Once Churchill, Roosevelt and Stalin had outlined the broad
brush strokes of their separate spheres of influence at Moscow, Yalta

and Potsdam, none of the Big Three powers was inclined to tolerate any major deviation from the political systems they themselves represented. This was now the age of the superpower, and local political differences were obliged to take second place behind superpower politics. Civil wars in individual countries would become mere expressions of a new continent-wide battle between the forces of communism, supported by the USSR, and those of capitalism, supported by the USA. Those idealists who truly hoped that 'free peoples' would be allowed to 'work out their own destinies in their own way' were about to be sorely disappointed.[5]

Political Violence in France and Italy

At the end of the Second World War, after the dust had settled a little, the people of Europe began to look about themselves for ways to explain the events that they had just experienced. Questions that had lain dormant throughout the war years were now voiced openly. How had the world allowed itself to be dragged into a second devastating conflict so soon after the first? Why had Hitler not been stopped sooner? Why had their politicians not protected them from occupation, exploitation, devastation? Who was responsible, and why were they not being brought to account?

Unsurprisingly, many people now regarded the old establishment with contempt. Attempts were made to purge the continent's institutions, but for some people this was not enough. They argued that the entire political system was at fault, and that if people wanted to avoid future wars and injustices they should find new, more inclusive ways of governing themselves. A radical wind had begun to blow, that would bring with it some of the most violent and tragic episodes of the postwar period.

If the Allies needed a demonstration of just how much people's attitudes had changed, they were given one almost as soon as they set foot on the mainland. In September 1943, as they were busy driving the Germans out of southern Italy, British and American troops were surprised to discover that many of the villages they had liberated were now rising up in rebellion – not against the Allies, nor even against the Germans, but against the Italian state itself. After more than twenty years of Fascist rule, and generations of exploitation by absentee landlords, many of these villages had had their fill of outsiders. A perfect example was the village of Calitri, in the Campania. After liberation, the people of Calitri held a meeting in which they unanimously declared their intention to govern their own affairs in future. To signify their determination, they renamed the area around the village the Republic of Battocchio, after their leader, and declared their independence from the rest of Italy.[1]

In the grand scale of things this would have been a fairly insignificant event, had it been unique, but actually it was just one village amongst many in southern Italy, Sicily and Sardinia to take such an action. In each case, almost the first thing the villagers did was to set about occupying pieces of uncultivated land that belonged to local aristocrats, the state or the church. They had sound reasons for doing so. The villagers were hungry and regarded uncultivated land as a waste of resources that could be used both to feed themselves and to make a little money for the community. In many areas peasants still remembered the seizure of common land by greedy aristocrats during the Risorgimento – as far as they were concerned they were merely righting historic wrongs by taking back what was theirs.

Needless to say, the landowners did not quite see things the same way. More importantly, the new authorities (many of which, as we have seen, were not so new at all) were unequivocally on the side of maintaining the status quo. At Calitri Allied troops and carabinieri entered the village within just a few days, suppressed the republic and returned the land – still fallow – to its former owners. The same thing happened elsewhere. At Oniferi in Sardinia fighting broke out that lasted for two days, resulting in one villager being killed and several wounded. In Calabria the Peasant Republic of Caulonia, which saw revolts in Stignano, Stilo, Monasterace, Riace, Placanica, Bivongi, Camini, Pazzano and many other places, was also forcefully put down.[2]

That such events were even possible shows just how fractured the south of Italy had become in the wake of the war. Individual villages felt quite justified in declaring themselves independent republics because they were both physically and politically cut off from central government. They saw the temporary absence of leadership created by the war as a small window of opportunity to take power into their own hands.

More significantly, however, these events show the lengths that some villages were willing to go to in order to achieve social reform. Contrary to what one might expect, very few of these uprisings were organized by the Italian Communist Party, who by their own admission had virtually no presence in the south of Italy before 1945. They were spontaneous protests, organized locally by people who were sick of social injustice.[3]

The appetite for social reform after the war – not only in Italy but across the whole of Europe – was enormous. It was this appetite that led to the birth of dozens of new political parties across the continent; that spawned hundreds of new newspapers in which left-wing writers could argue about how best to bring about societal change; that inspired demonstrations in support of workers' rights, economic reform, and immediate action against social and legal injustice. The postwar period saw an explosion of left-wing expression that was effectively the rebirth of everything that had been so brutally suppressed during the Nazi occupations. Even the British, whose country had never been occupied, voted for social reform in the aftermath of the war: in the summer of 1945 they ejected Churchill's centre-right administration and elected the most radical left-wing government in British history.

In most of Europe, the political organizations best placed to take advantage of this swing to the left were the various Communist parties. Not only were they ideally suited to harnessing the continent-wide zeal for social reform, but they also had the moral kudos of having been the backbone of the armed resistance to Nazi rule. Taking into account its association with the Soviet Union, regarded by many as the true victor of the Second World War, communism began to seem like an unstoppable force in European politics. Our collective memories of the Cold War have rather obscured the fact that to huge sections of the European population the Communists were viewed as heroes, not villains.

Furthermore, their popularity was greatest not in those countries that would eventually form the Eastern Bloc, but in those countries that would end up to the west of the Iron Curtain. In the postwar elections in Norway and Denmark the Communists won 12 per cent of the popular vote, in Belgium 13 per cent, in Italy 19 per cent, in Finland 23.5 per cent and in the French elections of November 1946 they achieved a massive 28.8 per cent of the vote, making them the biggest political force in the country.[4] More importantly, throughout Europe the Communist Party had a vast pool of committed activists: there were 900,000 party members in France, for example, and two and a quarter million in Italy – far more than in Poland or even Yugoslavia. Communism in western Europe was a hugely popular, and largely democratic move-ment.[5]

There were many, however, who found this popularity profoundly disturbing. Churchill was railing against the totalitarian evils of social-ism, 'or in its more violent form communism', long before his famous 'Iron Curtain' speech at Fulton, Missouri.[6] Of the many groups that Charles de Gaulle mistrusted, the Communists easily topped the list. In Italy, the Christian Democrat leader Alcide De Gasperi confided to friends that he was 'afraid that the future republic will lean too much to the left. The unity of the Communists, their courage, their organization, their means, make them a block that has the same power as old-school fascism.'[7] Even the US State Department was worried about a 'pattern developing in Europe of attempt[s] by Communists to wield an influ-ence disproportionate to their real numbers and eliminate their opponents either by public stigmatism or epuration if possible'.[8]

Such fear and mistrust were born of the fact that communism is ideo-logically opposed to the very thing that many had been fighting for throughout the war: their national sovereignty. The ultimate goal of communism was not the liberation of France or Italy, but the merging of the working classes of all nations in a supranational brotherhood. What many European politicians were worried about, therefore, was that the Communists would put *class* interests above *national* ones. De Gaulle in particular could not help remembering that French Commu-nists had refused to fight Germany in 1939 and 1940 because Germany was still allied to the Soviets at the time. In other words, in a straight choice between France and the Soviet Union, they had chosen the Soviet Union.

On a more prosaic level, the Communists touched far too many sen-sitive spots for the majority of the European population to be comfortable with their rise in prominence. Not only were they opposed to all of the things that the middle classes held most dear, such as reli-gion, the family, and the sanctity of private property, but they also advocated violence to achieve their goals. According to their manifesto, the Communists desired nothing less than 'the forcible overthrow of all existing social conditions'.[9]

After years of savage conflict, the last thing most people wanted was a new class war. Unfortunately, in some areas this was exactly what they were about to get.

The Targets of Political Violence

Some extravagant claims have been made about the Communist parties of France and Italy, so it is necessary to make a couple of things clear straight away. Firstly, there is no evidence to suggest that the Communist Party leadership in these countries intended to seize power immediately after the war. Neither did they authorize political violence – indeed, they appear to have done whatever they could to discourage it. The leader of the Italian Communist Party (PCI), Palmiro Togliatti, made personal visits to the most unruly areas of the country in order to tell regional and provincial PCI leaders to take better control of their members and ensure that the killings stopped. He regularly asserted, both in private and in public, that any movement for social change must be carried out by democratic, non-violent means. He even went so far as to expel from the Party some of those who advocated violence.[10] Likewise the leader of the French Communist Party (PCF), Maurice Thorez, made it quite clear that 'we must hold national unity dearer than what we ourselves cherish' – in other words, that the Communists must sacrifice their desire for radical social change for the sake of rebuilding the country. Both he and the Party leadership in general were regularly praised in government for their efforts to restore public order.[11]

However, just because the Party leadership expressed a wish to cooperate with their political rivals did not mean that the rank and file were equally willing. In both Italy and France there was a split between the 'politicians' and the 'partisans'. The latter, who had done all of the fighting, felt that they had earned the right to dictate policy to the former: in the words of Walter Sacchetti, one of the leaders of the Italian partisans, 'Siamo noi che vi abbiamo liberato' ('It was *we* who liberated *you*').[12] From the very beginning of the liberation in both countries there were many amongst the cadres who were disillusioned with the direction in which the Party leadership was taking them. Many partisans in the regions of France and Italy began to ignore instructions and take the law into their own hands. A minority went so far as to instigate small-scale purges of their traditional class enemies in their own areas. These were effectively revolutions in miniature.

It is difficult to see what exactly this violent minority were hoping to achieve. In the absence of support from their leadership it is unlikely that their actions would result in any long-term political gains – and yet their motives were often undeniably political. Perhaps the best way to make sense of their aims and objectives is to look at who their victims were, and show what, if anything, they had in common.

The first target of the Communists in these miniature revolutions was often the police force. This is perhaps not surprising, given the role that the police had played in propping up the discredited wartime governments. However, it seems that many of these attacks had nothing to do with whether the policemen in question had collaborated or not, but were the result of older grudges. In many parts of France, for example, Communists had been rounded up by police right at the beginning of the war because their loyalty to Stalin (who at the time was still allied to Hitler) made them a potential threat to national security. After the liberation, some French Communists deliberately targeted policemen who had taken part in these arrests, simply because the opportunity to avenge themselves was too good to miss.[13]

One such victim was Abel Bonnet, the police chief in Cognac. Bonnet was a staunch patriot who had been wounded and decorated in the Great War, and who had bravely taken part in various Resistance activities during the occupation. However, local Communists also remembered that he had ordered the arrest of several of their militant comrades in 1939. When Cognac was liberated by members of the FTP in September 1944, this fact came back to haunt him. Bonnet was arrested and taken to nearby Angoulême, where he was kept in a coal cellar for two months. Here he was beaten about the head with a revolver and almost strangled to death. By the time he was released he could no longer walk unaided, and was suffering from a burst ear-drum from the repeated beatings he had received. At no point had he ever been interrogated, or even accused of any crime. On the one occasion when he was brought before the local FTP leader, 'Commandant Pierre', he asked why he had been arrested, but received the cryptic reply, 'I only take orders from Stalin.'[14]

Bonnet's story is corroborated by another man who was imprisoned in the same cellar in Angoulême. Félix Sanguinetti was a *résistant*, but belonged to the Gaullist Armée Secrète – a group that was supposedly

8. Areas liberated by the French Resistance alone, as of 23 August 1944

allied to the FTP, despite their ideological differences. When brought before Commandant Pierre, Sanguinetti was told the same thing: 'De Gaulle, Koenig and the rest, to hell with them. I only have one boss, and that's Stalin.' Then he too was put in the cellar, where he witnessed the continuing barbarity of his captors.[15]

It is impossible to tell how many policemen in France and Italy were targeted for their anti-Communist past rather than any active collaboration with the occupiers – but a wealth of anecdotal evidence suggests that it was reasonably common in both countries. It is quite likely that many others were also branded as 'fascists' or 'collaborators' simply as a way of undermining their authority: if the police were not to be trusted, then the people were much more likely to rely on the partisan militias to uphold law and order instead. This was certainly a Communist tactic that was used to great effect in eastern Europe.

Another traditional enemy 'class' were the bosses – factory owners and managers who exploited the workers for profit. Many of the industrial cities in northern Italy and central and southern France saw a temporary inversion of power after the war, with workers setting up committees to investigate the wartime actions of their employers. In Lyon alone there were 160 'patriotic committees' inside the city's factories and businesses at the start of 1945, who took it upon themselves to arrest dozens of directors and employers, despite the fact that they were not supposed to do this without the official permission of the local prefect.[16] In Turin the workers took over the Fiat factory, and the managing director only narrowly escaped being shot on the factory floor. A visitor from the US State Department in May 1945 reported that the factory was being patrolled by armed gunmen and 'Management is virtually ignored.'[17] In the months after the liberation several high-profile Italian businessmen were killed, including the Christian Democrat industrialist Giuseppe Verderi, and Arnaldo Vischi, the vice-director of the biggest industrial complex in Emilia-Romagna.[18]

Even more vulnerable were members of the aristocracy, particularly if any link with the Fascists could be found. In Emilia-Romagna alone 103 landowners were murdered in the aftermath of the war.[19] The most famous example was the killing of the Manzoni counts at their country house near Lugo in the province of Ravenna. The counts were three brothers, all avowed Fascists, who were major local landowners and the most powerful family in the area. They had managed to avoid

the popular justice during the liberation itself. But in the aftermath of
the war they refused to renegotiate sharecropping contracts with their
tenants, or to put right the wartime damage that had been done to
their land, and this proved to be their undoing. On 6 July 1945, having lost patience, a group of ex-partisans broke into the house and
shot not only the three brothers but also their mother, their maid and
their dog. After the killings the entire population of the local village
descended upon the villa and distributed the family's clothes and
belongings amongst themselves: the episode had the flavour of a peasants' revolt against a feudal system that had oppressed them for
decades.[20]

In France too the aristocracy was targeted, regardless of whether or
not they had collaborated. The Duc de Lévis-Mirepoix, for example,
who had nothing to incriminate him but his title, only narrowly escaped
being sentenced to death by the 'People's Tribunal' in Pamiers because
the new prefect for Ariège closed the tribunal down. Pierre de Castelba-
jac, a count from Tarbes, to the north of Toulouse, was not quite so
lucky. It seems that there was little evidence that this man had actively
collaborated, but when his captors found his membership card for
Croix-de-Feu (a prewar far-right political party), this was considered
incriminating enough. He was beaten, then executed shortly afterwards.[21]

Similar events occurred across France, although the targeting of
minor aristocrats was particularly bad in Charentes, the Dordogne,
the Limousin and Provence.[22] In Vienne, a baron named Henri Reille-
Soult was imprisoned in a pigsty for several weeks, and regularly
beaten, before finally being executed in October 1944. Far from being
a collaborator, he had been part of a British intelligence network during the war.[23] Count Christian de Lorgeril, a decorated war hero in
Carcassonne, was apparently executed simply because of his title and
his monarchist views. According to L'Aube, the daily newspaper of
the Mouvement Républicain Populaire, he was tortured horrifically
before his death: the spaces between his fingers and toes were split,
his hands and feet were crushed, he was stabbed repeatedly with a
red-hot bayonet, and finally placed in a bath of petrol and set on
fire.[24]

Another favourite target, and traditional enemy of the Communist
Party, was the clergy. In Toulouse there were city-wide rumours that

the fascist Milice had set up gun posts in the towers of the local churches – a rumour that goes some way towards explaining why churches in the city were vandalized and machine-gunned during the August 1944 uprising. There are numerous examples across south-west France of clergymen being beaten, tortured and executed by members of the Resistance, often without any convincing evidence that they had collaborated in any way.[25] In Italy too the clergy were occasionally targeted, either because they were suspected of aiding Fascists or because they insisted on denouncing the Communist Party from the pulpit.[26]

Finally, and most importantly, some of the more radical Communist factions began to attack their democratic rivals. In the immediate aftermath of the liberation of France there were definite attempts by various Communist leaders to take control of local areas, particularly in the south-west of the country. The Gaullist Commissaire de la République in Toulouse was forced to fight off a concerted attempt by Communist leaders to usurp him, and only did so in the end by winning military backing from one of the Resistance commanders.[27] In Nîmes, the Gaullist prefect was repeatedly threatened by local Communist leaders, and on one occasion was almost arrested by them. He was saved only by the opportune arrival of the Commissaire de la République, Jacques Bounin.[28]

In Italy the violence against political rivals was more extreme. The centre of this violence was what became known as the 'Red Triangle', or even the 'Triangle of Death' – that area of Emilia-Romagna between Bologna, Reggio Emilia and Ferrara. In the summer of 1945 a series of high-profile murders occurred there that put a serious strain on the fragile alliance between Christian Democrats and Communists. On 2 June an engineer called Antonio Rizzi and his son Ettore were murdered in Nonantola. Both were confirmed anti-Fascists – Ettore had even been a partisan – but they were also Christian Democrats. These were not hot-blooded crimes, but rather that particular brand of political murder that the Italians call *omicidi eccellenti* (in other words, the 'necessary' killing of notable people who are in one's way). Six weeks later, in the same town, a Christian Democrat member of the Liberation Committee was also murdered. Similar killings of Christian Democrats also occurred in Bomporto (8 June), Lama Mocogno (10 June), and Medolla (13 June).[29]

9. Italy, 1945–6

Area relinquished to Yugoslavia, 1945
Main area of peasant land occupations, Calabria
'Red Triangle', Emilia-Romagna

SWITZERLAND
AUSTRIA
HUNGARY

VAL D'AOSTA
• Aosta
TRENTINO ALTO ADIGE
FRIULI-VENEZIA GIULIA
LOMBARDY
• Schio
• Milan
VENETO
• Trieste
Padua
Venice

FRANCE
Turin •
PIEDMONT
YUGOSLAVIA
Genoa •
Reggio Emilia
Ferrara
LIGURIA
Modena
EMILIA-ROMAGNA
Bologna
• Ravenna
Imola

Pisa •
Florence •
Ancona
TUSCANY
MARCHES
• Perugia
UMBRIA

N

CORSICA

LAZIO
ABRUZZI
• Rome
MOLISE

SARDINIA

CAMPANIA
APULIA
• Bari
Naples •
BASILICATA
• Brindisi
• Taranto

• Cagliari

Mediterranean Sea

Cosenza •
CALABRIA
• Caulonia

Adriatic Sea

• Palermo
SICILY
• Catania

0   100 miles
0   100 km

The following year, after anti-Communist feeling had already begun to harden, a second series of *omicidi eccellenti* occurred in the same region. It began in June 1946 with the aforementioned murder of the Christian Democrat industrialist Giuseppe Verderi and ended in August with the killings of the liberal lawyer Ferdinando Ferioli, the socialist mayor of Casalgrande, Umberto Farri, and a captain of the carabinieri named Ferdinando Mirotti.[30]

It must be stressed that all of the stories above are anecdotal, and do not add up to a Communist conspiracy to seize power in either France or Italy at a national level – indeed, as I have already mentioned, it seems that the Communist Party leadership did its utmost to rein in the more extreme factions on its fringes. They understood, as some of their members did not, that the objective conditions for revolution did not exist in either country.

Some local leaders, however, who lacked this breadth of vision, appear to have believed that the time for revolution had already arrived. The sheer number of violent stories from both France and Italy show that there was a significant proportion of the Party that remained committed to violence. Some members appear to have been driven by revenge, or a sense that justice would be done only if they meted out that justice themselves. Others were more calculating, and targeted class enemies regardless of the role that their victims had played during the occupation. Some wanted to intimidate their political rivals into silence. Others seemed to be trying to induce a state of terror amongst the population, much as they had done during the war. While their actions lacked focus, and their motives appeared diverse, the common denominator was the belief that the revolution was not only imminent, but had already arrived.

In the years to come, many in the Italian and French Communist parties would blame their leadership for failing to realize the potential of such immediate, violent action. They were proud of their successes at a local level – where for a time Communists were in control of several cities and one or two entire regions of Italy and France – and believed that this might have been translated into national success, if only their party leaders had seized the initiative. But without proper coordination from the centre, their piecemeal attempts at revolution were doomed to falter and eventually fizzle out.

This does not mean, however, that the political violence of the immediate postwar period had no effect. On the contrary: the effects were far-reaching, but very different from what local agitators had been hoping for.

The Reaction

The belligerence of former partisans and rank-and-file Communist Party members did not go unnoticed. In the immediate aftermath of the war it was put down to the general atmosphere of spontaneous lawlessness that accompanied the liberation – an argument that many historians still subscribe to today.[31] Later, when continuing violence demonstrated that this was not merely a short-lived phenomenon, fears began to mount. Rumours spread that the Communists were out of control or, worse still, that they were part of a more organized conspiracy to seize power. In Paris, stories circulated that the south-west of the country was undergoing a reign of terror, that Toulouse had declared itself a republic and that de Gaulle's representative there, Pierre Bertaux, had been imprisoned by the Communists. It took a visit to Paris from Bertaux himself to dispel the myths.[32] In Italy there were widespread whispers of an insurrection in Milan and Turin, along with rumours that economic collapse and a Communist takeover of the whole country were imminent. The party's enemies certainly used such rumours to their best advantage, and stoked up people's fears. Some Italian anti-Communists themselves admitted that such scaremongering was groundless, and had been deliberately propagated by 'right-wing elements anxious to stir up anti-Communist feeling'.[33]

In the south of Italy, landowners, businessmen, police chiefs, magistrates and other middle-class notables used the memory of the land occupations in 1943 to oppose the institution of left-wing administrators. They feared for their property, their wealth and their own positions of influence – but it was their argument that communism brought civil unrest that most swayed the Allied Military Government in newly liberated areas. As a consequence right-wing candidates, and even some ex-Fascists, were appointed to positions of local power simply as a method of keeping communism at bay.[34]

In the north of Italy, where the violence during the liberation had been much more intense, the right and centre-right parties made the fear of left-wing violence a cornerstone of their campaigning. From January and February 1947, references to the 'Triangle of Death' in Emilia-Romagna began to appear in newspapers such as *La Stampa* and *Corriere della Sera*.[35] In March an article in *L'Umanità* spoke of 'Red Squadristi' conducting a campaign of 'ideological and physical terror'.[36] This was a transparent attempt to snatch the moral high ground away from the left by portraying former partisans not as heroes but as violent thugs.

In France too, lurid stories of partisan violence became common-place in the press during the late 1940s. In 1947, the socialist Prime Minister Paul Ramadier pointed to the upsurge in strike action – which had come about mainly because of spiralling inflation, food shortages and plummeting living standards – and claimed that it was merely the result of Communist agitation. On 5 May he dismissed the Communists from government. Thereafter several Communist 'conspiracies' were uncovered, such as the infiltration of the Ministry of Ex-Servicemen. Rumours even spread of an 'International Brigade' being formed within France.[37]

However, no matter how much French and Italian politicians denounced Communist agitation at a domestic level, it was Communist action on the international stage that was the real cause for concern. What truly scared those of the centre and the right was not the piece-meal violence in their own regional cities, but the more wholesale repression that was taking place in eastern Europe. French and Italian newspapers carried increasingly worrying stories from countries such as Hungary, Romania and Bulgaria, with the implication that the same repression would overwhelm Italy and France if the Communists were ever allowed to take power.

This was also a subject that worried the Western Allies, and particularly the Americans. On 19 February the American ambassador to France claimed that Paris was 'a veritable hive of Comintern agents' and that the 'Soviet Trojan horse' was 'so well camouflaged that millions of Communist militants, sympathizers, and opportunists have been brought to believe that the best way to defend France is to identify French national interests with the aims of the Soviet Union'.[38] Shortly afterwards Dean Acheson went so far as to say that, considering the strength of the Communists in every area of society, a Soviet takeover of

France could occur at any moment.[39] In Italy, meanwhile, diplomats in Rome spoke of a 'psychosis of fear' building up in the country, and warned the US State Department that 50,000 or more trained and armed Communists were preparing themselves for possible insurrection in northern Italy.[40] What this shows is that if scaremongering was rife within Italian and French society, then it was amply reflected in Allied circles. Indeed, there were times when the Americans seemed to be even more afraid of civil unrest in these countries than the French and Italians themselves. They threw their considerable weight behind the anti-Communist political parties, and threatened to withdraw all aid if the Communists ever won power at the elections.[41]

In both countries, the government response to such fears was heavy-handed, but effective. After yet another rash of strikes and riots in the autumn of 1947, and some alarming acts of sabotage such as the derailment of the Paris–Tourcoing Express, the French Minister of the Interior, Jules Moch, announced a complete mobilization of the forces of order, including the call-up of all the country's reserves and conscripts. During a tumultuous debate in parliament the Communist deputy for Hérault was expelled from the chamber, and the government shepherded through a whole series of emergency measures aimed at quelling the unrest.[42]

In Italy, where Communist indignation was inflamed both by the Party's heavy defeat at the 1948 election and by the attempted assassination of Palmiro Togliatti that July, civil unrest became even worse than in France. The Communists announced their frustration through a series of strikes, riots, kidnappings, and even the sabotage of the country's north–south railways.[43] In reaction, the Italian government launched a programme of anti-Communist measures in which trade unionists, former partisans and Communist Party members were arrested en masse. This was a blatant attempt at intimidation, as can be seen by the results of the arrests. Of the 90–95,000 Communists and ex-partisans arrested between the autumn of 1948 and 1951, only 19,000 were ever prosecuted, and only 7,000 were found guilty of any crime – the rest were held for varying periods in 'preventative custody'. It was the hardcore members, and particularly the ex-partisans, who were treated most harshly. Of the 1,697 ex-partisans arrested between 1948 and 1954, 884 were condemned to a total of 5,806 years in prison. Some of them were tried for crimes carried out during the liberation,

despite the supposed amnesties that had been granted in 1946. Regardless of whether these people deserved their sentences, this 'trial of the
Resistance' was far more harsh than the purge of Fascists had ever
been. The message was clear: the 'heroes' of 1945, who had liberated
the north of Italy from Fascist rule, had finally become the new
enemy.[44]

The Myth of the Communist 'Lost Victory'

Given the strength of fear that prevailed at all levels in France and Italy
in the aftermath of the war, the question inevitably arises: just how
likely was it that the Communists might have taken power? At the time
the threat was obviously taken very seriously, but with the benefit of
hindsight it has to be said that such an outcome was never really on the
cards. The Communists never managed to win as much as a third of the
vote in either country, and even with the socialists at their side only
fleetingly came close to winning an absolute majority in France. The
only real hope they had of seizing power was to convince their coalition
partners to grant them not only the premiership but control of all the
important ministries. But as Allied observers in Italy noted in July 1945,
the parties of the right and the centre would never have allowed this to
happen because they were certain that the Communists were intent on
creating a one-party state: 'To permit the Left to come to power would
be equivalent to signing their own death warrants.'[45] In both countries
the Communists were repeatedly blocked from most of the important
positions of government.

The only way that the Communists might have won absolute power,
therefore, was through a full-blown revolution. Even if the Italian and
French populations had been inclined towards such an outcome, this
was not something that the Western Allies would ever have allowed. In
the months after the liberation, the British and Americans had huge
armies stationed in both countries which were more than capable of
putting down a Communist insurrection. Later on, when the Allied
presence diminished, America asserted its authority through economic
rather than military power. De Gasperi's expulsion of the Communists
from the Italian government was made possible only by a massive injection of aid to the country. Likewise, the French knew that if they were

to have any hope of rebuilding their shattered economy they would have to rely on American money.[46]

The idea that the Communists might have won power, or have been able to seize it, was therefore nothing but an illusion. Both countries were dependent on the Allies, and neither government had any real power without the support of America. The more astute members of the Communist parties in both countries recognized this. As Pietro Secchia, a former member of the PCI's northern directing committee, wrote in 1973:

> Young people today who read certain romanticized histories of our war of liberation have the impression that we held *power*, and that we were unable or worse, unwilling, to retain it (for some unknown reason), to bring about if not the proletarian revolution, which was quite out of the question, at least a regime of progressive democracy. The fact is that on account of the conditions in which the war of liberation developed in Italy and in Europe, *we* (when I say 'we' I mean the anti-fascists, the CLNAI) never held *power*, nor were we capable of capturing it.[47]

Togliatti and Thorez have been much criticized by left-wingers for their decision to steer their parties down the democratic route after the war. Many of their comrades blamed them for a failure to seize the initiative and bring about the social reform that so many had longed for. But both leaders were realists, and understood that the conditions in France and Italy were not right for violent social revolution. They strongly believed that the democratic route was the only possible way forward for communism in France and Italy, even though that route was unlikely ever to win them any real power.

History appears to have vindicated their decision. For an example of the chaos that might have ensued if they *had* gone down the revolutionary road, one need only turn one's gaze upon events that were taking place simultaneously on the other side of the Adriatic. In Greece, where Communist politicians did opt to walk out of the democratic arena, a bloody civil war was beginning that would prove even worse than the savage occupation of the Nazis. As I shall show in the next chapter, with British and American help this civil war would culminate in the complete annihilation of the Communist Party in Greece, and a brutal suppression of left-wing politics for the next thirty years.

*

I began this chapter with a description of the spontaneous land occupations by peasants in the south of Italy in 1943–4, and it seems worthwhile to finish it with an explanation of how those events affected the region in the months and years to come. While not nearly as dramatic as the events in Greece, these land occupations and the reaction to them were perhaps more representative of the sort of thing that was going on across the rest of western Europe. They also demonstrate that, contrary to Marxist doctrine, many of the most important battles between socialists and 'reactionaries' would occur not in the cities but in the countryside.

The peasant uprisings demonstrated a new and unexpected assertiveness on the part of the southern Italian peasantry that many found deeply inspiring. In an attempt to capture the mood of the moment, the Italian Minister for Agriculture, Fausto Gullo – a Communist – put forward a programme of agricultural reform. At a stroke, the most exploitative sharecropping contracts were banned. Intermediaries between the peasant and landowner – notorious for exploiting and intimidating peasants – were also banned. In addition, peasants started to be granted a bonus if they sold any excess produce to government granaries (a move that not only ensured a living wage for peasants, but also partially undermined the extremely damaging black market in food). The most crucial decree, however, stipulated that all uncultivated or poorly cultivated land could be occupied and farmed by peasants for a limited period, provided they first form themselves into cooperatives.[48]

The southern Italian peasantry, ignored and exploited for so long, greatly appreciated being acknowledged by the state at last, and immediately mobilized themselves into cooperatives. Gullo's land reforms proved to be a massive propaganda success for the Communist Party. 'Less than a year ago the peasants were completely foreign to us, and to a great extent hostile,' claimed a report from the PCI federation of Cosenza (Calabria) in the summer of 1945. 'But now they are coming to us, trustingly, and in great numbers . . . This is due above all to the extensive action we have carried on in the Province for the assigning of uncultivated lands and over the question of agrarian contracts.'[49] This surge in popularity for the Communist Party mirrors what happened in large parts of eastern Europe when land was likewise redistributed from the aristocracy, the church, the middle classes or from Volksdeutsch farmers.

Unfortunately for the Italian peasants, such legal measures to alleviate their abysmal poverty failed completely. Local officials, many of whom remained unchanged since Fascist times, simply refused to implement the social reforms required of them by law. All requests to work uncultivated land had to be heard by a local commission, which was always dominated by the landowners themselves and the local magistrate. As a consequence in Sicily, for example, 90 per cent of requests were denied.[50]

Frustrated by the failure of the local authorities to abide by the spirit of the law, the peasants of the Mezzogiorno embarked on a second period of land occupations in 1949 that was even more widespread than the first. According to some estimates about 80,000 peasants took part, but the vast majority of them were ejected from the land they occupied even more brutally than they had been in 1943.[51] In Caulonia they were threatened by local farmers who brought their own vigilantes to disperse them. At Strongoli the military used tear gas to disperse them. At Isola the father-in-law of the secretary of the Chamber of Works was assassinated as a warning to the peasants. But the worst event occurred near Melissa, where the carabinieri opened fire on an apparently peaceful crowd of about 600, killing an unknown number. According to some reports, the majority of those killed and injured were shot in the back as they were trying to run away.[52]

In the light of such events it is easy to see why so many left-wing Italians criticized the Communist Party leadership for putting their faith in a corrupt political establishment. During the following decades, despite their continued popularity with voters, the Communists were always sidelined, and the reformist agenda they championed was shelved. The political bullying continued into the next decade and beyond, as did the poverty, particularly amongst the southern Italian peasantry. Togliatti might have spared the country a civil war, but for many Italians the aftermath of the liberation represented a missed opportunity to overturn the injustice of generations.

24

The Greek Civil War

There are some moments in history – thankfully rare – when the fate of millions hangs on the decisions of a single man. One such moment occurred on the evening of 9 October 1944, during a conference between Churchill and Stalin in Moscow. This conference was smaller and less important than any of the 'Big Three' conferences at Tehran, Yalta and Potsdam. The Americans were not present, and Roosevelt had telegraphed both Churchill and Stalin to insist that any agreements should be made by 'the three of us, and only the three of us'. Despite this, Churchill produced what he called a 'naughty document' – a half-sheet of paper on which he had written a series of percentages showing the respective spheres of influence of Britain and the USSR in the postwar world. Romania, for example, would be under 90 per cent Russian influence, and only 10 per cent 'others'. Bulgaria would be 75 per cent Russian and 25 per cent 'others'. Hungary and Yugoslavia would both be split 50/50. There was only one country that would come firmly under the British sphere: Greece would be 90 per cent British (in accord with the USA) and only 10 per cent Russian. To signify his agreement over these percentages, Stalin reached over and marked the document with a big blue tick.[1]

Much has been made of the seemingly casual way that the postwar fate of these five countries was sealed, but in reality it was simply the culmination of months of secret talks between the diplomats of both countries. Nevertheless, it was extremely significant. I will return to what happened in Hungary and Romania in the next chapter. The important point for the moment is that Stalin was willing to ratify British influence in Greece – a decision that was to have profound effects in that country for the next thirty years.

*

The British had always been interested in Greece. It dominated the eastern Mediterranean and the approaches to the Middle East and the Suez Canal, and was therefore vital to British strategic interests. Churchill had been willing to risk coming to Greece's aid when Germany invaded in 1941, and despite a disastrous defeat had always been determined to return. In October 1944, just a few days before the Moscow conference began, the British had once again landed in the Peloponnese. In this respect, Stalin's big blue tick was merely a recognition of the reality on the ground: British troops were already marching towards Athens.

However, British authority in Greece was not quite the fait accompli that it seemed. The British were not the only force fighting for control of the country. As in Italy and France there were also significant numbers of partisans here – indeed, long before the British arrived these *andartes* already controlled most of the Greek mainland, forcing the German occupiers to stick to the main towns. By far the biggest resistance group was the National Liberation Front, EAM, and its military wing the Greek People's Liberation Army, ELAS.[2] While these groups ostensibly represented a broad church of *andartes*, in reality they were both dominated by the Greek Communist Party, which in turn owed loyalty to Stalin. The British had tried throughout the war to counterbalance the strength of the left by supplying arms and funds to alternative resistance organizations, but no amount of funding could change the fact that the Communist-led EAM and ELAS were vastly more popular than all the other resistance organizations put together.[3]

Arguably, therefore, Russian influence in the country was already just as important as British influence, and certainly more than the 10 per cent granted by Churchill's scrap of paper. Had Stalin instructed the Greek Communists to seize control of the country, it is quite possible that they could have done so. The Red Army was already within touching distance of the north of the country on the borders of Bulgaria, and the Communist Partisans of Yugoslavia were also linking up with their comrades in northern Greece. The British presence in October 1944 was tiny compared to that of EAM/ELAS; and when they arrived in Athens they found that the *andartes* had already liberated the city. Despite this, there was no attempt by the Communist Party to seize power at a national level. This was partly because the resistance were fairly disorganized, and partly also because there were many non-Communists within the EAM structure who threatened to withdraw their support if

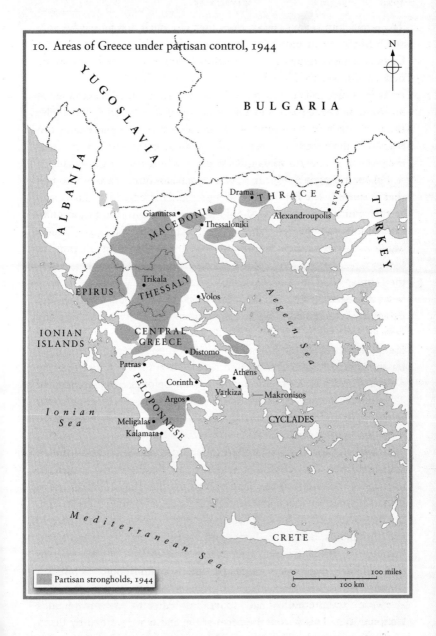

10. Areas of Greece under partisan control, 1944

N

YUGOSLAVIA

BULGARIA

ALBANIA

THRACE

Drama

Giannitsa

MACEDONIA

Thessaloniki

Alexandroupolis

EVROS

TURKEY

EPIRUS

Trikala

THESSALY

Volos

Aegean Sea

IONIAN
ISLANDS

CENTRAL
GREECE

Distomo

Patras

PELOPONNESE

Corinth

Athens

Varkiza

Makronisos

Ionian
Sea

Argos

Meligalas

Kalamata

CYCLADES

Mediterranean Sea

CRETE

Partisan strongholds, 1944

0   100 miles

0   100 km

the organization were to seize power for itself. But it was mostly because Stalin had kept his word: in the run-up to the Moscow conference he had sent a mission to Greece to instruct Communists there to cooperate with the British.[4]

As in France and Italy, there were many amongst the rank and file of the Communist Party – and even some within the leadership – who could not understand why they should stand back and allow others to take control. In a bitter speech to the Communist Party's Central Committee in the summer of 1944, EAM general secretary Thanasis Hadzis complained that the resistance was being betrayed. EAM/ELAS had spent several years fighting the occupier and establishing their power across most of Greece: why should they now bow to the British? 'We cannot follow two paths,' he insisted. 'We must make our choice.'[5] Many Greek resistance leaders suspected the British of wanting to reduce Greece to a virtual colony ruled by a puppet government, just as the Germans had done before them.

In the weeks after the liberation, tensions between the British and EAM/ELAS increased. The British military hierarchy mistrusted the motives of the *andartes* and, as in France, regarded them as a volatile group of amateurs with a tendency to fire off their weapons seemingly for the sake of it. Churchill himself claimed that he was fully expecting a clash with EAM, and sent instructions to the officer in command of Allied forces in Greece, General Ronald Scobie, to expect a coup d'état at any moment. If it materialized, Scobie's instructions were to use all force necessary 'to crush ELAS'.[6]

Conversely, members of EAM/ELAS were extremely mistrustful of British motives. They could not help noticing that the British continued to support the return of the Greek king, and that they appeared to be protecting some former collaborators rather than bringing them to trial. They also seemed to be supporting the appointment of some fiercely anti-Communist officials to key security posts. When, for example, following liberation George Papandreou's so-called 'government of national unity' appointed Colonel Panagiotis Spiliotopoulos as military commander of the Athens area in October 1944, the British refused to intervene. Spiliotopoulos had actively coordinated right-wing anti-Communist groups during the occupation, and was regarded by ELAS as a collaborator. Neither did they intervene when a group of senior Greek army officers in Italy began to speak openly of overthrowing the

Papandreou government and replacing it with an extreme right-wing administration.[7] Such attitudes, combined with the unfortunate tendency of some British officials, in the words of the American ambassador, to treat 'this fanatically freedom-loving country . . . as if it were composed of natives under the British Raj', meant that it was only a matter of time before some kind of dramatic split occurred.[8]

That split came at the beginning of December, less than two months after the liberation of Athens, when the ministers who represented EAM in Papandreou's cabinet resigned en masse. Their gripe was the same as that of the resistance parties in France and Italy: they were unwilling to disarm themselves and hand over control to a newly formed National Guard, at least until right-wing former collaborators had been comprehensively weeded out from the ranks of the police. Unlike France, however, there was no single, charismatic leader who was strong enough, and politically astute enough, to take on both the Communists and the purge of the police. And unlike Italy, the Communists themselves were not quite united enough to agree, however reluctantly, to a compromise agenda. Neither did the Allies have a strong enough presence in the country to compel the two sides to come to an agreement: British forces in Greece were only a fraction of the size of the massive Allied armies that were currently stationed in France and Italy. The political stalemate produced a tension that was tangible at all levels of society. As the writer George Theotokas wrote in his diary, 'It only needs a match for Athens to catch fire like a tank of petrol.'[9]

On 3 December, the day after the EAM ministers walked out of the government, demonstrators took to the streets of Athens. They congregated in Syntagma Square where, for reasons that remain a mystery even today, the police opened fire, killing at least ten and injuring over fifty. British troops who were present maintain that this was simply because the Athens police lost their nerve, but some Greek leftists claimed that it was a deliberate act of provocation.[10] Whatever the motives for opening fire, it unleashed the same cycle of violence that had been in abeyance for only a matter of weeks.

Remembering the brutality of the Greek security forces during the occupation, EAM supporters immediately blockaded and attacked police stations across the city. For the sake of law and order, British forces were now obliged to step in. At first they were pinned down in central Athens by ELAS snipers, but gradually they broke out into the south of the city and into the 'Red' suburbs, where they fought running street battles with former Greek resistance fighters. It was the only time during the war or its aftermath when Allied troops in western Europe found themselves fighting the very resistance groups they were supposed to have liberated. With true colonial hauteur, Churchill informed General Scobie that he was free 'to act as if you were in a conquered city where a local rebellion is in progress'.[11] Accordingly, British batteries of 25-pounders opened fire on the 'Communist' suburb of Kaisariani, and RAF fighter planes even strafed ELAS positions in the pine woods and apartment blocks overlooking the centre of Athens. For the terrified non-combatants who found themselves caught in the crossfire, this was the last straw: women and children were being wounded and killed in attacks by the British that appeared completely indiscriminate. When British medics visited a first-aid post in the suburb of Kypseli they had to pretend to be American in order to avoid being lynched by angry Athenians. Some of those who had been wounded when the Royal Air Force strafed a local square told them that 'they had liked the English, but now they knew that the Germans were gentlemen'.[12]

Over the course of December 1944 and January 1945 the fighting at last began to develop into a class war, with all its worst characteristics. On the one side were the fiercely fanatical EAM/ELAS fighters, who by now were convinced that the British were trying to reinstate both the monarchy and a right-wing dictatorship; on the other side was an uneasy coalition of British troops, Greek monarchists and anti-Communists, many of whom were equally convinced that EAM was trying to stage a Stalinist revolution. Events escalated when the British rounded up some 15,000 suspected left-wing sympathizers and deported over half of them to camps in the Middle East. The *andartes* responded by seizing thousands of bourgeois hostages in Athens and Thessaloniki and marching them through the snow up into the mountains. Hundreds of these supposed 'reactionaries' – often only identified as such because of their relative wealth – were executed and buried in mass graves.[13]

By the end of January both sides were exhausted by the fighting. That February they signed a peace agreement at the seaside town of Varkiza, in which ELAS agreed to disband and lay down their weapons, and the provisional government agreed to press forward with the purge of collaborators. An amnesty was declared for all political offences committed between 3 December 1944 and 14 February 1945, except for 'common-law crimes against life and property which were not absolutely necessary to the achievement of the political crime concerned'.[14]

Had both sides stuck to the agreement then perhaps the matter might have rested there. But, as would soon become apparent, the government had no real power over the right-wing bands that were now forming all over the country, nor even its own security forces. A backlash against EAM/ELAS was about to begin that would eventually lead to civil war.

The Character of Communist Resistance

It is easy to feel sympathy with the resistance fighters in France, Italy and Greece who, despite fighting courageously and successfully for the liberation of their countries, were often not only denied any reward by their postwar governments, but actively suppressed. Members of the Communist resistance were prevented from taking any positions of real power in the postwar governments of all three countries. Former heroes were arrested for deeds that many regarded as legitimate acts of war, and prosecuted with a ferocity that was conspicuously lacking in the official handling of collaborators. And to add insult to injury, stories of their heroic wartime exploits were brushed aside in favour of more dubious myths about Communist 'crimes' during the various purges across Europe. Influential people on the right made sure that the threat of Communist disorder, and even revolution, was exaggerated at every possible opportunity.

However, it is important not to dismiss *all* the claims made by the right. The left-wing resistance groups were not made up entirely of innocent idealists, struggling against the forces of tyranny for a better world – there were also many brutal realists who were more than willing to use tyranny themselves in order to push through their ideological reforms. It is impossible to paint the struggle between right and left in black-and-white terms: the methods, motives and allegiances of both sides are too tangled to unravel with anything approaching simplicity. Nowhere is this better exemplified than in Greece during and after the war. Here, more than in any other country, terror was freely employed by *all* sides upon a frightened population who found it increasingly difficult to avoid being sucked up into the war of ideologies.

The wartime rise of EAM was something completely new in Greece. The country had no tradition of mass ideological movements before the occupation, and politics tended to be something that was imposed upon the country from the top down, with little relevance to the working classes, particularly in the countryside. During the war, however, the brutal occupation of the Germans, Italians and Bulgarians, coupled with hunger and privation, had a deeply radicalizing effect upon the Greek population. Farmers, workmen and even women, who had previously had little use for politics, now saw it as the only way to bring sanity to a world gone mad with destruction. They turned to EAM in their hundreds of thousands, because EAM offered not only the possibility of resistance to occupation but the promise of a better world once the war was over.

The achievements of EAM at a local level are phenomenal, particularly since they occurred during a brutal war when their very existence was considered illegal by the occupying authorities.[15] In a time of famine they organized land reform, and the even distribution of food stocks. They instituted a new and highly popular form of 'people's justice' that was conducted in villages rather than in local towns, heard by local juries rather than expensive lawyers and judges, and conducted in demotic rather than in formal High Greek, which was like a foreign language to most Greek peasants. They created almost a thousand village cultural groups across Greece, sponsored dozens of travelling theatre groups and published newspapers that were read throughout the country. They created countless schools and nurseries that provided education for those who had never before had the opportunity. They encouraged youth groups, and the emancipation of women – indeed, it was EAM who first gave Greek women the vote in 1944. They mended roads and created unprecedented communications networks. These achievements were particularly notable in the remoter parts of the Greek mountains that had been all but ignored by prewar politicians. According to Chris Woodhouse, a British secret agent in Greece during the war, 'EAM/ELAS set the pace in the creation of something that Governments of Greece had neglected: an organized state in the Greek mountains'. It was only thanks to EAM that the 'benefits of civilization and culture trickled into the mountains for the first time'.[16] Their popularity in many parts of

Greece was founded upon their ability to change people's lives for the better, and their willingness to engage not only with village notables but with ordinary people.

However, there was another side to EAM that was not quite so benign. To begin with, they would brook no competition. Unlike in France and Italy, where, generally speaking, the different resistance groups cooperated with each other to oust the Germans, EAM/ELAS spent much of their time fighting other resistance groups rather than the occupier. In April 1944, for example, ELAS units executed Colonel Dimitrios Psarros in Roumeli, not because he was a traitor but because he was the head of a rival resistance group. Many of the survivors of this group, which was called National and Social Liberation (EKKA), promptly joined the collaborationist 'Security Battalions' on the grounds that they now believed EAM/ELAS were a greater evil than the Germans.[17] The Communists also targeted the National Republican Greek League, EDES, a resistance group in central and western Greece, requisitioning their members' food, their animals and eventually threatening their lives if they did not leave EDES and join EAM instead. As a consequence, many EDES members also defected to the Security Battalions; meanwhile many prominent EDES members, including their leader Napoleon Zervas, nurtured close ties with the collaborationist government and even the Germans in an unofficial anti-Communist alliance.[18]

After the war EAM members claimed that their excesses were merely 'patriotic wrongful acts' which, 'since they are linked to the patriotic struggle . . . cannot be considered punishable'.[19] But the fact that they acted so violently against other resistance organizations shows that for all their nationalist rhetoric – even the acronym ELAS was a deliberate evocation of the Greek word for Greece, 'Ελλάς' – the majority of the resistance leadership was more concerned with the class war than it was with the war of national liberation. The Communists even opposed the British, despite the arms and money they supplied to Greek resistance groups of all political persuasions, because they were suspicious of Churchill's monarchist sympathies.[20]

In areas where EAM/ELAS maintained absolute power, the people often found themselves subject to the whims of petty Communist dictators whose rule could be terrifyingly bloody. In the far north-east of the country, for example, a leader of an ELAS band who took the nom de guerre 'Odysseus' apparently went mad with power. After stamping out

black-market activity in most of the Evros region, he turned his attention to 'traitors', a category that appeared to contain anyone who
questioned his authority or who displayed any kind of Anglophilia.
Many people were killed merely because members of Odysseus's band
had personal grudges against them. When a special mounted 'Death
Battalion' was sent out with a list of 'informers' to be killed there was
an argument amongst the battalion's members over some of the names
on the list. The intervention of their commander, 'Telemachus', is chilling: 'This is a revolution,' he said. 'And things have to be done – even if
a few innocents are killed, it won't matter in the long run.' The situation
in Evros became so bad that eventually ELAS had to send a new leader
to the area. Odysseus was arrested, tried and executed, and a more
measured form of law and order was restored to the area.[21]

Perhaps the most famous *andarte* of the war was Aris Velouchiotis,
who ruled large parts of central Greece like a despot. One of the found-
ers of ELAS, Aris had learned about the use of terror as a method of
control in the years before the war when the police were cracking down
on communism: he was arrested and tortured until he was willing to
sign a renunciation of his party activities. The brutality he suffered
appears to have rubbed off on him. Now himself in a position of power,
he thought nothing of executing his own men for crimes as innocuous
as stealing chickens – a form of exemplary justice that virtually wiped
out indiscipline within the ranks of his band. Neither was he much concerned by the execution and torture of people he considered traitors or
criminals. In the autumn of 1942, for example, he ordered the arrest of
four respected family men in the village of Kleitso and tortured them
mercilessly and unceasingly for almost a week. Their crime was the
stealing of some wheat from the village storeroom – many years later,
however, one of the store guards confessed to the village priest that all
four men were innocent, because he himself had been the one to steal
the wheat.[22]

Apologists for EAM often blame such excesses on rogues and maver-
icks who were impossible to control in a country fragmented by war.
However, there is much evidence to suggest that such repression was
more centrally organized – if not on a national level then at least on a
regional one. In some parts of central Greece and the Peloponnese, terror was a deliberate and semi-official EAM method of controlling the
population. Lists of names were drawn up by committees, submitted to

other committees for approval and then passed on to special assassination squads who would execute the people on the list, often without even knowing what they were supposed to be guilty of. The bureaucratic nature of what would come to be known as the 'Red Terror' was chilling.[23]

In the Peloponnese, terror was directed not only at traitors but at 'reactionaries' – in other words, anyone who had voiced opposition to the Communist Party in the past. A distinction was made between 'active' reactionaries, who were executed, and 'passive' ones, who were supposed to be sent to concentration camps in the mountains – but in the event many of those who were sent to the mountains were executed when they got there.[24] Many village mayors, village doctors, merchants and other notables were killed, whether or not they had ever opposed the Communist Party – it was enough that they were *potentially* disloyal to EAM/ELAS.

Some local ELAS leaders, such as Theodoros Zengos, who controlled the area around Argos and Corinth, appear to have demanded a fixed quota of 'reactionaries' to be executed in every village under their jurisdiction.[25] In the absence of reactionaries and collaborators, their families would be targeted. In February 1944, the Communist newspaper of Achaia province ran an article warning members of the collaborationist Security Battalions to defect to the resistance. 'Otherwise we will exterminate them, we will burn their houses and we will destroy all their kin.'[26]

Such terror baffled the population, because it was a completely new phenomenon. Political arguments, uprisings, even coups had happened before in Greece, but they had been relatively bloodless affairs; they had certainly not resulted in Greeks killing Greeks on anything like the scale that was now, suddenly, the norm. Suspected reactionaries were taken to camps in the mountains, often remote monasteries, which were every bit as horrific as the Gestapo prisons. Here they were frequently tortured, starved and finally executed by having their throats slit.[27] Sometimes entire villages were written off as traitors, and massacres carried out on the population. In the Peloponnesian village of Heli, for example, ELAS took between sixty and eighty hostages, mostly old men and women, slaughtered them and threw their bodies into a well.[28]

Such terror was not unique to Greece, of course: terror was a method of control that the Nazis imposed upon most of occupied Europe, and

Greece was no exception. Just as in other countries with large partisan movements, the Nazis were not the only ones to employ this tactic: it was also employed by those very Greeks who were supposed to be fighting to free the nation. And for a while, at least, it worked – dissent was stamped out in EAM-controlled areas, reactionaries and their families fled to the towns and Communist control became absolute. But it also drove many into the arms of the Germans, and particularly to the German-backed Security Battalions. One Battalion in the Peloponnese, for example, was set up by Leonidas Vrettakos, whose main motivation was to exact revenge for his brother, who had been killed by ELAS in the autumn of 1943.[29] 'I went to the Germans,' explained another Battalionist whose parents had both been killed by EAM. 'What should I have done since there was no one else to turn to?'[30]

During 1943 and 1944 the collaborationist Security Battalions began to develop and expand, largely in response to Communist terror. Unfortunately the Battalions were often equally brutal, and in many areas launched a programme of random arrests, torture, execution, razing the homes of suspected EAM supporters and the general looting of food, livestock and possessions. Sometimes this was merely a case of indiscipline amongst troops that had been recruited from thuggish elements in the towns, but in other cases it was inspired by a rabid anti-communism that did not discriminate between the innocent and the guilty.

One British liaison officer in the Peloponnese summed up the escalating violence between the two sides as follows:

> ELAS had at last found their real enemies – a Right Wing element armed . . .
> ELAS' attitude to them was one of extreme hostility; and many of the
> worst ELAS atrocities were carried out against SB prisoners and against
> their families, who were normally removed to concentration camps. ELAS'
> fury against the Security Battalions grew with what it fed on, and the
> Battalions themselves proved no less masters of the arts of intimidation
> and terrorisation.[31]

Further north, in Thessaly and Macedonia, the growth of anti-Communist sentiments led to the formation of other German-backed organizations, such as the openly Fascist National Agricultural Federation of Anti-Communist Action, EASAD, which presided over a reign of terror in the city of Volos.[32] In Macedonia, a far-right paramilitary group commanded by Colonel George Poulos conducted countless atrocities, including the massacre of seventy-five of their fellow Greeks at Giannitsa.[33]

In the face of such extreme violence from both sides it became increasingly difficult for the ordinary citizens of Greece to maintain any kind of moderation. As in those areas of Italy that were similarly contested between Communists and Fascists, many Greeks faced the difficult choice of joining collaborationist militias (and finding themselves on a Communist blacklist), or joining EAM/ELAS (and risking the lives, liberty and property of their families). There was often no middle way. This suited the Germans perfectly, who openly admitted that their intention was to sow dissension amongst the Greeks so that they 'could sit back as spectators and watch the fight in peace'.[34]

Perhaps the most tragic aspect of all this was the highly personal nature of the violence. Villages across the country became split by their political standpoints, and disagreements that might in the past have been settled by an argument in the local *kafenia* now led to blood feuds that could see whole families murdered. Furthermore, while different families within the same village were often identified with one political group or the other, often their arguments had nothing to do with politics at all. Sharecroppers denounced one another to EAM in order to get their hands on each other's crops; villagers accused one another of treachery in order to settle personal squabbles or feuds; professional rivals denounced one another in order to eliminate competition. In such instances, tensions that already existed in the community were allowed to escalate beyond all proportion, with EAM/ELAS (or their opponents) acting as the catalyst.

There are countless examples of how the influence of political forces allowed purely personal grudges to get out of hand. I shall give just one, which is the blood feud between the Doris and Papadimitriou families, as unravelled by the historian Stathis N. Kalyvas.[35]

In 1942 a young shepherd named Vassilis Doris fell in love with Vassiliki Papadimitriou, a girl who lived in the village of Douka in the mountains west of Argos. Unfortunately she did not return his affections, and fell for his brother Sotiris instead. Embittered, Doris decided to get his revenge on her. He told some local Italian troops that Vassiliki was hiding weapons, and as a consequence the troops went to her house and badly beat her up.

The following year, when EAM came to the area, Vassiliki's family became prominent EAM supporters. They in turn wished to be avenged for what Doris had done, so they repeatedly denounced him as a traitor to EAM officials. Eventually one of their reports reached the provincial EAM committee. By now it was July 1944, and the regional Communist committee had begun their programme of weeding out reactionaries in the area. Accordingly, Vassilis Doris and his brother Sotiris were both arrested and taken to an EAM prison in the monastery of St George in Feneos. After a week here a guard came into the cells and called out twenty names, including those of Doris and his brother. They were told that they were being taken to the local ELAS headquarters, but in reality they were to be marched up the mountain to a cave where their throats would be slit.

Doris was no fool, and guessed what was about to happen to him. While members of the group were led away to the cave in twos he managed to untie his hands, so that when he was finally brought face to face with his executioners he was able to hit his guard and run away. In spite of the shots that were fired at him he escaped down the mountain and made his way to Argos. A day after his escape, EAM executed his other brother, Nikos, as an act of retribution.

Several months later, after the liberation, Doris got himself a weapon and returned to the area with the intention of avenging himself on Vassiliki Papadimitriou and her family once and for all. On 12 April 1945 he and a band of friends and relatives killed Panayotis Kostakis, a relative of the Papadimitriou family whom Doris believed had been involved in denouncing him to EAM. In reply, that June, two of the Papadimitriou brothers killed Doris's brother-in-law. The following February, Doris and his band attacked the Papadimitriou house and killed Vassiliki's mother and her young son Yorgos – and three months later they also hunted down and shot one of Vassiliki's brothers, her brother-in-law and her three-year-old niece. In the words of one of the villagers, 'Vassilis [Doris] and Vasso [Papadimitriou] began the whole affair; they survived, but everyone else around them was killed.'

This whole sorry story is a perfect example of how the war, and political forces that imposed themselves on a small Peloponnesian village, turned a minor personal problem into a cycle of violence and murder. Had the Italian occupiers of the region not acted on Doris's malicious tip-off, his resentment at being rejected by Vassiliki would probably have melted away harmlessly over time. Likewise, had EAM not over-reacted to the equally malicious denunciations by Vassiliki's family then the situation might not have become murderous. And finally, had the right-wing local authorities after the war arrested Doris rather than giving him carte blanche to hunt down his enemies, the cycle of violence could have been stopped in its tracks. When Doris and his associates were finally arrested and tried they were happy to pretend that they had been acting purely out of patriotism against a family who were violent EAM revolutionaries. It is a sign of just how comprehensive the anti-Communist backlash had become by 1947 that, despite the obviously personal nature of their crimes, both Doris and his accomplices were acquitted.

The Defeat of Communism in Greece

Given the entrenched positions of those at both ends of the political spectrum, and the intense and personal hatred that had developed between them, it was not entirely surprising that postwar attempts to steer the country back towards the centre failed. Papandreou's 'government of national unity' came under increasing attack from both sides. Even the British were unable to keep control, and large parts of the country were plunged into varying degrees of chaos for several years after the war was over.

The British have often been condemned for the part they played in propping up those on the Greek right and facilitating their subsequent reign of terror. For all their distrust of Communists, however, the British were more guilty of political naivety than of outright suppression. Their biggest mistake was during December 1944 when they succumbed to the demands of monarchist army commanders to rearm the Security Battalions and other right-wing collaborationist militias who were being held in camps outside Athens. Under attack from guerrilla forces, the British were in no position to refuse an offer of help, even if it did come from dubious sources. But as a consequence they allowed the new National Guard to become suddenly swamped with those same right-wing collaborators whom they had only recently defeated.

EAM had also been guilty of naivety. By resigning from Papandreou's

government, they had committed the first of a series of grave political
errors: their action, ironically, served to bring about the very develop-
ment that they had been protesting to avoid – an openly right-wing
National Guard. Over the following months many of these Guards
joined forces with right-wing bands and unleashed a White Terror on
the Greek countryside. Security Battalionists were released from prison,
suspected leftists and their families were attacked, and the offices of left-
wing groups were ransacked.

EAM's second mistake, though they can hardly be blamed for it, was
to stand by the terms of the Varkiza ceasefire agreement and hand over
at least some of their weapons to the authorities. Once disarmed, former *andartes* were no longer in a position to defend themselves, and
were often mercilessly pursued by their enemies. Those who refused to
disband, such as Aris Velouchiotis, were denounced by the Communist
Party, and eventually hunted down by government troops and massacred. In a scene of medieval barbarity, Aris's severed head was displayed
in the main square in Trikala.[36]

Greek right-wingers, by contrast, never even pretended to stand by
the terms of the ceasefire. They appeared to believe that the British
would support them 'under any and all circumstances', and therefore
felt free to act in whatever way they chose.[37] In the year after the Varkiza agreement, according to official sources, right-wing bands murdered
1,192 people, wounded 6,413 and raped 159 women – although the
true numbers are undoubtedly greater.[38] In some areas, particularly the
north and the Peloponnese, the police embarked on a programme of
mass arrests of anyone suspected of links with EAM. While the British
were always highly critical of such blatant persecution, they exerted
very little pressure on either the Greek government or rightist circles to
put a stop to it.[39] In the light of this, it is unsurprising that the Communists became extremely resentful of the British presence on Greek soil.
In years to come they would characterize the period of the 'White Terror' as a 'vast terrorist orgy of monarcho-fascism and the total
enslavement of the Greek people by foreign imperialists'.[40]

In the following months the Greek right made a concerted effort to
ensure that they controlled the country's armed forces, the National
Guard, the gendarmerie and the police. According to sources within the
Papandreou government, Communists were prevented from joining any
of these institutions because they could not be trusted not to betray

Greek national interests – but the term 'Communist' soon came to mean anyone with even moderately left-wing beliefs. Those already in the army or the police who were suspected of left-wing sympathies were immediately siphoned off into the reserves. These moves by the right were so extensive that many Allied observers began to fear that they were planning a coup d'état. At the very least they appeared to be trying to exercise improper influence over the forthcoming elections in March 1946.[41]

This brings us to the final great mistake of the Greek Communist Party. Incensed by the repeated breaches of the Varkiza agreement, the Communists decided to go against Soviet advice and abstain from the elections that March, thereby handing a massive victory to the royalist right. That autumn the monarchists secured the return of the king in a highly dubious referendum. At a local level right-wing officials used their new mandate to intensify anti-Communist repression. The gendarmerie expanded rapidly, and by September 1946 was more than treble the size it had been the previous year.[42] Violence escalated to a point where the government no longer controlled what was happening in the provinces. By the end of 1946 it was clear that many Greek leftists had no choice but to flee their homes and take to the mountains once more. The Communist Party formed the Democratic Army of Greece (Dimokratikos Stratos Ellados, or DSE) – the natural successor to ELAS – and civil war returned to the country.[43]

I will not give a blow-by-blow account of the next two years, in which the cycle of violence and counter-violence generally continued in much the same way as it had done during the war. The main difference now was that it was no longer the Germans, Bulgarians and Italians who supported the forces of the right against the Communists, but the British and Americans, who saw the maintenance of anti-communism as the lesser of two evils. Western aid poured into the country, as did British and American materiel, and the Greek government eventually employed the age-old British method of quelling uprisings – that of forcibly relocating tens of thousands of villagers to internment camps in order to starve out the guerrillas. The Greek Communists, by contrast, struggled to win support from outside the country. When Stalin refused to help them, they began to rely instead on Tito's Yugoslavian Partisans – an arrangement that lasted until 1948. But when the Greek Communist Party sided with Stalin after the Tito–Stalin split, even this backing was withdrawn, and the writing was on the wall. The civil war in Greece finally came to an end in 1949 with the complete collapse of the left.

Perhaps the most shocking aspect of this whole period of Greek history was the double standards that existed in the justice system. While the prosecution of Greek collaborators largely ceased in 1945, Greek Communists continued to be arrested and prosecuted in huge numbers. In September 1945, according to official figures, the number of leftists in prison outnumbered alleged collaborators by more than seven to one. The figures for executions were even worse. By 1948, according to American sources, only twenty-five collaborators and four war criminals had been judicially executed in Greece.[44] More than *a hundred times* that number of death sentences were carried out on leftists between July 1946 and September 1949.[45]

Those who were not executed often languished in jail for years or even decades. By the end of 1945 some 48,956 EAM supporters were behind bars, and the number would remain at around 50,000 until the end of the 1940s.[46] Even after the infamous internment camps on Makronisos were closed down in 1950 there were still 20,219 political prisoners in Greece and 3,406 in exile.[47] As late as the 1960s there were still hundreds of men and women in Greek prisons whose only crime was to have been members of the resistance groups that fought against the Germans.[48]

This 'trial of the resistance', as Italian historians call it, occurred in several countries after the war – but nowhere was it as harsh as it was in Greece. For twenty-five years the country was ruled by a combination of conservative politicians, the army and shadowy American-backed paramilitary organizations. The ultimate low point was between 1967 and 1974, when the country was taken over by a military dictatorship. During this time a law was passed which provided the final insult to the men and women who had fought for the liberation of Greece during the war: EAM/ELAS partisans were formally defined as state 'enemies', while former members of the Security Battalions, who had fought on the side of the Germans, were made eligible for state pensions.[49]

The Curtain Descends

The Greek civil war was to have profound effects for the rest of Europe. It was the first and bloodiest clash in what was soon to become a new,

Cold War between East and West, left and right, communism and capitalism. In some respects, what happened in Greece defined the Cold War. It not only drew the southern boundary of the Iron Curtain, but provided a stark warning to Communists in Italy and France, and indeed all over western Europe, about what might happen if they were tempted to try and seize control. But perhaps most importantly it drew the Americans back into Europe by forcing them to understand that isolationism was no longer an option. When the British announced that they could not afford to continue financing the Greek government's war against the Communists, the Americans were obliged to step in. They would remain in Greece, and at strategic points across the continent, for the rest of the century.

It was America's sudden involvement in Greece that gave rise to the Truman Doctrine – the US policy of containing what the American diplomat George F. Kennan called the Communist 'flood' that was threatening to wash over all of Europe.[50] On 12 March 1947 President Truman gave a speech to Congress declaring that it should now be United States' policy 'to support free peoples who are resisting attempted subjugation by armed minorities or by outside pressures', and that they should begin by granting a massive aid package to Greece and Turkey.[51] This was effectively drawing a line in the sand: eastern Europe might be beyond rescuing from communism, but the eastern Mediterranean would not be allowed to follow suit.

The logical conclusion of this new American policy was the announcement of the European Recovery Programme, otherwise known as the Marshall Plan after the incumbent US Secretary of State George Marshall, in June 1947. This massive aid package was ostensibly open to every European country including the Soviet Union, provided they embark on greater economic cooperation with one another. But while the stated purpose of the Marshall Plan was to combat chaos and hunger across the continent, the Secretary of State hinted heavily that priority would be given to those countries who were struggling to resist 'governments, political parties or groups which seek to perpetuate human misery in order to profit therefrom politically'.[52] In other words, while it professed to be a package of economic aid, the true purposes of the Marshall Plan were almost entirely political.[53]

The Soviets were infuriated by such diplomatic moves. While they had been willing to stand back from Greece, which, according to Stalin's agreement with Churchill, was firmly under the British and American 'sphere of influence', they were not prepared to accept any Western meddling in their own sphere. Stalin instructed all those countries under direct Soviet control to decline the American offer of Marshall Aid, and put concerted pressure on Czechoslovakia and Finland to do likewise. Thus, while sixteen countries did eventually sign up to the Marshall Plan, not a single future Communist state took part. Instead, under further Soviet pressure, they set up their own commercial treaties with the USSR. The split between the two halves of Europe was beginning to widen.

Perhaps the most important consequence of this chain of events was the Soviet decision to formalize their control over the other Communist parties of Europe. Just three months after the announcement of the Marshall Plan, the Soviets summoned all the Communist leaders to a meeting in the Polish town of Szklarska Poręba. Here they reformed the Communist International, or Comintern, under the new title of the Communist Information Bureau, or Cominform. At the same time they virtually instructed the western Communists to embark on a campaign of anti-American agitation – an instruction which was one of the main reasons for the sudden increase in strikes in Italy and France from the end of 1947. The age of autonomy and diversity amongst the Communist parties of Europe was well and truly over – from now on the Soviets would be calling all the shots.[54]

While it is quite probable that this chain of events would have happened in any case, it was the situation in Greece that proved to be the catalyst. The Greek civil war was therefore not merely a local tragedy, but an event of truly international significance. The Western powers recognized this, and seemed prepared to endorse almost any injustice as long as it held communism at bay.

For the ordinary people of Greece this merely added a new layer of misery to their experience. Not only were they caught between the extremist tendencies of their own countrymen – long after the Second World War was deemed to have finished – they had now also become a football in the new game between superpowers.

25

Cuckoo in the Nest: Communism in Romania

It is easy to criticize the actions of the Western governments in the aftermath of the war. In hindsight there were times when they seemed paranoid and overly willing to crush legitimate left-wing protest, even if it meant suspending the very democratic principles they claimed to be supporting. Injustices *did* occur. Lives *were* ruined. But the threat that faced the West was very real. Despite their heavy-handed and often badly managed approach, the Western governments truly believed themselves to be pursuing the least worst course.

In a straight choice between Stalinist communism and the flawed mix of democracy and authoritarianism espoused by the West, the latter was undoubtedly the lesser of two evils. The Communists in eastern Europe displayed a ruthlessness in their pursuit of power that made the Western governments seem like fumbling amateurs. Any of the dozen or so nations that fell behind the Iron Curtain might serve as a demonstration of this, but perhaps the best example is that of Romania, because the Communist takeover here was particularly rapid, and particularly vicious.

Romania was one of the few eastern European countries that had remained relatively untouched by the Second World War. Parts of it had been bombed extensively by the Allies, and the north-west had been ravaged by the approach of the Red Army – but in contrast to Poland, Yugoslavia and East Germany, where the traditional power structures were almost entirely swept away by the war, Romanian institutions remained largely intact. For the Communists to seize absolute power here, therefore, it was not simply a matter of imposing a new system upon a blank slate – the old system had first to be dismantled. The brutal and menacing way in which the traditional Romanian institutions were liquidated and replaced is a masterclass in totalitarian methods.

The August Coup

The story of postwar Romania begins in the summer of 1944 with a sudden and dramatic change of regime. Up until this point the country had been ruled by a military dictatorship under Marshal Ion Antonescu, and had been locked into a steadfast alliance with Germany. It had entered into the war fairly enthusiastically, and Romanian troops had fought alongside the Wehrmacht all the way to Stalingrad. Now that the tables had turned, however, it was becoming increasingly obvious that Germany was going to lose the war. Many in Romania realized that the only way to avoid devastation by the Red Army was to change sides. A broad alliance of opposition parties formed in secret and, convinced that Antonescu would stick with Hitler to the end, decided to oust him.

The driving force behind the coup was the leader of the National Peasant Party, Iuliu Maniu. It was Maniu who had first instigated the plot, and it was Maniu who was most involved in secret peace talks with the Allies. His party was by far the most popular opposition party during and after the war, and was expected to take most of the important government offices if the coup was successful. The other main plotters were politicians from the Social Democratic Party, the National Liberal Party, the Communist Party and – as the group's figurehead – the country's young monarch, King Michael.

After weeks of preparation, the coup was set for 26 August. The plan was for King Michael to invite Antonescu to lunch, and instruct him to open up new negotiations with the Allies. If he refused, the king would immediately dismiss him and appoint a new government made up of opposition politicians. This government would have been prepared beforehand, so that they could take over the reins of power immediately and seamlessly.

Unfortunately, events did not quite turn out as planned. The military situation had begun to deteriorate so rapidly that the marshal decided to leave for the front on 24 August, at short notice. Forced to improvise, the king decided to bring the coup forward a few days. On the after-

18. A tearful Corsican woman, accused of consorting with German soldiers, is ritually humiliated by her neighbours. By shaving her and stripping her naked they are effectively reclaiming her body for France.

19. Continued anti-Semitic violence sparked the flight of Jews from eastern Europe after the war. This ramshackle ship, the *Exodus 47*, was carrying Jews to Palestine before it was intercepted by the British.

NATIONALIST VIOLENCE, SPARKED BY THE WAR, CONTINUED LONG AFTER 1945

20. *Top* May 1946: Poles flee the village of Wąwolnica after it has been set alight by Ukrainian partisans.

21. *Bottom* Ukrainian victims after an attack by Polish nationalist forces on the village of Wierzchowiny, June 1945.

THE HUMAN CONSEQUENCES OF POSTWAR BORDER CHANGES

22. *Above* When south-east Poland became part of Ukraine, this family from Rudky was forced to pack up all its possessions and relocate to the new 'wild west' of Poland. The train journey took twelve days.

23. *Opposite* Nine million Germans were expelled from Silesia and Pomerania to make room for such families. Here German refugees crowd onto trains in Berlin.

24. *Above* Two protestors are shot dead by Athens police during an anti-government demonstration in December 1944. These events would mark the beginning of another five years of bloody civil war in Greece.

25. *Right* Tens of thousands of Greek civilians were interned on suspicion of having Communist sympathies. This girl makes use of the barbed wire to hang up washing, 1948.

26. *Left* Romania, 1946: after a sham election, the Communist stooge Petru Groza stands shamelessly beneath a picture of King Michael to deliver his victory speech.

27. *Below* Hungary, June 1947: members of the Freedom Party arm themselves with chairs when Communist thugs try to break up their meeting in Szeged.

28. *Top* Lithuanian folk hero Juozas Lukša (*centre*), with fellow partisans Klemensas Širvys (*left*) and Benediktas Trumpys (*right*) in 1950. Lukša would be betrayed and killed the following year.

29. *Bottom* Veterans of the Ukrainian Insurgent Army, pictured at an anniversary march in Lviv in 2009. Today's generation is unsure whether to remember them as heroes who resisted Soviet rule or villains who engaged in ethnic cleansing.

noon of the 23rd he invited Antonescu to the palace, where, after a brief but tense confrontation, he had the dictator arrested. The move appears to have taken Antonescu completely by surprise. When the king was interviewed by a British journalist a few months later, he claimed that they 'popped him into the palace strongroom for the night, where his language, I am told, is still remembered with admiration by the palace guards'.[1]

However, owing to the hurried nature of events, the plotters had not yet managed to agree how best to form the new government, so once again the king was left to improvise. After a quick conference with his advisers, he appointed a provisional cabinet on the spot. Shortly after ten o'clock that evening King Michael announced the coup d'état on radio. A pre-prepared declaration from the new Prime Minister, Constantin Sănătescu, was also read out. These announcements made it clear that Romania had accepted the armistice terms of the Allies; they also promised that the new government would be, in contrast to Antonescu's dictatorship, 'a democratic regime wherein public freedom will be both respected and guaranteed'.[2]

The Communists had played a fairly minimal role in events so far, but once the coup had been carried out they were by far the quickest to react. The first person to arrive at the palace after the coup was the Communist statesman Lucreţiu Pătrăşcanu, who immediately requested – and was granted – the post of Minister of Justice. It was not an unreasonable request: Pătrăşcanu had a legal background, and had helped to draft the king's proclamation to the nation. However, since none of the representatives of other political parties were given a specific portfolio until much later, the move was nothing if not bold. It also gave the impression that the Communists were being rewarded for taking a leading role: indeed Pătrăşcanu later exploited this impression by claiming, falsely, that he had been the *only* representative of the opposition to be consulted on the coming coup.[3]

Another lucky stroke for the Communists was the fact that they were given control of Antonescu and the other prisoners once the coup was over. Once again, there were good reasons for this. It was not thought to be a good idea to allow the military to take charge of Antonescu and his cabinet, since the soldiers might still feel some loyalty to their old commander and release him. The police were not to be trusted for the same reason. The plotters had therefore decided to hand the prisoners to a civilian militia group. The most likely group was Maniu's National Peasant Party volunteers; however, at the time of the coup they had already been sent to Transylvania to help fight against the Germans. The only other anti-fascist civilian militia was the Communist-trained 'Patriotic Guards'. Handing over the dictator to this group once again gave the impression that the Communists were far more influential in the coup than they actually had been.

The greatest gift to the Communists, however, was provided by the Allies during the armistice negotiations. While all sides had already accepted the general terms of the armistice by the time of the coup, the actual text was not finally agreed for another three weeks. One of the sticking points was over who amongst the Allies would be responsible for the country. The Soviets argued that since it was their army that had occupied Romania, they should be the ones to control it. Some British and American officials were concerned that the Soviets were acting as though Romania was 'Russia's own business': they argued that all three of the major Allies should take *joint* responsibility. In the end, however, it was the Soviets who got their way. The final wording of the armistice specified that the country would be controlled by an Allied Control Commission 'under the general direction and orders of the Allied (Soviet) High Command'. This would open the country to Soviet domination later on.[4]

The Communist Fight for Power

After the coup of 23 August 1944 there were three governments in quick succession. The first of these was a provisional government under General Sănătescu, which lasted just ten weeks. The Soviets were keen to dismiss this government for the simple reason that the Communists held very few positions of any power in it. Sănătescu was vulnerable on a couple of counts. Firstly, he had great difficulty in meeting Soviet demands for reparations, which led to accusations that he was reneging on his commitments as laid out in the armistice agreement.[5] But his true downfall lay in his failure to purge 'fascist elements' from society. In the first six weeks after the August coup, according to a report by the American Office of Strategic Services, only eight Romanian officials were dismissed for collaboration with the Germans.[6] While a handful of senior intelligence officers were arrested, the vast majority of the state security apparatus remained untouched. Worse still, former members of the fascist militia, the Iron Guard, could still be seen in Bucharest's bars and hotels 'boasting that no Government would dare to touch them'.[7] Some cabinet members did call for the immediate establishment of a tribunal for the trial of war criminals, but these calls were dropped when Iuliu Maniu raised legalistic objections. The Peasant Party leader claimed that his opposition to such a purge was in order to avoid further bloodshed, but there were widespread suspicions that he was really just trying to avoid anything that would cause thousands of former Iron Guards to switch their allegiance to the Communists overnight.[8]

Some sections of the population were understandably infuriated by such inaction, which made even the feeble purge in Italy look effective by comparison. The Romanian Communists capitalized on this popular anger, and did their best to stoke it up further. On 8 October they organized their first large demonstration in Bucharest, with some 60,000 protestors amassing in the city centre to demand that Sănătescu and his government resign. A large number of the protestors were undoubtedly genuine – but the Communists also used their influence within the trade unions to coerce more people to attend.[9]

Under pressure from both the Soviets and internal forces, General Sănătescu resigned on 2 November. However, he was immediately asked by the king to form a new caretaker government until an election could be organized. Sănătescu's new government contained more posts for the Communists, the most important of which was the appointment of their leader, Gheorghe Gheorghiu-Dej, as Minister of Transport. The Communist stooge Petru Groza, leader of the Ploughman's Party, was made vice-premier. However, the all-important Ministry of the Interior, which controlled the country's police forces, stayed with the National Peasant Party. Much to the disgust of the Communist Party it was awarded to Nicolae Penescu, who was fervently anti-Soviet. In an attempt to discredit the new Interior Minister, more demonstrations were organized, in which protestors were given the specific instruction to chant 'Down with Penescu'.[10] Such agitation increased steadily as the Communists tightened their grip on the trade unions, using both rhetoric and coercion to mobilize more and more people.

The second Sănătescu government was even shorter lived than the first. At the end of November two trade unionists were shot by Romanian soldiers during a drunken brawl, an event that the Communist-led National Democratic Front (NDF) made full use of. A huge funeral was organized for the two dead men, which became yet another mass demonstration against the government. The Communist press, meanwhile, raged about how 'Hitlerist Fascists' in the establishment were literally getting away with murder, and directly accused the National Peasant Party of supporting them. In protest at such harassment from the NDF, members of the Peasant Party and the Liberals withdrew from the cabinet en masse. Overwhelmed, Sănătescu was forced to resign, this time for good.[11]

The third post-coup government was formed on 2 December 1944. This time King Michael appointed his Chief of Staff, General Nicolae Rădescu – a non-party figure who was approved by the Soviets. In an attempt to put an end to the continued civil disturbances the king informed the Soviet Deputy Foreign Minister Andrei Vyshinski that if the Communist agitation continued he would be forced to abdicate and leave the country. Vyshinski was aware that such a move would cause chaos behind the Soviet front lines, and might even force the Soviets to take formal control of the country – an event that would not look good to their British and American allies. He therefore instructed the Romanian Communists to lower the temperature a little, and for a while at least the street demonstrations were stopped.[12]

The Communists did, however, use the government reshuffle to make further inroads towards power. They did not quite manage to gain overall control of the Interior Ministry, which Rădescu kept for himself, but they did get a prominent Communist appointed as his deputy. The new man, Teohari Georgescu, lost no time in seizing as much control for the Communists as he could. He installed his own men in nine of the sixteen prefectures in the provinces, and gave them strict instructions to take no orders from anyone but him. He began to introduce the Communist-trained 'Patriotic Guards' into the Romanian security police, the Siguranţa, and accelerated the Communist infiltration of the other branches of the security apparatus. By the time Rădescu realized what his deputy was up to it was already too late. When he ordered the disbanding of the 'Patriotic Guards' he was simply ignored. When he demanded Georgescu's resignation he was also ignored – his deputy simply carried on coming into the office and issuing orders to the regional prefects.[13]

Soon Rădescu's lack of control over his other deputy also became apparent. At the beginning of 1945 the vice-premier, Petru Groza, began openly encouraging peasants to seize land from the owners of large estates in anticipation of the forthcoming land-reform programme. On 13 February the Communist paper *Scînteia* reported that estates in the counties of Prahova and Dâmbovița had been occupied by peasants. At a cabinet meeting two days later Rădescu accused his deputy of fomenting civil war.[14]

Once again, the Communists organized demonstrations calling for the resignation of Rădescu, and by now their power was great enough to stage these rallies in several cities across the country. The situation came to a head on 24 February with a large demonstration outside the Interior Ministry itself. Rădescu, who was in the building, instructed the guards to fire into the air to disperse the crowd. In the ensuing confusion more shots were fired, this time from an unknown quarter, and some members of the crowd were killed. Rădescu, fed up with the constant provocation from the Communists, and losing his temper at now also being called a murderer, made a radio broadcast to the nation the same evening in which he called the Communist leaders Ana Pauker and Vasile Luca 'hyenas' and 'nationless and godless' foreigners. He was referring to the fact that many of the Romanian Communists were not actually 'Romanian' in the eyes of the population, but had Russian, Ukrainian, German or Jewish parentage; but he was also obliquely referring to their Soviet backers.[15] This appeal to Romanian nationalism did him no good, however, and the Communists continued to demand his arrest. In the aftermath of these events a joint commission of Soviet and Romanian doctors established that Rădescu's guards had almost certainly not shot into the crowd, since the bullets taken from the victims' bodies were not of a type that was used by the Romanian army. But by the time this became known it was immaterial. Rădescu had fallen into the same trap as Sănătescu before him, and his government was quickly becoming untenable.

The mass of strikes and demonstrations that occurred in Romania was essentially the same as what was happening in France and Italy. The difference was that in France and Italy the Allies stood firmly behind the government – partly for political reasons, but mostly for the sake of maintaining law and order – and provided vital moral, financial and military support. In Romania, by contrast, Allied support for the government was conspicuously lacking. The Soviets did not provide the country with financial aid – on the contrary, they were busy bleeding the country dry with constant requisitioning and demands for reparations. They did not provide moral support either, and there was no suggestion that they might use their considerable military presence to bring the civil unrest under control. By standing idly by while increasingly violent demonstrations took place, the Soviets were deliberately allowing the Romanian government to be undermined.

However, their support for Communist agitators was not merely passive. During the February crisis the Soviets made their position more or less clear. On 27 February 1945, the Soviet Deputy Foreign Minister Andrei Vyshinski went directly to see King Michael and demanded that he dismiss Rădescu, and install Petru Groza as Prime Minister in his place. While the king stalled for time, the Soviets turned up the heat by removing Romanian army units from Bucharest and replacing them with Soviet troops, who now occupied key positions in the city. The implied threat was obvious and, under further pressure from Vyshinski, Michael was compelled to dismiss Rădescu on 28 February. He stalled further over the institution of Groza and a Communist-dominated cabinet, but when Vyshinski made it clear that the Soviets were prepared to take over the Romanian state themselves, Michael had little choice but to capitulate. The Groza government came to power on 6 March 1945. Just six months after the coup, the NDF had managed to see itself officially installed in power.

The Dismantling of Democracy

Over the next year and a half Groza's government presided over the rapid disintegration of democracy in Romania. The National Peasant Party and the Liberals were almost entirely excluded from Groza's new cabinet: fourteen of the eighteen cabinet posts were given to NDF members, while the final four were given to breakaway members of the other parties, such as the dissident Liberal Gheorghe Tătărescu, who was made Deputy Prime Minister. The Communists held all the most important ministries, including those of Justice, Communications, Propaganda and, crucially, the Ministry of the Interior. They also held the deputy posts at the Agriculture and Communications ministries.[16]

Now, at last, the government machinery was subjected to a systematic purge and reorganization according to the Communist agenda. Having finally gained complete control of the Interior Ministry, Teohari Georgescu immediately announced a plan to eliminate 'fascists' and 'compromised elements' from the security forces. Of his 6,300 Interior Ministry officials, almost half were either placed on reserve or dismissed. Just a few weeks after the new regime came to power, several hundred police and counter-espionage officers were arrested.[17] The corps of detectives was given the specific task of hunting down all the former members of the Iron Guard who were still active. There is no doubt that a purge like this was needed, but the way that it was conducted also happened to serve other Communist and Soviet aims. Thousands of Patriotic Guards were now finally allowed to join the police force and the security services. The Soviet spy Emil Bodnăraş, who until now had been in charge of the Patriotic Guards, was given control of the dreaded Serviciul Special de Informaţii (SSI). Another Soviet spy, Alexandru Nicolski, was put in charge of moulding the corps of detectives into the basis for what would soon become the infamous Securitate. Herein lay the foundations of the future Romanian police state.

Having hijacked both the government and its security forces, the Communists now set about dismantling those other two pillars of democratic society: a free press and an independent judiciary. During the summer, the Justice Minister Lucreţiu Pătrăşcanu purged, dismissed or prematurely pensioned over 1,000 magistrates across the country. In their place he installed officials loyal to the Communist Party. He appeared to think nothing of summoning Supreme Court judges to his office in order to dictate their judgements to them, and eventually instituted a system whereby every judge would be accompanied in court by two 'Popular Assessors', who would have the ability to overrule him if his decisions were not in accord with Party policy.[18]

The subjugation of the press was even easier to achieve; indeed, it was already under way. From the very early days after the August coup the Soviets had regularly suspended the publication of newspapers that they deemed to be hostile, or closed them down altogether. For example, the largest National Peasant Party newspaper, Curierul, was closed

down on 10 January 1945 and part of its office space given instead to
the Communist paper, *Scînteia*. Similarly the Liberal paper, *Democratul*,
was suppressed because of its articles revealing that many of the areas
of Romania allegedly conquered by the Red Army had in fact been
taken by the Romanians themselves. Most ridiculously, the official Liberal newspaper, *Viitorul*, was suspended during the night of 17–18
February because the Soviets thought it was printing coded messages.
These messages turned out to be the 'suspicious' abbreviations at the
end of the name of the British military representative, Air Vice-Marshal
Donald Stevenson, OBE, DSO, MC.[19]

After a year of Groza's government the democratic press had all but
ceased to exist. On 7 June 1946 the US Department of State reported
that, out of a total of twenty-six newspapers published in Romania, the
National Peasant Party and the National Liberal Party were able to
publish only one daily newspaper each. The government, by contrast,
had ten daily papers and nine weekly or bi-monthly papers in Bucharest
alone. The Independent Social Democrat Party was not allowed to publish a newspaper at all. Despite numerous requests to the Ministry of
Information, they were fobbed off with the excuse that there was not
enough newsprint available.[20]

The Groza government was only ever supposed to be a caretaker government, pending elections. However, the NDF was unwilling to allow
elections until it could make sure of victory – Groza therefore procrasti-
nated continually while the Communist forces behind the scenes continued
to undermine all opposition. During its twenty months of rule it systematically terrorized Liberals, Peasants, Independent Socialists and anyone
else who opposed them. In August 1945 the government discovered two
'terrorist' plots that conveniently involved members of the National Peasant Party. On 15 March 1946 the former Prime Minister Rădescu was
beaten up by a group of men armed with clubs, an event that convinced
him that it would be sensible to flee the country. In May 1946 General
Aurel Aldea, the Interior Minister during the first Sănătescu government,
was arrested for 'plotting to destroy the Romanian state'. He was tried
alongside fifty-five 'accomplices', and on 18 November 1946 – the day
before the elections were to take place – sentenced to hard labour for life.[21]

In the run-up to the elections, the Communists and their collaborators made it as difficult as possible for the opposition parties. The

National Peasant Party repeatedly complained to the international community about the sort of political conditions they were obliged to endure:

> Meetings are not free. With the knowledge and tolerance of the government, notably of the Ministry of the Interior, armed bands have been organized. These bands attack public meetings and the heads of opposition parties; they kill, maim, and manhandle the adversaries of the regime. They possess automatic weapons. They make use of iron bars, knives and clubs; they are paid; most of the participants are convicted criminals. They not only enjoy complete immunity for any brutalities that they commit, including even murder, but they act under protection from the police and gendarmerie.[22]

One must remember when reading reports like this that they were written by people with a particular political agenda, in an atmosphere fraught with allegations and counter-allegations – nevertheless there is evidence from more neutral sources to suggest that such descriptions are not that far off the mark. An official Note of Protest from the British government claimed that 'gangs of roughs' had prevented opposition campaigning and broken up opposition meetings. There were also complaints by both the British and the Americans about the withholding of press and radio facilities to opposition parties, and the widespread falsification of electoral lists. When it came to the election itself, according to an editorial in the *New York Times*, 'the terrorization of the electorate, the suppression of the opposition, and the falsification of the election results were even more glaring than in Bulgaria, and approached Marshal Tito's standards in Yugoslavia'.[23]

The Communists stood in the 1946 elections on a single ticket with several other left-leaning parties that they had convinced to join them in what they called the 'Blocul partidelor democrate' ('Bloc of Democratic Parties'). When the votes were counted the Bloc officially received about 70 per cent of the vote, and 84 per cent of the seats in the new assembly. The National Peasant Party, by contrast, received only 12.7 per cent of the votes and 7.7 per cent of the seats; the rest went to other small parties.[24] However, independent sources at the time, as well as more recent research in the Communist Party's own archives, suggest that the true result was exactly the opposite: it was the National Peasant Party that had received the majority of the vote. The election had quite simply been rigged. In Someş, for example, the National Peasants had been credited with just 11 per cent of the vote when they had actually won more than 51 per cent. By falsifying the election results in this way the Communists had taken another huge step towards a monopoly of power.[25]

It was becoming obvious by now that, in the absence of any concerted pressure from the West, there was nothing that anyone could do to challenge absolute Communist rule in Romania. Unfortunately for Romanian democracy, the reaction of the West was indignant but completely ineffectual. During the two years that preceded the election, Britain and America had submitted several formal Notes of Protest, but there was never even a hint that they would back them up with serious action. The brazen way in which the Romanian Communist Party falsified the election results is a testimony to how confident they had grown that the West would remain apathetic – and indeed, while the British and Americans stated openly that they regarded the elections as invalid, neither country was bold enough to withdraw official recognition of the Romanian government. The Soviets understood their complaints as mere bluster, and history quickly proved them right. Ten weeks later, on 10 February 1947, the Allies signed a formal peace treaty with Romania, after which time the West effectively washed its hands of responsibility for the country.[26]

With both the election and the formalities of the peace treaty behind them, the Communists now launched a final round of arrests, this time with the intention of destroying the opposition once and for all. On 20 March, 315 members of the opposition parties were arrested on trumped-up charges. On the night of 4 May another 600 were arrested. On 2 June, the police in Cluj arrested 260 workers who had opposed the Communist Party. According to one, a member of one of the National Peasant youth organizations, they were taken to the local military barracks and later loaded onto trains heading in the direction of the USSR, before some of them escaped by tearing up one of the planks in the floor of their railway wagon. Many of those arrested were never formally charged. The majority were released after six months, presumably because by that time the authorities had made their point.[27]

Soon the security forces began to target the leadership of the opposition. On 14 July the former Interior Minister for the National Peasant Party, Nicolae Penescu, was arrested along with about a hundred other members of his party, including the Vice President Ion Mihalache, and the editor of the National Peasant newspaper *Dreptatea*. The premises of both the party and the newspaper were occupied by police, and the newspaper suppressed.

On 25 July the leader of the National Peasants himself, Iuliu Maniu, was also arrested. In a show trial that autumn he and the rest of the Peasant Party leadership were accused of conspiring with Britain and America, attempting to leave the country in order to set up an alternative government abroad, and otherwise plotting to undermine the Romanian government. In his defence Maniu quite reasonably claimed that the 'transgressions' he was being accused of were simply the normal democratic functions of any politician. It made no difference; he and Mihalache were sentenced to hard labour for life. Their co-defendants received sentences of hard labour or imprisonment that ranged from two years to life.[28]

The final major force of opposition, the king himself, was neutralized a couple of months later. At the very end of the year, under duress, he was forced to sign an act of abdication, and a few days later he fled the country. He did not return until after the fall of communism, in 1992.

Stalinism Unbound

With the last vestiges of opposition finally removed, the Communists were free to embark on their true agenda: Stalinization of the whole country. An assault on individual thought and expression saw a purge of teachers, the closing down of all foreign or religious schools, the banning of non-Communist textbooks and the enforced teaching of Stalin's interpretation of Marxist-Leninist precepts. Bourgeois children were denied education in favour of workers' children, and some students were thrown out of polytechnic schools on the grounds that their grandparents had once owned houses. Libraries were purged of any books that did not agree with a Stalinist world view. Poets and novelists were attacked in the Communist Party newspaper *Scînteia*, and their works either heavily censored or banned.[29]

Religion was especially targeted. Churches were stripped of their assets and their schools taken over by the state. The authorities placed bans on baptisms, church weddings and the public celebration of Christmas and

Easter, and Communist Party members were instructed not to attend any church services at all. The Catholic Church was put under the control of a new 'Catholic Committee for Action', and those who did not endorse the Committee's decrees were arrested. The Orthodox Church was purged, and its hierarchy filled with Communist Party members and others sympathetic to the regime. The Uniate Church, which had some 1.5 million members, was forced to merge with the Orthodox Church under state control. When Uniate priests refused to recognize this hijacking of their religious beliefs, they were arrested en masse. In November 1948 some 600 Uniate clergymen were under arrest. Several priests and bishops from all three religions were either killed or died under torture.[30]

The suppression of free speech was accompanied by a huge drive towards centralization and the abolition of private property. Everything from transport, industry and mining to insurance and banking was nationalized: by 1950 alone 1,060 major enterprises had been brought under state control, incorporating 90 per cent of the country's total industrial production. In the process, market mechanisms were destroyed, small businesses virtually disappeared, and the economy was placed in thrall to a 'State Planning Commission' and a Stalinist 'Five Year Plan'.[31]

Perhaps the greatest upheaval in the country, however, was brought about by the collectivization of farms. The land reforms introduced by the Groza government in March 1945 were deliberately calculated to increase support for the Communist-led NDF in the countryside. According to official figures, over a million hectares of land were expropriated from 'war criminals', those who had collaborated with the Germans, and landowners who had left their land uncultivated over the previous seven years. Everyone who owned more than fifty hectares of land was forced to relinquish it to the state, who then parcelled it out to the poorer peasants. In total, 1,057,674 hectares of land were distributed amongst 796,129 beneficiaries, giving them an average of 1.3 hectares each. While this was an extremely popular political move, it was much less successful economically: such small parcels of land were extremely inefficient, and without the same access to farm machinery that the old, large farms had had, food production dropped dramatically.[32]

Four years later, after the Communists had achieved absolute control of the country, they finally revealed their true agenda for the countryside.

At the beginning of March 1949, they announced that all farms up to fifty hectares, which had previously been exempt from Groza's land reforms, would now also be expropriated without compensation. Local militias and police forces immediately moved in and evicted an estimated 17,000 farming families from their homes.[33] In contrast to the Groza land reforms, these expropriations of land and property provoked widespread resistance. In the regions of Dolj, Arges, Bihor, Bucharest, Timişoara, Vlaşca, Hunedoara and parts of Western Transylvania peasants fought pitched battles in order to hold on to their lands, and in some cases the army were called in to suppress them. According to Gheorghe Gheorghiu-Dej in later years, mass arrests of peasants were carried out all over the country, as a result of which 'more than 80,000 peasants . . . were sent for trial'.[34] But now that there was no longer anyone to represent these people in government, or to protect them from the brutality of the new security forces, their resistance was futile.

The land expropriated from these peasants was used to set up almost a thousand collective farms, upon which brigades of landless or poor peasants were set to work. From the outset the project was an abject disaster. The government failed to set up anything like enough communal stations for tractors and other farm machinery: as a consequence crops could neither be properly sown nor properly harvested, resulting in drastic food shortages throughout the country. Having forced through this policy against the will of the people, just over a year later the government was obliged to scale back the programme drastically. The thrust for collectivization resumed in earnest the following year, and after ten years Dej was able to announce that 96 per cent of the total arable land in the country now belonged to state farms, collectives and agricultural associations.[35]

In the interest of balance, it is important to keep in mind the fact that some of the poorer peasants did find themselves better off under the new system. It is also worthwhile remembering that in the same year that thousands of Romanian peasants were fighting *against* land reform, in Italy they were protesting in their tens of thousands because land reforms were being actively prevented. None of this, however, excuses the brutal and anti-democratic way that collectivization in Romania was carried out. Both economically and in terms of sheer human misery, the programme was an unmitigated disaster.

*

The transformation that overtook Romania in the years 1944 to 1949 is quite astounding. In those few short years the country changed from a nascent democracy to a full-blown Stalinist dictatorship. That the Communists were able to achieve this through a largely political process, albeit a manipulated one, rather than through any kind of violent revolution is extraordinary. But the fact that Romania did not descend into the same kind of civil war that had engulfed Greece should not be taken to mean that the process was in any way peaceful. From the intimidation of trade union members to the arrest of politicians, from the massive and often unruly demonstrations in the cities to the repression of peasants and farmers in the countryside, violence, or the threat of violence, was omnipresent in Romania after the war.

Standing squarely behind this threat of violence, like the Romanian Communist Party's shadow, was the might of the Soviet Union. As I shall show in the coming chapters, the subjugation of Romania, and indeed of the rest of eastern Europe, would have been impossible without this towering presence. It is significant that the coup which ousted Marshal Antonescu from power in the first place had only ever been conducted in order to avoid the threat of annihilation from the Red Army. This threat remained in the background throughout the events I have described, and was the principal reason why resistance to the Communist Party's political manoeuvring was not greater.

Over the coming years the Romanian government was to become one of the most repressive regimes in the Eastern Bloc. It is painfully ironic that the coup of August 1944, which was conducted with the purpose of establishing democracy in Romania, should have heralded more than four decades of oppression that made Antonescu's dictatorship seem positively benign by comparison.

26

The Subjugation of Eastern Europe

The imposition of communism in Romania might have been brutal, but it was by no means unique. Historians of various nationalities tend to concentrate on the ways in which their own country's experience of communism was different from those around them. The French, Italian, Czech and Finnish experience in the immediate postwar period, for example, was one of a largely democratic Communist movement, whose leaders sought to win power through the ballot box. The Greek, Albanian and Yugoslav Communists, by contrast, were all members of a strictly revolutionary movement committed to overthrowing traditional power structures by force. In other countries the Communists sought to achieve power through a combination of these two approaches: a democratic surface, with a revolutionary undertow. In the words of Walter Ulbricht, leader of the East German Communists, '[I]t's got to look democratic, but we must have everything in our control.'[1]

If there appeared to be many different roads to communism in the aftermath of the war, however, these differences were outweighed by the similarities between countries. The first and most important thing the Eastern Bloc countries had in common was that they had almost all been occupied by the Red Army. While the Soviets always maintained that their army was only there to keep the peace, there were definite political overtones to their peacekeeping – in this respect their policy was the mirror image of the use of the British army in Greece. In Hungary, for example, the Communist leader Mátyás Rákosi implored Moscow not to withdraw the Red Army, for fear that without it Hungarian communism would 'hang in the air'.[2] Klement Gottwald, the man in charge of the Czech Communists, also asked for Soviet military detachments to be moved towards the Czech border during the February 1948 takeover, just for psychological effect.[3] Even if the Red Army was not actually used to impose socialism upon the population of eastern Europe, the threat was implicit.

Alongside the Red Army had come the Soviet political police, the NKVD. While use of the Soviet military to impose Communist rule was more often a threat than a direct reality, the NKVD took a much more hands-on approach, especially while the war was still going on. It was the NKVD's responsibility to ensure political stability behind the front lines, and as such they had carte blanche to arrest, imprison and execute anyone they saw as a potential threat. On the face of it, their aim was the same as that of the British and American administrations in western Europe – to prevent any kind of civil conflict in the interior that might draw resources away from the front – but the systematically ruthless way in which they and their local disciples rounded up and disposed of everyone they believed to be 'politically unreliable' clearly demonstrates that they had ulterior motives.

This was particularly obvious in Poland, where members of the Home Army (Armia Krajowa or AK) were hunted down, disarmed, arrested, imprisoned and deported. The AK was a potentially valuable fighting force, but as an alternative power base in Poland it was also a threat to future Soviet influence there.[4] For all their rhetoric, the Soviets were *never* only concerned with winning the war: they always kept one eye on the future political shape of the countries they were in the process of occupying.

A further method of ensuring Communist domination was through the use of Allied Control Commissions (ACCs). At the end of the war, the Allies set up these temporary commissions in all of the former Axis countries to oversee the business of the indigenous administrations. The ACC in Germany and Austria was more or less equally split between American, British, French and Soviet members, and arguments amongst these representatives often led to stalemate – and ultimately to the division of Germany. In Italy the ACC was dominated by members of the Western Allies. In Finland, Hungary, Romania and Bulgaria, by contrast, it was the Soviets who were firmly in control, with British and American members acting merely as political observers.

According to the armistice agreements in these countries, the Allied Control Commissions had the right to approve policy decisions made by each national government, as well as to authorize or veto appointments to particular government posts. The strict reason for this was to make sure that democratic principles were upheld, so that these former enemies could not return to their pro-fascist ways. However, it was up to the ACCs themselves to decide what was 'democratic' and what was not. In Finland and eastern Europe the Soviets routinely abused their powers to ensure that Communist policies were adopted, and that Communist personnel were appointed to key positions in government. The ACC was effectively a wild card that the local Communists could use whenever they found their plans blocked by other politicians.[5]

A perfect example was provided by Hungary in 1945, where the Allied Control Commission of almost a thousand members effectively formed a parallel government. It was the ACC which pressed for an early election that year, because they believed that this would favour the Communists. When, to their surprise, the Smallholders Party won a 57.5 per cent majority, the ACC prevented them from freely choosing how to form their government by backing Communist demands for control of the all-important Interior Ministry. The Soviet-dominated ACC also interceded in land reform, censorship, propaganda and the purging of wartime officials, and even prevented the Hungarian government from forming certain ministries that did not accord with Soviet plans for the country.[6]

Wherever the Communists came to power after the war, their modus operandi followed a common pattern. The most important thing was to get themselves appointed to positions of power. In the aftermath of the war, when coalition governments were first being set up across eastern Europe, they were very often headed by non-Communists. However, the positions of *real* power, such as that of Interior Minister, were almost always given to Communists. The Interior Ministry was what the Hungarian Prime Minister Ferenc Nagy called 'the all-powerful portfolio' – it was the nerve-centre which controlled the police and security forces, issued identity papers including passports and entry/exit visas, and granted licences to newspapers.[7] It was therefore the ministry that exerted the greatest power over both public opinion and people's everyday lives. The use of the Interior Ministry to crush anti-Communist sentiment was not unique to Romania – it happened throughout eastern Europe in the aftermath of the war. In Czechoslovakia, the crisis of February 1948 was directly caused by complaints that the Czech Interior Minister, Václav Nosek, had been using the police force specifically to further the causes of the Communist Party.[8] The Finnish Interior Minister, Yrjö Leino, openly admitted that when the police force was purged 'the new faces were naturally, as far as could be, Communists' – by December 1945 Communists made up between 45 and 60 per cent of the Finnish police force.[9]

Another important governmental post was that of Minister of Justice, who controlled the hiring and firing of judges, as well as the purging of 'fascist elements' from the administration. As I have shown, this was the first ministry that came under Communist control in Romania. It was also a key ministry for the Communist takeover in Bulgaria. From the moment the Fatherland Front seized power in Sofia in September 1944, the Communists used the Justice Ministry in conjunction with the police to purge the entire country of any possible opposition. Within three months some 30,000 Bulgarian officials had been dismissed from their jobs – not only policemen and civil servants, but also priests, doctors and teachers. By the end of the war 'People's Courts', sanctioned by the Justice Ministry, had tried 11,122 individuals and sentenced almost a quarter of them (2,618) to death. Of these, 1,046 executions were actually carried out – but estimates of the unofficial execution toll range from 3,000 to 18,000. As a proportion of the population this was one of the most rapid, comprehensive and brutal 'official' purges of any state in Europe, despite the fact that Bulgaria had never been fully occupied, and had not been involved in any of the wholesale savagery that had engulfed the other countries of the region. The simple reason for this was that, while the intelligentsia in other countries had already been destroyed by the Gestapo or their local equivalents, in Bulgaria the Communists had to do it all themselves.[10]

Other ministries were targeted in other countries, such as the Ministry of Information in Czechoslovakia and the Ministry of Propaganda in Poland, because these controlled the flow of information to the masses. In Czechoslovakia and Hungary, as in Romania, the Ministry of Agriculture was also a highly prized posting, since the Communists immediately recognized the potential of land reform to gain new members. I have already shown how quickly the Communists gained support in southern Italy by championing land reforms. In eastern Europe they were able to go much further: not only did they change the law, but they directly handed out parcels of land confiscated from large estates or evicted German families. They literally bought the support of millions of peasants.

If the Communists sought power on the national stage, they also did the same on a local level – but always with a view to how that power could be manipulated to further their cause nationally. The single most important task of every European government in the aftermath of the war was to keep the economy afloat. This meant keeping the factories and coal mines running, as well as ensuring that goods could be distributed throughout Europe. The Communists therefore aimed to gain a stranglehold on both industry and transport by infiltrating trade unions and workers' committees in factories. In this way the Communist parties were able to organize massive strikes whenever the national leadership needed a 'spontaneous' show of popular support against their rivals in the government. In Czechoslovakia such demonstrations were deliberately used to make the February 1948 coup seem like a genuine revolution. In all the Eastern Bloc countries, as well as in France, Italy and Finland, workers regularly went on strike in the pursuit of overtly political aims: in a continent that was constantly hovering on the brink of starvation, control of the workforce was an extremely powerful tool.

It was this desire to mobilize large groups of people that led to the next major objective of the Communist Party, which was to recruit as many members as possible, as quickly as possible. In the early days following the war none of the Communist parties was particularly fussy about who joined. They recruited thugs and petty criminals, whom they found useful for filling the ranks of their new security organizations. Likewise they recruited members of the previous regime, who were only too happy to do whatever was necessary to avoid prosecution for war crimes. Bankers, businessmen, policemen, politicians and even clergymen hurried to join the Communist Party as the best insurance policy against charges of collaboration: what the French called 'devenir rouge pour se faire blanchir' (to become red in order to whiten oneself).[11] There were also many 'fellow travellers' who joined up simply because they saw which way the wind was blowing. However, even factoring in these people fails to explain fully the rapid expansion of Communist numbers throughout central and southern Europe. When the Soviet tanks were approaching the borders of Romania in 1944 there were only some eighty Communist Party members inside Bucharest, and fewer than 1,000 members in the country as a whole. Four years later membership had reached one million – a thousandfold increase.[12] In Hungary, membership increased from only around 3,000 to half a million in a single year (1945);[13] while in Czechoslovakia the 50,000 Party members of May 1945 increased to 1.4 million within three years.[14] A large proportion of these new members must have been genuinely enthusiastic supporters.

At the same time as broadening their own power base, the Communists worked hard at weakening the power of their opponents. This was achieved partly by maligning rival politicians in the press, which they controlled both through Soviet censorship and through the ever-increasing Communist presence in the media unions. During the February 1948 crisis in Czechoslovakia, for example, Communist control of the radio stations made sure that Klement Gottwald's speeches and calls for mass demonstrations received maximum publicity; by contrast, the other parties' appeals to the country were silenced when union members in the paper mills and print works prevented them even from printing their newspapers.[15] Similar 'spontaneous' censorship by union members occurred in almost every eastern European country.[16]

Aware that it was impossible to discredit all of their opponents at once, the Communist parties of each country started by nibbling round the edges. This was what the Hungarians called 'salami tactics' – removing one's rivals a single slice at a time. Each slice would dispose of a group who could conceivably be accused of collaboration, or indeed any other crime. Some of these people truly were collaborators, but many others were arrested on trumped-up charges, such as the sixteen leaders of Poland's Home Army (arrested in March 1945), the Bulgarian Social Democrat leader, Krustu Pastuhov (arrested in March 1946), or the leader of the Yugoslav Agrarians, Dragoljub Jovanović (October 1947).

Next, the Communists would seek to engineer splits amongst their rivals. They would try to discredit certain factions of other parties, and pressurize their leaders into disowning these factions. Or they would invite rivals to join them in a united 'front', causing rifts between those who trusted the Communists and those who did not. This tactic was especially successful with the Communists' strongest rivals on the left, the Socialists and the Social Democrats. Eventually, having split them time and time again, the Communists would swallow what was left of these parties whole. The Socialists in East Germany, Romania, Hungary, Czechoslovakia, Bulgaria and Poland all came to an end by being officially merged with the Communist parties.

Despite such deft manoeuvres, none of the Communist parties of Europe ever managed to attain enough popularity to win absolute power at the ballot box. Even in Czechoslovakia, where they legitimately won an impressive 38 per cent of the vote in 1946, they were still obliged to govern through compromise with their opponents.[17] In other countries the lack of faith from the voting public often took the Communists by surprise. The heavy defeat at the Budapest municipal elections in October 1945, for example, was considered nothing less than 'a catastrophe', and left their leader Mátyás Rákosi slumped in a chair 'as pale as a corpse'.[18] He had made the mistake of believing his own propaganda reports about Communist popularity.

In the face of such widespread scepticism, the Communists inevitably resorted to force – at first by covert means, and later through the use of open terror. Popular opponents from other parties were threatened, intimidated, or arrested on false charges of 'fascism'. Some died in suspicious circumstances, such as the Czech Foreign Minister, Jan Masaryk, who fell from a window of the Foreign Ministry in March 1948.[19] Others, such as Bulgaria's most powerful opposition politician, the leader of the Bulgarian Agrarian National Union Nikola Petkov, were tried by kangaroo courts and executed. Many, like Hungary's Ferenc Nagy and Romania's Nicolae Rădescu, responded to threats by eventually fleeing to the West. And it was not just the rival leaders who suffered: the full force of state terror was unleashed on anyone who opposed them. In Yugoslavia, for example, the chief of the secret police, Aleksandar Ranković, later admitted that 47 per cent of arrests carried out in 1945 had been unjustified.[20]

During the course of such repression, elections across the region quickly became a sham. 'Undesirable' candidates were simply removed from the electoral lists. Alternative parties were listed together with the Communists in a single 'bloc' so that voters had no proper choice between parties. The electorate itself was directly threatened by gangs of security policemen at polling stations, and by ensuring that voting was not anonymous. When all else failed, the counting of the votes was simply rigged. As a consequence, the Communists and their allies were finally 'voted in' by some frankly improbable margins: 70 per cent in

Bulgaria (October 1946), 70 per cent in Romania (November 1946), 80 per cent in Poland (January 1947), 89 per cent in Czechoslovakia (May 1948), and an absurd 96 per cent in Hungary (May 1949).[21]

As in Romania, it was only once the Communists had gained uncontested control of the government that they finally embarked on their true programme of reform. Until this point their stated policies across most of Europe were always fairly conservative: land reform, vague promises of 'equality' for all, and the punishment of those who had acted badly during the war. From 1948 onwards (and even earlier in Yugoslavia) they began to reveal their more radical objectives, such as the nationalization of businesses, and the collectivization of land, which occurred across the rest of Communist Europe in much the same way as it did in Romania. It was also around this time that they started to justify all their previous actions by enacting empty laws against the people and institutions they had already destroyed.

The final piece of the jigsaw was to embark on the terrifying internal purges that would weed out every potential threat from inside the Party structure itself. In this way the last vestiges of diversity were eliminated. Independent-minded Communists such as Władysław Gomułka in Poland and Lucrețiu Pătrășcanu in Romania were either ousted from power or imprisoned and executed. In the wake of the Soviet–Yugoslav split, former supporters of Tito were arrested, tried and executed: in this way Albania's former Interior Minister, Koçi Xoxe, was eliminated, as was the former head of the Bulgarian Communist Party Traicho Kostov. In the late 1940s and early 1950s the whole of eastern Europe descended into a terrifying purge, where everybody and anybody could find themselves under suspicion. In Hungary alone, a country with a population of less than 9.5 million, some 1.3 million faced tribunals between 1948 and 1953. Almost 700,000 – more than 7 per cent of the entire population – received some kind of official punishment.[22]

It is no coincidence that this is exactly the same process that had overwhelmed Soviet Russia in the decades before the war. Since the opening of the Russian archives in the 1990s it has become increasingly clear that it was the Soviets who were pulling the strings. The evidence for this is now incontrovertible: one need only read the postwar correspondence between Moscow and the future Bulgarian premier Georgi Dimitrov, in which the Soviet Foreign Minister virtually dictates the composition of the Bulgarian cabinet, to see the extent of Soviet meddling in the internal affairs of eastern European countries.[23]

From the moment the Red Army entered eastern Europe, Stalin was determined to make sure that a political system was installed here that mirrored the system in his own country. In a conversation with Tito's deputy Milovan Djilas he famously stated that the Second World War was different from past wars because 'whoever occupies a territory also imposes upon it his own social system. Everyone imposes his own system as far as his army can reach.'[24] The threat of the Red Army was certainly instrumental in ensuring the establishment of communism across the region – but it was the ruthlessness of Communist politicians, Soviet and otherwise, which took the policy all the way to its logical conclusion. Through the use of terror, and a total intolerance for any kind of opposition, they created not only a strategic buffer between the Soviet Union and the West, but a series of replicas of the Soviet Union itself.

27

The Resistance of the 'Forest Brothers'

The Communist takeover of eastern Europe was not a peaceful process. Fighting often broke out between Soviet sympathizers and those who sought to resist them, workers rioted in response to Communist brutality and peasants armed themselves against the new authorities in order to oppose collectivization. In most cases these were fairly spontaneous expressions of popular anger, and were quickly suppressed. Sometimes, however, a more organized form of resistance grew up.

This was particularly the case in those parts of Europe that already knew what it was like to be in thrall to the Soviets. In the Baltic States especially, and in what was to become western Ukraine, nationalist movements sprang up whose members were highly organized, fiercely patriotic, and prepared to fight to the death. Unlike their neighbours to the south they were under no illusions about Stalin's intentions. Having already suffered Soviet occupation at the beginning of the war, they did not regard the immediate postwar years as something new, but rather as the continuation of a process that had begun in 1939 and 1940.

The struggle of the anti-Soviet resistance is one of the most underappreciated conflicts of the twentieth century, particularly in the West. For over ten years hundreds of thousands of nationalist partisans fought a doomed war against their Soviet occupiers in the forlorn hope that the West would eventually come to their aid. This war would last well into the 1950s, and would result in tens of thousands of deaths on all sides.

The greatest resistance occurred in western Ukraine, where the total number of men and women involved in partisan activities between 1944 and 1950 probably reached 400,000.[1] The situation in Ukraine, however, was immensely complicated and involved elements of ethnic cleansing, as I have already shown.

A 'purer' version of anti-Soviet resistance took place in the Baltic States, and particularly in Lithuania, which, according to Swedish intelligence reports, had 'the best organized, trained and disciplined of all the anti-Communist guerrilla groups'.[2] In all three Baltic countries the partisans were collectively known as the 'Forest Brothers'. In the proudly nationalist atmosphere that has predominated since the 1990s their exploits have, quite literally, become legendary.

The Battle of Kalniškės

In the autumn of 1944, after the Red Army had swept through the Baltic States, tens of thousands of Estonians, Latvians and Lithuanians went into hiding. They did not do so lightly. They abandoned homes and belongings, lost touch with family and friends for long periods and frequently went hungry. Some went to live with acquaintances, moving from place to place every couple of weeks, in order both to avoid outstaying their welcome and to avoid detection. The majority fled to the forests, where they often found themselves living without shelter or adequate clothing. The autumn brought rain, which turned many forest areas into virtual swamps; and winter – particularly the first two winters after the war – was extremely cold in this northern part of Europe. Those who were wounded or fell sick rarely had much hope of receiving adequate treatment.

It would be naive to imagine that everyone who subjected themselves to these conditions did so out of mere patriotism. In 1944 their numbers were swelled by local men trying to avoid conscription into the Red Army, along with others whose past political associations gave them reason to fear the Soviets. Later on they were joined by families fleeing deportation, farmers resisting collectivization or new groups of political enemies of the Soviet Union. But at the centre of these people was a strong, organized core who were dedicated to fighting for democracy and the independence of their countries. Many of them were military men of one sort or another: 'good soldiers', in the words of one Lithuanian partisan leader, 'who are not afraid of laying down their lives for the homeland'.[3] This central group supervised the division of people

N

FINLAND   *Gulf of Finland*

Tallinn•   Khotla-Järve•   •Narva

HIIUMAA   •Kautla

                 ESTONIA

                                  Lake Peipsi

SAAREMAA   Pärnu•   RUSSIA
                        •Viljandi   Tartu•
*Baltic
Sea*   *Gulf of   LIVONIA   Pelsen•   •Pskov
                 Riga*

Ventspils•   •Valmiera
                                    •Cēsus   ABRENE
                 Jūrmala• •Riga   LATVIA

•Liepāja   •Ogre   •Madona   LATGALE
                        •Jelgava
                                               •Rēzekne
      •Mažeikiai *Venta*

Klaipéda•   •Siauliai   •Daugavpils
                                    Zarasai•
                 LITHUANIA Panevėžys•

      Jurbarkas *Nemunas* •Kėdainiai
                          •Jonava
                 Kaunas•
                 Šešupe   Vilnius•   BELORUSSIA
                 •Kalniškės •Alytus
                          Varėna•

                                               •Minsk

0   50 miles
|————————————|
0   100 km   Lithuania's gains in territory after the war
                             Latvia's and Estonia's losses in territory
11. The Baltic countries   Forests

into military-style units, the digging of bunkers and construction of forest shelters, the gathering of food and supplies and – most importantly – the organization of partisan operations.

Right from the beginning, these fearless men and women embarked on some very ambitious operations indeed, especially in Lithuania. In the north-east of the country partisan units of 800 men or more fought pitched battles against the Red Army. In the centre, large groups of fighters terrorized Soviet officials, and even conducted attacks on their offices and security buildings in the centre of Kaunas. In the south they set elaborate ambushes for NKVD troops, assassinated Communist leaders and even attacked prisons in order to free their comrades who had been captured.

There is no room here to give anything like a complete list of the battles and skirmishes that were fought in the first twelve months after the Soviets arrived.[4] Instead I will describe just one, which has, over the years, come to symbolize all of the others. The Battle of Kalniškės happened exactly a week after the Second World War had officially come to an end, in a forest in the south of Lithuania. The battle was between a large detachment of NKVD troops from a garrison in the nearby town of Simnas, and a small but determined group of local partisans led by Jonas Neifalta, code named Lakūnas ('Pilot').

Neifalta was an inspirational leader, well known in the region for having resisted both the Nazis and the Soviets. A former army officer, he had been on a Soviet hit list ever since their first occupation of the country in 1940. He had been caught in the summer of 1944, and was wounded by a bullet to the chest, but had managed to escape from the hospital where the Soviets had put him under guard. After recovering at the farm of a relative, he and his wife, Albina, had taken to the forest that autumn. They spent the next six months gathering followers, training them, and conducting hit-and-run operations on local Soviets and their collaborators.

Determined to put a stop to Neifalta's activities once and for all, a large force of NKVD troops marched to the Kalniškės forest on 16 May 1945. They surrounded the area where Neifalta was hiding and gradually began to close in on him. Realizing they were trapped, Neifalta and his followers withdrew to a hill deep in the forest and prepared themselves for battle. They defended themselves heroically, inflicting heavy casualties on the Soviets with small arms and grenades – over 400 of them, according to the partisans themselves (although Soviet forces put the real number at only a fraction of this). After several hours of fighting, however, they began to run out of ammunition. Neifalta realized that their only hope of survival was to try to break through the Soviet cordon. Using the last of their ammunition, two dozen or so managed to burst through the Soviet lines, and escaped to take refuge in the nearby marshes of Žuvintas. They left behind them the bodies of forty-four partisans – more than half their total strength – including Neifalta's wife, who had died with a machine-gun in her hands.

Neifalta himself lived to fight another day, but it did not take long for fate to catch up with him. That November, in a secluded farmstead nearby, he and his comrades were once again surrounded, and Neifalta was killed in the resulting firefight.[5]

When the people of Lithuania remember the anti-Soviet insurgency of the 1940s and 1950s, these are the stories they tell. Such battles have become a symbol of everything the Lithuanians wish to remember about their own bravery and the nobility of their cause.

Looked at objectively, however, the Battle of Kalniškės also demonstrates many of the reasons that such resistance was doomed to failure. To begin with, the Soviets were better supplied than the partisans – it was not *they* who had run out of ammunition. The Soviets also vastly outnumbered the partisans at Kalniškės, as they did in virtually every other battle of the time. While some 100,000 people are thought to have been involved in the Lithuanian resistance between 1944 and 1956 – and Estonia and Latvia boasted another 20,000–40,000 each – this was nothing compared to the millions of soldiers that the Soviets could call on once Germany had been defeated.[6] At a local level this meant that the Soviets could afford to lose dozens or even hundreds of men in a single battle. The partisans could not.

Regardless of how noble or brave we might believe the Lithuanian resistance to have been, their conduct of operations against the Soviets was seriously flawed. While the partisans were very good at hit-and-run raids, they could never hope to match the strength of their enemies during a pitched battle. The Battle of Kalniškės is a perfect example of what happened when such groups were forced to fight on Soviet terms. A much more sensible way to fight would have been to split into small groups, only coming together just before an attack and then dispersing again – and indeed, these were the tactics that the partisans would later switch to. But until the summer of 1945 they insisted on maintaining large groups of fighters in specific locations. As Neifalta learned to his cost, larger groups were much easier to find, and much easier to destroy.

What happened at Kalniškės was symptomatic of what was going on all over the country: the Soviets were seeking out individual groups of partisans and picking them off one by one. The partisans found it very difficult to resist this, because they had no coordinated strategy at a national level. The national bodies who had guided them in the early days were wiped out by the Soviet secret police in the winter of 1944–5, and attempts to reunify the resistance did not materialize again until 1946. Local partisan leaders like Jonas Neifalta therefore tended to be isolated: they had very little contact with leaders in other districts, and fought for purely local objectives. Coordinating their actions with other groups of partisans on a large scale was impossible.

The desperate last stand at Kalniškės was therefore symbolic of all kinds of failings on the part of the resistance: a lack of resources, a high casualty rate, flawed tactics, and an absence of any coherent, nation-wide strategy. The only advantages they had over their attackers were their passion for a cause worth fighting for, and their fanatical courage. Such qualities should not be underestimated, however, especially when it comes to their capacity for inspiring future generations of resisters.

As for Jonas Neifalta himself, he too was symbolic of both the partisans' bravery and their flaws. He inspired his followers by leading from the front, and shared all the same dangers and hardships as his men. This was not a style of leadership that was designed to last very long: Neifalta outlived his fallen comrades at Kalniškės, but only by six months.

The Soviet Terror

The Soviet campaign against the partisans was every bit as efficient, and every bit as ruthless, as their seizure of political power in eastern Europe. It had to be. The Soviets were extremely concerned about both the extent and the determination of the resistance they encountered in Lithuania. In the early days their main priority had to be the war with Germany, and they simply could not allow a partisan war to disrupt supply lines to the front. In 1944 the head of the NKVD, Lavrenti Beria, ordered Lithuania to be cleared of partisans 'within a fortnight', and dispatched one of his most trusted subordinates, General Sergei Kruglov, to tackle them.[7] Amongst the troops Kruglov had at his disposal were the special units who had just finished conducting the mass deportation of the Crimean Tatars to Kazakhstan.

Kruglov was a ruthless but brilliant strategist, who understood instinctively that the partisans could not be defeated by a military approach alone. From the very beginning he involved local Lithuanian militias in as many anti-insurgency operations as possible, specifically in order to give the impression that this was a civil war rather than a war against Soviet occupation. Under his leadership any and all methods were sanctioned, provided they furthered the anti-partisan cause, and his troops embarked on a conscious and deliberate campaign of terror.

One of the cornerstones of Soviet methods was the use of torture. This usually took the form of beating prisoners, a practice that was so common, and so violent, that in one district of Latvia 18 per cent of police suspects were reported to have died during interrogation.[8] Other methods included the administering of electric shocks, burning the skin with cigarettes, slamming doors on prisoners' hands and fingers, and waterboarding. One former partisan suffered the same torture as the hero of George Orwell's *1984*: Eleonora Labanauskienė was locked into a toilet stall the size of a telephone booth, along with fifty rats released from a cage.[9] Such torture was officially frowned upon by the authorities, but in reality it was sanctioned at every level of the Soviet administration. Stalin himself had claimed before the war that the use of torture was 'absolutely correct and useful' because it 'brought results and greatly accelerated the unmasking of enemies of the people'. The Soviet secret police continued to use Stalin's endorsement as an excuse for torture at least until the end of the 1940s.[10]

While torture did provide the authorities with intelligence, it also had other, less welcome, results. All partisan memoirs state with pride that the 'Forest Brothers' would rather die than surrender, and there are numerous stories of partisan units trying to shoot their way out of hopeless situations rather than giving themselves up peacefully. This is not mere myth: Soviet reports also describe the extraordinary determination of partisans in both Ukraine and Lithuania to die fighting. For example, a Lithuanian police report from January 1945 describes how security troops surrounded a house containing twenty-five partisans who refused to surrender even after the house was set on fire. Five of these partisans broke out and crawled across a field towards a machine-gun crew in an attempt to silence it. They were shot one by one, but did not give up advancing until they were all dead. The rest of the group carried on firing from the burning house until it finally collapsed and buried them.[11] Such determination was only partly born of bravery. The certainty that they would be tortured, and perhaps the fear of what they might reveal under interrogation, provided a strong incentive for partisans never to be taken alive.

The use of torture was just one element of a system that was designed to terrorize both the partisans and their support networks amongst the civilian population. Other methods of intimidation included the public hanging of local guerrilla leaders, the deportation of those suspected of links to the resistance, and the display of dead bodies in market squares. In his memoir, Juozas Lukša gives half a dozen examples of dead partisans being propped up in villages, sometimes in obscene poses, as a method of terrorizing the population – even his own brother's body was treated this way. Sometimes the NKVD would force local residents to come and look at the bodies, and their reactions were observed in order to discover where their loyalties lay. 'If they saw people passing by the corpses who revealed sadness or pity, they would go out and arrest them and torture them, demanding that they reveal the names and surnames of the dead men.' There are numerous stories of parents being shown their dead children, and being obliged to show no emotion for fear of betraying themselves.[12]

The price of revealing one's loyalties in situations like this could be high. Zealous security officials thought nothing of targeting the friends and family of known partisans if they thought it might flush the insurgents out into the open. The very least such people could expect was arrest and interrogation, followed by the threat of deportation to Siberia. This was perhaps another reason that partisans were so reluctant to give themselves up during a siege. Many who found themselves surrounded would hold a grenade to their heads and blow themselves up, specifically so that the Soviets would not be able to identify them and so be able to target their families. Occasionally the Soviets would attempt surgical reconstruction, but 'Even a father could not recognize his son under these circumstances.'[13]

Sometimes Soviet security troops would resort to even more brutal methods amongst the general population. The burning of homes and farms was quite widespread in Lithuania as a method of punishing suspected partisans and terrorizing their communities. Eventually the practice was banned by the chief of the security troops himself, but it seems that his main objections were not on the grounds that the practice was unlawful, but because he suspected that some troops were targeting innocent civilians as a way to avoid fighting the real partisans.[14] An internal investigation revealed that it was not only the buildings that were being burned down – sometimes civilians were burned at the same time. For example, on 1 August 1945 an NKVD unit commanded by a Lieutenant Lipin set fire to a house in the village of Švendriai near Šiauliai. According to one of the other soldiers present, the family who owned the house were inside at the time:

> Private Janin set the house on fire from the outside. When an old woman, crossing herself, came out of the house, followed by a girl, Lipin told them to go back. Then the old woman and the girl started to run. Lipin took out his pistol and began shooting at each of them but missed. One soldier shot down the old woman, while Lipin ran after the girl and shot her at close range. Then he ordered two soldiers to take the bodies and to throw them through the window into the house. The soldiers took the old woman by the hands and feet and threw her into the burning house, then did the same with the corpse of the girl. Soon an old man and the elder son ran out of the house through another door. Soldiers opened fire but could not get them. Then I and two other soldiers were ordered to catch and kill the son, but we failed as it was dark and he escaped. On returning to the house we started combing the rye field. We found the old man there, he was wounded and was crawling through the rye. One of the soldiers finished him off and we brought the corpse to the house . . .

The next morning, the soldiers returned to the burned-out house to fetch the body of the old man as proof that they had eliminated a group of 'bandits'. Inside the house they saw the corpse of a teenager who had been burned alive. Not wishing to pick up the burned bodies, they instead stole a pig and two sheep belonging to the family and returned to their posts.[15]

There are also, of course, numerous examples of *partisans* being burned alive inside houses when they refused to give themselves up, but testimonies like this are proof that the practice was more indiscriminate than even the Soviets were prepared to sanction. The problem with random terror was that it drove people to join the resistance, both through sheer disgust at the things they were forced to witness and through fear that they themselves might end up being the security troops' next victims. It also stiffened the resolve of the partisans, and gave them a cause truly worth fighting for. Soviet doctrine advocated a much more targeted form of terror, to be directed exclusively at those who could be proven to support the resistance: everyone else should be made to feel relatively safe as long as they shunned the partisans at all costs. However, official policy was never properly enforced, and sadistic local officers often got away with perpetrating random acts of terror for years.

As the partisan war progressed, Soviet anti-insurgent methods became much more sophisticated. In 1946, whole bands of pseudo-partisans were set up to help catch the real ones. Such groups would pretend to be guerrillas from another region and, having arranged a meeting with the real partisans, would kill them all, along with any witnesses. They also murdered and robbed civilians in the name of the partisans, thereby giving the whole movement a bad name.[16]

As well as creating bands of false partisans, the Soviets developed methods of inserting their own agents into real partisan cells. Sometimes they would use Communists, or Baltic expats who had been living in the Soviet Union during the war, but more often they would attempt to recruit former members of the resistance to turn against their ex-comrades. Their biggest pool of recruits came from the amnesties in 1945 and 1946. According to the terms of these amnesties, partisans would be granted immunity from prosecution if they agreed to renounce their ways and hand in at least one weapon. In practice, however, the security apparatus threatened such people with deportation unless they also agreed to provide intelligence on their comrades, and even rejoin partisan groups as NKVD agents. Faced with these two equally unpalatable alternatives, the majority did the only thing they could do: they agreed to work for the security forces, but then did nothing. Some, however, succumbed to pressure and began to betray their former friends.

Perhaps the greatest success of the Soviet spies was the infiltration of the central organizing body of the Lithuanian resistance. In the spring of 1945 the security service had recruited a doctor named Juozas Markulis, who became one of their most valuable agents. Over the following months Markulis managed to convince the partisans that he headed an underground intelligence group, and became so trusted that when the partisans attempted to create a new overarching underground organization, the General Democratic Resistance Movement (Bendras demokratinis pasipriešinimo sąjūdis, or BDPS), he was elected as one of the top leaders. The police gained a certain amount of control over this committee through Markulis, who used his position to encourage partisans to demobilize and put their weapons away. Promising to make the men fake documents, he succeeded in getting hold of lists of partisan members and even photographs. Through these and other activities, several regional leaders were arrested, killed and, in the case of one region in the east of the country, replaced by one of Markulis's fellow agents.[17]

By the beginning of the 1950s the Soviets had set up specialist groups devoted to finding and monitoring partisan cells in specific localities. These groups were dedicated to building up a complete picture of the partisans they hunted – their names and code names, behaviour, methods of camouflage and signalling, their supporters and their contacts within other groups – before moving in and eliminating them.[18] As partisan numbers began to dwindle, and their support amongst the general population drained away, there was little that the resistance could do to protect themselves against these groups. One by one the last remnants of the partisans were hunted down and destroyed.

Partisans or 'Bandits'?

In his history of the Estonian partisans, the former Prime Minister of Estonia Mart Laar tells the story of Ants Kaljurand, a legendary figure in the resistance who became known as 'Ants the Terrible'. According to the story, Ants had a habit of announcing his arrival in any particular area by mail. On one occasion he notified the manager of a restaurant in Pärnu that he would be coming to lunch on a certain day, at a certain time, and that he was expecting a particularly tasty meal. The restaurant manager promptly informed the local authorities. When the day arrived hordes of plain-clothed NKVD men surrounded the restaurant, ready to leap out and capture the famed partisan leader. But Ants fooled them all by arriving in a Russian car marked with Russian army tags, and by dressing in the uniform of a high-ranking Soviet officer. Unsuspecting, the NKVD men left him alone. After enjoying a hearty meal, Ants left a generous tip and put a note under his plate reading 'Thank you very much for the lunch, Ants the Terrible.' By the time the NKVD men realized what had happened, he and his stolen Russian car were long gone.[19]

Stories like this demonstrate one of the major problems with getting to grips with what happened during the partisan war in the Baltic countries. It is plainly unthinkable that any partisan leader would make a habit of announcing his arrival to strangers by mail, or that he would risk such stunts purely for the sake of a meal – and yet such stories are recounted again and again as if they are true. The Lithuanian partisan Juozas Lukša recognized the importance of such mythology to inspire the people, but acknowledged that much of it was nonsense: 'People sympathized with the partisans,' he wrote in 1949; 'therefore, tales of their heroic deeds were often exaggerated to the extent that only a skeleton of the truth remained.'[20]

Given our present-day sympathy for all those who struggled against Soviet repression, it is easy to fall into the trap of hero worship. But however much we might like to imagine the partisans as Robin Hood figures, the majority of them did not fit this romantic image at all. Most joined the resistance not out of bravery but to avoid arrest, or deportation or being drafted into the Red Army. And they only remained in the forests while the benefits outweighed the risks: the vast majority of partisans returned to civilian life within two years.[21]

While most partisans chose to resist out of a sense of nationalism, there were many who hid from the Soviets merely because they had collaborated with the Germans in one way or another, and wanted to avoid punishment. Some had been heavily involved in anti-Semitic pogroms and massacres during the war. The Ukrainian partisan movement in particular was founded on a violently racist ideology – but in the Baltic States, too, there was a dark history to some partisan units. The 'Iron Wolf' regiment in Lithuania, for example, had started out as a fascist organization during the war. While the racist basis of the group had declined substantially by the summer of 1945, there were still anti-Semitic elements to the stories they told.[22] It is perhaps unsurprising that some figures in the West were suspicious of their motives. In Britain, for example, the Archbishop of Canterbury made a speech suggesting that the Baltic partisans were fascists whose deportation was justified. While his comments were certainly misguided, they contained enough truth for some of the mud to stick.[23]

Even more problematic for the partisans was the Soviet assertion that they were not freedom fighters, but mere 'bandits'. It was easy to refute such claims while they were engaging in pitched battles against Soviet army units – but it was much more difficult once they were obliged to direct their efforts against civilian targets. As I have shown, the partisans in Lithuania suffered such heavy losses in the early days that they were forced to change their tactics. From the summer of 1945 onwards, the vast majority of people they killed were civilians – mostly Communist officials and those who collaborated openly with the Soviets. The same pattern occurred in western Ukraine – and in Latvia and Estonia, where the resistance was never strong enough to openly challenge Soviet forces, civilian collaborators were the main target from the very beginning. Innocent people inevitably got killed, and goodwill towards the partisans began to drain away.

Table 3: Total deaths inflicted by the partisans, 1944–6[24]

Year	Category targeted	Western Ukraine	Lithuania	Latvia	Estonia	Western Belarus	Total
1944	Soviet forces*	3,202	413	No data	10	251	3,876
	Civilians	2,953	262	–	57	76	3,348
1945	Soviet forces*	2,539	1,614	509	175	332	5,169
	Civilians	4,249	1,630	262	141	296	6,578
1946	Soviet forces*	1,441	967	231	129	116	2,884
	Civilians	1,688	2,037	177	125	135	4,162

Note: *'Soviet forces' includes members of the Red Army, NKVD troops, police, militia, and local Soviet activists.

The partisans were therefore forced to walk a fine line. In order to succeed they had to portray themselves as an alternative authority to the new government, capable of enforcing their own will upon the people. And yet this had to be done without alienating those people. On the one hand they were obliged to punish anyone who collaborated too enthusiastically with the Soviets, but on the other hand they had to acknowledge that many of these local officials did not have any choice but to collaborate. In areas where they were strong they were able, for a time at least, to impose their own form of law and order on the countryside. In areas where they were weak, however, their only course lay in disrupting law and order. Amongst a population that was tired out from years of chaos and bloodshed, it became increasingly difficult to maintain support.

Like their Soviet counterparts, the partisans sometimes resorted to terror in order to impose their will. Sometimes this terror was simply the result of anger, frustration, or the heat of battle. In the Estonian town of Osula, for example, in March 1946, partisans launched an attack on the local 'destruction battalion', or Estonian volunteer militia. The attack was partly an attempt by the resistance to stamp their authority on the local area, but also an act of revenge for certain militia atrocities. Partisan leaders drew up a list of guilty officials and imprisoned them in the local pharmacy pending execution. According to the testimony of witnesses, the partisan operation soon degenerated into something of a frenzy:

> The Forest Brothers set about killing the others according to their list. Soon they realized that the list didn't include all the ones they wanted. Some of the men had gotten crazed with killing, and they started shooting women and children who were not on the list. The entire families of some authorities who had caused exceptional suffering to a few Forest Brothers were wiped out. For a while, the women succeeded in stopping the bloodshed. In one instance, they drove the partisans away from the wife of the destruction battalion commander, saying that a pregnant woman should not be killed.[25]

A total of thirteen people are reputed to have been executed that day before the partisans dispersed and headed back into hiding.

On other occasions there were colder, more political reasons for terrorizing individual communities. For example, in an apparent attempt to bring a halt to the Soviet land reforms, partisans in Lithuania occasionally attacked peasants who had been granted land confiscated from larger estates. According to Soviet reports from Alytus province, some thirty-one families were attacked by partisans in August 1945 for this reason, and forty-eight people killed:

Among the killed were 11 persons from 60 to 70 years old, 7 children from 7 to 14 years old and 6 girls from 17 to 20 years old. All victims were poor farmers who had received land [confiscated] from kulaks . . . None of the killed worked for party or other administrative agencies.[26]

In later years, when farms were being forcibly collectivized, the partisans resorted to burning crops, destroying the communal farm machinery and killing livestock. However, since these collective farms were still expected to provide their quotas for government warehouses, the only people to suffer were often the farmers themselves. In order to gather supplies during this time the partisans often had no choice but to break into communal stores. Since these stores now belonged to the community as a whole, it was the community as a whole that suffered. According to some historians, as the years went by the actions of the partisans began to look less like resistance and more like social obstructionism.[27]

Many people also began to question what the continued violence and chaos was supposed to achieve. It had become increasingly obvious that the partisans were fighting a lost cause, and most civilians simply wanted the violence to stop. Forced reluctantly into taking sides, many now sacrificed their nationalist ideals for the sake of stability. Informing on resistance groups became much more common towards the end of the 1940s, not only by paid informers and former partisans who had been coerced into changing sides, but by ordinary members of the public. By 1948, the majority of arrests and killings of partisans – more than seven out of ten – came as a result of intelligence. In other words, they were betrayed.[28]

The End of the Resistance

One of the greatest mistakes of the Baltic partisans was to imagine that the war they were fighting was predominantly a military one. In reality they were being attacked on several fronts at once – not only militarily, but also economically, socially and politically. The Soviets understood from the outset how much the guerrillas relied on their local, rural communities for support. They therefore set about dismantling these communities with a ruthlessness that left the fighters reeling.

The first blow came in the immediate aftermath of the war, when the Communists embarked on the same programme of land reform that they were practising elsewhere in Europe. This was an issue that genuinely divided the population, with the poor and the landless naturally much more in favour of it than those who would be forced to give up parts of their property. Middle-class farmers were much more likely to join the partisans than the poorer peasants – this created an embryo of a class struggle, and allowed the authorities to portray the partisans as reactionaries.[29] This might seem like a subtle point, but it was an important political victory for the Communists, who could claim that they were the champions of the poor. Combined with other political scoops, such as the award of Vilnius to Lithuania – a city that they had always claimed, but never controlled – it meant that not everyone was quite so willing to support the partisans as some nationalists in the Baltic States would have it.

The second blow came in the late 1940s, when the Soviets once again resorted to the policy of deportation of their political enemies. Between 22 and 27 May 1948, over 40,000 people were deported from Lithuania; the following March a further 29,000 joined them.[30] In Latvia, the deportation of 43,000 people to Siberia effectively ended the hopes of the resistance.[31] While in the short term these events swelled the numbers of people willing to flee to the forest and join the partisans, it destroyed their support networks amongst the general population. From this point on, the partisans could no longer rely on their communities to provide them with food and other supplies. Instead they were forced to go out and requisition what they needed, thereby alerting the authorities to their presence.

The final blow to the partisan supply lines was the policy of collectivization of land, which effectively took agriculture out of the hands of individuals altogether. Once all farms were owned or controlled by the state, there were no longer any sympathetic individual farmers for the partisans to rely on. Collectivization in the Baltic States was even more rapid than in other countries in the Communist bloc. At the beginning of 1949 only 3.9 per cent of Lithuanian farms were collectivized, only 5.8 per cent of Estonian farms, and only about 8 per cent of Latvian farms. When the policy of collectivization was formally announced, many farmers resisted, but after large numbers of them were punished with deportation the remainder hurried to comply with the new ruling.

By the end of the year 62 per cent of Lithuanian farms had been put under state control. In Estonia and Latvia, where the partisans were not so strong, and resistance less organized, the figures were 80 per cent and 93 per cent, respectively.[32]

With their homegrown support networks destroyed, the only possible salvation for the partisan cause was to get help from the West.[33] In desperation they dispatched envoys westwards to drum up support. The best known of these was the Lithuanian partisan Juozas Lukša, who travelled on foot across the border with Poland, and finally ended up in Paris in early 1948. He carried with him letters to the Pope and to the United Nations describing the brutal deportations that were taking place in his country. But his attempts to win the West over to his cause came to nothing. Apart from a few half-hearted efforts by Western intelligence agencies, the Baltic partisans were largely left to fend for themselves.[34]

In 1950, when Lukša returned to Lithuania, the struggle had turned into a lost cause. The hordes of active partisans who had filled the forests between 1944 and 1947 – numbering up to 40,000 at their peak – had now fallen to just a couple of thousand. By the summer of 1952 there were probably only 500 left.[35] Lukša's return was treated as a major event by the Soviets. He was hunted down by literally thousands of NKVD troops, who combed the forests of Punia and Kazlų Rūda in search of him. In the end he was betrayed by someone he thought was a friend, lured into an ambush and shot.[36] One by one, the same fate befell every other partisan leader in Lithuania. By 1956, twelve years after their struggle had begun, the last of the partisan groups in Lithuania was finally destroyed.[37]

Nations of Martyrs

Despite the terrifying efficiency of the Soviet security forces, the partisan cause was never entirely defeated. Even after the capture in 1956 of the last great partisan leader, Adolfas Ramanauskas – code-named Vanagas ('Hawk') – some forty-five partisans remained at large in the forests of Lithuania. As late as 1965 two Lithuanian guerrillas were surrounded by police: they shot themselves in order to avoid being taken prisoner. The last Lithuanian partisan, Stasys Guiga, was sheltered by a village woman for over thirty years, and managed to evade capture until his death in 1986.[38]

In Estonia two brothers, Hugo and Aksel Mõttus, were finally caught by the police in 1967. They had lived for twenty years in cold, damp forest bunkers, during which time they lost their father, their brother and their sister to hunger and sickness. They buried each of them in the forest. In the summer of 1974, the Soviet authorities shot the partisan Kalev Arro, whom they had stumbled upon in a village in Võrumaa. But the last Estonian partisan was not killed until four years later, in September 1978, when the KGB tried to arrest August Sabbe. Sabbe tried to escape from them by leaping into the Võhandu river, but drowned.[39]

During the height of the Cold War, when the Baltic States were firmly under the Soviet thumb, it was impossible to avoid the conclusion that such men had wasted their lives. Like those forgotten Japanese soldiers who continued to hold out on remote Pacific islands until the 1970s, or the lonely figure of Manuel Cortés, a Spanish republican who hid from Franco until 1969, these last partisans had continued fighting a war long after the rest of the world had moved on.[40] They had gambled on a new conflict starting up between America and the USSR, and paid the price for this misjudgement with their own lives and the imprisonment and deportation of their loved ones. For all their courage and patriotism, their resistance to Soviet authority ultimately seemed to have made no difference.[41]

And yet one cannot deny the influence that the partisan war had on later resistance movements. The Soviet handling of the partisans and their families, while brutally effective in the short term, served only to create a huge pool of people who were permanently disaffected. It was these people, who were excluded from normal participation in society, and whose children were denied proper jobs and access to higher education, who would later become some of the most active members of the Baltic dissident movement.[42]

Through the 1960s, 70s and 80s the people of the Baltic States continued to resist Soviet repression, and while they never again took up arms against the Soviets, they were still inspired by the memory of the partisan wars. Partisan stories were told and retold; partisan songs were sung in private, a practice later mirrored in the 'singing revolution' in Tallinn. Partisan memoirs were reproduced and distributed throughout the region, such as Juozas Lukša's *Partizanai*,[43] which would become a

runaway bestseller in Lithuania shortly after its declaration of independence in 1990. The partisan war so inspired one of Estonia's first
post-Soviet prime ministers that he too later wrote a book about it.[44]

The story of the Battle of Kalniškės, which I recounted at the beginning of this chapter, is a perfect example of how the partisan war
inspired later generations, and continues to do so. In the years after the
battle, the story passed into local folklore, and songs were written to
commemorate the heroic last stand. Far from fading with time, the story
actually gathered resonance. In the 1980s, former partisans returned
and created a shrine to their fallen comrades, and ceremonies of remembrance were conducted on the battle's anniversary. In 1989 this became
a new source of tension with the Soviets. Soldiers stationed at the nearby
Soviet garrison deliberately held practice firing sessions during the anniversary, and fired over the heads of the people gathered there. Later,
during the night, soldiers tore down the shrine. After independence,
however, a new monument was created, and the bodies of the partisans
killed at Kalniškės were exhumed and given a proper burial. Today the
battle is still commemorated in an annual ceremony attended by former
partisans and their families, representatives of the Lithuanian government and army as well as local politicians and schoolchildren. The event
has come to symbolize not only the heroism of Lithuania's partisans,
but the wider struggle for Lithuanian independence that lasted almost
half a century.[45]

It is not so easy, now, to dismiss the struggle of the Forest Brothers as
a pointless sacrifice. Their doomed uprising is no longer only a self-
contained story with a tragic ending – since the early 1990s it has also
become part of a much longer story that ends with the independence of
all three Baltic States. In this context, the sacrifices made by the partisans and their communities have been at least partially vindicated.
Despite the tens of thousands of deaths on all sides, the lives wasted in
exile and the lives spent in hiding, the people of Lithuania, Latvia and
Estonia now look back on the deeds of the Forest Brothers as a worthwhile cause, and a source of national pride.

28

The Cold War Mirror

On 29 January 1948, as part of a mass programme of political suppression, a sixteen-year-old girl – who is still alive today but who wishes to remain anonymous – was arrested with her mother and sent into exile. After spending a year in a distant prison camp, she was transferred to a place called the 'Special School for the Reeducation of Women'. Here, and in a subsequent prison camp, she was subjected to a brutal regime of indoctrination and torture until she eventually agreed to sign a declaration of repentance from her previous political beliefs. 'That was one of the most tragic moments of my life,' she told an interviewer decades later. 'For one month I didn't get out of bed . . . My nightgown was pink and it turned black. I did not even want to wash myself or change my clothes. I suffered a mental breakdown.'[1]

These events did not take place behind the Iron Curtain, but in Greece. The prison camps were not in Kazakhstan or Siberia, but in the Aegean Sea, on the islands of Ikaria, Trikeri and Makronisos – places dedicated not to Communist persecution but to the persecution of Communists. The girl in question was from a family known to have left-wing views, and as such was considered a danger to the Greek state.

There is an unpleasant symmetry between the way Communists were treated in some parts of western Europe and the way 'capitalists' were treated in the east. The mass arrests carried out by the Greek authorities in the aftermath of the Second World War were not dissimilar to the mass arrests that occurred in the Baltic States and western Ukraine, and were conducted for the same reasons – to break the back of the resistance. Greece, like many countries on the western side of the Iron Curtain, also deported tens of thousands of political suspects abroad – to the Middle East, care of the British, rather than to Siberia care of the

Soviets. Government-backed militias subjected large sections of the population to waves of rape, looting and murder that were every bit as random and brutal as anything that happened in eastern Europe.

There are also parallels between the way in which the right seized power in Greece and the way the left seized power in the Eastern Bloc. Right-wing conservatives were not the dominant force in Greek politics, and yet they managed to sideline the much more popular Communists – just as the powerful traditional parties were sidelined in Hungary, Romania and Bulgaria. The deliberate infiltration of the police for political gain was just as cynical on both sides. In Greece this led the Communists to resign from the cabinet in protest as early as December 1944 – an event which found its mirror image just over three years later when the traditional parties resigned from the Czech cabinet over the same issue. The Greek right, like the Communists in eastern Europe, used both the media and the courts to demonize and punish their political opponents. Neither were they above sabotaging the democratic process. The Greek elections in March 1946 were marred by abstentions and intimidation of the electorate, just as the elections in the Baltic States were; and the referendum on restoring the Greek monarchy later the same year was every bit as rigged as the elections in Romania.

In each case such behaviour was possible only because the dominant authority had the backing of a foreign superpower. Behind the Iron Curtain it was the Soviet Union who dictated the actions of the Communists, while in Greece it was the British, and later the Americans, who guaranteed the actions of the right. Without the intervention of outsiders it is difficult to see how the Communists would ever have gained power in most of eastern Europe – just as it is difficult to see how they could have failed to gain power in Greece. Little wonder that the people of both regions felt bitter about the meddling of foreigners. If the Romanians and Poles protested that they were being ensnared by 'foreigners without God or country', so too could some Greeks legitimately bemoan their 'enslavement . . . by foreign imperialists'.[2]

It was not only in Greece that the behaviour of the 'democratic' government mirrored the behaviour of the Communist governments of eastern Europe. The trend for sidelining and demonizing political opponents was the same across the continent, even if it was not quite so extreme as it was in Greece. For example, the ejection of Communists

12. The division of Europe in the Cold War

Legend:
- States which became Communist between 1945 and 1948
- Yugoslav gains from Italy, 1945
- The 'Iron Curtain'
- Germany since 1945

N

North Sea

SWEDEN
FINLAND

NORWAY
Helsinki
Lake Ladoga
Oslo
Stockholm
Tallinn
Leningrad
ESTONIA

DENMARK
Riga
LATVIA
Moscow
Copenhagen
Baltic Sea
LITHUANIA
Vilnius
SOVIET UNION
Kaliningrad
Minsk
HOLLAND
Gdansk
BELARUS
Amsterdam
Szczecin
EAST
Berlin
POLAND
Brussels
GERMANY
Warsaw
BELGIUM
Bonn
Wrocław
Kiev
LUX.
WEST
Prague
Kraków
Lwów
UKRAINE
FRANCE
GERMANY
CZECHOSLOVAKIA
Bratislava
MOLDOVA
Bern
Vienna
Budapest
SWITZ.
AUSTRIA
HUNGARY
ROMANIA
Bucharest
Black Sea
Belgrade
YUGOSLAVIA
BULGARIA
ITALY
Sofia
Istanbul
Rome
Tirana
ALBANIA
GREECE
TURKEY
Mediterranean Sea
Athens

0   200 miles
0   200 km

from the governments of Italy, France, Belgium and Luxembourg in 1947 mirrored the ejection of traditional politicians from the eastern European governments. The consequences for democracy may not have been quite so disastrous, but the intentions were the same: to neutralize the opposition, and to curry favour with a superpower sponsor. It was these superpowers who held all the important cards, and their influence was just as strong in both halves of Europe. American attempts to direct policy in the West were just as meddlesome as Soviet attempts to control governments in the East. It was only the methods that were different: America used the 'carrot' of Marshall Aid while the Soviets used the 'stick' of military coercion.

I do not want to carry this comparison too far, because the capitalist model of politics was self-evidently more inclusive, more democratic and ultimately more successful than Stalinist communism. But it is also true to say that the conduct of those 'democratic' countries in the aftermath of the war was often far from perfect. In some instances it was demonstrably worse than the Communists' – the treatment of peasants in the south of Italy, for example, who were denied the land reforms they had been promised by government, compares badly with the progressive attitude in eastern Europe during the early days of Communist rule. Neither side had a monopoly on virtue. In a continent as large and diverse as Europe, it is always unwise to generalize.

And yet, at the time, such generalization was increasingly apparent. Ideologues from the left characterized everyone who did not share their world view as 'fascist imperialists', 'reactionaries' and 'bloodsuckers'. Ideologues from the right portrayed anyone with even moderately left-wing views as 'Bolsheviks' or 'terrorists'. As a consequence, those in the middle were increasingly forced to take one side or the other – generally whichever side appeared strongest at the time. In the words of one of the fathers of international communism, 'one either leans to the side of imperialism or to the side of socialism. Neutrality is mere camouflage and a third road does not exist.'[3] The consequences of picking the wrong side, particularly in eastern Europe or Greece, could be fatal.

As I have shown, this conflict of ideologies was not new to the post-war period. Leftist partisans and rightist militias had regularly fought each other while the main war was still in progress, and sometimes even agreed local ceasefires with the Germans in order to concentrate more fully on fighting each other. Local civil wars ran alongside the main war not only in Greece but in Yugoslavia, Italy, France, Slovakia and Ukraine. For fanatics on both sides, what really mattered was not so much the national war against German occupation, but the more deep-rooted struggle between those with nationalist ideals and those with Communist ones.

In this ideological struggle between right and left, the defeat of Germany in 1945 was significant only because it removed the most powerful sponsor of the right in Europe. It did not mean that the ideological war was over. Far from it: for many Communists the Second World War was not a discrete event, but merely a staging post in a much larger process that had already lasted decades. The defeat of Hitler was not an end in itself, but a springboard from which the next stage of the struggle would be launched. The Communist seizure of control throughout eastern Europe came to be viewed as part of the same process, which would end, according to Marxist doctrine, with the 'inevitable' victory of communism throughout the world.

It was only the presence of the Western Allies, and especially the Americans, that prevented communism from spreading still further across Europe. It is no wonder, therefore, that Communists in the postwar years portrayed the Americans as imperialist conspirators, just as they demonized the bourgeois opposition in Hungary or Romania as 'Hitlero-fascists'. In the Communist mind there was no fundamental difference between dictators such as Hitler and more democratic figures such as President Truman, Imre Nagy or Iuliu Maniu – all were representatives of an international system that exploited workers, and tried continually to stamp out socialism.

As for the Americans, they soon found themselves being dragged towards the opposite pole. The war against communism was not something that they had planned on entering, but by becoming involved in the Second World War they also necessarily became embroiled in the larger political process of right against left. In their policing of Europe during the aftermath of the war they inevitably found themselves bogged down in the numerous local conflicts that broke out between the two factions – and in each case they instinctively took the side of the right, even in those instances where it meant standing behind a brutal dictatorship, such as in Greece. With time, and experience, they too began to demonize their opponents, and by the 1950s the measured approach of Americans like Dean Acheson or George C. Marshall had given way to the violent rhetoric epitomized by Senator Joe McCarthy. McCarthy's portrayal of American Communists as 'a conspiracy on a scale so immense as to dwarf any previous such venture in the history of man' was every bit as irrational as eastern Europe's anti-Americanism.[4]

It was the polarization of Europe, and ultimately the whole world, into these two camps that was to become the defining characteristic of the second half of the twentieth century. The Cold War was unlike any conflict that had ever been waged before. In its scale it was just as vast as either of the two world wars, and yet it was not fought predominantly with guns and tanks, but through the hearts and minds of civilians. To win these hearts and minds, both sides proved willing to employ whatever means were necessary, from the manipulation of the media to the threat of violence or even the incarceration of young Greek girls in political prison camps.

For Europe, and for Europeans, this new war would simultaneously show the importance and the impotence of the continent on the world stage. As in both of the global wars of the previous thirty years, Europe was still the main theatre of conflict. But for the first time in their history, Europeans would not be the ones pulling the strings: from now on they would be mere pawns in the hands of superpowers outside the borders of their own continent.

Conclusion

In his memoirs of the late 1940s and 50s, published after his death following the famous 'umbrella assassination' in London in 1978, the
Bulgarian dissident writer Georgi Markov told a story that is emblem-
atic of the postwar period – not only in his own country, but in Europe
as a whole. It involved a conversation between one of his friends, who
had been arrested for challenging a Communist official who had jumped
the bread queue, and an officer of the Bulgarian Communist militia:

> 'And now tell me who your enemies are?' the militia chief demanded.
>
> K. thought for a while and replied: 'I don't really know, I don't think I
> have any enemies.'
>
> 'No enemies!' The chief raised his voice. 'Do you mean to say that you
> hate nobody and nobody hates you?'
>
> 'As far as I know, nobody.'
>
> 'You are lying,' shouted the Lieutenant-Colonel suddenly, rising from
> his chair. 'What kind of a man are you not to have any enemies? You clearly
> do not belong to *our* youth, you cannot be one of *our* citizens, if you have
> no enemies! . . . And if you really do not know how to hate, we shall teach
> you! We shall teach you very quickly!'[1]

In a sense, the militia chief in this story is right – it was virtually impossible to emerge from the Second World War without enemies. There can
hardly be a better demonstration than this of the moral and human legacy of the war. After the desolation of entire regions; after the butchery
of over 35 million people; after countless massacres in the name of
nationality, race, religion, class or personal prejudice, virtually every person on the continent had suffered some kind of loss or injustice. Even
countries which had seen little direct fighting, such as Bulgaria, had been

subject to political turmoil, violent squabbles with their neighbours, coercion from the Nazis and eventually invasion by one of the world's new superpowers. Amidst all these events, to hate one's rivals had become entirely natural. Indeed, the leaders and propagandists of all sides had spent six long years promoting hatred as an essential weapon in the quest for victory. By the time this Bulgarian militia chief was terrorizing young students at Sofia University, hatred was no longer a mere by-product of the war – in the Communist mindset it had been elevated to a duty.

There were many, many reasons not to love one's neighbour in the aftermath of the war. He might be a German, in which case he would be reviled by almost everyone, or he might have collaborated with Germans, which was just as bad: most of the vengeance in the aftermath of the war was directed at these two groups. He might worship the wrong god – a Catholic god or an Orthodox one, a Muslim god, or a Jewish god, or no god at all. He might belong to the wrong race or nationality: Croats had massacred Serbs during the war, Ukrainians had killed Poles, Hungarians had suppressed Slovaks, and almost everyone had persecuted Jews. He might have the wrong political beliefs: both Fascists and Communists had been responsible for countless atrocities across the continent, and both Fascists and Communists had themselves been subjected to brutal repression – as indeed had those subscribing to virtually every shade of political ideology between these two extremes.

The sheer variety of grievances that existed in 1945 demonstrates not only how universal the war had been, but also how inadequate is our traditional way of understanding it. It is not enough to portray the war as a simple conflict between the Axis and the Allies over territory. Some of the worst atrocities in the war had nothing to do with territory, but with race or nationality. The Nazis did not attack the Soviet Union merely for the sake of *Lebensraum*: it was also an expression of their urge to assert the superiority of the German race over Jews, Gypsies and Slavs. The Soviets did not invade Poland and the Baltic States only for the sake of territory either: they wanted to propagate communism as far westwards as they were able. Some of the most vicious fighting was not between the Axis and the Allies at all, but between local people who took the opportunity of the wider war to give vent to much older frustrations. The Croat Ustashas fought for the sake of ethnic purity. The Slovaks, Ukrainians and Lithuanians fought for national liberation. Many Greeks and Yugoslavs fought for the abolition of the monarchy

– or for its restoration. Many Italians fought to free themselves from the shackles of a medieval feudalism. The Second World War was therefore not only a traditional conflict for territory: it was simultaneously a war of race, and a war of ideology, and was interlaced with half a dozen civil wars fought for purely local reasons.

Given that the Germans were only one ingredient in this vast soup of different conflicts, it stands to reason that their defeat did not bring an end to the violence. In fact, the traditional view that the war came to an end when Germany finally surrendered in May 1945 is entirely misleading: in reality, their capitulation only brought an end to one aspect of the fighting. The related conflicts over race, nationality and politics continued for weeks, months and sometimes years afterwards. Gangs of Italians were still lynching Fascists late into the 1940s. Greek Communists and Nationalists, who first fought one another as opponents or collaborators with Germany, were still at each other's throats in 1949. The Ukrainian and Lithuanian partisan movements, born at the height of the war, were still fighting well into the mid-1950s. The Second World War was like a vast supertanker ploughing through the waters of Europe: it had such huge momentum that, while the engines might have been reversed in May 1945, its turbulent course was not finally brought to a halt until several years later.

The hatred demanded by the Bulgarian militia chief in Georgi Markov's story was of a very specific kind. It was the same hatred that Soviet propagandists like Ilya Ehrenburg and Mikhail Sholokhov demanded during the war, and that political commissars tried to promote amongst the army units in eastern Europe throughout the period. If the student he was terrorizing had had any knowledge of Stalinist theory – something that would become a central part of every Bulgarian student's education in the years to come – he would have known precisely who his enemies were.

The angry, resentful atmosphere that pervaded throughout Europe in the aftermath of the war was the perfect environment for stirring up revolution. Violent and chaotic as it was, the Communists did not see this atmosphere as a curse but as an opportunity. Before 1939 there had always been tensions between capitalists and workers, lords and peasants, rulers and subjects – but they had usually been local, short-lived affairs. The war, with its years of bloodshed and privation, had inflamed these tensions beyond anything that the prewar Communists could have imagined. Large sections of the population now blamed their old governments for dragging them over the abyss into war. They despised businessmen and politicians for collaborating with their enemies. And, when much of Europe was on the brink of starvation, they hated anyone who appeared to have come out of the war better off than them. If workers had been exploited before the war, then during the war that exploitation had reached its utmost extremes: millions had been enslaved against their will, and millions more had been quite literally worked to death. It is unsurprising that so many people throughout the continent turned to communism after the war: the movement not only appealed as a refreshing and radical alternative to the discredited politicians who had gone before, but gave people an opportunity to vent all the anger and resentment that had built up during those terrible years.

Hatred was the key to Communist success in Europe, as the innumerable documents urging party activists to promote it make clear. Communism not only fed off animosity towards Germans, Fascists and collaborators; it also nurtured new revulsion for the aristocracy and the middle classes, for landowners and kulaks. Later, as the world war gradually became the Cold War, these passions were easily translated into a revulsion for America, capitalism and the West. In return all these groups also abhorred communism in equal measure.

It was not only the Communists who saw violence and chaos as an opportunity. Nationalists too understood that the tensions ignited during the war could be used to promote an alternative agenda – in their case, the ethnic cleansing of their countries. Many nations exploited the new hatred of Germans in the aftermath of the war to expel the ancient Volksdeutsch communities who had lived throughout eastern Europe for hundreds of years. Poland harnessed the wartime hatred for Ukrainians to launch a programme of expulsion and forced assimilation. Slovaks, Hungarians and Romanians embarked on a series of population exchanges and anti-Semitic groups exploited the violent atmosphere to chase the few remaining Jews off the continent. These groups aimed at nothing less than the creation of a series of ethnically pure nation-states across central and eastern Europe.

Nationalists never achieved their aims in the aftermath of the war – partly because the international community would not let them, but also because the needs of the Cold War took priority over everything else. But when the Cold War came to an end, the old nationalist tensions began to resurface. Issues that many thought were long dead were suddenly resurrected with a passion that made the events of fifty years earlier seem like yesterday.

The most spectacular example occurred after the fall of communism in Yugoslavia. Yugoslavia was the one eastern European nation that had not carried out a programme of ethnic expulsions and deportations after the war. As a consequence, Serbs, Croats and Muslims still lived in mixed communities across the region – a fact that was to have disastrous consequences when civil war broke out in the early 1990s. The perpetrators of this civil conflict used the Second World War and its aftermath as a direct justification for their actions, and resurrected many of the old symbols of ethnic tension from 1945. In a conscious re-enactment of those times they indulged in mass rape, civilian massacres and ethnic cleansing on a massive scale.

Other, less dramatic but no less significant incidents have been occurring in many parts of Europe since the fall of communism. In 2006, for example, a student in Slovakia named Hedviga Malinova told police that she had been beaten up for using her Hungarian mother-tongue. The accusation was widely publicized, and reawakened tensions between Slovaks and Hungarians inside the country. The Slovakian Interior Minister accused the student of lying, the police charged her with false testimony, and the uncomfortable relationship between Slovakia and its Hungarian minority seemed just as alive as it ever was in 1946.[2]

Across the border, Hungary has seen the return of a similar, but even more insidious national hatred: anti-Semitism is on the rise in a way that hasn't been seen since the 1940s. In a letter to the *Washington Post* at the beginning of 2011, an award-winning Hungarian pianist, András Schiff, claimed that his country was being swept by a wave of 'reactionary nationalism', characterized by an increasing hatred for Gypsies and Jews.[3] As if unaware of the irony, the Hungarian right-wing press immediately responded by claiming that only Jews were capable of accusing Hungary of such crimes. Zsolt Bayer, for example, wrote in the newspaper *Magyar Hírlap*: 'A stinking excrement called something like Cohen from somewhere in England writes that "a foul stench wafts" from Hungary. Cohen, and Cohn-Bendit, and Schiff . . . Unfortunately, they were not all buried up to their necks in the forest of Orgovány.'[4]

Such sentiments demonstrate that the recent rise in anti-Semitism across Europe is *not* merely a product of the relatively new tensions in the Middle East. Traditional forms of hatred towards Jews are also alive and well. The same could be said for the rise in animosity towards Gypsies since the fall of communism, particularly in the Czech Republic, Poland and Hungary. In Bulgaria riots broke out in the autumn of 2011, after a series of racist demonstrations against Gypsies.[5]

The re-emergence of such problems tempts one to consider that perhaps the nationalists of the 1940s were right to attempt the creation of ethnically homogeneous states after all. If there were no national minorities in countries like Slovakia or Hungary, then such issues would never arise. The problem with this idea, apart from the obvious moral implications, is that an ethnically homogeneous state is almost impossible to achieve. Poland came closest in the immediate aftermath of the war by expelling or hounding out its populations of Germans, Jews and Ukrainians. But even here it proved impossible to expel everyone – particularly the Ukrainian minority, which was perhaps the ethnic group most ingrained in Polish society. In the end, the Poles resorted to Operation Vistula, the controversial programme of enforced assimilation that broke up Ukrainian communities and dispersed them across the north and west of the country. This repressive measure was deemed a complete success at the time – and yet, today it is becoming quite obvious that the assimilation programme did not work. Since the 1990s, Łemkos and Ukrainians have increasingly asserted their communal ethnic rights. They have formed political lobbies and pressure groups, and have repeatedly demanded the return of the property that was taken from them after the war. Rather than solving the problem, Operation Vistula merely stored up new problems for the future.

Even the *total* expulsion of a nation's ethnic minorities has not proved to be a guarantee against such issues. The expulsion of Germans from many countries in the 1940s, especially Poland and Czechoslovakia, was probably the most widespread and complete of all the ethnic deportations after the war. It created a resentment within Germany that has never since dissipated. From the 1950s to the 1980s, the expellees formed one of the most powerful pressure groups in Germany, one that was, in the words of Lucius Clay, 'largely reactionary and certainly planning to go home'.[6] Much like Łemkos and Ukrainians in Poland, these people are continuing to lobby for the return of the lands and property stolen from them in the aftermath of the war. The prospect of having to deal with the claims of these expellees fills most eastern European governments with dread. In 2009, for example, President Václav Klaus of the Czech Republic refused to sign the Lisbon Treaty that granted the European Union new powers, because of fears that certain parts of it might open the door for Germans to mount legal claims against his country. Klaus held up the treaty for several weeks until the Czechs were granted an opt-out from the relevant clauses. The expulsion of the Germans in the aftermath of the war did not solve the minorities problem in Czechoslovakia, as it then was – it merely exported it.

One might expect the problem of expellees to fade away as the older generations gradually die out, but unfortunately even this does not seem to be happening. Many of the most vocal 'expellees' in Germany and elsewhere are not those who actually experienced the expulsions, but their children and grandchildren. One need only look at what has happened in the Crimea to see how nationalist tensions are transmitted down the generations. In 1944, the Crimean Tatars were deported from their homelands by Stalin, who decreed that they should be dispersed through Soviet central Asia as a punishment for collaborating with the Germans during the war. After the break-up of the Soviet Union in 1991, a quarter of a million Tatars decided to return to their homelands in the Crimea. They moved into derelict houses and renovated them. They formed illegal settlements on vacant land, and constantly pestered the Ukrainian authorities to register them as lawful tenants. When the police threatened to evict them, they protested violently, and some even doused themselves in petrol and set themselves on fire. The striking thing about these 'returnees' is that the vast majority of them were not, strictly speaking, 'returning' at all: they had been born and raised in central Asia. They had given up reasonably prosperous and secure lives there in order to move to a homeland they had never seen before, and where they were not welcome.[7]

The Importance of National Myths

The passion that drives such people comes from the stories and myths that they have been exposed to, and which are repeated throughout their communities. Tatars imbibed the agony of their deportation with their mothers' milk, and have repeated these stories daily for over sixty years. In their minds the Crimea has been elevated to some kind of promised land. In the words of one Tatar, 'For the Soviet people, the thirties, the forties, the fifties – are history. For Crimean Tatars, they are now . . . They live history.'[8] Likewise, German expellees endlessly reminisce about the horrors of their trek westwards while Ukrainians talk of the brutality of Operation Vistula as if it were yesterday. Such stories are repeated so frequently not merely because they happened, but because they serve a purpose: they are the glue that binds these national groups together.

The West is not immune to such myth-building. Norwegians, Danes, Dutch, Belgians, French and Italians have all built stories around the injustices they suffered during the Second World War, and by endlessly repeating them have managed to build the impression that each people was more or less united against Fascists and Nazi invaders. Thus, for decades, the more messy realities of widespread collaboration were conveniently swept under the carpet. Collaborators themselves have also built myths about the injustices they suffered after the liberation. Stories of extreme violence against innocent members of the political right, if repeated often enough, give the impression that *everyone* in these countries suffered equally, regardless of their political persuasion.

The victors too have their myths. The Second World War has become something of a national industry in Britain. Films, dramas and documentaries about the war appear on television daily, and books about it perennially grace the bestseller lists. The war is present at all national occasions, whether it is in the chants and songs of English football fans during the World Cup, or the fly-past of Spitfires and Lancaster bombers on state occasions. Like the Americans, the British think back to the Second World War as a time when their 'greatest generation' saved the world from the evil of Nazism. Like the Americans, the British prefer to believe that they did this virtually single-handedly. For example, folk memory has it that the British stood alone during the Battle of Britain in 1940–41; there is rarely any acknowledgement that one in five of the fighter pilots who defended the country came from Poland, Czechoslovakia, Belgium, France or parts of the British Empire.

The problem with such deeply cherished myths is that they inevitably end up conflicting with someone else's equally cherished myths. One man's vengeance is another man's justice. If the Sudeten Germans remember their expulsion from the Czech borderlands as a time of atrocity, the Czechs commemorate it as a time when historic wrongs were finally put right. If some Polish Ukrainians applaud apologies for Operation Vistula in the liberal press, some Ukrainian Poles see them as a national betrayal. And if the British see the Lancaster bomber as a symbol of pride, many Germans remember it only as a symbol of indiscriminate destruction.

A columnist from the Serbian newspaper *Vreme* put it thus, in the aftermath of the breakdown of the former Yugoslavia:

> Revenge or forgiveness. Remembrance or oblivion. These postwar challenges are never carried out according to heavenly justice: there will be more unjust vengeance and undeserved forgiveness. Already the policies of remembrance and oblivion are not pursued in a way that will serve peace and stability. The Serbs would like to forget exactly those things that the Croats or Bosniaks would like to remember and vice versa. If by chance any of the sides remember the same event, it is a crime for one and a heroic deed for the other.[9]

The sentiments apply equally to the aftermath of the Second World War, and to most other nations across the eastern half of Europe.

Another problem with the constant repetition of national myths is that they inevitably become so mixed up with half-truths, and even downright lies, that it is often impossible to disentangle them. What is important to people who feel aggrieved is not the factual content of their stories, but their emotional resonance. Almost every statistic quoted in this book is contested by some national group or another. For example, German expellee organizations still claim that two million Germans were massacred during the expulsions from eastern Europe, when even a glance at the government statistics they claim to quote shows this to be a gross distortion of the facts. Words like 'Holocaust' and 'genocide' are bandied about without thought for their actual meaning, and Polish prison camps like Łambinowice and Świętochłowice are labelled 'extermination camps' as if the hundreds of people who died in them are somehow equivalent to the millions shovelled into ovens at Sobibor, Bełzec and Treblinka.

Competing national groups across Europe routinely promote their

own statistics and denigrate those of their rivals with little regard for
the probable reality. Thus the generally accepted number of 60–90,000
Poles killed by Ukrainian nationalists during the war is often ignored by
'historians' from both sides: Poles multiply the number by five, and
Ukrainians divide it by five.[10] Likewise, Serbs have historically always
inflated their wartime death toll by some 700,000; while Croats similarly inflate the number killed by the Yugoslav state after the war was
over.[11] Political factions in the West are equally happy to use spurious
statistics. For decades the French right wing told stories about 105,000
Vichyites murdered in cold blood by the Resistance after the war. The
accepted figure now is actually just a few thousand.[12] So widespread are
these bogus figures that even serious historians occasionally repeat
them, thus propagating them still further.

If such myths and false figures promote antagonism amongst relatively small national and political minorities, they are even more
insidious when they begin to seep into the mainstream. Since the end of
the twentieth century the whole of Europe has experienced a marked
shift to the right, with far-right groups gaining more influence than at
any time since the Second World War. These groups are attempting to
shift the onus of blame away from the Nazis and Fascists who set the
whole cycle of atrocity and counter-atrocity in motion, and towards
their left-wing rivals. But when the far right begins to promote a specific
view of history we should be just as cautious as we have become accustomed to being when the Communists do the same.

An example of how history has been manipulated for political gain
occurred in Italy in 2005, when government ministers announced a
brand-new national day of remembrance. The events they wished to
commemorate had occurred in 1945, when the borderlands in the
north-east of the country had been overrun by Yugoslav Partisans. In a
frenzy of ethnic cleansing similar to what was happening in other parts
of Yugoslavia, thousands of Italian civilians were massacred or thrown
alive into the region's deep natural chasms. To mark the sixtieth anniversary of these events, and also the anniversary of the treaty which
signed over the north-eastern corner of the country to Yugoslavia, the
authorities planned to hold a series of commemoration ceremonies.
One of these ceremonies took place in Trieste, near the border, which
had been the scene of some of the Yugoslav atrocities. Controversially,
it was attended by Italy's Foreign Minister, Gianfranco Fini, whose

political party – the National Alliance – was the successor to the post-war neo-Fascist movement.

In a speech on the official day of remembrance, the Italian Prime Minister, Silvio Berlusconi, told his country, 'If we look back to the twentieth century we see pages of history we'd prefer to forget. But we cannot and should not forget.'[13] By invoking history in this way, however, the Italian government was being extremely selective in what it was choosing to remember. Thousands of Italians were indeed massacred by Yugoslavian Partisans in 1945 – but one needed only to look back a further four years to see that it had not been the Yugoslavs or the Communists who had set the process in motion. It was the Italian Fascists who had invaded Yugoslavia in the first place, who had committed the first atrocities, and who had installed the Ustashas – one of the most repulsive regimes in wartime Europe – in power.

In fact, the commemoration had nothing to do with 'history' and a lot to do with politics. At a time when Italy was becoming increasingly sensitive about immigration from eastern Europe, it suited Italian nationalists to portray their Slav neighbours as villains. But it was more than just an attempt to demonize foreigners. The whole event, which came barely a week after the international commemoration of the liberation of Auschwitz, was a deliberate attempt to provide Italy with its own homegrown holocaust. Italians were casting themselves as the victims, and their next-door neighbours as the perpetrators of atrocity. Just as importantly, especially from Gianfranco Fini's point of view, it challenged the traditional emphasis on the Italian people being the victims of *Fascist* atrocities. The villains in this commemoration were not from the political right, but from the left. It was a subtle way of shifting the blame for the events of the war away from Gianfranco Fini's predecessors, the Italian Fascists.[14]

Some historians have suggested that hatreds and rivalries between Europe's competing national and political groups will always exist as long as we continue to commemorate the events of the war and its immediate aftermath. The commemoration in 2005 certainly did nothing to promote friendly relations with Italy's north-eastern neighbours. Perhaps George Santayana's famous aphorism that 'those who cannot remember the past are condemned to repeat it' should be reversed – that is, it is *because* we remember the past that we are condemned to repeat it. The depressing re-emergence of national hatreds in the last two decades might seem to suggest so.[15]

If I truly believed remembrance to be the cause of continuing hatred, however, then I would never have written this book. To rake over the old coals of war, to repeat the very stories that are the source of so many antagonisms, would have been irresponsible in the extreme. If one follows the logic of this argument, there should be no books about this period at all, nor any newspaper articles, films or TV documentaries – the transmission of these stories from one generation to another becomes nothing better than the repetition of a vicious cycle. Remembrance, and even memory itself, becomes a sin – the only virtuous policy would be one of deliberate forgetting.

But forgetting is not an option. To begin with, events on the scale described in this book are impossible to forget. As the various efforts by the Communists to repress cultural memory during the Cold War have demonstrated, attempts to forget the past merely lead to further resentment, and ultimately to a dangerous distortion of the facts. Distorted facts are far more dangerous than actual ones. But neither should we want to forget. The events that have formed the world around us, and that continue to shape the world today, are important not only to historians but to everyone. It is our memory of the past that makes us who we are, not only on a national level but also on an intensely personal one.

The immediate postwar period is one of the most important times in our recent history. If the Second World War destroyed the old continent, then its immediate aftermath was the protean chaos out of which the new Europe was formed. It was during this violent, vengeful time that many of our hopes, aspirations, prejudices and resentments first took shape. Anyone who truly wants to understand Europe as it is today must first have an understanding of what occurred here during this crucial formative period. There is no value in shying away from difficult or sensitive themes, since these are the very building blocks upon which the modern Europe has been built.

It is not our remembering the sins of the past that provokes hatred, but the way in which we remember them. The immediate postwar period has been routinely neglected, misremembered and misused by all of us. Berlusconi and Fini's version of history omits any serious acknowledgement of Italian wrongdoing; the Crimean Tatar view of history glosses over their people's collaboration with the Nazis; the German expellees try to present the history of their own suffering as equivalent to the suffering of the Jews.

Those who wish to harness hatred and resentment for their own gain always try to distort the proper balance between one version of history and another. They take events out of context; they make blame a one-sided game; and they try to convince us that historical problems are the problems of today. If we are to bring an end to the cycle of hatred and violence we must do precisely the opposite of these things. We must show how competing views of history can exist alongside one another. We must show how past atrocities fit into their historical context, and how blame necessarily attaches itself not just to one party, but to a whole variety of parties. We must strive always to discover the truth, particularly when it comes to statistics, and then put that truth to bed. It is, after all, history, and should not be allowed to poison the present.

Despite the many depressing examples of how history has been used to resurrect old hatreds, there are also symbols of hope. Amongst the many examples I could cite, I will choose one – that of the relationship between Germany and Poland. In the aftermath of the war the hatred between Germans and Poles seemed permanent and irreversible. The Poles loathed the nation that had ravaged their country, murdered millions of its civilians and created a string of concentration camps – perhaps the most potent symbols of evil in the entire twentieth century – on Polish territory. The Germans in return felt bitter about the 'Slavic' brutality that saw the rape and murder of millions of *their* civilians, the looting of their homes and farms in Pomerania, Silesia and East Prussia, and the removal of thousands of square miles of German territory, which was handed over by the international community to Poland.

In 1965, however, the Polish bishops made an offer of reconciliation and forgiveness to Germany. In 1970 a treaty was drawn up between Poland and West Germany. Millions of Poles were allowed to visit their near neighbour and discover for themselves what ordinary Germans were like. A Polish–German commission was set up to revise history textbooks, to correct inaccurate statistics and to prevent historical episodes from being overtly manipulated for political reasons. The events of the past were not forgotten, but they were put within their proper context. Today Germans and Poles generally regard one another's nations as friendly. Residual hatreds tend to be confined to small groups only – the expellees on one side, and the older generations of Poles on the other. Both of these groups are now dying out, or losing ground with the passage of time.

For most young people in both Poland and Germany, the events of the war and its immediate aftermath are no longer much of an issue. National rivalries may still come to life occasionally for the duration of a football match, but chants and slogans of Polish and German football fans are generally just as sporting as the football itself. As for *real* hatred – the sort that used to be demanded as a duty by political commissars and war veterans – that is now regarded by most young people as little more than ancient history.[16]

Acknowledgements

The research for this book has been a monumental task, and could never have been accomplished without a vast amount of help from individuals and institutions across Europe. I am deeply grateful to the K. Blundell Trust for the generous grant which allowed me to pay for a significant part of my research. I am particularly indebted to Joanna Pyłat, Barbara Herchenreder, Kasia Piekarska, Irena Kolar and Anna Pleban for their help in gathering and translating Polish and Ukrainian documents, and for putting me in touch with numerous Polish eyewitnesses to postwar events. I could never have understood the intricacies of the Czech and Slovak sources without the assistance of Michaela Anderlova, Martina Horackova and Dasha Conolly; and Alexandra Sherley was a godsend when it came to translating Croatian documents. My attempt to struggle through Italian, French and German source material was greatly eased by Jennie Condell, John Conolly and my multilingual sisters Natalie and Sarah. My mother-in-law, Zsuzsi Messing, also worked tirelessly translating huge passages of Hungarian books and documents.

The staff of dozens of institutions across Europe and in the United States were uniformly helpful, but special mention must go to the British Library, whose astonishingly broad foreign-language collections are second to none. I am also very grateful to Dr Richard Butterwick and Dr Bojan Aleksov of the School of Eastern European and Slavonic Studies at University College London for introducing me to some of the researchers mentioned above; and to Peter Hart of the Imperial War Museum for selflessly sharing his expertise in the early days of my research.

I would especially like to thank all those who agreed to let me interview them about their often painful experiences, most notably Ben

Helfgott, Andrzej C. (who wishes to remain anonymous), Barbara Paleolog, Stefa Baczkowska, Hanka Piotrowska, Maria Bielicka, Marilka and Alik Ossowski, and Zbigniew Ogrodzinski. It was their input that first brought my drier archival research to life.

As always I am much obliged to my brilliant literary agents, Simon Trewin and Ariella Feiner of United Agents, and Dan Mandel of Sanford J. Greenburger Associates. They excel in all the areas where I am at my most incompetent.

I must also thank my equally brilliant editor, Eleo Gordon, without whose help this book would have been twice as long and half as interesting. But thanks are also due to the unsung heroes at Penguin, whose expertise in sales, marketing, publicity, design and production are so essential to any book. Special mention must go to Penguin's foreign rights team who have almost single-handedly made this book a commercial possibility.

Lastly, as in so many other areas of my life, my greatest thanks must go to my wife Liza for her help, patience, love and all-round support throughout the years that it took to write this book. It would have been impossible without her.

Sources

ARCHIVES

Archives Nationales, Paris
Archiwum Państwowe (AP – State Archive), Szczecin
Archiwum Wschodnie, Ósrodek Karta (AWK – Eastern Archive), Warsaw
Bundesarchiv, Koblenz
Centralne Archiwum Wojskove (CAW – Central Military Archive), Warsaw
Imperial War Museum, London, Department of Documents (IWM Docs) and
    Sound Archives (IWM Sound)
The National Archives of the United Kingdom (TNA; formerly known as the
    Public Record Office), London
Polski Ósrodek Społeczno Kulturalny (POSK – Centre for Polish Arts and Cul-
    ture), London
The Sikorski Institute, London
United Nations Relief and Rehabilitation Administration (UNRRA) archives,
    New York
United States Holocaust Memorial Museum, New York
US National Archives and Records Administration (NARA), Maryland, USA
Zentrum gegen Vertreibungen, Berlin

OFFICIAL PUBLICATIONS

Biuro Odszkodowań Wojennych przy Prezydium Rady Ministrów, *Sprawozdanie
    w Przedmiocie strat i szkód wojennych Polski w latach 1939–1945* (Warsaw,
    1947)
Burger, G. C. E., J. C. Drummond and H. R. Stanstead (eds.), *Malnutrition and
    Starvation in Western Netherlands September 1944–July 1945* (The Hague:
    General State Printing Office, 1948)
Centraal Bureau voor de Statistiek, *Oorlogsverliezen 1940–1945: Maandschrift
    van het Centraal Bureau voor de Statistiek* (The Hague: Belinfante, 1948)
Central Statistical Office, *Statistical Digest of the War* (London: HMSO, 1951)

Coles, Harry L. and Albert K. Weinberg (eds.), *Civil Affairs: Soldiers Become Governors* (Washington, DC: US Govt Printing Office, 1964)

Croatian State Commission for Establishing Crimes of Occupying Forces and their Assistants, *Crimes in the Jasenovac Camp* (Banja Luka: Becjead, 2000)

European Union Agency for Fundamental Rights, European Union Minorities and Discrimination Survey: Main Results Report (Vienna: European Union Agency for Fundamental Rights, 2009)

Foreign Relations of the United States (FRUS), available online at http://uwdc.library.wisc.edu/collections/FRUS/

HM Government, *Statistics Relating to the War Effort of the United Kingdom* (London: HMSO, 1944)

House of Commons Parliamentary Debates (Hansard) (London: HMSO, 1942–5)

International Committee of the Red Cross, *Report of the International Committee of the Red Cross on its activities during the Second World War (September 1, 1939–June 30, 1947)*, vol. I: *General Activities* (Geneva: ICRC, 1948)

Istituto Centrale di Statistica, *Morti e Dispersi per Cause Belliche Negli Anni 1940–45* (Rome: Istituto Centrale di Statistica, 1957)

Maddison, Angus, *The World Economy: Historical Statistics* (Paris: OECD, 2003)

Maschke, Erich (ed.), *Zur Geschichte der deutschen Kriegsgefangenen des zweiten Weltkrieges*, 15 vols. (Bielefeld: Ernst & Werner Gieseking, 1962–74)

Schieder, Theodor (ed.), *Documents on the Expulsion of the Germans from Eastern-Central Europe*, trans. G. H. de Sausmarez, 4 vols. (Bonn: Federal Ministry for Expellees, Refugees and War Victims, 1958–60)

United States Army, Office of the Surgeon General, *Preventative Medicine in World War II*, vol. V: *Communicable Diseases transmitted through Contact or by Unknown Means* (Washington, DC: US Government Printing Office, 1960)

United States Strategic Bombing Survey, *Over-all Report (European War)* (Washington DC: US Government Printing Office, 1945)

War Office, *Statistical Report on the Health of the Army, 1943–1945* (London: HMSO, 1948)

Webster, Sir Charles and Noble Frankland, *The Strategic Air Offensive against Germany 1939–1945* (London: HMSO, 1961)

NEWSPAPERS AND JOURNALS

Le Courrier de Genève
Daily Express
Défense de la France
Écrits de Paris
Journal Officiel

Le Monde
Múlt és jövő
New York Times
Newsweek
New York Review of Books
Le Peuple
Res Publica
Time
The Times

FILM AND TELEVISION

Le Chagrin et la Pitié, two parts (Laboratoires Gennevilliers for Télévision Rencontre, 1969; Marcel Ophüls)
The Last Nazis, part II (Minnow Films for BBC, 2009; Charlie Russell)
Millions Like Us (Gainsborough Pictures, 1943; Frank Launder and Sidney Gilliat)
A Shadow Over Europe (BBC, 2002; Charles Wheeler)

BOOKS AND ESSAYS
Travel guides

Baedeker, Karl, *Das Generalgouvernement: Reisehandbuch von Karl Baedeker* (Leipzig: Karl Baedeker, 1943)
Ministry of Culture & Art and Ministry of Reconstruction of the Country, *Warsaw Accuses: Guide-book to the exhibition arranged by the Office of Reconstruction of the Capital together with the National Museum in Warsaw* (Warsaw: Muzeum Narodowe, 1945)

Histories and academic studies

Abzug, Robert H., *Inside the Vicious Heart* (Oxford University Press, 1987)
Alessandrini, Luca, 'The Option of Violence – Partisan Activity in the Bologna Area 1945–1948', in Jonathan Dunnage (ed.), *After the War: Violence, Justice, Continuity and Renewal in Italian Society* (Market Harborough: Troubador, 1999)
Alexander, G. M., *The Prelude to the Truman Doctrine: British Policy in Greece, 1944–1947* (Oxford: Clarendon Press, 1982)
Ammendolia, Ilario, *Occupazione delle terre in Calabria 1945–1949* (Rome: Gangemi, 1990)

Anušauskas, Arvydas (ed.), *The Anti-Soviet Resistance in the Baltic States* (Vilnius: Genocide and Resistance Research Centre of Lithuania, 2000)

Arad, Yitzhak, *Belzec, Sobibor, Treblinka: The Operation Reinhard Deathcamps* (Bloomington: Indiana University Press, 1999)

Aron, Robert, *Histoire de l'épuration: De l'indulgence aux massacres, Novembre 1942–Septembre 1944* (Paris: Fayard, 1967)

Bacque, James, *Other Losses: The Shocking Truth behind the Mass Deaths of Disarmed German Soldiers and Civilians under General Eisenhower's Command* (Toronto: Stoddart, 1989)

Baerentzen, L., J. Iatrides and O. Smith (eds.), *Studies in the History of the Greek Civil War, 1945–1949* (Copenhagen: Museum Tusculanum, 1987)

Barber, John and Mark Harrison, *The Soviet Home Front, 1941–1945: A Social and Economic History of the USSR in World War II* (London and New York: Longman, 1991)

Battaglia, Achille, *I giudici e la politica* (Bari: Laterza, 1962)

Bauer, Yehuda, *Flight and Rescue: Brichah* (New York: Random House, 1970)

Beck, Earl R., *Under the Bombs* (Lexington: University Press of Kentucky, 1986)

Beevor, Antony, *Berlin: The Downfall 1945* (London: Penguin, 2003)

———, *Stalingrad* (London: Viking, 1998)

Beevor, Antony and Artemis Cooper, *Paris After the Liberation* (London: Penguin, 1995)

Beevor, Antony and Luba Vinogradova, *A Writer at War: Vasily Grossman with the Red Army 1941–1945* (London: Pimlico, 2006)

Benz, Wolfang and Angelika Königseder (eds.), *Das Konzentrationslager Dachau* (Berlin: Metropol, 2008)

Berlière, Jean-Marc with Laurent Chabrun, *Les policiers français sous l'Occupation* (Paris: Perrin, 2001)

Beschloss, Michael, *The Conquerors: Roosevelt, Truman and the Destruction of Hitler's Germany, 1941–1945* (New York: Simon & Schuster, 2002)

Bethell, Nicholas, *The Last Secret* (London: Futura, 1976)

Betts, R. R. (ed.), *Central and South East Europe 1945–1948* (London and New York: Royal Institute of International Affairs, 1950)

Bischof, Günter and Stephen E. Ambrose (eds.), *Eisenhower and the German POWs: Facts against Falsehood* (Baton Rouge and London: Louisiana State University Press, 1992)

Blom, J. C. H. et al. (eds.), *The History of the Jews in the Netherlands*, trans. Arnold J. Pomerans and Erica Pomerans (Oxford and Portland, OR: Littman Library of Jewish Civilization, 2002)

Borgersrud, Lars, 'Meant to be Deported', in Kjersti Ericsson and Eva Simonsen (eds.), *Children of World War II* (Oxford and New York: Berg, 2005)

Bosch, Manfred, *Der Neubeginn: Aus deutscher Nachkriegszeit Südbaden 1945–1950* (Konstanz: Südkurier, 1988)

Boshyk, Yury (ed.), *Ukraine during World War II: History and its Aftermath* (Edmonton: University of Alberta, 1986)

Botting, Douglas, *In the Ruins of the Reich* (London: Methuen, 2005)

Bourdrel, Philippe, *L'épuration sauvage* (Paris: Perrin, 2002)

Bourke, Joanna, *Rape: A History from 1860 to the Present Day* (London: Virago, 2007)

Brossat, Alain, *Les tondues: Un carnaval moche* (Paris: Hachette/Pluriel, 1992)

Brosse, Thérèse, *War-Handicapped Children* (Paris: UNESCO, 1950)

Buisson, Patrick, *1940–1945: The Erotic Years* (Paris: Albin Michel, 2009)

Bunting, Madeleine, *The Model Occupation: The Channel Islands under German Rule, 1940–1945* (London: HarperCollins, 1995)

Burleigh, Michael, *Moral Combat* (London: Harper Press, 2010)

——, *The Third Reich: A New History* (London: Pan, 2001)

Cohen, Rich, *The Avengers* (London: Jonathan Cape, 2000)

Cohen-Pfister, Laurel and Dagmar Wienroeder-Skinner (eds.), *Victims and Perpetrators: (Re)Presenting the Past in Post-Unification Culture* (Berlin and New York: Walter de Gruyter, 2006)

Conquest, Robert, *A History of Modern Russia from Nicholas II to Putin* (London: Penguin, 2003)

Conway, Martin, 'Justice in Postwar Belgium: Popular Passions and Political Realities', in István Deák et al. (eds.), *The Politics of Retribution in Europe* (Princeton University Press, 2000)

Crainz, Guido, *Padania: Il mondo dei braccianti dall'Ottocento alla fuga dalle campagne* (Rome: Donzelli, 1994)

Crampton, R. J., *Bulgaria* (Oxford University Press, 2007)

Dahl, Hans Fredrik, 'Dealing with the Past in Scandinavia', in Jon Elster (ed.), *Retribution and Reparation in the Transition to Democracy* (New York: Cambridge University Press, 2006)

Dallas, Gregor, *Poisoned Peace: 1945 – The War that Never Ended* (London: John Murray, 2006)

Dallin, Alexander, *German Rule in Russia 1941–1945: A Study of Occupation Policies* (London and Basingstoke: Macmillan, 1981)

Davidson, Eugene, *The Death and Life of Germany: An Account of the American Occupation* (London: Jonathan Cape, 1959)

Davies, Norman, *God's Playground: A History of Poland* (Oxford University Press, 2005)

——, *Rising '44: The Battle for Warsaw* (London: Pan, 2004)

Davies, Norman and Roger Moorhouse, *Microcosm* (London: Pimlico, 2003)

Dawidowicz, Lucy S., *The War against the Jews 1939–1945* (Harmondsworth: Pelican, 1979)

de Zayas, Alfred, *Nemesis at Potsdam* (London: Routledge & Kegan Paul, 1977)

——, *A Terrible Revenge: The Ethnic Cleansing of the East European Germans*, 2nd edn (New York: Palgrave Macmillan, 2006)

Deák, István et al. (eds.), *The Politics of Retribution in Europe* (Princeton University Press, 2000)

Dean, Martin, *Robbing the Jews: The Confiscation of Jewish Property in the Holocaust, 1933–1945* (New York: Cambridge University Press, 2008)

Deletant, Dennis, *Communist Terror in Romania: Gheorghiu-Dej and the Police State, 1948–1965* (London: Hurst & Co., 1999)

Derry, T. K., *A History of Modern Norway 1814–1972* (Oxford: Clarendon Press, 1973)

Diederichs, Monika, 'Stigma and Silence: Dutch Women, German Soldiers and their Children', in Kjersti Ericsson and Eva Simonsen (eds.), *Children of World War II* (Oxford and New York: Berg, 2005)

Dondi, Mirco, *La lunga liberazione: Giustizia e violenza nel dopoguerra italiano* (Rome: Riumiti, 2004)

Drakulić, Slavenka, *Balkan-Express: Chroniques de la Yougoslavie en Guerre* (Paris: Éditions Mentha, 1992)

Dreisziger, Nándor (ed.), *Hungary in the Age of Total War (1938–1948)* (New York: Columbia University Press, 1998)

Drolshagen, Ebba D., *Wehrmachtskinder: Auf der Suche nach dem nie gekannten Vater* (Munich: Droemer, 2005)

Dunnage, Jonathan (ed.), *After the War: Violence, Justice, Continuity and Renewal in Italian Society* (Market Harborough: Troubador, 1999)

Dupuy, R. Ernest and Trevor N. Dupuy, *The Harper Encyclopedia of Military History*, 4th edn (New York: HarperCollins, 1993)

Dushnyck, Walter, *Death and Devastation on the Curzon Line: The Story of the Deportations from Ukraine* (New York: Committee Against Mass Expulsion/ Ukrainian Congress Committee of America, 1948)

Dutton, Donald G., *The Psychology of Genocide, Massacres, and Extreme Violence: Why 'Normal' People Come to Commit Atrocities* (London and Westport, CT: Praeger Security International, 2007)

Eby, Cecil D., *Hungary at War: Civilians and Soldiers in World War II* (Philadelphia: Pennsylvania State University Press, 1998)

Elkins, Michael, *Forged in Fury* (New York: Ballantine Books, 1971)

Ellwood, David W., *Italy 1943–1945* (Leicester University Press, 1985)

Elster, Jon (ed.), *Retribution and Reparation in the Transition to Democracy* (New York: Cambridge University Press, 2006)

Ericsson, Kjersti and Dag Ellingsen, 'Life Stories of Norwegian War Children', in Kjersti Ericsson and Eva Simonsen (eds.), *Children of World War II* (Oxford and New York: Berg, 2005)

Ericsson, Kjersti and Eva Simonsen (eds.), *Children of World War II* (Oxford and New York: Berg, 2005)

Farmer, Sarah, *Martyred Village* (London and Berkeley: University of California Press, 2000)

Fisch, Bernhard, *Nemmersdorf, Oktober 1944: Was in Ostpreußen tatsächlich geschah* (Berlin: Edition Ost, 1997)

Fischer-Galati, Stephen, *Twentieth Century Romania*, 2nd edn (New York: Columbia University Press, 1991)

Fishman, Sarah, *The Battle for Children: World War II, Youth Crime, and Juvenile Justice in Twentieth Century France* (Cambridge, MA: Harvard University Press, 2002)

Florentin, Eddy, *Quand les Alliés bombardaient la France 1940–1945* (Paris: Perrin, 1997)

Fowkes, Ben, *Eastern Europe 1945–1969: From Stalinism to Stagnation* (Harlow: Pearson Education, 2000)

Friedländer, Saul, *The Years of Extermination: Nazi Germany and the Jews 1939–1945* (London: Weidenfeld & Nicolson, 2007)

Frumkin, Gregory, *Population Changes in Europe Since 1939* (New York: Augustus M. Kelley Inc., 1951)

Gaillard, Lucien, *Marseilles sous l'Occupation* (Rennes: Ouest-France, 1982)

Gaškaitė-Žemaitienė, Nijolė, 'The Partisan War in Lithuania from 1944 to 1953', in Arvydas Anušauskas (ed.), *The Anti-Soviet Resistance in the Baltic States* (Vilnius: Genocide and Resistance Research Centre of Lithuania, 2000)

Gilbert, Martin, *The Boys* (London: Phoenix, 1997)

——, *The Day the War Ended* (London: HarperCollins, 1995)

——, *The Holocaust: The Fate of European Jewry 1932–1945* (New York: Henry Holt, 1985)

——, *The Routledge Atlas of the Holocaust*, 4th edn (London and New York: Routledge, 2009)

Ginsborg, Paul, 'The Communist Party and the Agrarian Question in Southern Italy, 1943–1948', *History Workshop Journal*, vol. 17 (1984)

Giurescu, Dinu C., *Romania in the Second World War (1939–1945)*, trans. Eugenia Elena Popescu (New York: Columbia University Press, 2000)

Glantz, David, *Leningrad: City under Siege 1941–1944* (Rochester: Grange Books, 2005)

Glanz, Susan, 'Economic Platforms of the Various Political Parties in the Elections of 1945', in Nándor Dreisziger (ed.), *Hungary in the Age of Total War (1938–1948)* (New York: Columbia University Press, 1998)

Gringauz, Samuel, 'Jewish Destiny as the DP's See It: The Ideology of the Surviving Remnant', *Commentary* (Journal of the American Jewish Committee), vol. 4, no. 6 (December 1947)

——, 'Our New German Policy and the DP's: Why Immediate Resettlement is Imperative', *Commentary*, vol. 5, no. 3 (June 1948)

Gross, Jan T., *Fear: Anti-Semitism in Poland after Auschwitz* (New York: Random House, 2006)

Grüttner, Michael, Rüdiger Hachtmann and Heinz-Gerhard Haupt (eds.), *Geschichte und Emanzipation* (Frankfurt: Campus Fachbuch, 1999)

Gyurgyík, László, *Changes in the Demographic Settlement and Social Structure of the Hungarian Minority in (Czecho-)Slovakia between 1918–1998*, trans. Jószef D. Lőrincz (Budapest: Teleki László Foundation, 1999)

Hackett, David A. (ed.), *The Buchenwald Report* (Boulder, CO: Westview Press, 1995)

Harrison, Mark (ed.), *The Economics of World War Two* (Cambridge University Press, 1998)

Hastings, Max, *Armageddon* (London: Macmillan, 2004)

———, *Bomber Command* (London: Pan, 1999)

Herbert, Ulrich, *Hitler's Foreign Workers: Enforced Foreign Labor in Germany under the Third Reich*, trans. William Templer (Cambridge University Press, 1985)

Herzog, Dagmar (ed.), *Brutality and Desire: War and Sexuality in Europe's Twentieth Century* (Basingstoke: Palgrave Macmillan, 2009)

Hionidou, Violetta, *Famine and Death in Occupied Greece, 1941–1944* (Cambridge University Press, 2006)

Hirschfeld, Gerhard, *Nazi Rule and Dutch Collaboration: The Netherlands under German Occupation 1940–1945*, trans. Louise Willmot (Oxford, New York and Hamburg: Berg, 1988)

Hitchcock, William I., *Liberation: The Bitter Road to Freedom, Europe 1944–1945* (London: Faber & Faber, 2009)

Hitchins, Keith, *Rumania 1866–1947* (Oxford University Press, 1994)

Hodgson, John H., *Communism in Finland: A History and Interpretation* (Princeton University Press, 1967)

Hondius, Dienke, *Return: Holocaust Survivors and Dutch Anti-Semitism*, trans. David Colmer (Westport, CT: Praeger, 2003)

Huyse, Luc, 'The Criminal Justice System as a Political Actor in Regime Transitions: The Case of Belgium, 1944–50', in István Deák et al. (eds.), *The Politics of Retribution in Europe* (Princeton University Press, 2000)

Iatrides, John O. (ed.), *Greece in the 1940s: A Nation in Crisis* (Hanover and London: University Press of New England, 1981)

Ionescu, Ghita, *Communism in Rumania, 1944–1962* (London: Oxford University Press, 1964)

Israel, David L., *The Day the Thunderbird Cried* (Medford, OR: Emek Press, 2005)

Janics, Kálmán, *Czechoslovak Policy and the Hungarian Minority, 1945–1948*, trans. Stephen Borsody (New York: Columbia University Press, 1982)

Jedlicki, Jerzy, 'Historical Memory as a Source of Conflicts in Eastern Europe', *Communist and Post-Communist Studies*, vol. 32, no. 3 (1999)

Johr, Barbara, 'Die Ereignisse in Zahlen', in Helke Sander and Barbara Johr (eds.), *Befreier und Befreite: Krieg, Vergewaltigung, Kinder* (Frankfurt-am-Main: Fischer Taschenbuch, 2006)

Judt, Tony, *Postwar: A History of Europe Since 1945* (London: Pimlico, 2007)

Jurčević, Josip, *The Black Book of Communism in Croatia: The Crimes of Yugoslav Communists in Croatia in 1945* (Melbourne: Croatian Herald, 2006)

Kalyvas, Stathis N., 'Red Terror: Leftist Violence during the Occupation', in Mark Mazower (ed.), *After the War Was Over* (Princeton and Oxford: Princeton University Press, 2000)

Kenez, Peter, *Hungary from the Nazis to the Soviets: The Establishment of the Communist Regime in Hungary, 1944–1945* (New York: Cambridge University Press, 2009)

Kochavi, Arieh J., *Post-Holocaust Politics* (Chapel Hill and London: University of North Carolina Press, 2001)

Kondufor, Yuri (ed.), *A Short History of the Ukraine* (Kiev: Naukova Dumka, 1986)

Kontler, László, *A History of Hungary* (Basingstoke: Palgrave Macmillan, 2002)

Krawchenko, Bohdan, 'Soviet Ukraine under Nazi Occupation, 1941–4', in Yury Boshyk (ed.), *Ukraine during World War II* (Edmonton: University of Alberta, 1986)

Krivosheev, G. F. (ed.), *Soviet Casualties and Combat Losses in the Twentieth Century* (London: Greenhill, 1997)

Kucera, Jaroslav, *Odsunové ztráty sudetoněmeckého obyvatelstva* (Prague: Federalni ministerstvo zahranicnich veci, 1992)

Laar, Mart, *War in the Woods: Estonia's Struggle for Survival*, trans. Tiina Ets (Washington, DC: The Compass Press, 1992)

Levi, Fabio, 'Italian Society and Jews after the Second World War: Between Silence and Reparation', in Jonathan Dunnage (ed.), *After the War: Violence, Justice, Continuity and Renewal in Italian Society* (Market Harborough: Troubador, 1999)

Lewkowicz, Bea, '"After the War We Were All Together": Jewish Memories of Postwar Thessaloniki', in Mark Mazower (ed.), *After the War Was Over* (Princeton and Oxford: Princeton University Press, 2000)

Lilley, J. Robert, *Taken by Force: Rape and American GIs during World War Two* (Basingstoke: Palgrave Macmillan, 2007)

Lowe, Keith, *Inferno* (London: Viking, 2007)

Macardle, Dorothy, *Children of Europe: A Study of the Children of Liberated Countries, their War-time Experiences, their Reactions, and their Needs, with a Note on Germany* (London: Victor Gollancz, 1949)

MacDonogh, Giles, *After the Reich* (London: John Murray, 2007)

Mankowitz, Zeev W., *Life between Memory and Hope: The Survivors of the Holocaust in Occupied Germany* (Cambridge University Press, 2002)

Marcuse, Harold, *Legacies of Dachau* (Cambridge University Press, 2001)

Marko, Augustín and Pavol Martinický, *Slovak–Magyar Relations: History and Present Day in Figures* (Bratislava: Slovak Society for Protection of Democracy and Humanity, 1995)

Marrus, Michael R., *The Unwanted: European Refugees in the Twentieth Century* (New York: Oxford University Press, 1985)

Marx, Karl and Friedrich Engels, *The Communist Manifesto*, trans. Samuel Moore (Harmondsworth: Penguin, 1967)

Mayne, Richard, *Postwar: The Dawn of Today's Europe* (London: Thames & Hudson, 1983)

Mazower, Mark, *The Balkans* (London: Weidenfeld & Nicolson, 2000)

———, *Inside Hitler's Greece* (New Haven and London: Yale University Press, 1995)

Mazower, Mark (ed.), *After the War Was Over* (Princeton and Oxford: Princeton University Press, 2000)

McCarthy, Joseph R., *America's Retreat from Victory: The Story of George Catlett Marshall* (New York: The Devin-Adair Company, 1951)

McKinstry, Leo, *Spitfire: Portrait of a Legend* (London: John Murray, 2007)

Milward, Alan S., *The Reconstruction of Western Europe 1945–51* (London: Methuen, 1984)

———, *War, Economy and Society 1939–1945* (Berkeley and Los Angeles: University of California Press, 1979)

Miroszewski, Kazimierz, *Centralny obóz pracy Jaworzno: Podobóz Ukraiński (1947–1949)* (Katowice: Śląsk, 2001)

Misiunas, Romuald and Rein Taagepera, *The Baltic States: Years of Dependence 1940–1990* (London: Hurst & Co., 1993)

Modona, Guido Neppi, 'Postwar Trials against Fascist Collaborationists and Partisans: The Piedmont Experience', in Jonathan Dunnage (ed.), *After the War: Violence, Justice, Continuity and Renewal in Italian Society* (Market Harborough: Troubador, 1999)

Molnár, Miklós, *A Concise History of Hungary* (Cambridge University Press, 1996)

Moorhouse, Roger, *Berlin at War: Life and Death in Hitler's Capital 1939–45* (London: Bodley Head, 2010)

Morgan, Philip, *The Fall of Mussolini* (Oxford University Press, 2008)

Morgan, Sarah, 'The Schio Killings: A Case Study of Partisan Violence in Postwar Italy', *Modern Italy*, vol. 5, no. 2 (2000)

Morgenthau, Henry, Jr, *Germany Is Our Problem* (New York and London: Harper and Bros, 1945)

Myant, Martin, *Socialism and Democracy in Czechoslovakia, 1945–1948* (Cambridge University Press, 1981)

Naimark, Norman, *Fires of Hatred* (Cambridge, MA: Harvard University Press, 2002)

———, *The Russians in Germany* (Cambridge, MA: Harvard University Press, 1997)

Naimark, Norman and Leonid Gibianskii (eds.), *The Establishment of the Communist Regimes in Eastern Europe, 1944–1949* (Boulder, CO: Westview Press, 1997)

Nichol, John and Tony Rennell, *The Last Escape: The Untold Story of Allied Prisoners of War in Germany 1944–45* (London: Viking, 2002)

Nissen, Henrik S. (ed.), *Scandinavia during the Second World War*, trans. Thomas Munch-Petersen (Minneapolis: University of Minnesota Press, 1983)

Nøkelby, Berit, 'Adjusting to Allied Victory', in Henrik S. Nissen (ed.), *Scandinavia during the Second World War*, trans. Thomas Munch-Petersen (Minneapolis: University of Minnesota Press, 1983)

Nováček, Silvestr, *Drang nach Westen: Vystěhování Němců z Brna a odsun z jihomoravského pohraničí* (Czech Republic [no city]: Orego, 1996)

Novick, Peter, *The Holocaust and Collective Memory* (London: Bloomsbury, 2000)

——, *The Resistance versus Vichy* (London: Chatto & Windus, 1968)

Nowak, Edmund (ed.), *Obozy w Lamsdorf/Łambinowicach (1870–1946)* (Opole: Centralne Muzeum Jeńców Wojennych w Łambinowicach-Opolu, 2006)

Nurowski, Roman (ed.), *1939–1945 War Losses in Poland* (Poznań and Warsaw: Wydawnictwo Zachodnie, 1960)

Olsen, Kåre, *Schicksal Lebensborn: Die Kinder der Schande und ihre Mütter*, trans. Ebba D. Drolshagen (Munich: Knaur, 2004)

——, 'Under the Care of the Lebensborn', in Kjersti Ericsson and Eva Simonsen (eds.), *Children of World War II* (Oxford and New York: Berg, 2005)

Overmans, Rüdiger, *Deutsche militärische Verluste im Zweiten Weltkrieg* (Oldenbourg: Wissenschaftsverlag, 2000)

——, 'German Historiography, the War Losses, and the Prisoners of War', in Günter Bischof and Stephen E. Ambrose (eds.), *Eisenhower and the German POWs: Facts against Falsehood* (Baton Rouge and London: Louisiana State University Press, 1992)

Overy, Richard, *Russia's War* (London: Allen Lane, 1997)

Pansa, Giampaolo, *Il sangue dei vinti* (Milan: Sperling, 2005)

Pavlowitch, Stevan K., *Hitler's New Disorder: The Second World War in Yugoslavia* (London: Hurst & Co., 2008)

Pavone, Claudio, *Una guerra civile: Saggio storico sulla moralità nella Resistenza* (Turin: Universali Bollati Boringhieri, 2006)

Pearson, Raymond, *National Minorities in Eastern Europe 1848–1945* (London: Macmillan, 1983)

Pelle, János, *Az utolsó vérvádak* (Budapest: Pelikán, 1995)

Petacco, Arrigo, *A Tragedy Revealed: The Story of Italians from Istria, Dalmatia and Venezia Giulia, 1943–1956*, trans. Konrad Eisenbichler (University of Toronto Press, 2005)

Pike, David Wingeate, *Jours de gloire, jours de honte* (Paris: Société d'Édition d'Enseignement Supérieur, 1984)

Piotrowski, Tadeusz, *Vengeance of the Swallows* (Jefferson, NC: Macfarland, 1995)

Piscitelli, Enzo, *Da Parri a De Gasperi: Storia del dopoguerra 1945–1948* (Milan: Feltrinelli, 1975)

Porch, Douglas, *Hitler's Mediterranean Gamble* (London: Weidenfeld & Nicolson, 2004)

Prażmowska, Anita, *Civil War in Poland 1942–1948* (Basingstoke: Palgrave Macmillan, 2004)

Proudfoot, Malcolm J., *European Refugees 1939–52* (London: Faber & Faber, 1957)

Ray, John, *The Second World War* (London: Cassell, 1999)

Rees, Laurence, *Auschwitz* (London: BBC Books, 2005)

———, *World War Two behind Closed Doors* (London: BBC Books, 2008)

Richter, Heinz, *British Intervention in Greece: From Varkiza to Civil War* (London: Merlin Press, 1985)

Rioux, Jean-Pierre, *The Fourth Republic 1944–1958*, trans. Godfrey Rogers (Cambridge University Press, 1987)

Roberts, Andrew, *The Storm of War* (London: Allen Lane, 2009)

Rousso, Henry, 'The Purge in France', in Jon Elster (ed.), *Retribution and Reparation in the Transition to Democracy* (New York: Cambridge University Press, 2006)

Rubenstein, Joshua, *Tangled Loyalties: The Life and Times of Ilya Ehrenburg* (London and New York: I. B. Tauris, 1996)

Rumanian National Committee, *Persecution of Religion in Rumania* (Washington, DC: Rumanian National Committee, 1949)

———, *Suppression of Human Rights in Rumania* (Washington, DC: Rumanian National Committee, 1949)

Rumpf, Hans, *The Bombing of Germany*, trans. Edward Fitzgerald (London: White Lion, 1975)

Sack, John, *An Eye for an Eye: The Untold Story of Jewish Revenge against Germans in 1945* (New York: Basic Books, 1993)

Sander, Helke and Barbara Johr (eds.), *Befreier und Befreite: Krieg, Vergewaltigun Kinder* (Frankfurt-am-Main: Fischer Taschenbuch, 2006)

Sayer, Derek, *The Coasts of Bohemia: A Czech History* (Princeton University Press, 1998)

Schöpflin, George, *Politics in Eastern Europe* (Oxford and Cambridge, MA: Blackwell, 1993)

Sebag-Montefiore, Simon, *Stalin: The Court of the Red Tsar* (London: Weidenfeld & Nicolson, 2003)

Sebald, W. G., *On the Natural History of Destruction* (London, 2004)

Service, Robert, *A History of Modern Russia* (London: Penguin, 2003)

Shephard, Ben, *After Daybreak* (London: Pimlico, 2005)

———, *The Long Road Home: The Aftermath of the Second World War* (London: Bodley Head, 2010)

Siemaszko, Ewa, 'Bilans Zbrodni', *Biuletyn Instytutu Pamięci Narodowej*, nos. 7–8 (July–August 2010)

Siemaszko, Władisław and Ewa Siemaszko, *Ludobójstwo dokonane przez nacjonalistów ukraińskich na ludności polskiej Wołynia 1939–1945*, 2 vols. (Warsaw: Wydawn. von borowiecky, 2000)

Siklos, Pierre L., *War Finance, Reconstruction, Hyperinflation and Stabilization in Hungary, 1938–48* (Basingstoke: Macmillan, 1991)

Skolnik, Fred and Michael Berenbaum (eds.), *Encyclopaedia Judaica*, 22 vols. (Farmington Hills, MI: Thomson Gale, 2007)

Snyder, Timothy, *The Reconstruction of Nations: Poland, Ukraine, Lithuania, Belarus, 1569–1999* (New Haven and London: Yale University Press, 2003)

Spector, Shmuel, *Holocaust of Volhynian Jews*, trans. Jerzy Michalowicz (Jerusalem: Yad Vashem, 1990)

Spoerer, Mark, *Zwangsarbeit unter dem Hakenkreuz* (Stuttgart: Deutsche Verlags-Anstalt, 2001)

Staněk, Tomáš, *Internierung und Zwangsarbeit: Das Lagersystem in den böhmischen Ländern 1945 –1948* (Munich: R. Oldenbourg, 2007)

———, *Odsun Němců z Československa 1945–1947* (Prague: Academia/Naše vojsko, 1991)

———, *Retribuční vězni v českých zemích 1945–1955* (Opava: Slezský ústav Slezského zemského muzea, 2002)

———, *Verfolgung 1945: Die Stellung der Deutschen in Böhmen, Mähren und Schlesien* (Vienna, Cologne and Weimar: Böhlau Verlag, 2002)

Starkauskas, Juozas, 'The NKVD-MVD-MGB Army', in Arvydas Anušauskas (ed.), *The Anti-Soviet Resistance in the Baltic States* (Vilnius: Genocide and Resistance Research Centre of Lithuania, 2000)

Statiev, Alexander, *The Soviet Counterinsurgency in the Western Borderlands* (New York: Cambridge University Press, 2010)

Steinberg, Jonathan, *All or Nothing: The Axis and the Holocaust, 1941–1943* (London and New York: Routledge, 1990)

Storchi, Massimo, *Uscire dalla guerra: ordine pubblico e forze politiche, Modena 1945–1946* (Milan: Angeli, 1995)

Strods, Heinrichs, 'The Latvian Partisan War between 1944 and 1956', in Arvydas Anušauskas (ed.), *The Anti-Soviet Resistance in the Baltic States* (Vilnius: Genocide and Resistance Research Centre of Lithuania, 2000)

Takala, Hannu and Henrik Tham, *Crime and Control in Scandinavia during the Second World War* (Oslo: Norwegian University Press, 1989)

Taylor, Frederick, *Dresden* (New York: HarperCollins, 2004)

Tec, Nechama, *Defiance: The True Story of the Bielski Partisans* (Oxford University Press, 2008)

Tismaneanu, Vladimir, *Stalinism for all Seasons* (Berkeley: University of California Press, 2003)

Tolstoy, Nikolai, *Stalin's Secret War* (New York: Holt, Reinhart and Winston, 1981)

Tomasevich, Jozo, *War and Revolution in Yugoslavia: Occupation and Collaboration* (Stanford University Press, 2001)

Tooze, Adam, *The Wages of Destruction* (London: Penguin, 2007)

Tsaruk, Iaroslav, *Trahediia volyns'kykh sil, 1943–1944 rr.* (Lviv: I. Krypiakevych Institute of Ukrainian Studies, 2003)

Uehling, Greta Lynn, *Beyond Memory: The Crimean Tatars' Deportation and Return* (London and New York: Palgrave Macmillan, 2004)

United States Holocaust Memorial Museum, *The Confiscation of Jewish Property in Europe 1933–1945: Symposium Proceedings* (New York: USHMM Center for Advanced Holocaust Studies, 2003)

Upton, A. F., *The Communist Parties of Scandinavia and Finland* (London: Weidenfeld & Nicolson, 1973)

van der Zee, Henri, *The Hunger Winter: Occupied Holland 1944–5* (London: Jill Norman and Hobhouse, 1982)

Vardys, V. Stanley and Judith B. Sedaitis, *Lithuania: The Rebel Nation* (Boulder, CO: Westview Press, 1997)

Vědecká Konference 'Národní podoby antisemitismu', *Retribuce v ČSR a národní podoby antisemitismu* (Prague: Institute of Contemporary History, 2002)

Veyret, Patrick, *Lyon 1939–1949: De la collaboration industrielle à l'épuration économique* (Châtillon-sur-Chalaronne: La Taillanderie, 2008)

Virgili, Fabrice, *Shorn Women: Gender and Punishment in Liberation France*, trans. John Flower (Oxford and New York: Berg, 2002)

Voglis, Polymeris, 'Between Negation and Self-Negation: Political Prisoners in Greece, 1945–1950', in Mark Mazower (ed.), *After the War Was Over* (Princeton and Oxford: Princeton University Press, 2000)

Warring, Anette, *Tyskerpiger – under besættelse og retsopgør* (Copenhagen: Gyldendal, 1994)

———, 'War, Cultural Loyalty and Gender', in Kjersti Ericsson and Eva Simonsen (eds.), *Children of World War II* (Oxford and New York: Berg, 2005)

Watson, Peter, *A Terrible Beauty* (London: Phoenix, 2001)

Weitz, Margaret Collins, *Sisters in the Resistance: How Women Fought to Free France, 1940–1945* (New York: John Wiley & Sons, 1995)

Werner, Hermann, *Tübingen 1945* (Stuttgart: Konrad Theiss Verlag, 1986)

Werth, Alexander, *Russia at War* (London: Barrie & Rockliff, 1964)

Willis, F. Roy, *The French in Germany 1945–1949* (Stanford University Press, 1962)

Wilson, Kevin, *Bomber Boys* (London: Weidenfeld & Nicolson, 2005)

Winterton, Paul, *Report on Russia* (London: Cresset Press, 1945)

Withuis, Jolande and Annet Mooij (eds.), *The Politics of War Trauma: The Aftermath of World War II in Eleven European Countries* (Amsterdam: Askant, 2010)

Woller, Hans, *Die Abrechnung mit dem Faschismus in Italien, 1943 bis 1948* (Munich: Oldenbourg, 1996)

Wyman, Mark, *DPs: Europe's Displaced Persons, 1945–1951* (Ithaca and London: Cornell University Press, 1998)

Yekelchyk, Serhy, *Ukraine: Birth of a Modern Nation* (Oxford University Press, 2007)

Žerjavić, Vladimir, *Yugoslavian Manipulations with the Number of Second World War Victims* (Zagreb: Croatian Information Centre, 1993)

Collections of documents

Anon., *Komu sluší omluva: Češi a sudetští němci (Dokumenti, fakta, svědectví)*

Beneš, Edvard, *Speech delivered by President E. Beneš on the Old Town Square, Prague, on His Return to Czechoslovakia, May 16th 1945* (Prague: Orbis, 1945; repr. Prague: Erika, 1992)

Białecki, Tadeusz et al. (eds.), *Źródła do dziejów Pomorza Zachodniego: Niemcy na Pomorzu Zachodnim w latach 1945–1950* (Szczecin University, 2004)

Borodziej, Włodzimierz and Hans Lemberg (eds.), *Die Deutschen östlich von Oder und Neiße 1945–1950: Dokumente aus polnischen Archiven*, 4 vols. (Marburg: Herder Institut, 2003–4)

Cannadine, David (ed.), *Blood Toil Tears and Sweat: Winston Churchill's Famous Speeches* (London: Cassell, 1989)

Clogg, Richard (ed.), *Greece 1940–1949: Occupation, Resistance, Civil War: A Documentary History* (Basingstoke: Palgrave Macmillan, 2002)

Dziurok, Adam (ed.), *Obóz Pracy w Świętochłowicach w 1945 roku* (Warsaw: Instytut Pamięci Narodowej, 2003)

Misiło, Eugeniusz (ed.), *Akcja 'Wisła'* (Warsaw: Archiwum Ukraińskie, 1993)

———, *Repatriacja czy deportacja?: Przesiedlenie Ukraińców z Polski do USSR 1944–1946* (Warsaw: Archiwum Ukraińskie, 1996–9)

Pustejovsky, Otfrid, *Die Konferenz von Potsdam und das Massaker von Aussig am 31 Juli 1945* (Munich: Herbig, 2001)

Rupić, Mate et al. (eds.), *Partizanska i komunistička represija i zločini u Hrvatskoj 1944–1946: Dokumenti* (Slavonski Brod: Hrvatski institut za povijest, 2005)

Spieler, Silke (ed.), *Vertreibung und Vertreibungsverbrechen 1945–1948: Bericht des Bundesarchivs vom 28 Mai 1974, Archivalien und ausgewählte Erlebnisberichte* (Bonn: Bundesarchiv Koblenz & Kulturstiftung der Deutschen Vertriebenen, 1989)

Stalin, Generalissimo Josef, *War Speeches, Orders of the Day and Answers to Foreign Press Correspondents during the Great Patriotic War July 3rd, 1941 – June 22nd, 1945* (London: Hutchinson, 1946)

Trgo, Lt Gen. Fabijan (ed.), *The National Liberation War and Revolution in Yugoslavia: Selected Documents*, trans. Anđelija Vujović, Karin Radovanović and Madge Tomašević (Belgrade: Military History Institute of the Yugoslav People's Army, 1982)

Memoirs, reportage, eyewitness accounts, diaries and letters

Acheson, Dean, *Present at the Creation: My Years at the State Department* (New York: Norton, 1969)

Adler, Hans Guenther, *Theresienstadt 1941–1945: das Antlitz einer Zwangsgemeinschaft – Geschichte, Soziologie, Psychologie* (Tübingen: Mohr, 1955)

Andreas-Friedrich, Ruth, *Battleground Berlin: Diaries 1945–1948*, trans. Anna Boerresen (New York: Paragon House, 1990)

Anon., *The Day War Ended: Voices and Memories from 1945* (London: Weidenfeld & Nicolson, 2005)

———, *A Woman in Berlin* (London: Virago, 2006)

Becker, Hans, *Devil on My Shoulder*, trans. Kennedy McWhirter and Jeremy Potter (London: Four Square Books, 1958)

Bertaux, Pierre, *Libération de Toulouse et de sa région* (Paris: Hachette, 1973)

Blunt, Roscoe C., *Foot Soldier: A Combat Infantryman's War in Europe* (Cambridge, MA: Da Capo Press, 2002)

Bodson, Herman, *Agent for the Resistance* (College Station: Texas A&M University Press, 1994)

Bohec, Jeanne, *La plastiqueuse à bicyclette* (Paris: Mercure de France, 1975)

Byford-Jones, W., *Berlin Twilight* (London: Hutchinson, 1947)

Churchill, Winston, *The Second World War*, 6 vols. (London: Cassell, 1948–54)

Clay, Lucius D., *Decision in Germany* (London: Heinemann, 1950)

De Gasperi, Maria-Romana (ed.), *De Gasperi scrive: corrispondenza con capi di stato, cardinali, uomini politici, giornalisti, diplomatici*, 2 vols. (Brescia: Morecelliana, 1974)

de Gaulle, Charles, *Mémoires de Guerre*, vol. II: *L'Unité 1942–1944* (Paris: Plon, 1956)

Dimitrov, Georgi, *The Diary of Georgi Dimitrov 1933–1949*, trans. Jane T. Hedges, Timothy D. Sergay and Irina Faion (New Haven and London: Yale University Press, 2003)

Djilas, Milovan, *Conversations with Stalin*, trans. Michael B. Petrovich (London: Rupert Hart-Davis, 1962)

———, *Wartime* (New York and London: Harcourt Brace Jovanovich, 1977)

Donat, Alexander, *The Holocaust Kingdom: A Memoir* (London: Secker & Warburg, 1965)

Ehrenburg, Ilya and Vasily Grossman (eds.), *The Black Book*, trans. John Glad and James S. Levine (New York: Holocaust Library, 1981)

Eisenhower, Dwight D., *Crusade in Europe* (London: Heinemann, 1948)

Esser, Heinz, *Die Hölle von Lamsdorf: Dokumentation über ein polnisches Vernichtungslager* (Bonn: Landsmannschaft der Oberschlesier e.V., 1969)

Farge, Yves, *Rebelles, soldats et citoyens* (Paris: Grasset, 1946)

FitzGibbon, Theodora, *With Love* (London: Century, 1982)

Frommer, Benjamin, *National Cleansing: Retribution against Nazi Collaborators in Postwar Czechoslovakia* (Cambridge University Press, 2005)

Fuykschot, Cornelia, *Hunger in Holland: Life during the Nazi Occupation* (New York: Prometheus, 1995)

Geddes, Giorgio, *Nichivo* (London: Cassell, 2001)

Grassmann, Ilse, *Ausgebombt: Ein Hausfrauen-Kriegstagebuch* (Hamburg: Haymarket Media, 2003)

Gruschka, Gerhard, *Zgoda: Ein Ort des Schreckens* (Neureid: Ars Una, 1996)

Haukelid, Knut, *Det demrer en dag* (Oslo: Nasjonalforlaget, 1947)

Iatrides John O. (ed.), *Ambassador MacVeagh Reports: Greece 1933–1947* (Princeton University Press, 1980)

Jacobs, Ingeborg, *Freiwild: Das Schicksal deutscher Frauen 1945* (Berlin: Propyläen, 2008)

Kaps, Johannes, *The Tragedie of Silesia 1945–46* (Munich: Christ Unterwegs, 1952)

Karapandzich, Boriwoje M., *The Bloodiest Yugoslav Spring, 1945: Tito's Katyns and Gulags* (New York: Hearthstone, 1980)

Kardorff, Ursula von, *Diary of a Nightmare: Berlin 1942–1945*, trans. Ewan Butler (London: Rupert Hart-Davis, 1965)

Kennan, George F., *Memoirs 1925–1950* (Boston and Toronto: Little, Brown, 1967)

Klemperer, Victor, *To the Bitter End: The Diaries of Victor Klemperer 1942–45*, trans. Martin Chalmers (London: Weidenfeld & Nicolson, 1999)

Kopelev, Lev, *No Jail for Thought*, trans. and ed. Anthony Austin (London: Secker & Warburg, 1977)

Kovaly, Heda Margolis, *Prague Farewell*, trans. Franci Epstein and Helen Epstein (London: Gollancz, 1988)

Lane, Arthur Bliss, *I Saw Poland Betrayed: An American Ambassador Reports to the American People* (New York and Indianapolis: Bobbs-Merrill, 1948)

Levi, Primo, *Survival in Auschwitz and The Reawakening: Two Memoirs*, trans. Stuart Woolf (New York: Summit Books, 1986)

Lewis, Norman, *Naples '44* (London: Collins, 1978)

Lotnik, Waldemar, *Nine Lives* (London: Serif, 1999)

Lukša, Juozas, *Forest Brothers: The Account of an anti-Soviet Lithuanian Freedom Fighter 1944–1948*, trans. Laima Vincė (Budapest and New York: Central European University Press, 2009)

Manus, Max, *Det blir alvor* (Oslo: Steensballes Boghandels, 1946)

Markov, Georgi, *The Truth that Killed*, trans. Liliana Brisby (London: Weidenfeld & Nicolson, 1983)

Moorehead, Alan, *Eclipse* (London: Granta, 2000)

Mosley, Leonard O., *Report from Germany* (London: Gollancz, 1945)

Müller, Jens, *Tre kom tilbake* (Oslo: Gyldendal, 1946)

Mungone, G., *Operazione rossa* (Padua: Tipografia Gori di Tognana, 1959)

Nagy, Ferenc, *The Struggle behind the Iron Curtain*, trans. Stephen K. Swift (New York: Macmillan, 1948)

Nicolson, Nigel, *Long Life* (London: Weidenfeld & Nicolson, 1997)

Nossack, Hans Erich, *Der Untergang* (Hamburg: Ernst Kabel Verlag, 1981)

Olsen, Oluf, *Contact* (Oslo: Erik Qvist, 1946)

———, *Vi kommer igjen* (Oslo: Erik Qvist, 1945)

Owen, James and Guy Walters (eds.), *The Voice of War* (London: Viking, 2004)

Padover, Saul, *Psychologist in Germany: The Story of an American Intelligence Officer* (London: Phoenix House, 1946)

Patton, George S., *War as I Knew It* (Boston: Houghton Mifflin, 1947)

Polcz, Alaine, *One Woman in the War* (Budapest and New York: Central European University Press, 2002)

Prcela, John and Stanko Guldescu (eds.), *Operation Slaughterhouse: Eyewitness Accounts of Postwar Massacres in Yugoslavia* (Philadelphia: Dorrance & Co., 1970)

Robinson, Austin, *First Sight of Germany, May–June 1945* (Cambridge: Cantelupe Press, 1986)

Roosevelt, Elliott, *As He Saw It* (New York: Duell, Sloan and Pearce, 1946)

Ruhl, Klaus-Jörg (ed.), *Unsere verlorenen Jahre: Frauenalltag in Kriegs- und Nachkriegszeit 1939–1949, in Berichten, Dokumenten und Bilden* (Darmstadt: Luchterhand, 1985)

Saint-Exupéry, Antoine de, *Flight to Arras*, trans. Lewis Galantière (Harmondsworth: Penguin, 1961)

Schuetz, Hans A. D., *Davai, Davai!: Memoir of a German Prisoner of World War II in the Soviet Union* (Jefferson, NC, and London: McFarland & Co., 1997)

Sington, Derrick, *Belsen Uncovered* (London: Duckworth, 1946)

Smith, Lyn, *Forgotten Voices of the Holocaust* (London: Ebury Press, 2005)

Toth, Zoltan, *Prisoner of the Soviet Union*, trans. George Unwin (Woking: Gresham Press, 1978)

Truman, Harry S., *Memoirs*, vol. II: *Years of Trial and Hope* (New York: Signet, 1965)

Vachon, John, *Poland 1946: The Photographs and Letters of John Vachon*, ed. Ann Vachon (Washington, DC, and London: Smithsonian Institute Press, 1995)

von Einsiedel, Count Heinrich, *The Shadow of Stalingrad: Being the Diary of a Temptation* (London: Alan Wingate, 1953)

Voute, Peter, *Only a Free Man: War Memoirs of Two Dutch Doctors (1940–1945)* (Santa Fe, NM: The Lightning Tree, 1982)

Wilson, Francesca, *Aftermath: France, Germany, Austria, Yugoslavia, 1945 and 1946* (London: Penguin, 1947)

Wolff-Mönckeberg, Mathilde, *On the Other Side: To My Children from Germany 1940–1945* (London: Peter Owen, 1979)

Woodhouse, C. M., *Apple of Discord* (London: Hutchinson, 1948)

Notes

INTRODUCTION

1. Dean Acheson memorandum to Harry Hopkins, 26 December 1944, *Foreign Relations of the United States (FRUS)*, 1945, vol. II, pp. 1059–61. Pope Pius XII's address to the Sacred College of Cardinals, *New York Times*, 3 June 1945, p. 22.
2. 'Europe: The New Dark Continent', *New York Times* magazine, 18 March 1945, p. 5.

PART I – THE LEGACY OF WAR

1. Samuel Puterman, quoted in Michał Grynberg (ed.), *Words to Outlive Us: Eyewitness Accounts from the Warsaw Ghetto* (London: Granta, 2003), p. 440.
2. Acheson, p. 231.

CHAPTER I – PHYSICAL DESTRUCTION

1. Baedeker, pp. 85–94.
2. Davies, *Rising '44*, p. 556.
3. Ibid., pp. 666–7.
4. Ibid., p. 439.
5. Ministry of Culture & Art, *Warsaw Accuses*, pp. 19–24; and Davies, *God's Playground*, p. 355.
6. Ministry of Culture & Art, *Warsaw Accuses*, pp. 19–24.
7. Vachon, p. 5, letter of 10 January 1946.
8. Hastings, *Armageddon*.
9. HM Government, *Statistics*, p. 9; see also The National Archives (TNA): Public Record Office (PRO) CAB 21/2110 and *Daily Express*, 29 November 1944.
10. Ray, pp. 95–6.
11. Hitchcock, p. 44.

12. Florentin, p. 430.

13. Gaillard, p. 113.

14. Rioux, p. 471.

15. According to Ferenc Nagy, p. 129.

16. See Judt, p. 16; and Werth, p. 864.

17. Werth, p. 709.

18. See Kondufor, p. 239; and Krawchenko, p. 15.

19. Valentin Berezhkov, quoted in Beevor, *Stalingrad*, p. 418.

20. Werth, p. 837.

21. Kennan, pp. 280–82.

22. United States Strategic Bombing Survey (USSBS), *Over-all Report (European War)*, 1945, p. 72. Tooze has 3.8 million, p. 672; and the German Federal Statistics Office in Wiesbaden calculated 3.37 million – see Hastings, *Bomber Command*, p. 352.

23. The 202,000 British homes damaged beyond repair represented just over 1.5 per cent of the total: HM Government, *Statistics*, pp. 31–2; see also TNA: PRO CAB 21/2110.

24. See Rumpf, pp. 128–9. The British Bombing Survey Unit has Berlin 33 per cent, Hanover 60 per cent, Hamburg 75 per cent, Duisburg 48 per cent, Dortmund 54 per cent, Cologne 61 per cent; see Webster and Frankland, vol. IV, pp. 484–6. The United States Strategic Bombing Survey has other figures again: e.g. Hamburg at 61 per cent – see Lowe, p. 318.

25. Robinson, diary entry for Monday, 28 May 1945.

26. Philip J. C. Dark, IWM Docs 94/7/1, typescript account, 'Look Back This Once: Prisoner of War in Germany in WWII'.

27. Herbert Conert, quoted in Taylor, p. 396. For Dresden as moonscape see Kurt Vonnegut, *Slaughterhouse 5* (London: Vintage, 1991), pp. 130–31.

28. Klemperer, p. 596, diary entry for 22 May 1945.

29. Colonel R. G. Turner, IWM Docs, 05/22/1, letter to his mother, 11 July 1945.

30. Janet Flaner quoted in Sebald, p. 31.

31. USSBS, *Over-all Report*, p. 95. For prewar populations, see Maddison, pp. 38–9.

32. Taras Hunczak, 'Ukrainian–Jewish Relations during the Soviet and Nazi Occupations', in Boshyk, p. 47; and Kondufor, p. 239. The prewar population of Hungary was 9,227,000: see Maddison, p. 96.

33. Lane, p. 26.

34. Werth, p. 815.

35. Anne O'Hare McCormick, 'Europe's Five Black Years', *New York Times Magazine*, 3 September 1944, p. 42.

36. Ibid., pp. 42–3.

37. Judt, p. 17. Early estimates by SHAEF (15 December 1944) are slightly lower at 500,000 acres (202,000 hectares); see Coles and Weinberg, p. 826.

38. Nøkelby, p. 315.

39. Mazower, *Inside Hitler's Greece*, p. 155; Judt, p. 17; and Hitchcock, p. 228, has a larger estimate of 1,700 villages.

40. Tomasevich, p. 715.

41. Judt, p. 17. In Ukraine alone 28,000 villages were destroyed: see Krawchenko, p. 15.

42. Stalin, *War Speeches*, p. 7.

43. Quoted in Andrew Gregorovich, 'World War II in Ukraine', *Forum: A Ukrainian Review*, no. 92 (Spring 1997), available online at http://www.infoukes.com/history/ww2/page-26.html.

44. Order to SS-Obergruppenführer Prützmann on 3 September 1943, quoted in Dallin, p. 364.

45. See Glanz, pp. 170 and 186.

46. Judt, p. 17.

47. Tomasevich, p. 715.

48. For Finland and Norway see Nøkelby, p. 315; for Poland see Jan Szafrański, 'Poland's Losses in World War II', in Nurowski, pp. 68–9; for Holland, France and the USSR see Judt, p. 17; for Greece see Judt, p. 17 and Hitchcock, p. 228; for Italy see UNRRA statistics quoted in Hitchcock, p. 234, and Vera Zamagni, 'Italy: How to Lose the War and Win the Peace', in Harrison, p. 212; for Yugoslavia see Tomasevich, p. 715; for Ukraine see Kondufor, p. 239.

49. Philip J. C. Dark, IWM Docs 94/7/1, typescript account, 'Look Back This Once: Prisoner of War in Germany in WWII', entry for 19 April 1945.

50. Levi, pp. 288–9.

51. Ibid., p. 367.

CHAPTER 2 – ABSENCE

1. Nossack, p. 67.

2. Ibid., p. 98.

3. Ibid., p. 68. Lowe, *passim*.

4. Working out statistics for war deaths is an extremely difficult matter, complicated by lack of proper data, changes in territory, problems over what constitutes a 'war death', huge population movements, and so on. For complicating factors in each country see Frumkin, *passim*.

5. Based on prewar Polish territory: see Frumkin, pp. 60 and 117. For comparison, see Maddison, pp. 38 and 96.

6. Frumkin (p. 168) and Dupuy and Dupuy (p. 1309) give vastly differing figures; but Britain's Central Statistical Office (pp. 13, 37 and 40) gives 63,635 civilians killed by the war, and 234,475 in the armed services – so I have assumed these figures to be the most reliable. Milward gives 611,596 deaths including those from the Commonwealth – see his *War, Economy and Society*, p. 211.

7. France: Frumkin gives 600,000, as does Rioux, p. 18; but Milward gives

497,000 deaths in *War, Economy and Society*, p. 211, and, like Rioux, mentions a possible further 300,000 indirect war casualties (from malnutrition etc.). Holland: Frumkin gives 210,000, p. 168, as does the Centraal Bureau voor de Statistiek, p. 749, and possibly 70,000 indirect war casualties. Belgium: Frumkin gives 88,000, p. 168, and estimates 27,000 of these were Jews; Martin Gilbert gives 24,387 Belgian Jews, *Atlas of the Holocaust*, p. 231. Italy: Frumkin gives 410,000, p. 103; but official Italian government statistics show 159,957 military casualties and 149,496 civilian casualties, making a total of 309,453 – see Istituto Centrale di Statistica, pp. 3–11.

8. Estimates vary wildly, depending on definitions of German borders, German nationality, cut-off dates for war dead, estimates for deaths in Soviet prison camps, etc. Frumkin inaccurately gives 4.2 million German deaths (p. 83); Overmans gives over 6 million, of which 4,456,000 are military deaths – see *Deutsche militärische Verluste*, pp. 333–6. Milward also gives 6 million, *War, Economy and Society*, p. 211. According to the USSBS *Over-all Report*, p. 95, 305,000 German civilians were killed by Allied bombing; but the more comprehensive Statistisches Bundesamt in 1962 gives 570,000 – see their *Wirtschaft und Statistik*, 1962, p. 139.

9. Frumkin has 160,000 deaths, plus 140,000 from famine, pp. 89–91. However, the number of famine deaths was actually far higher: 250,000 according to a Red Cross study; see Mazower, *Inside Hitler's Greece*, p. 41. Many historians put famine deaths at 350,000: see Hionidou, pp. 2, 158. Maddison, p. 44, has the prewar Greek population at 7,156,000.

10. Frumkin has 430,000 war deaths (p. 94); Glanz estimates between 420,000 and 450,000, p. 169. Maddison has the prewar Hungarian population at 9,227,000 (p. 96).

11. The most reliable figure is 1,027,000: see discussions in Tomasevich, pp. 718–50, and Croatian State Commission, pp. 19–26. According to Maddison, p. 96, the prewar population of Yugoslavia was 16,305,000.

12. This percentage is an educated guess by Misiunas and Taagepera, p. 356.

13. Frumkin has Polish deaths at 5.8 million, including 3.2 million Jews (p. 122), but official Polish statistics in 1947 put the figure at 6,028,000 (which, unofficially, includes 2.9 million Jews) – see Biuro Odszkodowańjennych przy Prezydium Rady Ministrów. See also Davies, *God's Playground*, p. 344 and Jan Szafrański, 'Poland's Losses in World War II', in Nurowski, p. 44. The prewar population of Poland was 34.8 million – see note 5.

14. Estimates differ wildly: see Krivosheev, p. 83; and Barber and Harrison, p. 206. Milward has just 17 million, *War, Economy and Society*, p. 211. Overy, p. 288, has 25 million, and notes that the official figure by Khrushchev in 1956 was 20 million, and by Gorbachev in 1991 was 25 million.

15. Yekelchyk, p. 151. See also Krawchenko, p. 15, who has 6.8 million. Kondufor has 5 million, p. 222.

16. Statiev, p. 64.

17. Edith Baneth, quoted in Smith, p. 318.

18. Moorhouse, p. 183.

19. Victor Breitburg quoted in Anon., *The Day War Ended*, p. 200.

20. See Friedländer, p. 219, for lower prewar figure; and Snyder, pp. 74 and 86, for higher prewar figure, and the postwar percentage. See also Skolnik and Berenbaum, vol. XX, p. 531.

21. Skolnik and Berenbaum, vol. XX, pp. 670, 674.

22. Skolnik and Berenbaum, vol. XIV, p. 294.

23. Spector, pp. 357–8.

24. Gilbert, *Atlas of the Holocaust*, p. 232. According to the Nuremberg evidence the figure was 5.7 million, though later estimates put it at 5,933,900 – see Dawidowicz, pp. 479–80.

25. Alicia Adams, quoted in Smith, p. 317. The figure she gives is exaggerated: of 17,000 Jews at the beginning of the war, only 400 remained at the time of Soviet liberation. See Skolnik and Berenbaum, vol. VI, p. 24.

26. Quoted in Beevor and Vinogradova, p. 251.

27. Quoted ibid., p. 253.

28. Celina Liberman testimony in Anon., *The Day War Ended*, p. 184.

29. Gilbert, *Atlas of the Holocaust*, p. 229. Dawidowicz gives 3 million survivors, but includes 868,000 Russian Jewish survivors: see p. 480.

30. Gilbert, *Atlas of the Holocaust*, p. 154; Dawidowicz, p. 446.

31. Steinberg, *passim*.

32. Gilbert, *Atlas of the Holocaust*, p. 140; Dawidowicz, pp. 464–5.

33. Gilbert, *Atlas of the Holocaust*, p. 230.

34. Hondius, p. 97.

35. There has been some wild exaggeration about the numbers of Serbs killed during the war. This figure is probably the most accurate; see Tomasevich, pp. 727–8.

36. Zbigniew Ogrodzinski, personal interview, 30 October 2007. The same thing occurred in Transnistria; see Werth, pp. 814–15.

37. Major A. G. Moon, IWM Docs 06/126/1, typescript memoir, p. 50.

38. Milward, *War, Economy and Society*, p. 215.

39. National minorities in December 1945 accounted for only 10 per cent of the population of eastern Europe: see Pearson, p. 229.

40. Farmer, *passim*.

41. For statistics on Lidice see Anon., *Komu sluší omluva?*, p. 70; and Sayer, pp. 231 and 369, fn. 45.

42. Miloslava Kalibová interview in Charles Wheeler's BBC documentary *A Shadow Over Europe*, 2002.

43. Miloslava Kalibová interview with Carmen T. Illichmann, 'Lidice: Remembering the Women and Children', *UW-L Journal of Undergraduate Research*, 8 (2005).

44. Saint-Exupéry, p. 63.
45. Major A. G. Moon, IWM Docs 06/126/1, typescript memoir. In Berlin there were almost two women for every man: see Naimark, *Russians*, p. 127.
46. See Barber and Harrison, p. 207; also Mark Harrison's essay 'The Soviet Union: The Defeated Victor', in Harrison, p. 286; and Milward, *War, Economy and Society*, p. 212.
47. See Macardle, pp. 107, 202, 231. See also Brosse, p. 29.
48. Byford-Jones, p. 52.
49. Ibid., p. 55.
50. Macardle, p. 80. This is a conservative figure: UNESCO figures from 1946 suggest 1.7 million; see Brosse, p. 30.
51. TNA: PRO FO 938/310.
52. Andrzej C., personal interview, 3 March 2008.
53. Brosse, p. 29.
54. Andrzej C., personal interview, 3 March 2008.
55. According to Red Cross estimates in 1948, Brosse, p. 28.
56. For official figures in various countries, see Macardle, pp. 58, 80, 107, 156, 200, 206 and 287.
57. See, for example, Lucie Cluver and Frances Gardner, 'The Mental Health of Children Orphaned by Aids: A Review of International And Southern African Research', *Journal of Child and Adolescent Mental Health*, 19 (1) (2007), pp. 1–17. This compares AIDS orphans with orphans from other causes (including war) and non-orphans.

CHAPTER 3 – DISPLACEMENT

1. According to Tooze, p. 517, foreign labour in Germany reached a peak of 7,907,000 at the end of 1944. See also IWM Docs 84/47/1, statistical tables kept by Miss B. F. N. Lewis; Spoerer, p. 222; Proudfoot, p. 159.
2. For number of bombing evacuees see TNA: PRO WO 219/3549. For German refugees fleeing the Red Army, see Tooze, p. 672. See also Beevor, *Berlin*, p. 48.
3. For the various conflicting figures for British and American prisoners of war, see Nichol and Rennell, pp. 416–20.
4. For the total number of displaced in *all* of Germany, Tooze has 20 million, p. 672. For figures on individual groups within this total see Spoerer, p. 212; Hitchcock, p. 250; Proudfoot, pp. 158–9; Marrus, pp. 299, 326.
5. Proudfoot, p. 34.
6. Derek L. Henry, IWM Docs 06/126/1, typescript memoir, p. 93.
7. Padover, p. 273.
8. Mrs E. Druhm, IWM Docs 02/28/1, manuscript memoir.
9. Major A. G. Moon, IWM Docs 06/126/1, typescript memoir, p. 58.
10. Andrzej C., personal interview, 11 February 2008.

11. Mrs E. Druhm, IWM Docs 02/28/1, manuscript memoir.

12. Marilka Ossowska, personal interview, 17 November 2007.

CHAPTER 4 – FAMINE

1. For Spain see *New York Times* magazine, 18 March 1945, p. 51; for Switzerland see Milward, *War, Economy and Society*, p. 255.

2. See Hionidou, esp. ch. 4.

3. Ibid., p. 162.

4. According to the Red Cross: see Mazower, *Inside Hitler's Greece*, p. 41. For figures ranging from 100,000 to 450,000 see Hionidou, pp. 2, 158.

5. For German requisitions and the subsequent Dutch hardship, see van der Zee, *passim*, and Fuykschot, pp. 124–50.

6. For reports on Holland, see TNA: PRO FO 371/39329, 20 May 1944; and AIR 8/823, 'Interview between the Prime Minister and Dr Gerbrandy, Prime Minister of the Netherlands', 5 October 1944. For statistics on emergency supplies shipped to Holland, against those shipped to Belgium, see WO 106/4419, and FO 371/49032. See also Hitchcock, pp. 98–122.

7. NARA RG 331 SHAEF G-5, entry 47, box 27, Military Government Branch, Main HQ, First Canadian Army, Weekly Report no. 27, period 13–19 May 1945.

8. *The Times*, 7 May 1945.

9. For the lower figure see Hitchcock, p. 122; for the higher figure see Hirschfeld, p. 53.

10. Himmler to Seyss-Inquart, 7 January 1941, quoted in Hirschfeld, p. 46.

11. Tooze, p. 264.

12. Ibid., p. 539.

13. Calorific intake figures in Judt, p. 21; Tooze, p. 361.

14. Letter of 4 February 1945, in Wolff-Mönckeberg, p. 107.

15. Tooze, p. 419.

16. For rations in liberated Holland, see TNA: PRO WO 32/16168, Montgomery message to Eisenhower. For rations in German-occupied Holland, see Burger et al., pp. 20–24. For Rotterdam, see Hitchcock, p. 114.

17. Quoted in Mazower, *Inside Hitler's Greece*, p. 33.

18. Tooze, p. 467.

19. Ibid., p. 366.

20. Ibid., pp. 479–80. At a weekend party just before the invasion of Russia began, Himmler told colleagues, 'The purpose of the Russian campaign is to decimate the Slavic population by thirty millions'; see Rees, *Auschwitz*, pp. 53–4.

21. See, for example, the many stories in Geddes, *passim*.

22. Krawchenko, p. 27.

23. For the lower figure see Spoerer, p. 72; for the higher figure see Tooze, p. 482, who claims that a further 600,000 were executed. See also Herbert, p. 141.
24. Glantz, p. 220.
25. TNA, FO 1005/1631, Reports on conditions in Germany, 1945–1946.
26. *New York Times*, 9 September 1944: '$100,000,000 in Aid Sent to Italians'; *Daily Express*, 6 September 1944: 'Finished with War, Rome Cries for Bread'; *New York Times*, 8 December 1944: 'Housewives Riot on Prices in Rome'.
27. Hitchcock, p. 234.
28. See Macardle, p. 206.
29. Ruth Irmgard testimony in Jacobs, p. 72.
30. Botting, p. 168; Lewis, p. 61.
31. Macardle, p. 201.
32. R. J. Hunting, IWM Docs 10519 P339, typescript memoir, pp. 272–4.
33. Quoted in Hitchcock, p. 277.

CHAPTER 5 – MORAL DESTRUCTION

1. Lewis, pp. 25–6.
2. Ibid., pp. 42–3, 56–7.
3. Blunt, p. 56.
4. Macardle, pp. 94, 206.
5. Moorehead, p. 66.
6. Quoted in Byford-Jones, p. 38.
7. Hionidou, ch. 4.
8. See, for example, Tec, p. 91.
9. Anon., *A Woman in Berlin*, pp. 57–60.
10. Andrzej C., personal interview, 11 February 2008.
11. Risto Jaakkola and Henrik Tham, 'Traditional Crime in Scandinavia During the Second World War', in Takala and Tham, pp. 38–51.
12. Fishman, p. 85.
13. Brosse, p. 80.
14. Zbigniew Ogrodzinski, personal interview, 30 October 2007; Captain I. B. Mackay, IWM Docs 94/8/1, typescript memoir, p. 130.
15. Moorehead, p. 66.
16. Porch, p. 518.
17. Lewis, p. 100.
18. Botting, p. 183. See also TNA: PRO FO 1050/292, letter from anti-Fascist parties of Germany on increase in brigandage, 31 January 1946; and FO 1050/323 for Berlin statistics in 1945.
19. Anon., *A Woman in Berlin*, p. 209.
20. Andreas-Friedrich, p. 20, entry for 9 May 1945.
21. Polcz, p. 92.

22. Alik Ossowski, personal interview, 17 November 2007; Maria Bielicka, personal interview, 28 January 2008.

23. Maria Bielicka, personal interview, 28 January 2008.

24. Milward, *War, Economy and Society*, p. 282.

25. Ibid., p. 283.

26. Quoted in Mazower, *Inside Hitler's Greece*, pp. 60–61.

27. The Great Decree, no. 16/1945, para. 10: see Frommer, p. 353.

28. Lt Gen. Sir Frederick Morgan to the Foreign Office's Under Secretary of State, 14 September 1946, IWM Docs 02/49/1.

29. Margaret Gore interview, IWM Sound, 9285, reel 4.

30. Pavone, pp. 475–91.

31. Lt Gen. Sir Frederick Morgan to the Foreign Office's Under Secretary of State, 14 September 1946, IWM Docs 02/49/1.

32. Quoted in Hitchcock, p. 252.

33. According to the *New York Times*, 23 August 1944.

34. Dutton, pp. 114–22.

35. Photographic evidence of such mutilation exists in the Italian Foreign Ministry Archive, Archivo Storico Diplomatico Jugoslavia (Croazia) AAPP B.138 (1943) – see Steinberg, pp. 30, 271.

36. See Hitchcock, p. 229.

37. According to the Jewish eyewitness Yakov Groyanowski, quoted in Friedländer, p. 318.

38. De Zayas, *Terrible Revenge*, p. 45.

39. Snyder, p. 172.

40. Lotnik, p. 59.

41. See Konrad Kwiet, 'Erziehung zum Mord: Zwei Beispiele zur Kontinuität der deutschen "Endlösung der Judenfrage"', in Grüttner et al., p. 449.

42. Bourke, p. 359.

43. Polcz, p. 104.

44. Kopelev, p. 57.

45. Central Statistical Office, pp. 48–50. See also 'Combating Crime', *The Times*, 23 July 1946, p. 5; and 'A Problem Picture', *The Times*, 3 June 1948, p. 5.

46. Bourke, p. 378.

47. Quoted in Botting, pp. 35–6.

48. Werner, p. 88.

49. See Bosch, pp. 34, 52; and Willis, pp. 69–70: *perception* of the extent of rape by French colonial troops was worse than the reality.

50. Beevor and Vinogradova, p. 209.

51. Genia Demianova quoted in Owen and Walters, p. 134.

52. See Naimark, *Russians*, p. 70.

53. Polcz, pp. 89, 90, 105.

54. Quoted in de Zayas, *Terrible Revenge*, pp. 54–65.

55. See Alexander Solzhenitsyn, *Prussian Nights: A Narrative Poem*, trans. Robert

Conquest (London: Fontana, 1978), pp. 41, 51–3, 93–103; and Lev Kopelev's memoirs, pp. 50–56. See also Beevor, *Berlin*, p. 29.

56. Beevor and Vinogradova, p. 327.
57. Quoted in Andreas-Friedrich, p. 16, entry for 6 May 1945.
58. Kardorff, p. 217.
59. Ost-Dok 2/14, p. 106, quoted in de Zayas, *Terrible Revenge*, p. 45.
60. Judt, p. 20.
61. Johr, p. 54. According to Botting, p. 92, 90,000 women in Berlin sought medical assistance as a consequence of rape. See also Laurel Cohen-Pfister, 'Rape, War and Outrage: Changing Perceptions on German Victimhood in the Period of Post-unification', in Cohen-Pfister and Wienroeder-Skinner, p. 316.
62. Naimark, *Russians*, pp. 79, 94–5.
63. Johr, p. 59.
64. Kenez, p. 44.
65. Lilley, pp. 11–12.
66. Ruhl, p. 155. The official statistics for West Germany alone show 68,000 'Besatzungskinder', of which 3,194 were the product of rape; see the Statistisches Bundesamt figures quoted in Ebba D. Drolshagen, 'Germany's War Children', in Ericsson and Simonsen, p. 232. According to *Die Welt*, 17 August 1948, 2 million abortions were carried out in Germany each year after the war; see Naimark, *Russians*, p. 123.
67. For statistics on the huge outbreaks of VD throughout Europe see Naimark, *Russians*, p. 98; War Office, *Statistical Report on the Health of the Army*, p. 264; United States Army, Office of the Surgeon General, vol. V, p. 257; and Andreas-Friedrich, p. 84, entry for 18 August 1945.
68. For examples of how women who were not raped were affected by the postwar atmosphere see Lena Berg, quoted in Donat, p. 317; Yvette Levy, quoted in Hitchcock, p. 307; Muriel Heath, IWM Docs 98/25/1, manuscript booklet.
69. See, for example, the testimony of Ruth Irmgard in Jacobs, p. 77.
70. Naimark, *Russians*, p. 125. In England and Wales divorce rates tripled between 1939 and 1945: see Central Statistical Office, p. 54.
71. Kopelev, pp. 51, 55. See also Anon., *A Woman in Berlin*, p. 158; Naimark, *Russians*, p. 109.
72. Respectively, the words of Soviet soldiers according to Lena Berg, quoted in Donat, p. 317; a Soviet tank man quoted in Kopelev, p. 51, and a Soviet interpreter's words to the British military governor in Schwerin, Major A. G. Moon, IWM Docs, 06/126/1, typescript memoir, p. 56.
73. Beevor and Vinogradova, p. 327.
74. Kopelev, pp. 56–7.
75. Grassmann, p. 28; MacDonogh, p. 100.
76. Byford-Jones, p. 53.
77. Central Statistical Office, p. 51.

78. United States Strategic Bombing Survey, vol. I, pp. 89–90. See also Beck, p. 220, note 111.

79. *Newsweek* report from Stockholm correspondent, 11 June 1945, p. 56.

80. Borgersrud, p. 75.

81. "'I have looked into the souls of these Nazi boys – they are black'", *Daily Express*, 26 October 1944.

CHAPTER 6 – HOPE

1. Motto of Jean-Paul Sartre's *Les Temps modernes*: see Watson, p. 410.

2. Mayne, pp. 12–32.

3. Jens Müller, *Tre kom tilbake* (Oslo: Gyldendal, 1946); Oluf Olsen, *Contact* (Oslo: Erik Qvist, 1946) and *Vi kommer igjen* (Oslo: Erik Qvist, 1945); Knut Haukelid, *Det demrer en dag* (Oslo: Nasjonalforlaget, 1947); Max Manus, *Det blir alvor* (Oslo: Steensballes Boghandels, 1946).

4. Speech by Josip Broz Tito, 9 May 1945, reproduced as doc. 239 in Trgo, pp. 718–21.

5. Churchill speech, 13 May 1945, quoted in Cannadine, p. 258; VE Day speech, 8 May 1945, quoted on www.winston-churchill-leadership.com/speech-victory.html – accessed 23 September 2011.

6. Declaration of the new Romanian government, as broadcast on Radio Romania, 23 August 1944: see *FRUS, 1944*, vol. IV, p. 191.

7. Speech to meeting of Moscow Communist Party representatives, 6 November 1944, quoted in Stalin, *War Speeches*, p. 110.

8. FitzGibbon, p. 63. FitzGibbon, an Irish food writer, lived in London during the Blitz.

9. Mayne, p. 12.

10. At the time of writing, Croatia had just received the green light to join the European Union, and Serbia was expected to follow suit within a few months.

11. Drakulić, p. 35. For an expanded argument along these lines, and a Polish affirmation of Drakulić's experience, see Jan Gross, 'War as Revolution', in Naimark and Gibianskii, pp. 17–40.

12. Milward, *War, Economy and Society*, pp. 284–6.

13. FitzGibbon, p. 63.

14. Quoted in Owen and Walters, p. 80.

15. Quoted in Philip Morgan, p. 64.

16. Kovaly, p. 57.

17. Quoted in Kenez, p. 107.

18. Pelle, p. 151.

19. Gross, p. 40.

CHAPTER 7 – LANDSCAPE OF CHAOS

1. Dean Acheson memorandum to Harry Hopkins, 26 December 1944, *FRUS*, 1945, vol. II, pp. 1059–61.
2. *New York Times*, 3 June 1945, p. 22. See also *Newsweek*, 11 June 1945, p. 60.

PART II – VENGEANCE

1. Beevor and Vinogradova, p. 248.

CHAPTER 8 – THE THIRST FOR BLOOD

1. *Le Courrier de Genève*, 7 November 1944. Fisch, pp. 151–3, disputes the accuracy of this report, as well as the author's claims to have been an eyewitness.
2. Hermann Sommer, quoted in Spieler, p. 148.
3. See Fisch, pp. 165–7, who refutes claims that this happened in Nemmersdorf, but admits that it probably did occur elsewhere in East Prussia.
4. Hermann Sommer, quoted in Spieler, p. 147.
5. Kopelev, p. 37.
6. Quoted in Ehrenburg and Grossman, p. 236.
7. Quoted ibid., p. 234.
8. Quoted ibid., p. 38.
9. Fisch, pp. 141–53: for example, there were probably 26 killed in the village, but this was exaggerated to over 60.

CHAPTER 9 – THE CAMPS LIBERATED

1. Werth, pp. 889–90.
2. Quoted in Hitchcock, p. 288. See also Werth, pp. 892–3: Werth visited Majdanek in 1944 and witnessed the use of human ashes as fertilizer.
3. Werth, p. 896.
4. Ibid., p. 897.
5. See Arad, p. 368; Werth, pp. 890–99.
6. *Pravda*, 11 and 12 August 1944, 16 September 1944. See also Rubenstein, p. 426 fn. 82; Beevor and Vinogradova, p. 281.
7. Werth, p. 895; Rubenstein, p. 426 fn. 82.
8. Gilbert, *The Holocaust*, p. 711.
9. Vasily Grossman, 'The Hell Called Treblinka', in Ehrenburg and Grossman, pp. 399–429. See also Beevor and Vinogradova, pp. 280–306. For figures, see Burleigh, *Third Reich*, p. 650. The US Holocaust Memorial Museum puts the figure between 870,000 and 925,000: see their Holocaust Encyclopedia page for

Treblinka at www.ushmm.org/wlc/article.php?lang=en&ModuleId=10005193, accessed 27 September 2011.

10. US Holocaust Memorial Museum, Holocaust Encyclopedia page on Auschwitz, www.ushmm.org/wlc/article.php?lang=en&ModuleId=10005189, accessed 27 September 2011.

11. For a good comparison of the Nazi Holocaust and the Soviet gulag system, see Dallas, pp. 456–68.

12. See, for example, Burleigh, *Third Reich*, p. 752.

13. *Pravda*, 17 December 1944, quoted in Rubenstein, p. 220.

14. *Pravda*, 27 October 1944, quoted ibid., p. 426 fn. 82.

15. Anthony Eden speech to Parliament, 17 December 1942, Hansard, series 5, vol. 385, col. 2083.

16. TNA: PRO INF 1/251 Part 4: 'Plan to combat the apathetic attitude of "What have I got to lose even if Germany wins?"', 25 July 1941.

17. Roosevelt statement to reporters, 24 March 1944, quoted in Beschloss, p. 59. For American reluctance to believe in wholesale extermination see Abzug, pp. 5–19; and Marcuse, pp. 53–4.

18. Beschloss, p. 61.

19. Werth, p. 890.

20. Ibid., p. 898.

21. See Abzug, pp. 3–4; testimony of Dr Fritz Leo, TNA: PRO WO 309/1696.

22. See *New York Times*, 5 December 1944; Abzug, pp. 5–10.

23. Eisenhower, p. 446.

24. Patton, pp. 293–4.

25. Ibid., pp. 293–4.; see also Abzug, p. 27.

26. Hackett, pp. 103, 112–15.

27. Quoted in Abzug, p. 33.

28. Quoted in Marcuse, p. 54.

29. Ibid., pp. 54–5.

30. Abzug, p. 92. See also Percy Knauth's description of Buchenwald in *Time*, 30 April 1945.

31. Marcuse, pp. 51, 54.

32. Buechner later wrote a book about this incident called *The Hour of the Avenger* (Metairie, LA: Thunderbird Press, 1986), which has been criticized for distorting the facts and exaggerating the number of Germans killed. See Jürgen Zarusky, 'Die Erschießungen gefangener SS-Leute bei der Befreiung des KZ Dachau', in Benz and Königseder, pp. 113–16, and Israel, pp. 175–8. See also www.scrapbookpages.com/dachauscrapbook/dachauliberation/Buechner Account.html – accessed 13 September 2011.

33. Quoted in Abzug, p. 94.

34. Sington, pp. 20–25, 37; and Lt Col. R. I. G. Taylor quoted in Shephard, *After Daybreak*, p. 37.

35. Sington, pp. 49–50.

36. Lt Col. M. V. Gonin, IWM Docs 85/38/1, typescript account, 'The RAMC at Belsen Concentration Camp' (no date, c.1946), p. 5.

37. Testimony of Wilhelm Emmerich, 'Interim Report on the Collection of Evidence at Belsen-Bergen Camp', TNA: PRO WO 309/1696; figure of 18,000 given by Shephard, *After Daybreak*, p. 37.

38. Testimonies in 'Interim Report on the Collection of Evidence at Belsen-Bergen Camp', TNA: PRO WO 309/1696.

39. Ibid., p. 1.

40. Quoted in Shephard, *After Daybreak*, p. 55.

41. BSM Sanderson quoted by Major A. J. Forrest, IWM Docs 91/13/1, typescript memoir, ch. 17, pp. 5–6.

42. Derek L. Henry, IWM Docs, 06/126/1, typescript memoir, p. 95.

43. Spottiswoode speech from Movietone film quoted in Shephard, *After Daybreak*, pp. 76–7.

44. Abzug, p. 93.

45. Israel Gutman quoted in Gilbert, *The Day the War Ended*, p. 391.

46. Clay quoted in Gringauz, 'Our New German Policy', p. 510.

47. Ben Helfgott, personal interview, 19 May 2008.

48. Quoted in Gilbert, *The Boys*, p. 252.

49. Pinkus Kurnedz interview, IWM Sound, 9737, reel 3.

50. Szmulek Gontarz interview, IWM Sound, 10348, reel 4.

51. Alfred 'Freddy' Knoller interview, IWM Sound, 9092, reel 12.

52. Quoted in Gilbert, *The Boys*, p. 251.

53. Quoted ibid., p. 256.

54. Max Dessau interview, IWM Sound, 9236, reel 4.

55. Kurt Klappholz interview, IWM Sound, 9425, reel 23.

56. Peter Leo Frank interview, IWM Sound, 16690, reel 4.

57. Alfred Huberman interview, IWM Sound, 18050, reel 6.

58. Cohen, pp. 191–217; Sedlis quoted p. 191; slogan quoted p. 224. See also Mankowitz, pp. 236–8; and the more sensationalist account by Elkins, pp. 193–249, who changed the names of those he interviewed.

59. According to the *New York Times*, 24 April 1946, 2,238 prisoners fell sick, but none died. Other writers claim that this was a fiction created by American officials wishing to cover up their own lapses in security. See Cohen, p. 212.

60. Cohen, pp. 221–38.

61. Shlomo Frenkel, quoted in Mankowitz, p. 239.

CHAPTER 10 – VENGEANCE RESTRAINED:
SLAVE LABOURERS

1. Novick, *The Holocaust and Collective Memory, passim.*
2. Hitchcock, pp. 245–6.
3. Abzug, p. 61.
4. Tooze, p. 517.
5. Beck, p. 164.
6. Kardorff, pp. 152–3.
7. Beck, p. 143.
8. Major R. C. Seddon, IWM Docs 95/19/1, typescript diary, entries for 6 and 12 April 1945.
9. Major A. G. Moon, IWM Docs 06/126/1, typescript memoir, p. 46.
10. Botting, p. 282.
11. See, for example, Major A. J. Forrest, IWM Docs 91/13/1, typescript memoir, ch. 16, p. 4; ch. 18, pp. 11–12.
12. Bernard Warach, UNRRA welfare officer, quoted in Wyman, p. 38.
13. Derek L. Henry, IWM Docs 06/126/1, typescript memoir, pp. 92–3.
14. Mrs M. Heath, Welfare Officer of DP centre at Hanau, IWM Docs 98/25/1, manuscript diary, entry for 7 May 1945.
15. David Campbell of 180th Engineers, quoted in Abzug, p. 72.
16. Moorehead, pp. 241–2.
17. R. J. Hunting, IWM Docs 10519 P339, typescript memoir, p. 368; Mosley, p. 72.
18. Major A. J. Forrest, IWM Docs 91/13/1, typescript memoir, ch. 18, p. 7.
19. Ibid., ch. 17, p. 6.
20. Mosley, p. 80.
21. Ibid., p. 69.
22. Ibid., pp. 69–70.
23. Ibid., pp. 73, 80, 81.
24. Davidson, p. 54.
25. R. J. Hunting, IWM Docs 10519 P339, typescript memoir, pp. 378–9.
26. Major A. G. Moon, IWM Docs 06/126/1, typescript memoir, p. 34.
27. TNA: PRO FO 945/595, General Montgomery telegram to Foreign Office, 6 August 1945.
28. Undated newspaper clipping kept by Katherine Morris: 'Death warning to food rioters: U.S. may invoke military law', IWM Docs, 91/27/1.
29. Major A. G. Moon, IWM Docs 06/126/1, typescript memoir, p. 34.
30. For types and conditions of DP camps, see Wyman, pp. 38–60. For conditions in 1946 onwards, see Shephard, *Long Road Home*, pp. 267–99.
31. TNA: PRO FO 371/47719, telegram C-in-C Germany's political adviser to Foreign Office, 11 August 1945.
32. TNA: PRO FO 1005/1631 – 'Report on life in Germany during October 1945', p. 3; and Hitchcock, p. 279.

33. TNA: PRO FO 1032/1933 – JIC report, 'Possible dangers to the occupying power during the coming winter', 29 November 1945.

34. Lt Gen. Frederick Morgan to Foreign Office, IWM Docs 02/49/1.

35. See, for example, Moorehead, p. 240; Botting, p. 46; Andreas-Friedrich, p. 43.

36. See, for example, TNA: PRO FO 1005/1631 – 'Report on conditions in Germany during May 1946'.

37. Major A. G. Moon, IWM Docs 06/126/1, typescript memoir, p. 69.

38. Quoted in Shephard, *Long Road Home*, pp. 68–9.

39. Quoted in Hitchcock, p. 252. These observations were backed up by military personnel: see Coles and Weinberg, p. 858.

40. Francesca Wilson, p. 131.

41. Quoted in Hitchcock, p. 332.

42. Shephard, *Long Road Home*, p. 167; Hitchcock, pp. 275–6.

43. Kay Hulme, quoted in Shephard, *Long Road Home*, p. 167.

44. UNRRA mission statement, according to Kay Hulme, quoted in Hitchcock, p. 167.

45. Wyman, pp. 99–104.

46. Ibid., pp. 117–21.

47. Kay Hulme, quoted in Shephard, *Long Road Home*, p. 166.

48. Ibid., pp. 173, 204.

49. Ibid., p. 143.

50. Ibid., pp. 152–4. See also Acheson, p. 201; Hitchcock, p. 216.

51. Yvette Rubin story related by Jean Newman, quoted in Hitchcock, pp. 248–9.

52. Quoted ibid., p. 252.

CHAPTER 11 – GERMAN PRISONERS OF WAR

1. Churchill, vol. V, pp. 330; and Elliott Roosevelt, pp. 188–90.

2. For various readings of this episode see, for example, Rees, *Behind Closed Doors*, pp. 229–32; Beschloss, pp. 26–8; Burleigh, *Moral Combat*, pp. 351–2; Sebag-Montefiore, pp. 415–16.

3. Beschloss, p. 179.

4. Werner Ratza, 'Anzahl und Arbeitsleistungen der deutschen Kriegsgefangenen', in Maschke, vol. XV: *Zusammenfassung*, p. 208.

5. See Botting, p. 112; Eisenhower, p. 464; Overmans, 'German Historiography', p. 143.

6. Tomasevich, p. 756.

7. Kurt W. Böhme in Maschke, vol. X: *In amerikanischer Hand*, p. 11. See also Overmans, 'German Historiography', pp. 143, 147, 155.

8. Kurt W. Böhme in Maschke, vol. X: *In amerikanischer Hand*, p. 15.

9. See, for example, General Lee's memo to SHAEF, 2 June 1945, in NARA, quoted in Bacque, p. 51.

10. See, for example, Kurt W. Böhme in Maschke, vol. X: *In amerikanischer Hand*, *passim*; and Bischof and Ambrose, *passim*.

11. Anonymous diary of a German sergeant, entries for 17 and 20 May 1945, quoted by Kurt W. Böhme in Maschke, vol. X: *In amerikanischer Hand*, pp. 309–13.

12. Kurt W. Böhme in Maschke, vol. X: *In amerikanischer Hand*, p. 150.

13. Ibid., p. 148.

14. Ibid., pp. 151–2, 154.

15. Quoted in Bacque, p. 40.

16. Quoted by Kurt W. Böhme in Maschke, vol. X: *In amerikanischer Hand*, pp. 152, 154.

17. See Bacque, *passim*; Bischof and Ambrose, *passim*.

18. Werner Ratza, 'Anzahl und Arbeitsleistungen der deutschen Kriegsgefangenen', in Maschke, vol. XV: *Zusammenfassung*, pp. 207, 224–6. According to parish records, an additional 774 from smaller camps also died: see Kurt W. Böhme in Maschke, vol. X: *In amerikanischer Hand*, pp. 204–5.

19. See, for example, Albert E. Cowdrey, 'A Question of Numbers', in Bischof and Ambrose, p. 91; and Overmans, 'German Historiography', p. 169.

20. Werth, p. 413.

21. Quoted in Service, p. 284. See also Werth, p. 417, who quotes this poem slightly differently.

22. Quoted in de Zayas, *Terrible Revenge*, p. 40. For alternative renditions of this passage see also Werth, p. 414, and Tolstoy, pp. 267–8.

23. *Krasnaya Zvezda*, 13 August 1942, quoted in Werth, p. 414.

24. De Zayas, *Terrible Revenge*, p. 40.

25. Beevor, *Berlin*, p. 199.

26. *Défense de la France*, no. 44 (15 March 1944).

27. Von Einsiedel, p. 168.

28. See, for example, von Einsiedel, p. 164; Beevor, *Stalingrad*, pp. 386, 408.

29. Rupić et al., docs. 10 and 60 (pp. 60, 171); Kurt W. Böhme in Maschke, vol. I: *Jugoslawien*, pp. 104–34.

30. Istituto Centrale di Statistica, p. 10.

31. Giurescu, p. 157.

32. Schieder, vol. II, *Hungary*, p. 46. Glanz, p. 169, puts the figure higher at 850,000–900,000.

33. Toth, p. 5.

34. Schuetz, p. 21.

35. See, for example, Becker, pp. 73–4; and Toth, p. 7. Prisoners of the Yugoslav Partisans were also often denied water: see, for example, Kurt W. Böhme in Maschke, vol. X: *In amerikanischer Hand*, pp. 218–19.

36. Beevor, *Stalingrad*, pp. 408–9; Becker, pp. 77–81.

37. Becker, p. 87; Toth, p. 48.

38. Toth, p. 48.

39. Becker, p. 184.
40. Von Einsiedel, p. 206.
41. See Bischof and Ambrose, *passim*.
42. Source: Werner Ratza, 'Anzahl und Arbeitsleistungen der deutschen Kriegsgefangenen', in Maschke, vol. XV: *Zusammenfassung*, pp. 207, 224–26. In the 1990s Rüdiger Overmans compared these figures with several other sets of available data and found them to be broadly accurate; see his 'German Historiography', pp. 146–63.
43. Overmans, 'German Historiography', p. 152.
44. Ibid., p. 148.
45. Werner Ratza, 'Anzahl und Arbeitsleistungen der deutschen Kriegsgefangenen', in Maschke, vol. XV: *Zusammenfassung*, pp. 194–5.
46. Ibid., pp. 194–7.
47. Brian Loring Villa, 'The Diplomatic and Political Context of the POW Camps Tragedy', in Bischof and Ambrose, pp. 67–8.
48. Roosevelt quoted in Beschloss, p. 28.
49. For the original document see Morgenthau, prelim. pages; for discussion and agreement see Beschloss, pp. 125–31; Rees, *Behind Closed Doors*, pp. 302–8.
50. International Committee of the Red Cross, pp. 333–5.

CHAPTER 12 – VENGEANCE UNRESTRAINED: EASTERN EUROPE

1. See Gary B. Cohen, *The Politics of Ethnic Survival: Germans in Prague 1861–1914* (Princeton University Press, 1981), pp. 274–82.
2. While such torments were usually reserved for soldiers and SS men, occasionally civilians were also treated in the same way; see Staněk, *Verfolgung 1945*, p. 95.
3. Schieder, vol. IV: *Czechoslovakia*, pp. 390–91.
4. Ibid., p. 57; and Staněk, *Verfolgung 1945*, p. 94.
5. Testimony of 'F.B.', doc. 24, in Schieder, vol. IV: *Czechoslovakia*, p. 366.
6. See Schieder, vol. IV: *Czechoslovakia*, p. 49; and Staněk, *Verfolgung 1945*, pp. 89–90.
7. Staněk, *Verfolgung 1945*, p. 97.
8. Kurt Schmidt quoted in Report 29 in Schieder, vol. IV: *Czechoslovakia*, p. 404; see also for comparison p. 59, and Staněk, *Verfolgung 1945*, pp. 94–5.
9. For conditions in prisons see Staněk, *Retribuční*, pp. 36–8; for conditions in work camps see the same author's *Internierung und Zwangsarbeit*, pp. 111–32.
10. Kurt Schmidt quoted in Report 29 in Schieder, vol. IV: *Czechoslovakia*, pp. 404–5.
11. Report no. 26 by 'A.L.', quoted ibid., p. 389.
12. Staněk, *Retribuční*, p. 39.

13. Staněk, *Verfolgung 1945*, p. 210; Kucera, p. 24; Naimark, *Fires of Hatred*, p. 118.

14. See Staněk, *Verfolgung 1945*, p. 174; and Pustejovsky, p. 561. For emotive eyewitness accounts, see testimonies in Pustejovsky, pp. 315, 338–9; and Schieder, vol. IV: *Czechoslovakia*, pp. 68, 430.

15. Staněk, *Verfolgung 1945*, pp. 143–8.

16. Ibid., pp. 148–9.

17. Ibid., pp. 155–6.

18. See, for example, Beneš's speech in Anon., *Komu sluší omluva?*, p. 90.

19. Beneš, *Speech, May 16th 1945*, p. 5.

20. See Drtina's postwar pamphlet *My a Němci* ('We and the Germans'), pp. 5, 13, quoted in Schieder, vol. IV: *Czechoslovakia*, pp. 66–7 fn. 13; Staněk, *Odsun Němců*, p. 59.

21. Article in *Práce*, 14 July 1945, quoted in Petr Benařík, 'Retribuční soudnictví a český tisk', in *Vědecká Konference*, p. 23.

22. Staněk, *Odsun Němců*, p. 59.

23. Law reproduced as Annex 19 in Schieder, vol. IV: *Czechoslovakia*, p. 276.

24. *Frankfurter Allgemeine Zeitung*, 4 April 1988. See also Sayer, p. 243.

25. See, for example, the website of the Zentrum gegen Vertreibungen, www.z-g-v.de/english/aktuelles/?id=56#sudeten, accessed 3 October 2011; Schieder, vol. IV: *Czechoslovakia*, p. 128; and MacDonogh, p. 159. Staněk convincingly deconstructs such high figures, *Verfolgung 1945*, pp. 208–12.

26. See, for example, Nováček's description of the 'voluntary' deportation of Germans from Brno, p. 31.

27. Staněk, *Verfolgung 1945*, pp. 208–12.

28. Staněk, *Retribuční*, pp. 24–5. The official figure for under-fourteens was 6,093, which Staněk argues is an underestimate.

29. Maschke, vol. XV: *Zusammenfassung*, p. 197.

30. International Committee of the Red Cross, pp. 334, 336, 676; prisoners of war held by the French and American authorities were also forced to clear minefields, but civilians were never used. See also Staněk, *Retribuční*, pp. 28, 37.

31. Schieder, vol. IV: *Czechoslovakia*, p. 75, and eyewitness reports 27 and 59 on pp. 392, 441.

32. Ibid., pp. 75, 88, and eyewitness report of Dr Hermann Ebert, Report 66, p. 450.

33. Ibid., Report 24, pp. 373–4.

34. Adler, p. 214.

35. Kaps, Reports 193 and 195, p. 535.

36. Poster reproduced from Anon., *Tragedy of a People: Racialism in Czecho-Slovakia* (New York: American Friends of Democratic Sudetens, 1946), p. 2.

37. Later redesignated a 'labour camp', but the ethos did not change. See Dziurok, p. 17.

38. Gruschka, p. 42.

39. Testimony by Jadwiga Sonsala, doc. 35 in Dziurok, p. 115; see also Henryk Grus testimony, doc. 38 ibid., p. 120.

40. Testimony of Henryk Wowra, doc. 47 in Dziurok, p. 146.

41. According to Gruschka, p. 47. See also Dziurok, p. 146.

42. According to Edmund Kamiński, quoted in Dziurok, p. 133.

43. Testimony of Jadwiga Sonsala, doc. 35 in Dziurok, p. 115; Gruschka, pp. 48–9, 56.

44. Gruschka, pp. 55–6; and Nikodem Osmańczyk testimony, doc. 39 in Dziurok, pp. 123–4.

45. See Henryk Grus testimony, doc. 38 in Dziurok, pp. 121–2; and Gruschka, p. 50.

46. Dziurok, p. 27; and testimony by Józef Burda, doc. 42, pp. 130–31.

47. Testimony of Henryk Wowra, doc. 47 in Dziurok, pp. 25–6.

48. Doc. 7, Świętochłowice statistical report, 1 August 1945, doc. 7 in Dziurok, pp. 46–7.

49. Dziurok, pp. 21–5.

50. Doc. 6 in Dziurok, p. 45.

51. Gerhard Gruschka testimony, doc. 46 in Dziurok, p. 144.

52. Gruschka, p. 59.

53. Statement by R. W. F. Bashford, TNA: PRO FO 371/46990.

54. Testimony by Günther Wollny, German Federal Archives Ost-Dok 2/236C/297, quoted in Sack, pp. 109, 204.

55. See docs. 9 and 10 in Dziurok, pp. 49–50.

56. Doc. 21 in Dziurok, p. 78; see also pp. 17, 31.

57. Kaps, Report 195, pp. 537–8.

58. Sack, p. 67.

59. Kaps, Report 192, p. 532.

60. According to eyewitness report by 'P.L.' of Łódź, in Schieder, vol. I: Oder-Neisse, Report 268, pp. 270–78.

61. Testimonies by Christa-Helene Gause von Shirach and E. Zindler in Bundes-archiv, Ost-Dok 2/148/103 and Ost-Dok 2/64/18, quoted in Sack, p. 110.

62. Anonymous testimony, quoted in Esser, p. 40.

63. Anonymous testimony, quoted ibid., p. 41.

64. Anonymous testimony, quoted ibid., p. 42.

65. Anonymous testimony, quoted ibid., pp. 43–5.

66. Edmund Nowak, 'Obóz Pracy w Łambinwicach (1945–1946)', in Nowak, pp. 277–8.

67. Anonymous testimony, quoted in Esser, p. 38.

68. Anonymous testimony, quoted ibid., pp. 35, 37.

69. Anonymous testimony, quoted ibid., p. 46.

70. Anonymous testimony, quoted ibid., p. 40.

71. Anonymous testimony, quoted ibid., p. 39.

72. Anonymous testimony, quoted ibid., p. 33.

73. Nowak, p. 284.

74. Anonymous testimony, quoted in Esser, p. 39.

75. Anonymous testimony, quoted ibid., pp. 38, 44.

76. Ibid., pp. 51–61.

77. Anonymous testimony, quoted ibid., p. 32; and Polish Communist account quoted ibid., p. 59.

78. Ibid., p. 26; cf. his testimony in Kaps, Report 193, p. 534, which is identical except for the figures.

79. According to one of the prosecutors, Frantiszek Lewandowski, quoted in the *Sunday Telegraph*, 3 December 2000.

80. Esser, pp. 60, 98.

81. Nowak, pp. 283–4; Borodziej and Lemberg, vol. II, p. 379; Esser, pp. 99–127.

82. Spieler, p. 40.

83. Borodziej and Lemberg, vol. I, p. 98. Interestingly, this document claimed that the figure for Zgoda/Świętochłowice was a mere thirty deaths, and Lamsdorf/Łambinowice did not even figure.

84. See, for example, Ursula Haverbeck-Wetzel interview in Charlie Russell's TV documentary for the BBC, *The Last Nazis*, Part II, Minnow Films, 2009.

85. Order no. 19 from the Department of Prisons and Camps of the Ministry for Public Security: in Borodziej and Lemberg, vol. I, doc. 25, pp. 151–2.

86. Dziurok, pp. 93–100. See also www.ipn.gov.pl/portal.php?serwis=en&dzial=2&id=71&search=10599, accessed 3 October 2011.

CHAPTER 13 – THE ENEMY WITHIN

1. *Défense de la France* and Oslo *Dagbladet*; quoted in Novick, *Resistance versus Vichy*, p. 31 and Dahl, pp. 154–8.

2. TNA: PRO FO 371/38896, Major D. Morton, 'Conditions in France and Belgium', 3 October 1944. See also Conway, pp. 137–42.

3. Voute, p. 181.

4. TNA: PRO FO 371/48994, Sir H. Knatchbull-Hugessen to Churchill, 2 July 1945; see also Bodson, pp. 144–5.

5. Philip Morgan, pp. 224–6.

6. Pelle, pp. 193–5.

7. A report made by a doctor at the Drancy internment camp on the outskirts of Paris lists forty-nine people who were severely beaten during interrogation and sustained massive bruising, broken skulls and facial bones, burns to the soles of the feet and, in one case, injuries caused by prolonged electric shocks to the vagina and rectum: see Bourdrel, pp. 109–15. For other examples see ibid., pp. 509–10, 585–6; Fabienne Frayssinet, 'Quatre saisons dans les geôles de la IVe République', *Écrits de Paris*, July 1949, pp. 114–25; Aron, p. 572; Virgili, pp. 139–40.

8. *La Terre Vivaroise*, 29 October 1944, quoted in Bourdrel, pp. 316–17.

9. De Gaulle quoted by Philippe Boegner in Beevor and Cooper, p. 63; radio announcement 14 August 1944, quoted in Bourdrel, p. 346.

10. *Journal Officiel*, Parliamentary Debates, 27 December 1944, pp. 604–7; 12 March 1954, p. 831. See also Novick, *Resistance versus Vichy*, p. 84, and the discussion of figures in Berlière, pp. 321–5.

11. Beevor and Cooper, pp. 111–12.

12. Judt, p. 65; Sonja van 't Hof, 'A Kaleidoscope of Victimhood – Belgian Experiences of World War II', in Withuis and Mooij, p. 57.

13. For Belgium see Judt, p. 44; for Czechoslovakia see Annex 19 in Schieder, vol. IV: *Czechoslovakia*, p. 276; for Italy see Alessandrini, p. 64.

14. Novick, *Resistance versus Vichy*, p. 77.

15. TNA: PRO FO 371/49139, Duff Cooper to Anthony Eden, 11 January 1945.

16. *Le Peuple*, 5 September 1944, 'Une proclamation des partis . . .'.

17. Huyse, p. 161; Judt, p. 46; Rioux, p. 34, Derry, p. 405. Although the death penalty was still a part of the civil criminal code in Norway in 1902, and in Denmark as late as 1930, there had been no executions in either country since the nineteenth century: see Dahl, pp. 152–3; and Nøkelby, p. 319.

18. See the statistics for reported homicides in Dondi, pp. 97, 102.

19. TNA: PRO WO 106/3965A, memo from Sir Noel Charles to Foreign Office, 11 May 1945. More recent Italian studies suggest figures of 1,322 for Turin and 1,325 in Milan; see Pansa, pp. 55, 117.

20. Quoted in Philip Morgan, p. 218.

21. Testimony of Benito Puiatti and Eraldo Franza, quoted in Pavone, pp. 508, 768 fn. 11.

22. Judt, p. 42.

23. For more specific figures, and a discussion of how they were arrived at, see Rioux, p. 32, Rousso, pp. 93–7, 119, and Novick, *Resistance versus Vichy*, pp. 202–8.

24. For figures of 12–15,000 postwar killings, see Pavone, p. 511; and Philip Morgan, p. 167. For figures of up to 20,000, see Pansa, p. 371. For discussion of figures, see Pansa, pp. 365–72, and Philip Morgan, pp. 216–18.

25. Philip Morgan, p. 218.

26. Roberto Battaglia letter to the police chief of La Spezia, quoted in Pavone, p. 509.

27. Philip Morgan, pp. 85, 205; Jonathan Dunnage, 'Policing and Politics in the Southern Italian Community, 1943–1948', in Dunnage, pp. 34–9; Woller, pp. 90–91.

28. For a summary of the Italian failure to reform the court system see Achille Battaglia, *passim*; and Modona, pp. 48–58; see also Claudio Pavone, 'The General Problem of the Continuity of the State and the Legacy of Fascism', in Dunnage, p. 18.

29. Modona, pp. 53–4.

30. Pansa, p. 369. Judt, pp. 47–8, puts the figure at no more than fifty executions.

31. Dondi, pp. 142–4; Pansa, pp. 316–26.

32. Testimonies of Valentino Bortoloso and Pierina Penezzato, interviewed by Sarah Morgan, pp. 154–5.

33. Rousso, p. 103.

34. For percentages and statistics see ibid., pp. 106–8. For slightly different numbers see Judt, p. 46; Rioux, p. 34.

35. Conway, p. 134; Huyse, pp. 161–2.

36. Conway, pp. 134, 140, 148; Huyse, pp. 161–2.

37. TNA: PRO FO 371/47307, British Embassy in Copenhagen to Foreign Office, 3 August 1945.

38. Le Monde, 13 January 1945; Farge, pp. 243–50; Novick, Resistance versus Vichy, pp. 76–7.

39. Nøkelby, pp. 319–20; Derry, pp. 405–6; Judt, p. 45.

40. MacDonogh, pp. 359–61; Judt, p. 52.

41. Population figures taken from Maddison, pp. 38–9. Population of the Czech lands (Bohemia and Moravia) estimated from Maddison, p. 96 and Czech census data reproduced in Gyurgyík, pp. 38–9. Other data adapted as follows: Denmark and Norway: Dahl, p. 148. Belgium and Holland: Huyse, p. 161. France: Rousso, pp. 108, 110, 119–20, includes the 767 executions carried out by the Courts of Justice and the 769 carried out by military tribunals. Italy: Judt, pp. 47–8, Pansa, p. 369; figures for milder sanctions unknown. Czech lands: Frommer, pp. 91, 220, 243. Austria: MacDonogh, pp. 359–61; and Judt, p. 52.

42. Frommer, p. 38; Huyse, pp. 165–6.

43. Judt, p. 51; Huyse, pp. 163, 166–8; Frommer, pp. 272–7.

44. For these and other legal problems, see Novick, Resistance versus Vichy, p. 209; Huyse, pp. 159–69; Judt, pp. 44–5; Nøkelby, pp. 320–21.

45. TNA: PRO FO 371/48994, Sir H. Knatchbull-Hugessen to Churchill, 2 July 1945.

46. Huyse, p. 163.

47. See Tony Judt's seminal essay, 'The Past is Another Country: Myth and Memory in Postwar Europe', in Deák et al., pp. 296, 298.

48. MacDonogh, pp. 348–57; Judt, pp. 53–61; Botting, pp. 315–53.

49. Judt, p. 61.

50. See, for example, Fabienne Frayssinet, 'Quatre saisons dans les geôles de la IVᵉ République', Écrits de Paris, July 1949, pp. 114–25; and the story of the rape and torture of a forty-three-year-old woman in Villedieu-sur-Indre, in La Gerbaude, 1951, issue 2, quoted in Aron, p. 572. Compare these to the more dispassionate stories produced by official investigations in the Indre, in La Chauvinerie internment camp at Poitiers and the Drancy internment camp in Paris: Virgili, pp. 139–40; and Bourdrel, pp. 109–15, 509–10.

51. For a discussion of all the conflicting figures see Rioux, p. 32; Rousso, pp. 93–7, 119; Novick, Resistance versus Vichy, pp. 202–8.

52. See, for example, Mungone, p. x. For discussion of such figures, see Pansa, pp. 365–72; Philip Morgan, pp. 216–18.

53. Philip Morgan, pp. 166–7.
54. See note 24 above.
55. Pansa, p. x.

CHAPTER 14 – REVENGE ON WOMEN AND CHILDREN

1. Virgili, p. 173.
2. Quoted ibid., p. 26.
3. Police reports concerning persons arrested and accused of collaboration, interned at Jayat camp at Charente, Archives Nationales, Paris, 72 AJ 108 (AVIII); Virgili, p. 26; Warring, 'War, Cultural Loyalty and Gender', p. 46.
4. Kåre Olsen, 'Under the Care of the Lebensborn', p. 24.
5. For statistics on babies born to German fathers, see notes 36–40 below.
6. For surveys of attitudes of Danish women towards Germans, see Lulu Ann Hansen, '"Youth Off the Rails": Teenage Girls and German Soldiers – A Case Study in Occupied Denmark, 1940–1945', in Herzog, p. 151. See also Warring, 'War, Cultural Loyalty and Gender', pp. 44–5.
7. Virgili, p. 238.
8. Quoted ibid., p. 239.
9. Saint-Exupéry, p. 145.
10. Speech on the BBC, 8 November 1942, quoted in de Gaulle, p. 393; Christmas speech to the French people, 24 December 1943, p. 553; speech to Consultative Assembly, Algiers, 18 March 1944, p. 560.
11. Speech to Consultative Assembly, Algiers, 18 March 1944, quoted in de Gaulle, p. 562.
12. See Virgili, p. 80.
13. Derek L. Henry, IWM Docs 06/126/1, typescript account, pp. 48, 52; Captain Michael Bendix, IWM Docs 98/3/1, typescript account, p. 30.
14. Major J. A. S. Neave, IWM Docs 98/23/1, typescript diary, entry for 3 September 1944, p. 157.
15. Female resident of Bonnières by the Seine, quoted by Major A. J. Forrest, 12 September 1944; see IWM Docs 91/13/1, typescript memoir, ch. 10, p. 3.
16. Bohec, p. 186.
17. Weitz, pp. 149, 170.
18. Major A. J. Forrest, IWM Docs 91/13/1, typescript memoir, ch. 8, p. 11.
19. Lt Richard W. Holborow, IWM Docs 07/23/1, typescript memoir, pp. 135–6.
20. La Marseillaise, 3 September 1944, quoted in Virgili, p. 191.
21. Leaflet from the Comité Départemental de la Libération, Troyes, quoted in Virgili, p. 191.
22. Virgili, p. 189.
23. Warring, Tyskerpiger, pp. 156–73; Diederichs, pp. 157–8.
24. Bunting, pp. 235, 258–9.

25. As quoted in Dondi, p. 126. A more literal translation would be: 'And you beautiful young girls/ who go with fascists/ your beautiful tresses/ will soon be shaved.'

26. Novick, *Resistance versus Vichy*, pp. 69, 78.

27. Rousso, p. 98. According to Diederichs, head shaving took place in at least one Dutch village in a deliberate and coordinated attempt to stave off a general 'day of reckoning', p. 157.

28. Virgili claims that the supposed channelling of violence is inconclusive, but agrees that it provided a focus for communal unity, pp. 93–4, 172.

29. Virgili, pp. 65, 94. See also the many examples in Brossat, *passim*.

30. See, for example, the photographs in Warring, *Tyskerpiger*, pp. 100–101, 161.

31. Virgili, p. 192.

32. Rousso, p. 98. Also variously reported as 'My heart is France's, but my body is mine', Arletty obituary, *Daily Telegraph*, 27 July 1992; and 'My heart is French, but my arse is international' ['Mon coeur est français mais mon cul est international'] according to Buisson, p. 9.

33. Virgili, p. 52.

34. Anthony Eden interview in Marcel Ophüls's film documentary *Le Chagrin et la Pitié*, part II: 'Le Choix'.

35. Quoted in Virgili, p. 239.

36. Warring, *Tyskerpiger*, p. 146.

37. For the higher Dutch figure see Johr, p. 71; Diederichs, p. 153, puts the figure at only 16,000.

38. For Norwegian figures see Kåre Olsen, *Schicksal Lebensborn*, p. 7. Olsen believes the true figure to be between 10,000 and 12,000; however, only 8,000 of these children were officially registered by the German Lebensborn organization during the war, and the figure of 9,000 was the standard one used by the Norwegian War Child Committee.

39. Johr gives the range 85,000 to 100,000, p. 71. The figure of 85,000 appears to come from a German document dated 15 October 1943: later estimates put the figure as high as 200,000 – see Buisson, pp. 116–17; Roberts, p. 84.

40. Drolshagen, p. 9.

41. See Diederichs, p. 157.

42. *Lufotposten*, 19 May 1945, quoted and translated in Ericsson and Ellingsen, p. 94.

43. For a description of the work of this commission see Kåre Olsen, 'Under the Care of the Lebensborn', pp. 307–19.

44. For a description of the 2001 research programme and its findings, see Ericsson and Ellingsen, pp. 93–111.

45. Kåre Olsen, 'Under the Care of the Lebensborn', p. 26.

46. Borgersrud, pp. 71–2.

47. Ibid. There are no accurate figures relating to marriages between Germans

and Norwegian girls during the war, but Kåre Olsen estimates the number at around 3,000: see 'Under the Care of the Lebensborn', p. 26.

48. Borgersrud, p. 87.
49. Doctor's statement in 1990, quoted in Kåre Olsen, 'Under the Care of the Lebensborn', p. 29.
50. For these, and many other anecdotes, see Ericsson and Ellingsen, pp. 93–111.
51. Drolshagen, p. 101.
52. Borgersrud, p. 85.
53. Ericsson and Ellingsen, p. 109.
54. Ibid., pp. 105–6.
55. Drolshagen, p. 96.
56. Arne Øland, 'Silences, Public and Private', in Ericsson and Simonsen, p. 60.
57. Ibid.
58. Drolshagen, p. 118.
59. Ibid., p. 137.

CHAPTER 15 – THE PURPOSE OF VENGEANCE

1. Berek Obuchowski interview, IWM Sound, 9203, reel 5.
2. Dr Zalman Grinberg, quoted in Gilbert, *The Day the War Ended*, pp. 391–2.
3. See 'Attacks on Jews soar since Lebanon', *The Times*, 2 September 2006; and 'Anti-Semitic Attacks Hit Record High Following Lebanon War', *Guardian*, 2 February 2007.
4. Laurel Cohen-Pfister, 'Rape, War and Outrage: Changing Perceptions on German Victimhood in the Period of Post-unification', in Cohen-Pfister and Wienroeder-Skinner, pp. 321–5.

PART III – ETHNIC CLEANSING

1. Stalin's advice to Poland's postwar leader Władysław Gomułka on how to rid Poland of Germans, quoted in Naimark, *Fires of Hatred*, p. 109.

CHAPTER 16 – WARTIME CHOICES

1. Burleigh, *Third Reich*, pp. 449–50.

CHAPTER 17 – THE JEWISH FLIGHT

1. Roman Halter, letter to Martin Gilbert in *The Boys*, pp. 266–8. See also IWM Sound, 17183, reel 10.

2. Blom et al., p. 337.

3. Lewkowicz, p. 260.

4. Hondius, p. 104.

5. Report in *Neue Welt*, no. 1, quoted in Gringauz, 'Our New German Policy', p. 512.

6. Abba Kovner quoted in Bauer, p. 36; Gringauz, 'Jewish Destiny', p. 504.

7. Primo Levi, p. 373.

8. Hondius, pp. 55, 77.

9. Ibid., pp. 78–82.

10. Ibid., p. 80.

11. Fabio Levi, p. 26.

12. See, for example, Beevor and Cooper, p. 172; Hitchcock, pp. 267–72; Rioux, pp. 13–16.

13. Hondius, pp. 76, 79–80, 93–5.

14. F. C. Brasz, 'After the Second World War: From "Jewish Church" to Cultural Minority', in Blom et al., p. 337.

15. Rita Koopman, Ab Caransa, Gerhard Durlacher and Mrs 't Hoen quoted in Hondius, p. 100.

16. Quoted ibid.

17. Hitchcock, pp. 271–2.

18. Newspaper story quoted in Pelle, pp. 228–9.

19. Ethel Landerman testimony quoted in Shephard, *Long Road Home*, p. 393.

20. Quoted in Kenez, p. 158.

21. Hondius, pp. 77–8.

22. Myant, p. 103; Pelle, 151; Jean Ancel, 'The Seizure of Jewish Property in Romania', in United States Holocaust Memorial Museum, pp. 43–55.

23. Gross, p. 44.

24. See, for example, Kovaly, pp. 56–7; Dean, p. 357; Gross, pp. 39–51; Lewkowicz, p. 260; Gilbert, *The Boys*, pp. 268, 274.

25. For a detailed analysis of the events at Kunmadaras see Pelle, pp. 151–68.

26. Eszter Toth Kabai interview in *Haladás*, quoted ibid., p. 161.

27. Pelle, pp. 157–60.

28. Ibid., p. 160.

29. Kenez, pp. 159–60; Jewish historians claim that there were three deaths, and eighteen injured: see Éva Vörös, 'Kunmadaras Újabb adatok a pogrom történetéhez', *Múlt és jövő*, no. 4 (1994).

30. Pelle, pp. 161, 162.

31. Ibid., p. 173.

32. Fabio Levi, pp. 28–9.

33. Gross, pp. 47–51.

34. Siklos, p. 1.

35. Quoted in Eby, p. 287.

36. In Hungary, for example, not only was the entire top layer of the Communist hierarchy Jewish, but in 1945 around 14 per cent of ordinary members were

too, as compared with between 1 and 2 per cent of the population as a whole. See Kenez, p. 156.

37. Pelle, p. 206.
38. Ibid., p. 160.
39. Kenez, pp. 159–61; Pelle, pp. 212–30.
40. Letter, Mór Reinchardt to the president of the Hungarian Jewish Bureau, 5 August 1946, quoted in Pelle, pp. 166–7.
41. Ben Helfgott, personal interview, 19 May 2008.
42. Gross, p. 35.
43. Bauer, p. 15; Gross, p. 36.
44. Gross, pp. 74–5.
45. Ibid., p. 82.
46. The following description is based on Gross's digest of Polish documentary evidence about the massacre, pp. 81–117.
47. Quoted ibid., p. 89.
48. Ibid., pp. 93, 113.
49. Bauer, p. 210; Gross, p. 138.
50. Gross, p. 98. For a more sympathetic view of Communist action on the day, see Bauer, pp. 206–11. For a discussion of opposing views on responsibility for the pogrom, see Kochavi, p. 175.
51. Gilbert, *The Boys*, p. 275.
52. Ibid., p. 271.
53. Report, Joseph Levine to Moses Leavitt, 24 October 1945, quoted in Hitchcock, p. 334.
54. Kochavi, pp. 173, 227–8; Gross, p. 218.
55. Kochavi, pp. 175, 187; Bauer, pp. 216–23; Shephard, *Long Road Home*, pp. 186–9, 235–6.
56. Bauer, pp. 211–12. Other authors have different figures, based on different criteria, but all show the same pattern of a massive increase in July and August; see, for example, Gross, p. 43.
57. Gross, p. 43; Bauer, pp. 295, 298; Kochavi, p. 185.
58. Bauer, pp. 318–20. For similar statistics based on different time periods, see Prażmowska, p. 176; and Kochavi, p. 227. Proudfoot's Table 35 has slightly higher figures, based on immigration statistics to Israel.
59. Shephard, *Long Road Home*, pp. 190–99; Bauer, p. 319.
60. Bauer, pp. 319–21.
61. British Foreign Office to Washington, 5 October 1945, TNA: PRO FO 1049/81. Bevin quoted in Shephard, *Long Road Home*, p. 191.
62. Walid Khalidi, quoted in Shephard, *Long Road Home*, p. 356.

CHAPTER 18 – THE ETHNIC CLEANSING OF POLAND AND UKRAINE

1. Anonymous witness quoted in Dushnyck, pp. 15–16. See also Misiło, *Repatriacja czy deportacja?*, vol. II, pp. 24, 31, 39, 43; and Snyder, p. 194.

2. Anonymous witness quoted in Dushnyck, pp. 16–17.

3. Testimony of 2nd Lieutenant Bronisław Kuzma quoted in Dushnyck, p. 21.

4. Snyder, p. 194. Seventy names are listed by Dushnyck, but some survived their wounds: see pp. 18, 19, 31–2.

5. Snyder, pp. 182–7.

6. See, for example, ibid., esp. pp. 177, 200. Gross makes the same point about postwar anti-Semitism, pp. 260–61.

7. For the complicated divisions between the followers of Stepan Bandera (OUN-B) and followers of Andrii Melnyk (OUN-M), see Snyder, pp. 164–8; Yekelchyk, pp. 127–8, 141–4.

8. Snyder, pp. 158–62.

9. Testimony of Jan Szkolniaki, AWK II/2091.

10. Testimony of Mirosław Ilnicki, AWK II/3327.

11. Piotrowski, p. 89.

12. Testimony of Mieczysława Woskresińska, AWK II/2215/p.

13. See, for example, testimonies in AWK: II/36, II/594, II/737, II/953, II/1144, II/1146, II/2099, II/2110, II/2353, II/2352, II/2451, II/2650, II/2667. For German, Soviet and Polish reports, see Snyder, pp. 169–70 and related endnotes.

14. Kliachkivs'kyi and Stel'mashchuk quoted in Statiev, p. 86.

15. See, for example, the massacres of Ukrainians in Piskorowice, Pawłokoma and Wierzchowiny by Polish militias: Misiło, *Akcja 'Wisła'*, p. 13; Piotrowski, p. 93; Statiev, p. 87.

16. Lotnik, pp. 65–6.

17. Testimony of Bronisław Kuzma, quoted in Dushnyck, p. 21.

18. Snyder, p. 194.

19. Statiev, pp. 87–8; Snyder, p. 205. See also Siemaszko and Siemaszko, vol. II, pp. 1038, 1056–7; and Siemaszko, p. 94. For a breakdown of other, wildly differing estimates, see Piotrowski, pp. 90–91.

20. See, for example, Siemaszko and Siemaszko, esp. Professor Ryszard Szawłowski's introduction, pp. 14–20, 1095–1102. See also Tsaruk's questioning of their figures, pp. 15–26.

21. Rees, *Behind Closed Doors*, pp. 222, 236.

22. Lane, p. 66.

23. Rees, *Behind Closed Doors*, p. 236; and Lane, pp. 55–88.

24. Lane, pp. 84–8.

25. House of Commons debate, 1 March 1945, Hansard, Series 5, vol. 408, col. 1625.

26. Conquest, pp. 133–4.

27. See Uehling, esp. pp. 79–107.

28. Snyder, pp. 182–7.

29. Statiev, p. 182. Snyder, p. 187. Yekelchyk, p. 147, gives a higher figure of 810,415 expelled from Ukraine.

30. Testimony of Maria Józefowska, AWK II/1999.

31. Statiev, p. 182; Snyder, p. 194; Yekelchyk, p. 147.

32. Testimony of Henryk Jan Mielcarek, AWK II/3332.

33. Statiev, p. 182. See also, for example, the eyewitness testimony of Anna Klimasz and Rozalia Najduch, AWK I/344.

34. Snyder, p. 196; Miroszewski, p. 11.

35. Wacław Kossowski, quoted in Snyder, p. 196.

36. Misiło, Akcja 'Wisła', doc. 42: Radkierwicz and Żymierski memo dated 16 April 1947, outlining 'Special action "East"', p. 93.

37. Misiło, Akcja 'Wisła' , doc. 44, pp. 98–9: Office of State Security document dated 17 April 1947. Ryszard Szawłowski denies any kind of ethnic cleansing involved in Operation Vistula: see his introduction to Siemaszko and Siemaszko, pp. 15, 1096.

38. Rozalia Najduch, interview, 1990, AWK I/344.

39. Anna Klimasz and Rozalia Najduch interview, 1990, AWK I/344.

40. Olga Zdanowicz, manuscript, AWK II/2280/p.

41. Anna Szewczyk, Teodor Szewczyk and Mikołaj Sokacz interview, 1990, AWK I/790.

42. Miroszewski, pp. 19–22.

43. Olga Zdanowicz, manuscript, AWK II/2280/p. Those being sent to Jaworzno also stopped at Auschwitz: see Miroszewski, p. 16.

44. See the testimony of former repatriation official Leon Dębowski, AWK II/457.

45. Miroszewski, p. 17.

46. Anna Szewczyk, Teodor Szewczyk and Mikołaj Sokacz interview, AWK I/790.

47. According to Anna Klimasz, AWK I/344. See also Karolina Hrycaj, typescript, AWK II/3404.

48. For an excellent analysis of how an idealized concept of 'home' becomes almost sacred to displaced people, see Uehling, esp. ch. 7.

49. Olga Zdanowicz, manuscript, AWK II/2280/p.

CHAPTER 19 – THE EXPULSION OF THE GERMANS

1. De Zayas, Nemesis, p. 42

2. Parliamentary debate, 23 February 1944, Hansard, Series 5, vol. 397, col. 937.

3. Schieder, vol. I: Oder-Neisse, p. 62.

4. Rees, Behind Closed Doors, p. 338.

5. Schieder, vol. I: *Oder-Neisse*, p. 62.

6. Lane, p. 185.

7. AP Szczecin, UWS, file ref. 939, 'Sytuacja ludności niemieckiej na Pomorzu Zachodnim według sprawozdania sytułacyjnego pełnomocnika rządu RP na okręg Pomorze Zachodnie', article from June 1945, pp. 13–15.

8. Centralne Archiwum Wojskove, Warsaw, IV/521/11/54, 'Sprawozdanie liczbowe z akcji wysiedlania ludności niemieckiej za okres od 19 do 30 czerwca 1945 roku'.

9. The same was true in Poland: see Prażmowska, p. 182.

10. Lane, p. 153.

11. *New York Times*, 13 November 1946, p. 26.

12. The following story is from Anna Kientopf, attested copy 15 August 1950, quoted at length in Schieder, vol. I: *Oder-Neisse*, doc. 291, pp. 289–95.

13. Kaps, Reports 136 and 162, pp. 405, 478.

14. Ibid., Reports 70, 71, 72 and 125, pp. 260–62, 379.

15. Białecki et al., docs. 27 and 30, pp. 64–9, 71–4.

16. See doc. 217 in Schieder, vol. I: *Oder-Neisse*, p. 233.

17. Instructions from the Republic of Poland's Ministry of Recovered Territories regarding the resettlement of Germans, 15 January 1946, reproduced as doc. 27 in Białecki et al., pp. 64–9. See also docs. 21 and 30 ibid., pp. 57, 71–4.

18. Agreement between British and Polish representatives of the Combined Repatriation Executive, reproduced as doc. 30 in Białecki et al., pp. 71–4.

19. For a selection of these press reports, see de Zayas, *Nemesis*, pp. 107–14.

20. See, for example, docs. 51 and 115 in Białecki et al., pp. 114–16, 192–4. See also *Manchester Guardian* report quoted in de Zayas, *Nemesis*, pp. 121–2.

21. Quoted in Davies and Moorhouse, p. 422.

22. Kaps, Report 51, pp. 234–5.

23. Ibid., Report 66, p. 253.

24. Ibid., Report 2, pp. 128, 130.

25. Byford-Jones, p. 50.

26. *FRUS*, 1945, vol. II, pp. 1291–2.

27. Ibid., pp. 1317–19.

28. De Zayas, *Nemesis*, pp. 122–4.

29. No accurate number for refugee deaths exists. For vague estimates by the German government, and vastly exaggerated claims of up to 2 million by German expellee groups, see Spieler, pp. 53–4; and de Zayas, *Terrible Revenge*, p. 156.

30. German Federal figures quoted in de Zayas, *Terrible Revenge*, p. 156.

31. Naimark, *Russians*, pp. 148–9.

32. Szczecin State Archives, UWS, Wydział Ogólny, sygn. 231, Pismo do ob. płk Z. Bibrowskiego szefa Polskiej Misji Repatriacyjnej w Berlinie, p. 29; Agreement between British and Polish representatives of the Combined Repatriation Executive, reproduced as doc. 30 in Białecki et al., p. 72.

33. Clay, pp. 314–15; Pieck quoted in Naimark, *Russians*, p. 149.

34. Red Cross reports in de Zayas, *Terrible Revenge*, pp. 131–2.

35. Clay, p. 315.

36. Franz Hamm, quoted in de Zayas, *Terrible Revenge*, p. 136.

37. Quoted in Naimark, *Russians*, p. 149.

38. Ibid., p. 149.

39. Testimony of Josef Resner, quoted in de Zayas, *Terrible Revenge*, p. 141.

40. Ibid., p. 142. See also Snyder, p. 210.

41. Davies and Moorhouse, p. 447.

42. Quoted in H. Schampera, 'Ignorowani Ślązacy', *Res Publica*, no. 6 (1990), p. 9.

43. Beneš, *Speech . . . May 16th 1945*, pp. 5, 19.

44. Schieder, vol. III: *Romania*, p. 68.

45. Janics, p. 120.

46. Ibid., pp. 133, 177. For statistics on the Hungarian minority see tables 1–3 in Gyurgyík, pp. 38–9.

47. *Čas*, 26 February 1946; *Obzory*, 11 October 1947; *Východoslovenská Pravda*, 3 November 1946: quoted in Janics, pp. 133, 152, 188.

48. Janics, p. 172.

49. For contrasting points of view on the Hungarian–Slovak population exchanges see Gyurgyík, p. 7, and Marko and Martinický, pp. 26–7. Both give similar figures.

50. Janics, pp. 136–9.

51. For Bulgarian statistics see Marrus, p. 353; for Karelian Finns see Proudfoot, p. 41.

52. Pearson, p. 229.

CHAPTER 20 – EUROPE IN MICROCOSM: YUGOSLAVIA

1. Report of district committee of Communist Party of Croatia in Nova Gradiška, 2 June 1945, reproduced in Rupić et al., doc. 52, p. 151.

2. Pavlowitch, pp. vii–xi. I am indebted to this book, and Tomasevich's *War and Revolution in Yugoslavia*, which is amongst the most impartial accounts of the war and its aftermath in Yugoslavia available in any language.

3. Pavlowitch, p. ix.

4. As with all such statistics, the number of deaths at Jasenovac has been vastly exaggerated for political purposes. For credible figures see Žerjavić, pp. 20, 29–30; Pavlowitch, p. 34; Tomasevich, pp. 726–8. In 1997, researchers at the Belgrade Museum of Victims of Genocide and the Federal Statistical Office assembled a list of 78,163 named people who had died at the Jasenovac camp: see Croatian State Commission, p. 27.

5. Tomasevich, p. 753.

6. Ibid., pp. 757–63; Bethell, pp. 118–22. For British estimates of numbers see TNA: PRO WO 170/4465, WO 106/4022 X/L 03659 and FO 371/48918 R 8700/1728/92. Yugoslav estimates appear to agree – see Tito's communication with Field Marshal Alexander of 17 May 1945 in Rupić et al., doc. 31, p. 116.

7. See Alexander's telegrams to AGWAR and AMSSO, 17 May 1945, TNA: PRO FO 371/48918 R 8700/G; and to the Combined Chiefs of Staff, TNA: PRO WO 106/4022. See also Bethell, pp. 131–5, 147–55; Tomasevich, pp. 773–4; Pavlowitch, p. 264. For eyewitness accounts of British deceptions see Nicolson, pp. 120–22 and testimonies by A. Markotic and Hasan Selimovic in Prcela and Guldescu, docs. XXIV and XXVII, pp. 279, 292.

8. Prcela and Guldescu, *passim*.

9. See the testimonies gathered by Kurt W. Böhme in Maschke, vol. I: *Jugoslawien*, *passim*.

10. In Prcela and Guldescu, doc. XIV, p. 215.

11. Account of 'Ivan P.', ibid., doc. XXXIV, p. 335.

12. Account of 'G.', ibid., doc. LV, p. 417.

13. Account of Hasan Selimovic, ibid., doc. XXVII, p. 294.

14. Branko Todorovic account, 25 June 1945, TNA: PRO FO 1020/2445.

15. In Prcela and Guldescu, doc. XXII, pp. 265–6.

16. Accounts of M. Stankovic, Zvonimir Skok and Ante Dragosevic, ibid., docs. XIV, XXIII and XXVI; pp. 213, 274 and 289.

17. Unnamed officer quoted in Karapandzich, pp. 72–3.

18. Account of 'L.Z.' in Prcela and Guldescu, doc. XXXII, p. 325. For corroboration of all the above from German witnesses, see Kurt W. Böhme in Maschke, vol. I: *Jugoslawien*, p. 108.

19. See Tomasevich, pp. 761, 765; Pavlowitch, p. 262.

20. Account of 'I.G.I.' in Prcela and Guldescu, doc. XLIV, p. 375.

21. Tomasevich, p. 774.

22. Accounts of 'I.G.I.' and 'M.L.' in Prcela and Guldescu, docs. XLIV and XLVI, pp. 375, 381.

23. Account of Ignac Jansa ibid., doc. XLV, pp. 377–9.

24. Report of Vladimir Zinger and others, Karapandzich, pp. 91–113. Accounts of 'J.F.' and 'S.F.' in Prcela and Guldescu, docs. XLII and XLIII, pp. 369–70.

25. Kurt W. Böhme in Maschke, vol. I: *Jugoslawien*, p. 108.

26. Account of 'K.L.V.' in Prcela and Guldescu, doc. XXXIX, p. 360.

27. Petacco, pp. 90–94.

28. Account of 'M.M.' in Prcela and Guldescu, doc. XXXVIII, p. 358.

29. Account of Milan Zajec ibid., doc. XLVII, p. 385.

30. See, for example, Kurt W. Böhme in Maschke, vol. I: *Jugoslawien*, pp. 107–34; and Rupić et al., doc. 87, p. 249.

31. Minutes of the first conference of the head of Odjel za zaštitu narodna for Croatia, July 1945, in Rupić et al., doc. 80, p. 236.

32. Mazower, *Balkans*, pp. 143–51.

33. Tomasevich, p. 765. 70,000 killings represents about 466 per 100,000 of population, as compared to 22 in France, and between 26 and 44 in Italy – see ch. 13. Werner Ratza gives 80,000 prisoners of war, including Germans but not Yugoslav civilians, in 'Anzahl und Arbeitsleistungen der deutschen Kriegsgefangenen', in Maschke, vol. XV: *Zusammenfassung*, pp. 207, 224–6.

34. Account by Dusan Vukovic in Prcela and Guldescu, doc. LXVII, pp. 461–4.

35. Accounts of Ivan S. Skoro and Franjo Krakaj ibid., docs. XXI and XXII, pp. 258, 268; and by a Red Cross nurse quoted by Kurt W. Böhme in Maschke, vol. I: *Jugoslawien*, p. 121.

36. Account of postwar trial by lawyer Henri Rochat, quoted in Marcel Ophüls's film documentary *Le Chagrin et la Pitié*, part II: 'Le Choix'.

37. Bodson, p. 145.

38. Report of Interior Ministry for Federative Croatia to Central Committee of the Communist Party of Croatia, 10 July 1945, in Rupić et al., doc. 67, p. 188.

39. Interview in *Encounter*, vol. 53, no. 6, reproduced in Karapandzich, p. 170.

40. Tito quoted in Djilas, *Wartime*, p. 449.

CHAPTER 21 – WESTERN TOLERANCE, EASTERN INTOLERANCE

1. Shephard, *Long Road Home*, p. 158; Hitchcock, pp. 50–55.

2. Hitchcock, pp. 92–7.

3. Snyder, pp. 186–7; Janics, pp. 136–9.

PART IV – CIVIL WAR

1. Eisenhower, p. 521.

CHAPTER 22 – WARS WITHIN WARS

1. Interview with former partisan 'G.V.', in Alessandrini, p. 68. For similar instances see Pavone, pp. 465–6.

2. See Pavone, who pioneered this view, *passim*.

3. See, for example, the treatment of Trotskyist leaders Joseph Pastor and Jacques Méker, in Bourdrel, pp. 216–27.

4. See Pike, p. 73.

5. President Truman's famous 'Truman Doctrine' speech, quoted in Kennan, p. 320.

CHAPTER 23 – POLITICAL VIOLENCE IN FRANCE AND ITALY

1. Ginsborg, p. 89.
2. Ammendolia, pp. 22–8.
3. Ginsborg, p. 88.
4. Only in Czechoslovakia did the Communists do better in free elections, achieving 38 per cent of the vote in 1946; see Rioux, p. 110; Ginsborg, p. 82; Judt, pp. 79, 88; Hodgson, p. 212.
5. Judt, p. 88.
6. Party political broadcast, 4 June 1945, quoted in Cannadine, pp. 271–7.
7. Letter, Alcide De Gasperi to Luigi Sturzo, April 1946, in De Gasperi, vol. II, p. 44.
8. Telegram from State Dept to Rome Embassy, 16 May 1945, quoted in Ellwood, pp. 184–5.
9. Marx and Engels, p. 120.
10. Philip Morgan, p. 213; Dondi, pp. 175–6.
11. Thorez quoted in Rioux, p. 55; Novick, pp. 74–5.
12. Quoted in Dondi, p. 175.
13. See Novick, p. 76; Bourdrel, pp. 679–84.
14. Bourdrel, pp. 486–9.
15. Ibid., pp. 489–90.
16. Veyret, p. 194.
17. Report in telegram, Kirk to State Department, 28 May 1945, quoted in Ellwood, p. 186.
18. Dondi, pp. 168, 176.
19. Ibid., p. 157.
20. L'Unità, 24 February 1953; see also Alessandrini, pp. 65–6; Philip Morgan, p. 211; and Pansa, p. 258.
21. Bertaux, pp. 63–6; Bourdrel, p. 571.
22. Aron, p. 564.
23. Ibid.
24. L'Aube, 16 November 1950, quoted in Bourdrel, p. 543.
25. See, for example, the treatment of various priests in Toulouse and Perpignan in Bourdrel, pp. 546–7, 559–60, 573.
26. See, for example, the killing of the priest Umberto Pessina in Emilia-Romagna on 18 June 1946: Dondi, pp. 176–7.
27. Bertaux, pp. 22–4.
28. Bourdrel, pp. 523–4.
29. Dondi, pp. 168–9.
30. Ibid., pp. 174–7.
31. See, for example, Storchi, and Crainz, *passim*. See also Piscitelli, pp. 169–70.
32. Bertaux, pp. 109–10.
33. American intelligence report by AFHQ Operations Division, quoted in Ellwood, p. 187.

34. Jonathan Dunnage, 'Policing and Politics in the Southern Italian Community, 1943–1948', in Dunnage, pp. 34–40.

35. Sarah Morgan, pp. 148, 158.

36. *L'Umanità*, 29 March 1947; Ambassador Dunn to Secretary of State, 1 April 1947, *FRUS*, 1947, vol. III, p. 878.

37. Rioux, pp. 123–5.

38. Ambassador Caffery to Secretary of State, 19 February 1947, *FRUS*, 1947, vol. III, p. 691.

39. Acheson quoted in Rioux, p. 113.

40. Ambassador Dunn to Secretary of State, 7 May 1947 and 18 June 1947, *FRUS*, 1947, vol. III, pp. 900, 924.

41. *FRUS*, 1948, vol. III, pp. 853–4.

42. Rioux, pp. 129–30.

43. 'Blood on the Cobblestones', *Time* magazine, 26 July 1948.

44. Alessandrini, p. 64; Dondi, p. 180.

45. Psychological Warfare Bureau report, 5 July 1945, quoted in Ellwood, p. 193.

46. Juan Carlos Martinez Oliva, 'The Italian Stabilization of 1947: Domestic and International Factors' (Institute of European Studies, University of California, Berkeley, 14 May 2007), pp. 18–30; Rioux, p. 114.

47. Quoted in Ellwood, p. 190.

48. Ginsborg, pp. 91–2.

49. Ibid., p. 94.

50. Ibid., p. 96.

51. Ammendolia, p. 39.

52. Ibid., pp. 45–9.

CHAPTER 24 – THE GREEK CIVIL WAR

1. For Moscow conference see Dallas, pp. 285–94.

2. EAM stands for Ethniko Apeleftherotiko Metopo; ELAS for Ethnikos Laikos Apeleftherotikos Stratos.

3. Mazower, *Inside Hitler's Greece*, pp. 140–42.

4. Michael S. Macrakis, 'Russian Mission on the Mountains of Greece, Summer 1944 (A View from the Ranks)', *Journal of Contemporary History*, vol. 23, no. 3, pp. 387–408; Mazower, *Inside Hitler's Greece*, pp. 296, 359–60.

5. Quoted in Mazower, *Inside Hitler's Greece*, pp. 295–6.

6. TNA: PRO WO 204/8832, SACMED to Scobie, 15 November 1944. See also Churchill to Eden, 7 November 1944, TNA: PRO FO 371/43695; Alexander, p. 66.

7. Mazower, *Inside Hitler's Greece*, pp. 364, 413 fn. 24.

8. Iatrides, *Ambassador MacVeagh Reports*, p. 660.

9. Quoted in Mazower, *Inside Hitler's Greece*, p. 362.

10. Ibid., p. 352.

11. TNA: PRO PREM 3 212/11, Churchill's order to Scobie, 5 December 1944: see Clogg, p. 187.

12. TNA: PRO WO 170/4049, 'Report on Visit to Greek Red Cross F.A.P., Platia Kastalia, Kypseli, 12 Dec 1944'; report by Ambassador Lincoln MacVeagh, 6 December 1944 in Iatrides, *Ambassador MacVeagh Reports*, p. 658.

13. See the many reports of ELAS hostages in TNA: PRO FO 996/1. See also WO 204/8301, 'Account of military and political events in Western Greece during the independent mission of 11 Ind Inf Bde GP', esp. appendix C.10; WO 204/9380, 'Report by Captain WE Newton on a visit to Kokkenia on 12th January 1945'.

14. For an English translation of the Varkiza Agreement see Richter, pp. 561–4; and Woodhouse, pp. 308–10.

15. See Mazower, *Inside Hitler's Greece*, pp. 271, 279–84.

16. Woodhouse, p. 147.

17. Ibid., pp. 84–6; Mazower, *Inside Hitler's Greece*, pp. 318, 325. EKKA stands for Ethniki Kai Koinoniki Apeleftherosi.

18. See Hagen Fleischer, 'Contacts between German Occupation Authorities and the Major Greek Resistance Organizations', in Iatrides, *Greece in the 1940s*, pp. 54–6; and Mazower, *Inside Hitler's Greece*, pp. 142, 329–30. EDES stands for Ethnikos Dimokratikos Ellinikos Syndesmos.

19. EAM member Konstantinos G. Karsaros, quoted in Kalyvas, p. 171.

20. Mazower, *Inside Hitler's Greece*, p. 290.

21. Ibid., pp. 318–20.

22. John Sakkas, 'The Civil War in Evrytania', in Mazower, *After the War Was Over*, p. 194.

23. Kalyvas, pp. 161–2.

24. Ibid., pp. 157, 159.

25. Ibid., pp. 148, 163.

26. *Odigitis*, 8 February 1944, quoted in Kalyvas, p. 157.

27. Kalyvas, pp. 153, 159.

28. Ibid., p. 154.

29. Mazower, *Inside Hitler's Greece*, p. 327.

30. Kalyvas, p. 151.

31. TNA: PRO HS 5/698 'General Report', pp. 8–9.

32. EASAD stands for Ethnikos Agrotikos Syndesmos Antikommounistikis Draseos.

33. Mazower, *Inside Hitler's Greece*, pp. 334–9.

34. TNA: PRO FO 188/438, 'Summary of a Letter dated Athens 22nd November 1944 from Mr Justice Sandström, Chairman of the Greek Relief Commission to the Supervisory Board of the Swedish Red Cross'.

35. The following example from Douka is dissected in greater detail by Kalyvas, pp. 171–5.

36. Mazower, *Inside Hitler's Greece*, p. 373.

37. See report of Charles F. Edson, to Lincoln MacVeagh, 29 March 1945, quoted in Clogg, p. 192.

38. Voglis, p. 75.

39. See reports by Charles F. Edson to Lincoln MacVeagh, 29 March and 4 July 1945, quoted in Clogg, pp. 192, 196; and Woodhouse report quoted in Richter, pp. 148–50.

40. Democratic Army of Greece radio proclamation to the Greek people, 24 December 1947, quoted in Clogg, p. 205.

41. See report by Charles F. Edson to Lincoln MacVeagh, 4 July 1945, quoted in Clogg, pp. 195–6.

42. See Mark Mazower's introduction in Mazower, *After the War Was Over*, p. 11.

43. See ibid., p. 7.

44. Eleni Haidia, 'The Punishment of Collaborators in Northern Greece, 1945–1946', ibid., p. 54.

45. According to British estimates, 3,033 people were executed as sentenced by extraordinary courts martial between 1946 and 1949, and 378 as sentenced by civil courts, making a total of 3,411; see TNA: PRO FO 371/87668 RG10113/11, Athens to Foreign Office, 6 April 1950.

46. P. Papastratis, 'The Purge of the Greek Civil Service on the Eve of the Civil War', in Baerentzen et al., p. 46. See also Mark Mazower, 'Three Forms of Political Justice, Greece 1944–1945', in Mazower, *After the War Was Over*, pp. 37–8.

47. TNA: PRO FO 371/87668, RG 10113/28. Voglis appears to misquote these figures, p. 75.

48. Mazower, *Inside Hitler's Greece*, p. 376.

49. Ibid.

50. See George F. Kennan's statement to the War College, 28 March 1947, Kennan, pp. 318–20.

51. Truman, p. 129.

52. George Marshall's speech at Harvard, 5 June 1947, quoted ibid., p. 138. See also Rioux, p. 114.

53. See Milward, *Reconstruction*, pp. 5, 56–61.

54. Judt, p. 143. For descriptions of Communist agitation in France and Italy, see Rioux, pp. 129–30; 'Blood on the Cobblestones', *Time* magazine, 26 July 1948; *FRUS*, 1948, vol. III (Western Europe), pp. 853–4.

CHAPTER 25 – CUCKOO IN THE NEST: COMMUNISM IN ROMANIA

1. Cedric Salter, interview with King Michael of Romania, *Daily Express*, 23 November 1944. For more detailed descriptions of Michael's coup d'état see *New York Times*, 27 August 1944, p. 12; Deletant, pp. 46–50; Ionescu, pp. 83–4.

2. Declaration of the new Romanian government, 23 August 1944, *FRUS*, 1944, vol. IV, p. 191.

3. Deletant, pp. 36–7, 49.

4. For the complete text of the Romanian Armistice see TNA: PRO WO 201/1602.

5. Ionescu, p. 88; Hitchins, pp. 502–5.

6. Deletant, p. 59.

7. *Daily Express*, 23 November 1944.

8. Ibid. and TNA: PRO WO 201/1602, digest of OSS reports sent from Foreign Office to Minister Resident, Cairo, 16 September 1944.

9. Ionescu, p. 98; Deletant, p. 57.

10. Ionescu, p. 103; Deletant, pp. 56–9.

11. Deletant, pp. 59–60. For Penescu's version of events see James Marjoribanks' minute to the Foreign Office on 2 December 1944, TNA: PRO FO 371/48547.

12. The truce lasted just three weeks: see the report by the Chief of Polish Intelligence, 1 February 1945, reproduced in Giurescu, doc. 1, pp. 134–44.

13. Deletant, pp. 61–3; see in particular the quotation of Georgescu's telegram to regional prefects 'not to carry out orders . . . given by General Rădescu, who has proved himself by his dictatorial action to be the enemy of our people'.

14. Ibid., pp. 63–4.

15. For the text of Rădescu's speech see Giurescu, doc. 4, pp. 174–5; see also Judt, p. 135.

16. Tismaneanu, pp. 89–90.

17. Deletant, p. 72: 2,851 Interior Ministry officials were placed on reserve, and 195 dismissed.

18. Rumanian National Committee, *Suppression of Human Rights*, pp. 67–8.

19. Ibid., p. 27; Winterton, p. 96.

20. Rumanian National Committee, *Suppression of Human Rights*, pp. 27, 36–7.

21. Deletant, pp. 68 fn. 32, 75–7.

22. Quoted by Rumanian National Committee, *Suppression of Human Rights* p. 40.

23. *New York Times*, 25 November 1946. For a brief description of the conditions in which the elections took place, see Hitchins, pp. 530–34.

24. The exact number of seats allocated in the 1946 parliament is disputed by both Romanian and other historians. For this reason I have given only the percentage of seats, which remains largely the same, rather than the number. See Hitchins, p. 534; Deletant, p. 78; Ionescu, p. 124; Betts, p. 13.

25. Deletant, p. 78; Tismaneanu, pp. 287–8 fn. 10.

26. Tismaneanu, p. 91; Fischer-Galati, p. 99; E. D. Tappe, 'Roumania', in Betts, p. 11.

27. Deletant, p. 79; *Le Figaro*, 18 March 1948; Rumanian National Committee, *Suppression of Human Rights*, p. 54.

28. Ionescu, pp. 133–6; Rumanian National Committee, *Suppression of Human Rights*, pp. 77–81.

29. Deletant, p. 88; *Le Figaro*, 26/27 March 1949; Rumanian National Committee, *Suppression of Human Rights*, pp. 109–10; Tismaneanu, p. 91.

30. For detailed descriptions of the suppression of all three branches of the Christian church in Romania, see Rumanian National Committee, *Persecution of Religion*; and Deletant, pp. 88–113.

31. Ionescu, pp. 161–70.

32. Ibid., pp. 111–12; Tismaneanu, p. 108.

33. Rumanian National Committee, *Suppression of Human Rights*, p. 90; Deletant, p. 87.

34. These claims, reported in *Scînteia* on 7 December 1961, must be treated with some caution, because the figures were used as evidence to incriminate Dej's former rivals Ana Pauker and Teohari Georgescu: see Ionescu, p. 201. A Securitate report from 1953 shows that in 1951 and 1952 alone, 34,738 peasants were arrested: see Deletant, p. 140.

35. Ionescu, p. 335; Deletant, p. 141.

CHAPTER 26 – THE SUBJUGATION OF EASTERN EUROPE

1. Quoted in Judt, p. 131.

2. Rákosi quoted in Kenez, p. 224.

3. In the end such military moves were not necessary; see Fowkes, p. 23.

4. See John Micgiel, '"Bandits and Reactionaries": The Suppression of the Opposition in Poland, 1944–1946', in Naimark and Gibianskii, pp. 93–104.

5. Jan Gross, 'War as Revolution', in Naimark and Gibianskii, p. 31.

6. Nagy, pp. 160–64; Kenez, pp. 61–6, 102.

7. Nagy, p. x.

8. Igor Lukes, 'The Czech Road to Communism', in Naimark and Gibianskii, p. 258.

9. Quoted in Upton, p. 258.

10. Crampton, pp. 309–11.

11. Novick, p. 75 fn. 38.

12. Tismaneanu, p. 87; Schöpflin, p. 65.

13. Kontler, p. 392. Schöpflin has figures of 2,000 Communist Party members in November 1944 rising to 884,000 in May 1948, p. 65.

14. Myant, pp. 106, 222. Schöpflin has figures of 40,000 Communist Party members at the end of the war rising to 2.67 million by October 1948, p. 65.

15. Myant, p. 204.

16. For Romania, see Rumanian National Committee, *Suppression of Human Rights*, p. 28; Deletant, p. 58 fn. 10; Giurescu, pp. 34–5.

17. Myant, pp. 125–9.

18. Z. Vas, quoted by Bela Zhilitski, 'Postwar Hungary 1944–1946', in Naimark and Gibianskii, p. 78.

19. Masaryk's death was probably suicide, but rumours persisted that foul play was involved; see Myant, p. 217; Judt, p. 139.
20. Fowkes, p. 28.
21. Crampton, p. 315; Tismaneanu, p. 288; Davies, *God's Playground*, p. 426; Myant, p. 225; Kontler, p. 409.
22. Molnár, p. 303. I have revised Molnár's estimate of a total population of 10 million downwards, in line with Maddison, pp. 96–7.
23. Correspondence between Dimitrov and Molotov in Dimitrov, diary entries for 15–29 March 1946, pp. 397–402.
24. Djilas, *Conversations with Stalin*, p. 105.

CHAPTER 27 – THE RESISTANCE OF THE 'FOREST BROTHERS'

1. Statiev, p. 106.
2. Quoted by Laima Vincė, afterword Lukša, p. 403.
3. Lionginas Baliukevičius quoted in Gaškaitė-Žemaitienė, p. 44.
4. For numerous examples of partisan battles, see Lukša, pp. 103–24. A chronology is available at www.spauda.lt/voruta/kronika/chronic1.htm, accessed 17 October 2011.
5. For descriptions of the Battle of Kalniškės see Lukša, pp. 119–21; and www.patriotai.lt/straipsnis/2009-05-22/jonas-neifalta-lakunas-1910-1945, last viewed 17 October 2011.
6. For the higher estimates see Misiunas and Taagepera, p. 86; for the lower estimates see Strods, p. 150, and Mart Laar, 'The Armed Resistance Movement in Estonia from 1944 to 1956', in Anušauskas, p. 217.
7. Beria quoted in Starkauskas, p. 50.
8. Statiev, p. 247.
9. Eleonora Labanauskienė testimony in Laima Vincė's afterword to Lukša, p. 375.
10. In July 1947, for example, the minister responsible for the secret police, Viktor Abakumov, quoted Stalin's 'directive' on torture as justification for its use: see Statiev, pp. 32–3, 247–9, 291–2.
11. Statiev, pp. 107–8, 112–13.
12. Lukša, pp. 210–11, 226–30, 305, 331, 335.
13. Lukša, p. 335. For other examples of this see ibid., pp. 203, 225, 228, 230, 240, 273; Vardys and Sedaitis, p. 84; Gaškaitė-Žemaitienė, p. 35; Statiev, p. 108.
14. Statiev, p. 289; Starkauskas, p. 51.
15. Testimony of Private Strekalov, quoted in Starkauskas, pp. 50–51.
16. The existence of such groups is confirmed by both Western and Soviet sources: see Misiunas and Taagepera, p. 91; Gaškaitė-Žemaitienė, p. 31.

17. Gaškaitė-Žemaitienė, p. 32; Statiev, p. 237.
18. Starkauskas, p. 60.
19. Laar, pp. 117–19.
20. Lukša, p. 124.
21. Misiunas and Taagepera, p. 86.
22. Lukša, pp. 101–3, 147.
23. According to Alfred Käärmann, quoted in Laar, pp. 183–4.
24. Table adapted from Statiev, p. 125.
25. Ilse Iher, quoted in Laar, p. 98.
26. Memo from Beria to Stalin, quoted in Statiev, p. 132.
27. Statiev, pp. 132–4, 137–8; Misiunas and Taagepera, pp. 92–3.
28. Starkauskas, p. 58.
29. Statiev, pp. 101–2.
30. Gaškaitė-Žemaitienė, p. 37.
31. Strods, pp. 154–5.
32. Misiunas and Taagepera, pp. 99, 102–3.
33. The partisans in all three countries knew this from the outset; see, for example, the programme of Relvastatud Võitluse Liit ('Armed Combat Alliance') quoted in Laar, p. 108.
34. Lukša, pp. 24–7.
35. Gaškaitė-Žemaitienė, pp. 38, 42. Based on pre-1989 figures, Misiunas and Taagepera, rather more optimistically, estimate 5,000 still active in 1950, p. 357.
36. See Laima Vincė's afterword to Lukša, pp. 385–8.
37. The last major partisan leader, Adolfas Ramanauskas, was captured in 1956, and executed on 29 November 1957. See Gaškaitė-Žemaitienė, p. 44.
38. Gaškaitė-Žemaitienė, pp. 43–4.
39. See Laar, pp. 196–206.
40. See 'Japan: The Last Last Soldier?', Time magazine, 13 January 1975; and Ronald Fraser, In Hiding: The Life of Manuel Cortés (London: Allen Lane, 1972).
41. For the argument that resistance simply made the Soviet repression worse, see Alexander Statiev's comparison of Lithuania and Belarus, pp. 117, 137–8.
42. Vardys and Sedaitis, p. 84.
43. Translated and updated as Forest Brothers; see Bibliography.
44. Laar, passim.
45. See www.patriotai.lt/straipsnis/2009-05-22/jonas-neifalta-lakunas-1910-1945.

CHAPTER 28 – THE COLD WAR MIRROR

1. Tassoula Vervenioti, 'Left-Wing Women between Politics and Family', in Mazower, After the War Was Over, pp. 109, 115.

2. Democratic Army of Greece radio proclamation to the Greek people, 24 December 1947, quoted in Clogg, p. 205; speech by Nicolae Rădescu quoted by Deletant, p. 67; Giurescu, doc. 4, pp. 174–5.

3. Mao Zedong, 1 July 1949, quoted in Conrad Brandt, Benjamin Schwartz and John K. Fairbank, *A Documentary History of Chinese Communism* (London: Allen & Unwin, 1952), pp. 453–4.

4. McCarthy, p. 168.

CONCLUSION

1. Markov, p. 16.

2. *The Economist*, 13 November 2010, p. 48.

3. *Washington Post*, 1 January 2011; see also István Deák, 'Hungary: The Threat', *New York Review of Books*, vol. 58, no. 7 (April 2011), pp. 35–7.

4. Quoted ibid., pp. 35–7. Orgovány was the site of a massacre in 1919, when counter-revolutionary officers murdered suspected Communists and non-political Jews; Cohn-Bendit is a left-wing opponent of the Hungarian government.

5. European Union Agency for Fundamental Rights, pp. 9, 15, 167–70 (available on http://fra.europa.eu/fraWebsite/attachments/eumidis_mainreport_conference-edition_en_.pdf, last viewed 12 October 2011).

6. Clay, p. 315.

7. Uehling, pp. 8–9.

8. Ibid., p. 10.

9. Quoted by Jedlicki, p. 230.

10. See Chapter 18, note 19, above.

11. Žerjavić, *passim*; Jurčević, p. 6. See also Tomasevich, p. 761 and Chapter 12, above.

12. See Chapter 13, note 51, above.

13. *Guardian*, 11 February 2005.

14. Philip Morgan, p. 231.

15. Jedlicki, p. 225.

16. Ibid., p. 227.

Index

Page references in *italic* indicate maps, which are also listed in full at the beginning of the book.